# The Promise of the West

# The Promise
## *of the*
# West

## THE GREEK WORLD
## ROME AND JUDAISM

## Alan E. Samuel

Routledge

*London and New York*

*First published in 1988 by*
*Routledge*
*11 New Fetter Lane, London EC4P 4EE*

*Published in the USA by*
*Routledge, Chapman & Hall, Inc.*
*in association with Methuen, Inc.*
*29 West 35th Street, New York NY 10001*

© *1988 Alan Samuel*

*Typeset by Scarborough Typesetting Services*
*and printed in Great Britain at the*
*University Press, Cambridge*

Library of Congress Cataloging in Publication Data
Samuel, Alan Edouard.
The promise of the West.
Bibliography: p.
Includes index.
1. Civilization, Classical.   1. Title.
DE60.S26   1987     938     87–7820

*British Library CIP Data also available*
*ISBN 0–415–00274–5*

*To Valerie*

# Contents

# Contents

# Plates

x

List of Plates

# Acknowledgments

The author and publishers would like to thank the following for permission to reproduce the plates appearing in this book:

The Ancient Art and Architecture Collection for nos 1, 3, 5, 18, 27 and 34
Archivi Alinari S.P.A. for nos 2, 6, 7, 8, 9, 10, 11, 12, 13, 14, 17, 20, 21, 22, 23, 24, 26, 28, 29, 31, and 33
The Bridgeman Art Library for no. 16
The British Museum for nos 4 and 25
La Salle University Art Museum, Philadelphia, Pa. 19141 for no. 30
The Metropolitan Museum of Art, New York, for nos 15 and 19
Popperfoto for no. 32

# Preface

For most of us, it is almost as hard to imagine the world of 1936 as it is to recreate the fifth century BC. The year 1936 began with the death of King George V, who had led Britain through the Great War. In March, the German government repudiated the Locarno pacts and reoccupied the Rhineland; in May, the King of Italy took the title of Emperor of Ethiopia, announcing the annexation of that country; in October, the Berlin–Rome axis was announced and in November came the German–Japanese alliance. Meanwhile, in France, the socialist Léon Blum's Popular Front government replaced that of the discredited Laval, and answered a national sit-down strike with a new program of social reform. A month later the Spanish Civil War broke out. The year ended with the Soviet Union adopting a new democratic Constitution and with the election of Franklin Roosevelt to a second term as American president. Throughout the industrialized world, workers remained without jobs, economies wallowed sluggishly. It was all just fifty years ago.

In 1936 Werner Jaeger's *Paideia*[1] had recently appeared, presenting ideas which seem much closer to us than the events of the 1930s. For all that we may impose a harsher judgment than Jaeger's on Hellenic antiquity, his vision of Hellenism as a coherent ideology is still an appealing one, and his braid of strands of history and literature in a unified presentation still provides a standard for intellectual historians. The effort has been repeated: Bruno Snell's *Die Entdeckung des Geistes* in 1946; Eric Dodds' *The Greeks and the Irrational* in 1964. Progressively less encomiastic, later books see the less rational, more "primitive," if you will, aspect of the Greek mentality, and are not so inclined to build their picture of Hellenism on the basis of the evidence of the high culture of the literary texts. The newest work in ancient history reaches out to the insights of anthropologists, psychologists, and economists to learn from the parallels provided by other, often radically different, societies. Modern approaches to Hellenism try to make hitherto ignored evidence and radically altered modes of interpretation yield concepts which will help us to come closer to understanding the Greeks and their culture.

This is not such a book. I do not intend to give an account of Greek civilization here, neither in an overall political-economic-social-cultural account nor in a more limited intellectual history of Hellenism. Rather I select from the written texts of Hellenism ideas, values, and concepts which I believe to have been influential in determining the ideology of western civilization. Naturally, in interpreting these texts in themselves and against their background, and in tracing the emergence of ideas in antiquity, among Jews and Christians as well as Greeks and Romans, I hope to bring to bear concepts of history and society which, if not demonstrably objectively correct, at least do not violate what evidence we have about the world of the ancient Mediterranean. In general, however, I do not intend to argue the validity of these concepts, and I give historical background primarily to facilitate understanding of my discussion of the texts. For the most part, disagreement about details of social structure, about events or chronology, do not materially affect my interpretations, although where I believe a scholarly controversy to be significant to the thread of my argument, I have indicated this and tried to give the reader some guidance into the issues at stake and the bibliography of the discussion.

Where I felt it essential to make my argument clear or to give the reader some sense of the nature of a text discussed, I have quoted in translation; otherwise I have merely indicated the contents of a work. Apart from Old Testament texts, the translations are my own. In many cases, the awkwardness of English wording is a deliberate device to indicate the distance between the flow of the Greek or Latin and normal English modes of expression. Language, if nothing else, shows the foreignness of those cultures.

Certain aspects of those cultures are indeed very foreign to us, a fact often noted today by those who challenge the long-standing tradition of thought and historiography which finds so much familiarity in the Greek and Roman past. But they are still closer to us than the remote past of humanity to which they are often compared. I believe that all human cultures which are contemporary or recent enough to have left us written evidence are much closer to our own than to that romanticized state of prehistoric nature which is sometimes re-created to explain something which is foreign to us. The foreignness of Greek culture must not obscure those aspects of it which have survived to mold our own. If we see familiarity in some texts and ideas, it is because in 2000 years we have not lost touch with them. These are the aspects of Hellenism with which I am primarily concerned. However, because I am not pursuing these ideas with the primary aim of understanding ancient culture, I make no attempt to explain, justify, or excuse notions on the basis of the matrix in which they were embedded. Once our comprehension of the context has advanced to the point of providing the possibility of understanding what a writer meant to communicate, we do the ideas no service if our response is limited by an argument that the ancient environment precluded a development with which we would have greater sympathy.

Because this work is taken up largely with connections rather than differences, the portrayal here of ancient culture and ancient writers is inevitably only a partial one. There are many important themes in fifth-century drama with which I do not deal, but this does not invalidate the significance of what I do discuss. So, too, my overall argument does not depend on agreement with all the individual interpretations. If I stress the rationality of Herodotus, for example, my argument does not require acceptance of my view that it dominated his writing, so long as I have made it clear that in historical writing in the mid-fifth century BC, this character of thought emerges. It is certainly true that some modern readers will argue that the mundane and rational dominate Herodotean thought, while others see him quite otherwise, but I have not found it necessary to reassess all the arguments here. For those interested in this sort of issue, or in a fuller explication of the historical background of these writers, or in fuller assessments of their work as literature, the recent books listed in the bibliographies offer evidence, argument, and further reading.

One of the great pleasures which accompanies the completion of a book is the contemplation of the obligations incurred in its preparation, and the formulation of suitable thanks. For a book such as this, the debts reach far back, not only to my teachers and colleagues over the years, but to the scholars and writers whose often illuminating, sometimes infuriating, views about antiquity, the modern world, and the nature of human beings inspired many of the notions in the pages which follow. In a more particular way, I want to express my appreciation for responses to some of these ideas which emerged from a presentation of some of the Socratic material to the Seminar of the Department of Philosophy at McMaster University in 1983; these encouraged me to continue in the direction in which I was then moving.

The year's leave which the University of Toronto kindly provided in 1983–4 was of inestimable help in permitting me the time to complete the manuscript, and I am grateful to that institution and to the Social Sciences and Humanities Research Council of Canada for the financial support involved. A fellowship of the John Simon Guggenheim Foundation made it possible for me to compress a great deal of research and writing into a short period and I particularly appreciate the courtesy and support which the officers of the foundation tendered me in the course of that year. To Professors Frank Gilliam, Naphtali Lewis, John Thomas, and William Willis go my thanks for all their help and encouragement as I was formulating this project.

I am particularly indebted to my wife Valerie, not only for the patience with which she tolerated my frequent preoccupation with reading, writing, and musing, but for her urging me to this study and her very active participation in the formulation of my ideas. I also remember with gratitude the wonderful home and garden in Marrakesh which Constant Brummer and Seve Søderlund made available, and to them as well as to Mohamed Lemchuan and Hassan go my thanks for their hospitality.

Of course, I am particularly grateful for the very specific suggestions from those who have read drafts of one or more chapters: Naphtali Lewis, Meyer Reinhold, John Rist, Michael O'Brien, Christopher Jones, Elaine Fantham, and the late and much-regretted Leonard Woodbury, all of whom very kindly devoted time to consider one or more chapters, and put their considerable knowledge at my disposal to improve my draft. Errors which remain, of course, are those of perversity or misunderstanding on my part.

I am also grateful to my friend Bruce Lewis, who arranged some technical assistance to make my revisions much easier to prepare; and to Sandra Martin, for her help in typing a number of chapters. I also appreciate the cooperation of Andrew Wheatcroft and the staff of Routledge, as well as the editorial contribution of Brigid Bell and Sarah Cahill of Methuen & Co, and I would also like to acknowledge the very useful comments of the anonymous readers of my original draft. For John Naylor, the managing director of Routledge, I reserve a special word of appreciation. It must be rare these days for an author to feel that a publisher has not only made a great contribution to his book, but has done so in an unfailingly friendly, humane, and perceptive manner.

*Toronto, May 1986*

# Part One
# The elements
# of Hellenism

# 1
# Introduction

Any philosophy, religion, or even history is based on some particular understanding of the nature of humanity. For that matter, literature of any sort calls
for assumptions about human nature and human behavior. The assumptions
may be explicit or left tacit; they may be argued or asserted; they may range
from the exclusively material to the ideal, but whatever they may be they are
there, and they influence or control the development of any human system of
thought. An individual shares with his society and his age most aspects of an
understanding of what it is to be human, and even the most creative of us will
affect the common inheritance only in very minor details. But that common
view differs from place to place, and even in one society changes over time, as
the insights or assertions of talented members of a group stimulate one another
and accumulate in a period of change. We can usually notice these changes once
they have taken place, and from a long perspective can see how a new ideology
of humankind has affected the actions of individuals and groups (or as some
might prefer it, how the actions of groups have formed ideology). So, for
example, although we know how new views of human psychology and
physiology, discoveries in anthropology and animal behavior, have made us
regard ourselves much more as part of nature, we do not yet know how all this
will motivate us or affect our behavior in groups or as individuals. We can,
however, look back to see how a new version of humanity in Christianity
wrought fundamental changes in western society, so that people lived in a new
world even before the Greek and Roman Mediterranean yielded to Europe,
Byzantium, and the lands of Islam.

As an old world of ideology was passing away, the arena in which the new
would emerge was changing too. What was, in AD 50, one world, focusing on
the Mediterranean but reaching in the east to the Euphrates, in the south to the
first cataract of the Nile in East Africa, to the Atlas Mountains in the west, and
in the north to Britain, the Rhine, and down the Danube, started to break apart
in two centuries. In the east, the remarkably durable Byzantine Empire lasted
until the fifteenth century, but in the west, everything south of the Pyrenees

3

was Arab by the early eighth century. Europe, as Henri Pirenne has said,[1] was forced to turn inland away from the Mediterranean, inevitably to create new social and political institutions. It was in this newly limited realm that many ancient ideas would eventually lodge, consciously taken up again by a civilization which was in fact rooted in a millennium of Greek history which had ended 1000 years before.

When Greek ideas again became more commonly known in Europe, they seemed different, because in the centuries between the rise of Christianity and Aquinas' confrontation with Aristotle, Christian thinkers had made a very different thing of their Hellenic heritage. Christian Europe's idea of the human being was very different from that of the Greek and Roman Mediterranean. On many points that define us there were different attitudes: the relation of human beings to God and to nature; human predilection for virtue or vice; the mainsprings of human motivation; the relation of individuals to society and the need for political living; the nature and interrelation of human mind, spirit, soul, and body. A Greek or Roman looked at these quite differently from how a Christian did, and, more significantly, had quite different ideas about which of them were more important for reflection and study, and even how to go about that study.

The difference in the ideological curriculum is the most important of all. What aspects of humanity we study and how we do it are determined in large measure by underlying, tacit assumptions about human nature, and those assumptions are not likely to be disturbed much by study so determined. It is only when people break with earlier approaches, start looking at different aspects of the human being, or interpret our characteristics quite differently, that we can construct a different view of our nature. For whatever reasons people start doing this, once they do it they remake the world, because they change the eye and the mind that perceive it. And, even if we do not know how it is all going to turn out, we know when we are in the middle of it, because the people who are roiling our thoughts are telling us to look at this or that anew, to pursue this path of research or that mode in literature and art. Their very language indicates what is happening, for they are forced to make up new words or use the old with very different meanings. Most of all, they come back again and again to the theme that there is a new curriculum, and to what makes it up. It does us very little good for that enlightened neoclassicist Alexander Pope to tell us that the proper study of mankind is man if he doesn't tell us in what classes to enrol.

We certainly do know today: psychology, anthropology, sociology, at the basic levels. Advanced students should go on to the specialized disciplines within those fields, and then expand their scope by learning about animal behavior and psychology. Ethology is good. The biological sciences are essential, and one cannot really work without some knowledge of human and animal physiology. So go the evaluations, passing by the once-exalted philosophy, theology, literature, and history. I am not deriding this curriculum, for it is the one to be pursued by anyone who wants to understand the contemporary ideology of the nature of humankind. When I put it down so baldly, however, it immediately becomes clear just how different it is from the curriculum of the nineteenth century, which for the most part reached back into late antiquity before coming up against a change in approach. That alone should jolt us into an awareness of how different we are from our great-grandparents, creatures changed in what we think we are and why we think we act.

The twentieth-century idea of humanity places us firmly in the animal kingdom, admittedly the most complex of those creatures which range from protozoa to mammals. The human animal is seen to have come about through a process of evolution which is not yet thoroughly understood, but which, if ever comprehended in all its details, will explain the existence of all animals, living and extinct, in a single system. We humans have some capabilities which certainly differ quantitatively from those of our nearest primate relatives, and the differences may be great enough to be qualitative as well. We are social, often territorial, aggressive animals. Our physiology, especially neural and cranial, is very complicated, operated by an incredibly delicate chemical system. We live a long time, remember a lot, and are prone to an activity known as thinking. What that process is, or what any of the other mental processes like curiosity or memory are, we do not know, but many of us have hopes of finding answers in a better understanding of details of anatomy, body chemistry, and cellular or molecular function. We have only begun to understand some of our psychological activities, but we have been making big strides in establishing some of the fundamental chemical processes by which we transmit our characteristics to successive generations. Still, despite claims to the contrary, we do not know to what extent our common human traits of territoriality, aggressiveness, and the like are uncontrollably genetic,[2] and how much is and has been influenced by environment. We, who have changed the world about us so much, are being told that we cannot do much about changing ourselves, and we continue to seek an understanding of what kind of creatures we are.

For a long time writers invested human beings with an attribute called a "soul" or "spirit" which differentiated us from the lower animals; but today, we try instead to define ourselves by what we call human consciousness. It is a term usually associated with something we do, arising, say many, out of one or more aspects of our physical makeup, although some, like Wilder Penfield,[3] unable to isolate in the brain any anatomical source of consciousness, try to explain it as some as yet unidentifiable energy within us. In general, however, we shy away from metaphysical explanations, because we assume that anything which is can be studied, and we take metaphysics as assertion, not investigation. However much we may accept the dictum that study is never entirely objective, that the act of study itself may affect and change the object

5

studied, we pursue our course because our notion of ourselves is so firmly rooted that we cannot offer or accept any assertions about ourselves that are not based in some measure on empirical observations.

This does not relieve us of our metaphysical problems, only of the activity which concerns them. Some people, who share but are uncomfortable with the current view of the human condition which deprives us of a known – known at least to some agency – role in this universe or even this world, worry about the "meaning" of life. Others cast about for a means of justifying the rules by which we live, seeking to find, with extra-human endorsements gone, some validations for the systems of ethics we adopt, and there are even claims that validation can be found in the processes of natural selection. The very existence of these problems illustrates the effects on the western world of this view of the human being as ultimately explicable purely physically, a point of view which reaches back beyond 2000 years of Christianity to share some of the attitudes of ancient ideology.

Hellenism had developed many interpretations of human nature and the constitution of the human being. From the *Iliad* to the tracts of Philo, Greek texts exhibit that wide-ranging variety in treatment of humanity and its relation to the cosmos that generated so much literature reflecting so many deeply felt intuitions. The explorations of the relationship between human ideas of justice and cosmic justice, if it existed, and the different answers offered show that from the *Iliad* and Hesiod on, Greeks never reached a consensus on that issue, just as they never achieved a coherent ideology of human social institutions in this world. In their explorations of these issues, however, they developed some attitudes about humanity which affected the evolution of their own culture, and, ultimately, determined some aspects of human development over the millennia. Bluntly put, the course of western civilization has not only been directed in a number of ways by Hellenic ideology, but many modern values are validated simply by their indissoluble relationship to western culture. In the course of the history of Greek civilization, certain attitudes about the nature of humanity and the proper modes of organizing human society and interaction became so basic to social and intellectual structures that they influenced both practical affairs and abstract thinking, and on some of these, our world, no less than that of the Greeks, is built.

Although the Greek tradition provided diversity in questions and solutions of ethics, spirituality, justice, injustice, and the like, the Hellenic approach to all these matters still rested on some fundamental assumptions about the nature of human beings and the world. Those assumptions made of humanity a central and organizing principle for the cosmos. While not all Greeks would have accepted the Protagorean view which made human understanding the only measure of anything which existed, Greeks tended to share an approach to understanding the cosmos in which anything important in the universe achieved its importance through its value and relation to humanity. The subtle might recognize that the importance accorded *by* humans came only from the measure of importance *to* humans, but the overall attitude was the basis of much Greek thought and religion. Deities and the cosmic order were reckoned with as they affected humans, and any superior forces which were acknowledged were not considered apart from their interaction with human life, at least in a general sense. Greeks did not generally hold notions that people were created to serve such superior beings or forces or even that these gods created humans, and Greek religion did not tend to "love God and do his commandments."

Even for those who thought superior forces acted for their own motives with no regard for humans, philosophy and ethics focused on the manner in which people could regulate their lives to make them as satisfying as possible in a world which they could not control. In philosophy, human happiness in this world was an important, and often the preeminent, goal, and its quest the subject of argument and doctrine, some of which proposed to make people independent of the world and cosmic forces. There was, in other words, no sublimation of the human will in the face of superior forces, but an assertion of independence, a separation of human activity from divine or cosmic acts, a claim that all people could control their individual fortunes by choosing a manner of life. Happiness could be made independent of luck, chance, the gods, or fate by freeing it from any dependence on material goods, social position, or even physical condition.

Throughout the thousand years of Greek literary and philosophical writing this fundamental valuation of humanity stands out. While many might argue over the importance to be allotted to individuals as against their societies, all started from the assumption that humanity was the focal species. Even during the periods in which some moderns think they detect a "crisis in confidence" or a "loss of faith," that fundamental Hellenic concept of the cosmos as the abode of humanity meant that human problems were dealt with as the primary concern of religious and philosophical thinkers. If the world seemed to be going badly, people did not generally rethink assessments of their value to the world, but rather how they were to deal with it. It is only with the emergence of Jewish Hellenism, when basically Jewish concepts emerge in Greek dress in the later Greek Jewish apocalyptic literature and Philo, that we see any movement away from this fundamental Hellenic attitude. Even during the first and second centuries, however much confronted with the spreading influence of Jewish and Christian thought, the fundamental ideological character of Hellenism remained uncontaminated. From the Stoicism of Marcus Aurelius to the sardonic satire of Lucian, Hellenism maintained its essential attitudes and made human happiness the criterion for valuing the worth of a philosophy or program of life.

This is the fundamental difference between Greek and Christian thought. No Christian thinker or writer proposed that conventional happiness in this world was the objective of life or the purpose of the commandments of their religion. Rather, humanity was subordinated to the will and plan – not necessarily known or understood – of a deity who rewarded conformity to the commandments for life in this world with an existence in the kingdom of the next. This is what Christian thinkers made of the apocalyptic vision of the New Testament, and it is a concept which elevates the aims and wishes of God far above the ordinary human perceptions of good and bad, pleasant and unpleasant, valuable and deleterious, and subordinates the importance of humanity to the purpose of God. It changes the Hellenic appraisal of humanity's value and establishes the Christian elevation of the deity that marks a new era in human history. For a long time thereafter, the central concern of human thought and the major efforts of most thinkers related to the understanding and elucidation of the deity's plan and will, and the role of humanity in conformity thereto. Many events hung on devoutly held but violently differing views of these matters, and the histories of individuals and states were intimately involved with theological and philosophical disputes over issues which emerged from these differences. People often fought – *pace* the modern materialists – as much or more over ideas in Christian Europe as they did over practical advantage in the Hellenic Mediterranean.

On the other hand, Christianity, influenced as it was by the Greek mode of thought of its leading adherents, was inevitably penetrated by Hellenic ideas. This penetration went beyond the abstractions of Platonic metaphysics and idealism, and incorporated some of the basic attitudes about the importance of humanity which did not coincide with the main thrust of Christian thought. This aspect of Hellenic thought, which in Christianity often created great difficulties for those attempting to accommodate it, has been preserved for us over the centuries and has been emphasized in modern western ideologies. In Christian Europe, the antinomy between this Hellenism and basic Christianity can be traced in theological disputes from the time of Augustine down to the Protestant Reformation and Calvinism, and it lies behind the differing valuations of faith or good works which can be seen as early as New Testament texts. It is present in some of the earliest expressions of Christian thought, and is reinforced by the influence of Hellenism during the second and third centuries, when Christians shared the Mediterranean with still-dominant Hellenic philosophy and religion.

Tracing the attitudes toward human nature and institutions in a thousand years of Hellenism is much more than an exercise in the definition of ancient culture. Insofar as some fundamental Hellenic judgements about the behavior of individuals and societies have persisted through the millennia to influence the societies which hold them, the identification of these ideas at the inception of the development of western society serves to validate them for current times. So as I discuss some manifestations of Greek ideology in literature, issues like the conflict between individual conscience and public law, or the emergence of the concept of the citizen and of citizen equality in the Greek city-state, or the tension between pragmatic philosophy and a push towards transcendence, I am not primarily interested in pursuing them to a full definition of Hellenism.

Rather I am concerned to follow those threads which ran through Greek life and influenced the development of Hellenism, and which then continued on to our own time to become part of the fabric of our own society. I am interested in them primarily as they are so much part of the warp and woof of western society as to be vital threads without which the weave would disintegrate, or, more precisely, would never have been woven.

Because my interest in this material is not primarily historical, is not concerned with its meaning for ancient society nor used to provide insight into that society, many modern issues in historical methodology lose their significance. The challenge to the force of ideas made by cultural materialists may be declined when we do not seek to make ideas part of a tightly linked chain of cause and effect, but allow for a dialectical relationship between intellectual conceptions and social arrangement. And the insights of more modern historical description, which deals with the interactions of groups and comprehends the effects of social and economic forces, need not prevent us from giving a prominence to individual accomplishment which a search for the exceptional requires. More important, I ignore the nexus between myth and social structure, the mutual implications between institutions and ideas. Nor is any suggestion of causation or influence which I may present crucial to the overall picture: while I think that ideas and texts once current tend to have an impact on people interested in such things and find this mode of presentation more coherent, the question of ancient influences is quite a different matter from that of the long-term impact of Greek ideas on the west.

Some of the best of our culture comes from this Hellenic inheritance, and a large part of the west's promise can be realized by pursuing and expanding upon some of the principles which have dominated the creation of western institutions in the past. The idea that the citizen has some rights against the sovereign collective has still to be realized fully in our societies, and there are expansions beyond the Greek notion of "citizen" justified in the modern world. And the first step toward public distribution of wealth in fifth-century BC Athens, although halted for two and half millennia, is part of the movement of society toward the current greater consciousness of economic "rights" alongside political rights.

I should make my own ideological orientation clear. I believe that the direction of change in the political, social, and economic structures of society in the first two-thirds of the twentieth century to be the right direction. I endorse the goals of those called "liberals" in American politics, goals which include a fuller sharing of society's wealth by all its members, the most complete protection of the weak against exploitation by the powerful, the guarantee that every member of society will be treated equally by all society's institutions, public as well as private. I also believe the relation of citizen to society to be such that the state has the right, indeed the obligation, to legislate in pursuit of these goals, so that, for example, it should require that women be paid equally with men for the same work, or for work of similar value.

I base these opinions, however, not merely on faith or political taste. I think these "liberal" goals emerge from the basic ideology of western society and are the natural stimuli of this society's dynamic. I believe that the push towards these goals and others like them is powered by attitudes and assumptions which control the very structure of our western world. In my view, these liberal ethics and many other values of our society are validated, for the western world at least, by their being embedded in the history of that society. This book, then, is an investigation of the manner in which some of these ideas first emerged and became part of western ideology. It is an exploration of Hellenism, the culture of the Greeks over the thousand years which ended with the emergence of Christianity, to find, not necessarily the essentials of that culture, but the aspects of that culture which have become the essentials of our own. Not every important aspect of Greek society will appear here, nor even will there always be a balanced and rounded picture of a particular literary or philosophical contributor to Hellenic culture, but I do hope to treat the elements of Hellenism which have served most to dictate the development of western society.

The converse of this is also true: not all the controlling elements of western ideology appear here. Some of the most important of these, after all, emerged after political and cultural Hellenism had ceased to develop as an integral culture, and although they may have been influenced by the nature of western society to which Hellenism gave the first direction, they are products of their own times. Such, for example, is the ethic of growth and technological advance, which has reached its fullest expression only in this century to give the strongest impetus to satisfying the material needs of the majority of the members of society. While I would argue for the validation of that ethic from the history of the west in the last 400 or 500 years, I do not look for its origins in Hellenism. Nor do I argue that everything about Hellenism is good; we have inheritances from the Greeks which have influenced history in what I might see as a deleterious way.

There is, however, much here for which we can be grateful, much that has given our society not only a promising future but even a present rewarding for many. It is a fair, if mundane, observation that the plenitude which has given me the leisure to write this book, and the reader the time to read it and the money to buy it, is a characteristic of our society for which most of us are glad. It may be less banal to observe that this very plenitude and its distribution emerges from a set of ideas and attitudes which are fundamental to the form which society has taken. And finally, it may be better than merely optimistic to hope that the western dynamic will continue to increase that plenitude, broaden its distribution, and increase the freedom available for its use.

# 2
# The environment of Hellenism

## *Gods and the land*

The history of Hellenism is one of political turmoil and change, as many Greek societies were impelled by events and ideas towards granting greater and greater participation in civic power and benefits to those whose claim rested primarily on mere membership in the state – that is, citizenship in the Greek sense. Resistance by the dominant to sharing power and wealth led to turmoil; change came when these pressures forced concessions. Both factors influenced ideology, were influenced by it, and developed in a cultural matrix in which political, social, and religious affairs continually interacted to make up the environment of Hellenism. All these aspects of Hellenism developed within the frame of a society made up of a number of quite independent and competitive units – city-states – which were characteristic of the Hellenic political order. That kind of state, which for some modern interpreters had roots in a tripartite structure of human society going back thousands of years to the dawn of society among Indo-European peoples of Eurasia, was an ideological construct as early as we have evidence of its existence in Greece. The state was, in essence, not a physical entity but a conceptual being, an aggregate of the people, their customs and laws, their family traditions and religious activities. It existed in space as well, however, and the residents of every Greek city were conscious of its physical aspect, expressed in the public and religious buildings within an agglomerate of housing, an urban or semi-urban center which controlled and depended on a countryside which provided food and other necessities. But even the physical city was an expression of the concept-ual, for, in general, only citizens, that is members of the city-state, could own any of the land on which it rested. There is no doubt that in some way, this fundamental sense of the relationship between the members, even the poorest members, of the state and the physical and political expression of the state had some influence on the evolution of Hellenic ideas and institutions, but the great diversity of the political expressions of this ideology of the state, from archaic family-focused organizations to the bureaucratic monarchies of the Greek east in the centuries after Alexander, shows how differently Greeks could structure their societies and distribute the material fruits of their collective effort.

11

The material fruits and the physical environment were much more uniform than the use made of them. The land, with rare exceptions, was poor, with only a thin layer of topsoil, and with only a few good arable stretches here and there in hilly or mountainous terrain. Except in the southern part of the Peloponnesus and in Thessaly, where good, open country could be found, communities generally clung to the littoral plains, and for many Greek city-states the sea provided an important supplement to the products of the land. But everywhere wealth was predominantly agricultural, and riches as well as livelihoods came from the land. Grains grew best on flat terrain, wine from grapes was a product of the hillsides, while olives and their oil came from trees which could grow even in the bad soils of the mountainsides and survive the dry Greek climate. Sheep grazed the hillsides and goats grubbed their food from the worst scrub, and in some places decent pastureland supported cattle and even horses. Some cities rested on a much better agricultural base than that I suggest here, and in those, the larger landowners could become very wealthy by Greek standards, but even in the cities with the poorest land, the peasantry which made up the vast majority of the population could find subsistence. When populations expanded to uncomfortable levels, rivalry for good land became a major and early cause of war, even though colonization took off some of the excess numbers.

The peninsula of Greece, or the Aegean area in general, did not tend to generate great social wealth. Archaeology shows that even in the late Bronze Age, when major palace centers seem to have focused wealth and collected it through trade as well as agriculture, the quantities of precious metals and luxury goods in Greece were small in comparison to the wealth of the oriental kingdoms of the Near East. And by 1000 BC with the collapse of these palace-centered kingdoms, even that level of material prosperity had slumped, and Greece saw several hundred years of rebuilding and population growth before the largest cities again reached high levels of prosperity.

That prosperity was, for the most part, limited to the comparatively few families in each city who owned enough land to produce a significant surplus. Often the uncertainties of agriculture and human life combined to push the marginal peasant into bankruptcy: circumstances which conspired to bring more and more of the smaller parcels into the possession of the wealthy who could survive adversity themselves and pick up the land of others by purchase or mortgage foreclosure. Many cities saw long periods of internal strife as citizen-farmers struggled to impose some restraints on the political, legal, and social power of the large landowners, and even when incomes were supplemented in some cities by revenues from trade, that wealth tended to be concentrated into the hands of a few and there were only very limited opportunities to create entrepreneurial fortunes. Public incomes were also slender; initial nearly non-existent public revenues might be supplemented by port and harbor dues, taxes, and fees imposed on non-citizen craftsmen and traders, or certain kinds of special taxes, but for the most part, whatever public functions required funding were paid for by individual citizens who were rewarded for their public-spiritedness by prestige and, in most cities, by the power which public activity, office, reputation, and expenditure united to preserve. Outside these aspects of public finance, military activity, as Max Weber noted,[1] served as a major catalyst in the creation of Hellenic society, and some cities, like Athens in the fifth century BC, attained very high levels of public revenue through war and imperial domination.

But most people saw little material benefit from wars, and most citizens, even as civic prosperity grew, could look at best to a reasonable diet, a little surplus for luxuries and arms, the services of women and slaves to make daily toil a little lighter, and an existence which could be burdened by war or disease but rarely lightened by unexpected windfalls. Most goods would be made at home, and what was bought, like pottery or weapons, would be manufactured by individual craftsmen who sold their own wares; or, in some circumstances, these might come from factories where a group of slaves worked for the profit of an owner. However, even in the largest urban center, Athens, the proportion of citizens involved in manufacture or trade would have made up a very small portion of the total citizen body, for at no time did any ancient city change the predominant agricultural orientation. Of course, precise quantification is impossible, but ancient societies could not have had a smaller percentage of the population devoted to food producing than the 75 per cent common in some modern agricultural economies. So for all the modernism of manufacture, commerce, and even overseas trade evident in a city like Athens, the age-old rhythms of farming and seasonal work on the land defined the daily life of most citizens.

That life, contrary to the prejudice of so many sedentary moderns who dislike the prospect of carrying stones out of fields, was not an experience of constant drudgery and grinding poverty. Even if most Greeks lived only at the level of subsistence agriculture, farming work would not have been unremitting. Today, Mediterranean peasants spend little more than a quarter of their daylight hours in their fields; the rest of life is taken up with walking to and from the village, talk, work around the house, repair of implements, tending to animals, more talk, and of course, festivals. Even today, religious festivals provide a major focus for social and cultural activity throughout the year, and in antiquity, they were equally important, or, with the diversity of divinities and cults, probably much more so.

The proliferation of Greek festivals and the opacity of the rituals performed at them are analogous to the complexity of Greek religion, and the difficulty of understanding Greek religious act, myth, and belief. Yet religion lies at the heart of Hellenism, for the world of divinity and human treatment of it was as much part of the environment as the earth and the work of planting and reaping. The diversity of religion is bewildering, however, in myth, ritual, and festival, not only across city-lines and diachronically, which perhaps is no more than should be expected, but within tight bounds of time and place. It filled

13

many days of the year: at Athens, for example, about one-third of the days of the year held some festival or another. What people did at these festivals, even if known to us, simply adds to the distance between our understanding and the meaning of Greek ritual act. The three days of the important Athenian festival of the Anthesteria comprised a day of drinking the new wine in a very formal way, such as each man drinking from his own cup and mixing bowl; this was followed by a day of mysterious rituals, doorposts of houses smeared with pitch, and men consuming laxatives; while on the third day, called "pots" day, a mixture of grains were boiled with honey, a meal which priests, at least, were forbidden to eat.[2] What such acts may mean has been the subject of interpretation from antiquity to the present, and in modern times, anthropology and psychology have offered interpretations which draw on our understanding of a variety of tribal societies and intuitions about human mentality. The rituals and myths of the Greeks, by analogy with those of other societies, have been given a wide range of meanings, from fertility to functional means of ordering society or ideas of the world to language-related structures which were complete in themselves as media of communication. I will make no attempt here to discuss the varied modern theories of Greek myth[3] or religion,[4] nor will I attempt a unifying theory of either, although I would warn against the romantic tendency to look at Greek religion as a stage or stages in human development, as though the religious acts of Greeks represent some mediation between religion in early human society and that which belongs to social structures of greater complexity and rational development. There is a great attraction in seeing both myth and religion among the Greeks as a kind of "language" expressing concerns about the world, and there is a good deal of force in John Gould's observation that "any religion must extend the range of the explicability of things beyond what men can derive from projection of their own self-awareness on to the external world,"[5] as well as his view that for the Greeks, if not for all humanity, "the essence of divinity lies in the paradoxical coexistence of incompatible truths about human experience."[6] As will be clear in the following chapters, I think that the perception of the combination of incompatibility and truth in the possible explanations of experience is a characteristic of Hellenism, and it is helpful to see that there is a religious expression of this idea. In this sense, Lévi-Strauss' idea of myth in its deeper structure[7] expresses the tension between opposites, although I do not find it useful to assert the concept for all human mythic thought, nor do I believe Hellenism's approach to incompatibility and truth to be a universal attitude. Christianity, after all, is based on the view that truth is unitary, and incompatibility is to be explained away, and, although secularists in the disordered modern world may welcome the perception of ambiguity inherent in Hellenism, philosophy and social theory and action for the most part still pursue the goals of unifying explanations and systems.

One of the most striking aspects of Greek religion and myth is their apparent naïvety and lack of intellectual content. Scholars and readers steeped in the verbal and argumentative aspects of Greek culture, from the speeches in Homer through Athenian tragedy to the disputations of philosophy and the law courts, are unwilling to believe that Greek religion does not go a great deal deeper than crude sacrifice or the tales of the gods which fill mythology books, although an acceptance of the surface meaning of myth would at least put us in the company of Greeks who themselves saw no sense deeper than the narrative.[8] While the so-called "Olympian" religion of epic and tragedy may be an overlay on an early chthonic or "earth" religion which has left traces in many practices, and many cult acts may have had origins quite different from their practitioners' interpretations, these connections had disappeared, their meanings lost, by the time we meet the Hellenism of our texts. So too, certain aspects of Greek religion may be found in the religions of other so-called Indo-European peoples from the Indus Valley to Ireland, but that would have little effect on the Greeks. We may understand the Eucharist better from historical criticism reaching back through the ancient world into the most antique; we understand modern people and their ideas only through a clarification of the conceptualization or multiple interpretations of the Eucharist today. So also, to understand Hellenism, we need to understand how religion made up part of the environment not only in Homeric times, but also in the fifth and fourth centuries BC, and later. While the evidence of practice is variegated enough to inspire ideas of comparing paleolithic hunting ritual to Greek practice,[9] we must not lose sight of the directness and purposefulness which are characteristic and prominent in the Greek approach to divinity. I think that any extensive survey of Greek texts in a number of genres forces the reader to come to terms with a portrait of a society which accepts the gods as active, affective, and responsive. While there is no doubt that ordinary belief might often be challenged, there is no doubt that the ordinary consensus in society held that divine powers intervened in human life according to some known principles, and that judgments about human action could be made on the basis of what gods did or didn't do.[10] It is a peculiar stubbornness of many modern students which prevents them from starting their investigation of Greek religion with Socrates' last words: "Crito, I owe a cock to Asclepius; now you give it, and don't neglect it."[11]

We have also been accustomed to draw distinctions between public religion, in which act focuses on the temples, altars, and sanctuaries of the gods named by Homer, Hesiod, and the tragedians, and the so-called "popular" religion. On the one hand, we have the brilliance and clarity of the great Olympian deities, like Athena, Apollo, Poseidon, and Hermes, with Zeus at their head and even comprehending such a foreigner as Dionysus. The Olympians lived in the light of the great festivals like the Panathenaic at Athens and the great games at Olympia, they communicated through oracles, and had their system explored openly in epic, tragedy, and hymn. Popular religion, on the other hand, we deduce from scattered references in our texts and from discoveries of artifacts related to them. There are traces of totemism and animism, fertility

15

*1* One of the original works of Greek sculpture which have survived, this bronze portrayal of the god Poseidon, his arm raised to hurl the trident, was saved from the melting furnace by the sea. Found in the waters off Cape Artemision, it probably sank there soon after it was made in the mid-fifth century BC. (National Museum, Athens)

cults, and magic which seem to have been the origin of some practices in public cult but are masked by later adaptations and rationalizations, and notions of spirits, monsters, and the like never died out among Greeks. Houses were provided with their protecting shrines and charms, and the public ways too had their guardians. The ubiquitous herms, busts of Hermes with protruding phallus, use this Olympian god – now as protector of travelers – in a restructuring of an earlier tradition which used the phallus as a talisman of protection. There is, no doubt, some truth in all this, and some validity to the distinction between "popular" and "Olympian" religion, although if recent investigations into Greek religion have done nothing else, they show us how the most common characteristics and myths of Olympian religion can be related to what some would call the most primitive religious practices of early humans.

A much more useful distinction shows how the deities and practices of our texts were part of the public, civic world of the Greek city. In matters which brought people into social contact, Olympian deities were the interested parties. Such were "the gods whom the city took cognizance of," whose neglect constituted the allegation against Socrates, or "the national gods" of Macedonia, whom Alexander always respected. Not only need they be propitiated and thanked in connection with the concerns of the body politic as a whole, it was to them that people had resort for enforcing and regulating the bonds between individuals and families which made the peculiar Greek state possible in the first place. It could be a complicated, time-consuming and variegated task to do all this, particularly in a society without a body of priests to take care of religious duties on a full-time or surrogate basis. Some rituals were affected by some of the population, others by most, and individual response might range from virtual neglect to the frantic behavior of Theophrastus' superstitious man. But the whole body of ritual, sacrifice, and act remained available as an explanation of events; public or personal good fortune or failure could be explained in terms of proper behavior toward the gods, although, as I will make clearer below, contradictions abounded and expectations were not always fulfilled.

The Greek orientation toward religion as a communal structure promoted another kind of collective worship, in which specifically formed groups performed their services to a deity or deities. These groups had their family and clan manifestations, but, quite early, they also evolved as associations in which membership could be deliberately chosen, even if in some instances eligibility was determined by family or citizenship status. The procedures of worship were usually prescribed in a liturgy known in detail to every member of the group. Membership in such an association required an affirmative act, often a series of acts, and in many instances there were various levels of participation which a new member reached progressively as initiation advanced further and further into full membership in the group. The so-called mystery religions were associations of this type. As they appear in our later texts, of the time after Alexander and in the Roman period, they offered their adherents a kind of transcendent experience of communion with the deity, a communion in which the *mystos*, or participant, became one with the god or even became the god itself. The initiate would be guided along the path by experienced members of the group who had already achieved the higher states, and he might in turn serve as guide or religious "father" to those who came after. What we know of the effect of the mysteries in earlier times, the fifth and fourth centuries BC, suggests that mysteries were deemed to benefit the initiates in the afterlife, but the prevalent Greek attitudes which had low regard for any existence after death in opposition to life indicate that the mysteries did not create a mood that was very widely expressed.

Religious associations of this sort existed in Greece from the earliest times of *polis* society. Some of them became semi-official, either connected with a city cult or accorded a special respect by the citizens. Such were the Eleusinian Mysteries, dedicated to the goddess Demeter, carried on at Eleusis, a suburb of Athens. Similar, although more obscure to us, were the practices of the Orphics, an association said by the Greeks to have been founded by Orpheus,

17

2 This relief found at Eleusis, the center of the Eleusinian mysteries near Athens, is one of the most famous – and finest – examples of fifth-century BC sculpture. In this portrayal of the divinities to whom the mysteries were dedicated, the goddess Demeter, at the left, gives the stalks of grain to the young Triptolemus, while from the right, Demeter's daughter Kore places a crown on the boy's head. Apart from specific symbols, such as the Eleusinian torch which Kore holds, nothing sets the divine figures apart from humanity. It is their actions and accidental properties, rather than their essential appearance or physical attributes, which distinguish gods from humans in Greek representational art.

18

and also the mysto-philosophical Pythagoreans, who followed the concepts of the south Italian Greek Pythagoras, relating the phenomena of the cosmos to numbers, in the way that harmonic chords are interrelated in numeric fashion. The worship of Dionysus was also carried on in mysteries, following cult practices which even as late as the fifth century BC were believed to have originated in the east, as Euripides' play *The Bacchae* makes clear. Not only Dionysus but other deities brought their worship from Anatolia and further east, and by the time we have evidence for them in texts and inscriptions of the fifth century and beginning of the fourth century BC, a number of so-called oriental mystery religions had become well-established in many parts of the Greek world and had become thoroughly Hellenized.

These religious activities existed side by side with the more public services of festivals and celebrations which were directly connected with city life. But like the worship attached to the Olympian deities, the mystery religions served the needs and desires of the worshippers. The service to the deity was fundamentally construed as a process by which the initiate gained something – communion, immortality, knowledge, health – rather than a devotion organized to benefit the deity. This was also a characteristic of what are perhaps the most famous Greek religious phenomena, the oracles. Delphi is the most noted,[12] but Zeus also spoke through priests at the oasis oracle at Siwah in the Libyan desert, and at Dodona in western Greece, a sacred place mentioned as early as the Homeric poems. By the fifth century individuals and states were consulting these oracles to aid decisions. Even the Lydian King Croesus asked Delphi in the sixth century if he should attack Persia, and was told that if he did, he "would destroy a great empire," an answer with an ambiguity he did not detect. The Greeks were aware of the riddling quality of some of these pronouncements, which in tradition represented the high point of Delphian prophecy, but they were, in a sense, only the tip of the iceberg which was the god's clarification of the future to humanity. The prophecy first came to the priestess at Delphi, and then was recorded by priests known as prophets. It may be that, as many modern accounts have it, the priestess spoke incomprehensible sounds while in a trance; then her prophecy was interpreted by priests in sometimes ambiguous words. On the other hand, the Pythian priestess herself was punished when she was proved guilty of false prophecy, and the prophecy she gave may have been direct and understandable. In any case, the god would never lie, but the priestess and priests might, and Greeks were aware of the possibility, but in general, they expected to be able to trust what Delphi told them. Certainly, while public or political oracles might be interpreted for suspect purposes, the private prophecies could be taken with greater confidence.

Apollo might advise, warn or predict; his son Asclepius specialized in curing the sick. Known early as a physician and worshipped as a hero, Asclepius' curative powers became so well known as time went on that centers of worship were devoted to him, places which provided the focus for the crippled and the

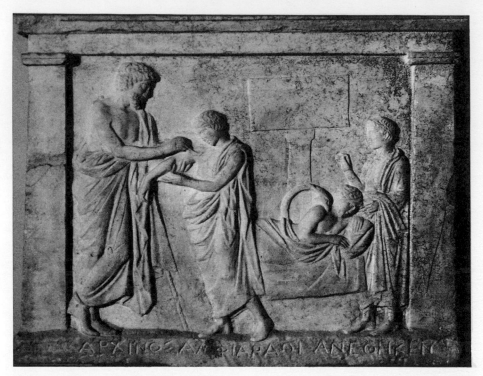

*3* Many representations of Asclepius were erected in so-called votive reliefs, sculptures, dedicated to the god in thanks for his help. Here, a work of the first half of the fourth century BC shows the god arranging cures, with what is presumably a bedridden patient in the background. (National Museum, Athens)

sick to appeal for help to the god. The *Aesculapeion*, as the god's precinct was called, combined the usual religious edifices with accommodation for visiting petitioners, with larger and larger buildings honeycombed with cubicles for the pilgrims who sought sleeping room while awaiting cures. That the cures came is amply attested. At Epidaurus, the best-known *Aesculapeion*, and at others across the Hellenic world, inscriptions erected by grateful worshippers record the benefactions of the god: the blind received sight; the lame and halt walked again; the ill and the suffering rose, cured, from their beds; the barren conceived and disfigurements vanished. All these and more were credited to the god, demonstrations of his efficacy and his care for humans, ample justification for the largess heaped upon his shrines.

All these strains of religious feeling were known and available to Greeks by the end of the fifth century BC. Not everyone would believe everything, and some might not believe anything of the systems of worship or what was said about divinity, but all Hellenes would understand the practices of people in the Greek cities which stretched from the coast of Lebanon to the Atlantic shores of Spain. And everywhere, Hellenic worship of the gods involved primarily the performance of cult acts in an effort to gain a deity's aid. Apart from the contact points in public festivals, oracles, mystery rituals, and the like, however, the divine and human spheres were quite separate, and religion had little to do with relationships amongst humans or the proprieties of humans' treatment of one another. Although a Greek like Hesiod might proclaim Zeus would punish evildoers, there is no sense that human injustice was in any way regarded as a crime against the god, and the gods did not prescribe detailed law like that set down for the Hebrews. It is, in fact, for precisely this reason that the question of divine justice emerged so often in Greek literature. Because the answers to ethical questions were not provided as part of religious faith, Hellenism tended to approach the question of moral order in philosophic and literary form rather than as part of a theological structure. In this way, service to the gods could be seen as perfectly adequate even when it was totally divorced from ethical action.

These characteristics of Hellenic religion changed little in the fourth century BC, although intellectuals continued to disparage consensus religion as it was practiced. The denigration of common religious practice and prevailing conceptions of the gods had been characteristic of the Sophists, and attitudes persisted despite the examples of vigorous legal action which Athenians took against some of those philosophers. It is quite clear that many of those who saw themselves as advancing human knowledge, "lovers of wisdom" or philosophers as Plato used the term, regarded most Greek ritual as benighted, and myths as invented stories about childishly conceived gods. They regarded ordered reason about the nature of the cosmos and the divinities in it as the only reliable means of understanding experience. The modern intellectual's willingness to accord validity to another way of understanding and communication, the logic of the "savage mind" as Lévi-Strauss calls it, would have seemed laughable to the Greeks. By the fourth century Plato would reject even the tragic mode of using divinities and myths to explore the apparent failings of human accommodation to the cosmic order, finding in the plays he knew as a youth a deceptive quality which betrayed reason's search for truth. While he was careful to couch his rejection of many common views and statements as betrayals of the principle that the gods should never be seen as anything but good, it was essential to his system that the sense of inherent contradiction and multiplicity of truth which lay at the heart of the consensus religious experience be banished from the arena of discussion. Ultimately, many intellectuals consigned all of religion to the side of Hellenism which we would call the "irrational," and insisted on incorporating the concerns of religion into the categories of verbal, explicit, and consequential language.

The same period which began the intellectuals' attempt to move the treatment of the ambiguities of life from myth and ritual into reasoned verbal analysis saw a great deal of interchange amongst Greeks and foreigners. Foreign cults came to the Greek world; there was a shrine to Isis at Athens before the end of the fourth century; Phrygian and Anatolian cults spread into the Hellenic world before Alexander began his expedition which carried so many Greeks east. But there is no reason to suppose that these new centers of eastern cult were established by Greeks, and their presence can easily enough be explained by the presence of large numbers of foreigners in Greek cities. There is certainly no evidence of Greek participation on any scale at this time. Still, Greeks got to know more about other deities, in an awareness which increased greatly after the conquests of Alexander established the Greeks in the east and gave an entirely new dimension to that contact as the Greeks came to lands where other gods had shrines. Alexander himself exemplified a typical Greek reaction to the gods he encountered. He was respectful, he worshipped appropriately, but he maintained all the observances due to his own particular Macedonian deities and Hellenic divinities in general. In much the same way, the kings who came after him maintained their Hellenism in the face of very diverse religious and social customs which they encountered in the east, and so did their Greek subjects. Eastern deities, like Isis, long known to Greeks, were approached in the Hellenic fashion, and alongside the old Egyptian temple worship of Isis grew up a clearly Greek cult, which spread rapidly through the Mediterranean world. At the same time, newly discovered deities, like Serapis, were represented as Greek divinities and also worshipped in Hellenic fashion, with temples, processions, and festivals in the Greek style. Whether these religions developed their own mysteries from the start or not, they did show early on the characteristics of offering communion with the deity, and extending special divine help, sometimes even a kind of immortality, to the worshipper. Later in time the Isis religion certainly had acquired its mysteries. In any case, the prestige of the older Greek mysteries was such that there were attempts to transfer them to the Greek centers of the new kingdoms set up after Alexander; for example, a suburb of Alexandria was named Eleusis, after the mystery center of Demeter near Athens, in order to serve as a location for mysteries in Egypt. Other mysteries, like those of Dionysus, or those of the Cabiri on the island of Samothrace, offered patterns to Isis worshippers, and if the new or transformed religions which swept out of the east had mysteries when they came to Greece and Italy, they came not as fundamentally "oriental" cults changing the religious atmosphere of the period, but Hellenized, with worship following the traditional Greek manner.

Hellenism it was, almost completely: religion still based on the traditional kinds of Greek ritual. In this there was no difference from another religious phenomenon emerging at the time, the so-called "dynastic cults," organized structures of worship, with royally appointed priests and priestesses, devoted to the service of the deified sovereigns. These dynastic cults began with a priesthood devoted to Alexander, and from this it was an easy expansion to cults of deceased kings of the royal line, and thence to living rulers. There is some argument about the point at which this transference was made in Egypt, but the question is merely one of detail. The establishment of cults to living sovereigns took place in the course of the third century BC in Egypt, and there, as well as in the realms of the Seleucids, were established and maintained by the crown, and were picked up by non-Greeks as well as Hellenes. The dynastic cult was a means of formally conferring honors on the king and members of his family, and despite its priests the sacrifices, rituals, and formalized actions were typically Hellenic, much like the public cults of the city-states to which it was often joined in the eastern kingdoms. The fundamental concepts had their inception in Hellenic ideas and in the practices of Alexander the Great and his father Philip, and they fitted in perfectly well with the services to traditional Greek deities which were carefully maintained by the kings in Egypt, Syria, and Macedonia.

The cults of the traditional Greek deities were far from being overwhelmed by the new religions focusing on eastern divinities. Cities carried on or even expanded their long-established practices, and worship and oracular consultation at Delphi continued unabated. The Olympic Games and the other major inter-city religious festivals continued, and new games were established in honor of kings or for other reasons in the centuries after Alexander. The gods kept in touch with humanity, and Artemis herself came in relevation to Magnesia on the Maeander in Asia Minor in the last quarter of the third century BC, as a result of which the city established games and asked the kings and other Greek cities to accept their new festival and to consider the city inviolate in the future. Similar actions show in the acceptance of Teos as sacred to Dionysus, and the establishment, often with the consent of a king, of sacred groves, rites, processions, or temples to one or another of the traditional Hellenic deities, and on a number of occasions the royal cult was joined to this worship. Thus the two centuries after Alexander saw in the Greek world and its newly acquired regions what was essentially a continuance of Hellenic traditions, with no religious features which were strikingly new or overturned earlier practice. The worship of the traditional Greek gods in public civic cult continued and prospered, joined by cults devoted to the deified sovereigns and their ancestors. Mystery religions, which had long flourished in Greek centers, continued their growth and became more and more diversified in the deities which they served. Private worship continued as well, as people sought help or advantage from the gods, and salvation of one sort or another, which had always been part of the promise of mystery religions, continued to be available in these as well as in the cults of Isis, Astarte, and other divinities which were spreading all through the Mediterranean lands.

The condemnation of intellectuals had made little impact on either the popularity or nature of traditional religious practice. As late as the second century of our era, while the Roman Emperor Marcus Aurelius might exemplify the rational and philosophical presentation of the alliance between divinity and virtue, the satirist Lucian still felt compelled to rail at what he saw as the absurdity and even fraud of the religion of his day. At the same time, the Christian rationalist, Clement of Alexandria, exhorted the Greeks to give up a religion which seems from his text to differ very little from what we understand from the writers of half a millennum earlier. As long as Hellenism existed as a relatively pure force, the society which it formed had a need for rendering non-human force as discontinuity, and treating divine power as multifaceted. As Plato saw, this was a most unsatisfactory and even improper representation of a divine power which ought to be seen as superior to human, but Greek religion had never evolved out of a sense of human subservience of an ethic of worship. Whatever its remote origins in prehistoric human experience might or might not have been, so long as it was part of Hellenism it was a complex of act and word, ritual and myth, through which humans, for the most part in their social matrix, attempted to project and establish patterns of behavior which were beneficial to themselves.

The Roman experience of all this was quite different from that of the Greeks. Although Roman religion was originally of the same polytheistic type as that of the Greeks, it had developed quite differently, and the sense of the spirits investing the world around them remained stronger among the Romans than it did among the Greeks. Although as time went on and Romans either adopted Greek cults of the Olympian deities or equated Greek gods to their own, that practice overlooked the very different roles which the Roman deities originally played in their society. Roman gods, so long as their conception remained insulated from the attractions of Greek representations, were more a part of nature, more related to the earth and the regular phenomena of the agricultural year, more inchoate in their visualization, more connected with the dead, with ancestors, with the individual in society, and with the society itself.

In some of this, the neighboring Etruscans, whose society stands out amongst peoples of the northern Mediterranean for its focus on respect and service to the dead, may have been influential. There were other characteristics of Roman religion which contributed to the important part ancestors played in Roman religious activity, which seems to preserve a closer connection between divinity and the social order than was the case for the Greeks. Some modern analysts see the early Roman triad of Jupiter, Mars, and Quirinus as a preservation of the old Indo-European partition of reality – and thus of the gods and the population as well – among the functions of sovereignty, with magical and legal aspects, the function of war, and the function of agriculture and reproduction. Similarly, Roman historical writing has been taken as a historicization of very old Indo-European myth.[13] Right or wrong, these suggestions illustrate how closely Roman religious history was tied into the social functions of the state, even in very early times, and they show how the Romans retained aspects of religion even through periods of drastic social change.

Whatever impact Etruscan and Greek conceptions had on the Romans, some sort of basic Romanism remained. Ancestors continued to play a very important part in religious activity; their images were carried about in processions and on some official occasions, and their spirits, the *manes*, were served in a formal cult. In other groups involved in family or household religion, the *lares*, who protected the family's fields, and the *penates*, who guarded its wealth, the spirits were undifferentiated and unnamed, and never developed the anthropomorphic representation so common among the Greeks. In addition to these protecting and ancestral spirits, an individual could pray to the *genius* – personal spirit, a kind of spiritual *alter ego* – which could act as a guide and inspiration, and the *genius* of the head of the household, on which the whole household depended to guide and empower the master, became part of the family cults and was worshipped along with all the other spirits. This family cult remained an important part of Roman religious activity, and it preserved its essential and particular characteristics, even as the public cult changed as the state grew from a small city-state to dominion over Italy. The Roman sense of integration of religion and society was so strong that despite the strong Roman conservatism in family, law, and custom, religious patterns could adapt as the state itself changed, and Latinistic cult became more acceptable as Rome moved closer to becoming the leading city of central Italy and to dominating the Latin states immediately to the south. Public worship, with temples, individual divinities, festivals, and services, became more like those of the Latins and, incidentally, those of the Greeks of south Italy. On the Capitoline Hill a temple provided a focus for three deities – still – but now named Jupiter, Juno, and Minerva. These are not simply Greek gods with Latin names, Jupiter for Zeus, Juno for Hera, and Minerva for Athena, for in the Roman conception, Jupiter and Juno were the divine embodiments of the father and mother of the household – *pater* and *mater*, master and mistress – and in the cult they had the central importance that these held in the family. Minerva was a Latin goddess who was credited with some of the attributes of Athena, and Mars, the war-related god of the earlier triad whose worship continued at Rome, was far more important than his equivalent Ares was to the Greeks; to him the Romans prayed before battle and to him they dedicated temples and spoils in thanks for his help.

These deities, as well as some of the others whose worship started up or whose cult was officially established in the city, were served by officially sanctioned procedures and by priests and priestly colleges who were actually appointed by the state. These priests were, in a sense, magistrates for the performance of divine affairs, and they had official status and great prestige in Rome. There were *flamens*, serving particular gods; *augurs*, who called upon the gods for omens to determine divine approval for proposed actions; there were the sacred dancers of Mars, the *Salii*. Women also participated in sacred colleges, like the most famous women's group, the Vestal Virgins, dedicated to the service of Vesta and the city's hearth. The most prestigious of these religious magistracies was that of the *pontifex maximus*, the "greatest pontifex," who headed and embodied the college of officials with the name *pontifex*, exercised independent power over religious practice, had wide-ranging authority of appointment and discipline of other priests, and served as an adviser on religious matters and law. The existence of these priestly colleges illustrates how closely religious matters were entwined with political life, a

25

Roman characteristic which affected the state's attitude toward foreign religions. Although Romans were tolerant of other religious traditions, and made no effort to "correct" other ideas or spread their own, their leaders often took pains to isolate Roman practice and Italy as a whole from what they saw as pernicious foreign influences. To the Senators, "the wogs began at Corfu," and the Greeks and the easterners could have all their erratic cults so long as they did not bring them to Rome. Despite this official attitude, the eastern cults did penetrate, and they remained or returned despite official sanctions like the suppression of the Bacchanalian mysteries in 186 BC. This and other suppressions and expulsions seem to have been directly related to those orgiastic cults which, with their secret and night-time rituals, raised the suspicions of sedate elders that all kinds of sexual and other immoralities were practiced under their protection. Still, the magistrates allowed the establishment of temples to the Greek gods in the late third century BC, and at the end of the Second Punic War the cult of the Phrygian Magna Mater was formally established, her votive object, the black stone of Pessinus, dutifully sent to Rome by the king of Pergamum. The worship was strictly regulated, however, illustrating the Roman tradition of official control of religion, and demonstrating the suspicion directed at the eastern cults. Nevertheless, Greek and Hellenized eastern religions penetrated Roman society more and more, and by the first century BC, as we see from the decorations of the villa dei Misteri at Pompeii, the mystery religions were incorporated into Roman life. By this time, shrines of Isis and other deities like Cybele, Attis, and Serapis had brought Hellenic religion to Rome, while healing religions prompted the establishment of great sanctuaries like that overlooking the sea at Praeneste. In all probability, by the end of the second century BC Rome was similar to most Mediterranean cities of the time, apart from the official state religion and the private family cults, with religious activities that could be found in Antioch, in Alexandria, in Athens, or westward to Massilia in France and Gades on the Atlantic.

Although Rome, even into imperial times, retained a sense of separateness from the Greek cities and the dynasties of the east, it did provide both a location and an opportunity for the expansion of Hellenic religion to the west. In Italy and more particularly Rome itself, Hellenism might confront an environment and social structures quite different from those of the Aegean area and further east, but it was able to maintain itself despite the differences. Government at Rome, like religion, was more formal, resting more on traditional custom and regulation, and law itself was a carefully and openly elaborated system reaching back, at least conceptually, to the historical development of the city of Rome. As the Romans saw it, even political change was, at least until the end of the second century BC, a structured and controlled interaction of classes which generated a desirable social evolution, and change was linear, rather than cyclical or alternating as it was portrayed so often by Greeks. As Hellenism encountered the Romans, it was affected by some of the fundamental attitudes of Roman thought, and although Hellenism retained its basic characteristics

26

even in adaptation, it was influenced in some manifestations by Roman ideology. The religious and social environment in which it was carried on was, in detail, quite different.

Even the physical environment of Italy is different. Much of the peninsula is more hilly than mountainous, and the agricultural land is better and more plentiful that that of Greece. The climate offers more to the farmer – more rain in many parts at least – and more variety. It can be colder in Italy, and while snow is rare in Rome, it is rarer still in Athens. Also, although there are mountains, less than a quarter of the territory is taken up with ranges above 2300 feet, so that passes are not so arduous, interior communications are easier, and the peoples of the peninsula are not forced out to the sea as were the Greeks. All this encourages different human institutions and activities. The Romans opened up roads and interior routes before they mastered the sea. They put more energy into domestic architecture, so far as we can determine, and in agriculture, despite official attempts to encourage the allocation of land in small lots to citizen-farmers, the nature and potential of the land were themselves an impetus for the development of very large estates, which attracted the capital, effort, and part-time residence of the wealthy at considerable distances from the city itself. Even all of Italy could not contain the ambitious or covetous, and southern France, Sicily, parts of Spain, and ultimately North Africa from Morocco to Egypt attracted Roman investment.

If the west operated on a greater scale, Hellenism could nevertheless adapt. Although throughout the Mediterranean, local particularism, cultural, linguistic, and religious, was able to survive the arrival of Greek civilization and Roman government, the urban environment in the constellation of cities across the Mediterranean which flourished under Roman rule provided fertile soil on which Hellenism could continue to live. Ultimately, Hellenism was an urban phenomenon, so much so that Aristotle could not imagine human life outside the context of the city-state. That city-state environment may have been encouraged in part by the isolating geography of Greece, and its institutions may have been molded by the exigencies of intra-city conflict of a sort very different from the Roman experience of war, but its structure proved adaptable to the very different circumstances of participation in territorial kingdoms and eventually the world-state of Rome. The city-state as an expression of human political power changed with time, but it always remained enough of a focus of human effort, activity, and concern to provide a background for cultural activities and to generate issues for Hellenism to consider. For 1000 years or more, whatever Hellenism did or created – and however it evolved – happened in these cities.

# 3

# In the beginning

## The nature and importance
## of Homeric epic

No Greek writer came close to Homer's influence on Hellenic thought, and no Greek poetry was so fundamental to education or known so thoroughly by later Greeks as the great epics, the *Iliad* and the *Odyssey*. Of the two, the *Iliad*, with its psychological depth and its inclusion of so many concepts in religion and philosophy which dominated later Greek thought, can safely be said to have had more influence on later Greek literature than any other single work. The poems were not only intellectually important; they were popular as well. In the periods of history for which we have good evidence, from the third century BC down to the fifth century of our era, remnants of the ancient books actually read by the Greek-speaking residents of Egypt, the papyri preserved in the sands of that country, give us a statistical demonstration of that popularity: of the literary texts discovered in Egypt at the present time of writing, Homer accounts for almost 800 pieces, while the next most common authors, Demosthenes and Euripides, account for only about 100 each. This pattern is consistent from the earliest pieces to the latest times before the Arab conquest of the country, and it amply justifies the statement that Homer was the most widely read author in antiquity. It is small wonder then, that the philosopher who was most concerned about the influence of poetry on thought, that is, Plato, regarded Homer as the most influential,[1] and argued that his work should be banned because the attitudes and the views of men and gods he expressed were not only wrong in themselves, but had a deleterious influence on opinion and behavior.

Just as Homeric epic filled roll after roll of papyrus in antiquity, modern studies of Homer fill whole ranges of library shelves today. For 200 years, scholars and critics have studied and argued about the language of the poems, about the authorship, whether one mind or a multiple was responsible for the epics, about the nature of the "oral" style, and about the society which the poetry reflects. The debates, like so many scholarly arguments, are never won or lost, but are simply outdistanced by events, as new discoveries, which began in the nineteenth century, about the Homeric age were joined by twentieth-

28

century revelations about the nature of the poetry itself. First came the stunning archaeological discoveries which demonstrated that the cities and civilizations of the *Iliad* had really occupied Greek soil, and as the results of the excavations of the nineteenth century blew away the mists that had shrouded these civilizations and given them the image of legend, the archaeologists of the twentieth century refined and expanded our knowledge of the development of Stone-Age and Bronze-Age Greece, so that by mid-century we knew that the occupants of these Bronze-Age cities were really Hellenes, in that they spoke a form of Greek, and some could even write.

No less an upheaval changed our understanding of the manner of the composition and transmission of the epics. Our concept of the oral nature of the poetry eventually shifted from one of memorized poetry, handed down over centuries by singers whom the Greeks called "rhapsodes" until the epics were finally written down in the sixth century BC. A much better explanation of this oral poetry came from Milman Parry's comparison of Homeric epic to the still vital oral tradition of early twentieth-century Serbo-Croatia, where the oral poet did not produce his song as a feat of memory, but rather fashioned a known narrative out of a repertoire of learned formulas which carry the concepts, description, and information which he needed for his songs. In this "formulaic diction," as it is called, the same words, phrases, and verses are used over and over again to describe specific people or report similar actions, so that in the *Iliad* and *Odyssey*, over a third of the verses are used more than once. The poet who operates in the tradition is, of course, limited by the content of the repertoire and the extent of his own knowledge of formulas in the repertoire and his own ingenuity in using them. The occasional very creative singer may enlarge the body and pass on to his successor the potential of greater scope. But because the formulas fit into metrical systems, they preserve old ideas, words, or information to the extent that the meter is rigid, and these metrical formulas can be compounded or excised almost at will to make a given recitation either short or long. So, essentially, runs the Parry thesis[2] on the nature of Homeric epic, the thesis which still commands the most support.

Although most modern analysts of the *Iliad* agree that the poem was created by oral composition of some sort, there is still a great deal of debate about the period in the history of Greek oral poetry during which the composition was vital, creative, and capable of producing works of the extraordinary quality and length of the Homeric epics. Some argue that they belong to the beginning of the first millennium BC, after the collapse of the great Bronze-Age centers which recent archaeology has discovered, while others insist that the main period during which the formulas were developed should be pushed back to the Bronze Age or even earlier. And in recent years, as we learn more about oral poetry in other societies, some of us who think about the poems have lost confidence in the explicit accounts of the "oral society" which produced the epics. Almost any concept of "Homer" is possible, and none is provable. In a way, it does not matter, because we have the text, and the text can tell us a great deal, although even here it is difficult to fit the information into a cognitive social context. It is possible to argue that the poetic and intellectual stance of the epics fits into some sort of picture of society affected by the international scene in the late Bronze Age, when the political arrangements in Mediterranean life were suffering a general disruption by invasions, pillage, and destruction. On the other hand, there is enough correlation between the society portrayed in the epics and that of the period of the so-called "dark ages," after the fall of the great centers, to allow some modern historians to insist that the only society "Homer" knew or could imagine was that of warring chieftains who lived a rude life of war and plunder in a social and economic structure less advanced than that which had been overturned by the turbulence which ended the Bronze-Age culture of the Aegean.[3] To some extent, the opinions are based on assumptions about the nature of the poetry and the kind of society which could produce it.

One thing is certain in all this. The ancient Greeks had practically no knowledge of the background to the epic, either the archaeological record or the nature of the oral poetry which the epic represents. No one in antiquity had any idea about the existence of Bronze-Age culture, let alone its nature, and the few relics which stood around Greece, like the monumental fortifications of Mycenae, were taken to have been the work of giants who inhabited the earth before the advent of humankind. Equally ignorant were they about oral poetry and what it could convey. Although they knew of rhapsodes, and were aware that the epics had been sung by them in earlier days, they had no idea of the essential nature of oral poetry, that long narrative poems like Homeric epic tended to be refashioned, even "recomposed," over the generations, and that their form and conceptions are the product of the interaction between audiences and creating singers. They certainly had no idea that this kind of composition can produce poetry as subtle and reflective as any produced by, let us say, Euripides, cogitating alone in his study. The Greeks certainly thought of the epics as produced by a single mind, "Homer" as a single and real person, wherever he hailed from, who was responsible for fashioning the entire poems, creating masterpieces from inspiration, not tradition.

For Homer was new; he was, for the Greeks, the beginning. Although they had a tradition of their poetry reaching back to Orpheus and Museaus, only a few pieces of song or oracle could even be attributed to those poets, so that the epic texts were, chronologically, the first to which Greeks could refer, and the sheer monumentality of the work, with its inclusion of both human and divine spheres of activity, assured it also of a primacy in thought. Homer always remained "the poet," and his work provided the touchstone for all poetry, drama, philosophy, and history which followed. The epics comprehended much that was essential to Greek culture and religion, and all accounts of the development of Greek thought and literature, whether written by ancients or moderns, start with them. They did more than express religious and philosophical truths, much more than serve as entertainment or purely intellectual literature, or as a model for later poetry, although they did all of these. They also provided the Greeks with the only record of that part of their past which preceded the organization and development of Greece as it was known in the historical period.

The events reported in the Homeric epics and in other poetry and narrative which came down through the dark ages into the historical period, tales, near-epics, and other oral poems which never made it into writing or perhaps even past the eighth century, conveyed to the Greeks a sense of their origins and their past. When Thucydides writes that at the time of the return to the Peloponnesus of the sons of Heracles all the peoples of southern Greece were uprooted and only Athens held out to provide continuity and some refuge for others, he is reporting information which, even if it had been put in writing before his own time, ultimately owes its existence to an oral tradition. The contents of the *Iliad* and the *Odyssey* preserve a significant amount of that tradition. Herodotus saw the Trojan War as part of a train of reciprocal wrongs exchanged between Europe and Asia, and Thucydides could use it as a measure against which to assess the size of the armaments and the importance of the Peloponnesian War. And the actions of specific heroes and the trains of events which they started were seen to have ramifications for their descendants and for the cities of Greece long after the war was over. Furthermore, this great armament and expedition of allied Greek states was a traditional representation of the essential unity of Hellenes in the face of the barbarian world, and symbolized that unity for all of their history. Finally, the events of the great war and the reactions and responses of the heroes to those events gave later Greeks historical perspective on their own conflicts, and a set of examples which they could accept as Hellenic behavior in military and even political conflict.

As important as were the historical implications facilitated by the tradition, the intellectual and perhaps religious effects were probably even greater. Representations of the gods and their behavior, descriptions of their relationships with each other and with humanity, interpretations of their role in the determination of human success or failure, and their effect on human action – all these appear in the epics. And the different senses of these affairs which we find there recur again and again in Greek literature and thought, sometimes unquestioned and sometimes seriously challenged or even denied, but always preserved as an aspect of the Greek mentality understandable to any Hellene. Furthermore, Homer provided an intellectual basis for Greek ideas. Here were attitudes toward mutual obligations, usually of nobles, and the requirements of behavior of inferior to superior and vice versa. The epics reflect a reasonably consistent code of conduct for warriors, and display the courtesies of combat and the values which a warrior class seemed to accept. It is clear what was "honorable" to the figures in the *Iliad*, and much of that is accepted in the scheme of the *Odyssey* as well. To help one's friends and hurt one's enemies is an understandable code, and one that could accept the deceit of an Odysseus as

31

well as the frank and open stubbornness of an Achilles. One could find in the epics not only the virtues of kings, princes, and soldiers, but of wives, children, and servants as well. In Homer the list of aspects of human relations, and what makes up *arete* or nobleness, is almost endless – surprisingly broad for two poems apparently limited in subject matter. It includes filial and wifely responsibilities and feelings, the expected duties of hosts and requirements of a guest, honors owed to friends and comrades, and the limits of maltreatment of enemies; it ranges from practices and courtesies at banquets to the appropriate treatment of the dead. Against the qualities of the epic heroes later Greeks could measure themselves and their own customs, and the epics could provide a touchstone common to all Greeks, however hostile their states or different their ways of life.

They could find even deeper meaning in the poems, ideas which never completely left the Greek sense of the relationship between people and nature. The sense of human weakness, of the individual's role as victim carrying out what are thought to be personal aims in order to achieve, often unknowingly, the will of the gods, remained with the Greeks for a long time. Inasmuch as Homer was fundamental to Greek education, it is small wonder that the Homeric view would strike impressionable sensibilities and permeate thought; it is therefore hardly surprising that Plato, in sketching his view of ideal education for an ideal state, would exclude Homer from that process. Homer included too many stories about gods and heroes which would not lead to the sort of behavior of which Plato approved. So too, the sense of fate in Homer, fate which was determined but which people would often try and always fail to elude, remained characteristic of many Greek thinkers and writers. The essential and inherent contradiction of this kind of behavior bothered later Greeks no more than it bothered the singers and audiences of the epics. Not confronted by the Christian dilemma of the necessity of free will to justify eternal reward and punishment, Greeks could live for centuries accepting both fate and the struggle against its dictates.

It is true that we can find differences between the world view of Homer and the ideas of some writers of the fifth and fourth centuries BC or later, but the similarities always remained stronger than the differences, and later centuries added to, rather than overturned, the concepts of the epics. Many have traced the evolution of religious, metaphysical, and ethical ideas from Homer to, say, Aristotle, and we have fairly good idea of how attitudes changed and new concepts grew as society was transformed from clan-orientated, family-dominated aristocratic structures to political states in which authority was vested and exercised in widely differing ways. For this, as for the Greeks, Homer marks the beginning, a state of evolution of Greek culture which is the first to have been recorded and written down, arrested by this writing at a certain stage.

When that stage was we really cannot say for certain. The world view of the *Iliad* and *Odyssey* may indeed be that of the dark ages, as so many think, but we must admit the possibility that intellectual and religious concepts as well as pieces of everyday life came along with the Bronze-Age formulas. Whatever the case may be, it is more a matter of antiquarian interest than it is relevant to an understanding of Greek culture, for the epics had their effect on later Greek

4 The Apotheosis of Homer, by Arcesilaos of Priene, third/second century BC. Priene, not so far from Homer's reputed birthplace, has left us this visual reminder of the respect paid to the poet long after the epics were created. (British Museum, London)

culture totally independent of their actual date. They were for the Greeks a single and simultaneous formulation; once in existence they brought their effects as a unity and exercised their influence continually. They maintained this influence as texts, and the nature of those texts stood completely independent of the reality of Bronze-Age civilization, the nature of oral poetry, the question of unitary or multiple authorship, or the temporal place of the civilization represented by the ideas in the texts. The mere fact that the *Iliad* and the *Odyssey* were regarded as so important that they were written down when so much else was let go is a testimonial to their significance to the Greeks, and once the poems were frozen, as it were, in writing, they were free to mold the future of Hellas, rather than be molded by the generations of bards who had sung them through the centuries.

The influence which the epics maintained through the centuries extended beyond the establishment of historical tradition, the framing of attitudes to the gods, and the representation of the proprieties of behavior for the members of a noble class. They preserved as well the deeper attitudes toward the role of human beings in the world, and they portray behavior, attitudes, and statements which conveyed tacit assumptions about the nature of the world, the gods, and humanity all the more powerful and influential for the very fact that they are not explicit but represent the givens and assumptions on which reasoned ideas are based. The world view of the epics would permeate later Greek thought and remain for a long time one of the basic influences on that thought on account of the very fact that it was carried with the directness of narrative and drama rather than as expository written prose. So long as it was transmitted as oral poetry, it maintained its similarity with drama as "heard" literature, presenting ideas which perforce must be expressed clearly and forcefully for listeners to perceive their meaning, and at the same time coming with the direct effect of dialogue rather than exposition. And once the epics had in fact been committed to writing, the drama could pick up many of these concepts along with newer ones, and present yet another century of this directness in conveying a cultural heritage.

This cultural heritage was also the more assimilable for being popular. The epic traditions, undoubtedly not only the product of the reflections of individual human beings but also nourished by the reactions and acceptances of audiences who heard them, maintained some common values until our texts were committed to writing.[4] The values of the *Iliad* may have been the values of a class, but they were, more surely than in the case of any later Greek work, the values of a whole class. The attitudes expressed by the heroes of the *Iliad* were meaningful and understandable to a whole social group, and perhaps, a whole society. More than any other work we have, the *Iliad* gives us insight into a broader collective than the writing of any individual.

That Hellenic mind was also transmitted broadly into later Hellenism, for the *Iliad* and *Odyssey* were the common heritage of all Greeks. While we are conscious that the ideas of a Pindar, a Herodotus, an Aeschylus, or a Plato must be seen in the first instance as the ideas of an individual, then secondarily in the context of a specific and individual city, and not just as generalized "Greek," we may take the influence of the epics as precisely such a general Greek phenomenon. They were not the property of one city or one group, but rather penetrated every literary and religious tradition and reached every corner of the Greek world. Homer was read from Spain and France in the west to the easternmost reaches of Egypt and Syria, and after the conquests of Alexander the Great the epics were carried even further east. Whatever was written or said in the Greek world, and wherever and whenever it was said, was done with an awareness of the epics, an awareness which frequently produced resurgences of their ideas and renewed the sense of humanity which can be found in them. Much that was new emerged in Greek thought in the centuries after the creation of the *Iliad* and the *Odyssey*, but novelty never replaced the past entirely, and whatever new ideas and concepts emerged out of new experience and new thought, the common Hellenic concepts in the epics persisted alongside them.

# 4

# The wrath of Achilles

## *A view of humanity's place in the cosmos*

What is the *Iliad* all about, not only in its plot but in its concepts? Is it possible for a poem which may have evolved over hundreds of years through the oral tradition of generations of bards to have a coherent intellectual stance? Can an epic of such length, passing as it did from place to place, through society after society, maintain consistency in its presentation of the situation of man in the universe, and be meaningful to listeners who come to it with their own world views? My answer to both these latter questions is "yes," although not out of a demonstration of the potentialities of either the tradition or the audiences, but out of the text itself, with its strong strain of philosophical and intellectual consistency.[1]

The bard asks the goddess to sing of the wrath of Achilles, and this is the theme which holds together this monumental poem of over 15,000 lines. That wrath, why it was justified, how it was maintained, renewed, redirected, and finally laid to rest, is more than theme, since it is the fundamental cause of all the events which fill book after book of fighting. For, after ten years of siege, the Greeks had victory within their grasp, when Thetis, Achilles' divine mother, prevailed upon Zeus to tilt the scales in favor of the Trojans to give meaning to Achilles' angry withdrawal from the Greek ranks. The wrath also elucidates values. Achilles was angry in the first place because of his own interpretation of honor and insult. When Agamemnon took Achilles' prize, the girl Briseis, in reposte for Achilles' advice that Agamemnon restore the seer Calchas' daughter to lift the plague fallen on the Greek host, the act laid open in a flash the whole system which recognized achievement, provided reward, and established the basis for feelings of self-worth. In the years of fighting at Troy, Achilles had not only distinguished himself and earned the emoluments of honor, he had done so at considerable cost and as the result of a deliberate choice of a glorious but short life in preference to a long but undistinguished existence. This was the choice that a noble of his stature would have been expected to make, and there is no suggestion that it had been a difficult one for him, but the compensation for the years he was giving up was the recognition he would receive, and the marks of honor which his prowess would bring him. Not only was Briseis one of these, but the cavalier treatment by Agamemnon was the antithesis of everything which Achilles believed that he had a right to expect.

In this value system, worth was measured and recognition gained from excelling – in combat, in games, in counsel, even in craftiness – and those to be outstripped were others of one's class. It was, as has been pointed out over and over again in so many different ways, an ethos of an aristocracy. Men awarded prizes and exchanged gifts as tokens of earned esteem, and their culture was not one in which people internalized, going their way in supreme self-confidence, assured of their own worth regardless of the opinions of others. Outward opinion in fact made worth, and then only when it was demonstrated by visible signs. Homeric men went to university solely for the diploma, not, as today's students do, for the sheer joy of learning and expanding their intellects. Agamemnon's slighting of Achilles was not only insult, suggesting that Achilles might deserve less than he thought he had earned, it actually *made* Achilles of less account. Achilles could hardly do less than attack Agamemnon, a resort to arms from which he was only held back by the intervention of Athena, and his failure to do so could only have been explained by divine action or, if modern secular feelings prevail, by some irrational aspect of Achilles' mentality. Withdrawal from combat, then, was an alternative to his first impulse, perhaps even a second-best alternative, because Achilles could only rely on demonstrating his excellence by default, rather than prevailing directly and immediately over Agamemnon.

But with Zeus' interference, the demonstration of Achilles' worth came in the thousands of lines which, until the end of Book viii, detailed the swelling success of the Trojans as they relentlessly forced the Greeks back upon their ships. Almost pushed into the sea, with Agamemnon himself suggesting that the assault on Troy be abandoned, the Achaeans hold another conference. Agamemnon accepts the advice to propitiate Achilles, and announces that he will offer him truly extraordinary gifts if he returns to the fighting. He explains his earlier actions as madness, a derangement due, he says, to *Ate*, that divine force which always lurks ready to strike men down, thus attributing his loss of reason to the stroke of an external force. This sense of madness, although later subject to some change and alternate interpretations, always played some part in the ethical approach to human motivation, and the Greek intellect and imagination continued to use Agamemnon's "madness" as one explanation for human error. The outcome of Agamemnon's return to rationality was the dispatch of an embassy to Achilles, to tell him of the army's need and Agamemnon's tribute. The embassy and its failure take us back to Achilles' wrath.

To some modern readers, the whole embassy episode seems to be a relatively late accretion to the *Iliad*. Certainly the designation of three envoys, Phoenix, Ajax, and Odysseus, followed immediately by the words, "So these two

5 The embassy to Achilles, on an Athenian vase of the early fifth century BC. Achilles, head bowed in sadness, listens to the words of Odysseus who is seated at the left. As is usual in the vase paintings of the scene, the aged Phoenix is present just as he is in the *Iliad* account, and the frequency with which this episode appears in vase painting illustrates the prominence which this part of the story had achieved.

walked along the strand," describing their trip to Achilles' tent, other dual grammatical forms, and the fact that, although Phoenix had been appointed leader, Odysseus led off and reported Agamemnon's offer to Achilles, makes the inclusion of Phoenix suspicious. Phoenix's message to Achilles therefore may not be reflective of the ethos of the rest of the poem. The response of Achilles, on the other hand, is quite a different matter. It provides no reason to suppose the embassy episode inconsistent with the rest of the *Iliad*, and indeed Achilles' response is an almost essential part of the story of his wrath. The wrath remains, its cause unchanged, but it now fits into an Achilles whose attitude toward glory has changed.[2]

His rejection of Agamemnon's peace offering is expressed not only as detestation of the king, but also as a disavowal in large part of the very concept which had elicited his initial feelings. Achilles had decided to participate in the Trojan expedition for the glory which would live after the short life it implied; it was the issue of that glory which had brought him to such wrath; now Agamemnon was not only unable to retrieve the damage of his insult by offering even greater honor, but Achilles was even questioning the principle itself. As he began his reply, Achilles points to the fact which was now of greatest concern to him: a man who fights bravely reaps the same fate as the coward – death. Whether a man does much or little, he comes to death. There are a number of other notions in this speech of Achilles, including his feeling that no subsequent recognition could compensate him for the "heart's affliction" he has already suffered, but nothing remotely touches in importance or stands out so notably as Achilles' discounting of the value of glory when measured against death. No one else, in the *Iliad* or the *Odyssey*, says anything remotely like this, and if there is any doubt that Achilles means here that glory is not worth dying for, he repeats the theme a little differently some lines later, following a stream of invective directed at Agamemnon. Of the fine rewards of war, cattle, fat sheep, horses, he says, they can be had for the taking, while a man's life cannot be brought back, neither filched nor returned by force, "once it has crossed the barrier of the teeth." And Achilles tells the envoys of his alternate fates; either he can stay at Troy to die young after winning eternal glory, or he can return home to live a long life but one without glory. He plans to return, and it is his advice to others to do the same.

I think that the transformation of Achilles' attitude is clear. He had originally decided for the everlasting glory which he would gain by his exploits at Troy, where he would die renowned for his valor and his fighting skill, but the blow to his glory administered by Agamemnon which brought his withdrawal from combat was a blow also to his confidence in the wisdom of his decision. He has, so to speak, rethought his life, and his second thoughts are very different from his first and bring him to a different life-principle. The glory which before justified everything was now insufficient. Achilles had really looked at death, and seen that it did not distinguish between brave man and coward. All the gifts, all the recognition, all the honor, all the cities, and all the daughters which Agamemnon could give fell short, not only because of the intensity of Achilles' hatred for the king, but because he was turning to another goal besides that of glory on which to set his pursuit of happiness and satisfaction. He would enjoy what he had and what had been won by his father as long as he could in a long life without glory.

So the envoys returned to the disappointed army, which, now urged on by Diomedes, readied itself to fight again the next day, still without Achilles. And on and on they fought, through six more books, more slaughter, more loss of men, and wounds of heroes. Finally, at the beginning of Book XVI as the Achaeans are at the brink of destruction, Achilles' beloved comrade Patroclus comes and pleads with him to allow some help to the army: if Achilles will not fight, will he not at least lend Patroclus his armor and let him join the battle? Thus, thinking Achilles had returned to the fray, the Trojans might slacken their attack and give the Achaeans some respite. Achilles' answer, mentioning again how Agamemnon took the girl Briseis from him as if he were "some wanderer without rights," contains a very interesting core, as he says he will let it be a thing of the past, that it was not in his heart to be angry forever. Achilles allows Patroculus to go off to battle, wearing his armor, but cautions him to limit his activity to driving the Trojans away from the Greek ships, but not to pursue or attack them, asserting concern both for his own prestige, which might be reduced by Patroclus' success, and for Patroclus' life.

The passage is a noted one. When Achilles tells Patroclus that he should hold back from pursuit of the Trojans to avoid detracting from Achilles' glory, so that they will give him back his woman with gifts in addition, he seems to overlook completely the fact that the offer had already been made and refused, and this passage is cited as evidence that the embassy episode is an intrusion. But the apparent inconsistency is easy to explain merely as a caveat on the part of Achilles that Patroclus not supplant Achilles and lose him the honor which has already been promised; or, alternatively, the inconsistency may lie in this short and relatively unimportant aspect of Achilles' speech and be the kind of thing which can easily happen in oral composition. In any case, both passages are in the *Iliad* which came down to the Greeks and therefore both must be considered; the most important part of the passage in Book XVI is Achilles' implication that his anger has passed. He seems to be moving back toward his old self, looking again for honor, wishing at the end of his speech that only he and Patroclus might emerge from the carnage. Now, he seems less confident in his earlier denigration of the value of such honor, less willing to depend for life's satisfaction on the long life and enjoyment of possessions back in Ithaca. He has gone from white-hot anger to bitter anger to a certain calm, a greater balance, and a willingness to help his old comrades in their worst need, a reacceptance of the traditions of honor and help for one's friends. And his hatred of Agamemnon drives him less.

This was not to last. Soon after Achilles armed the Myrmidons and sent them out with Patroclus, a leader and a force which together sent the Trojans reeling back with many of their best men killed, Patroclus himself lay dead in the dust, stripped of Achilles' magnificent armor by Hector. He had not followed Achilles' instructions and, caught up in the flush of his victories in battle, had pursued the Trojans to the very walls of the city, where, stunned by Apollo's blow and the wound of a javelin thrown at his back, he finally fell to Hector himself. Now the world changed again for Achilles. His grief at the news of Patroclus' death was unbounded, and his lamentations called his goddess-mother Thetis to his side, to tell her of his new resolve to take vengeance by killing the great Hector, even though it meant that his own death would come soon after. Sorrow is the emotion which moves him here, subduing the anger which we may be surprised to learn he still alludes to – if we still insist on consistency among all his speeches – and if we remember that it seemed to be gone when he sent Patroclus out to battle.

Thetis tells Achilles to delay his search for revenge while she goes off to Olympus to obtain new armor for him from the god Hephaestus, and Achilles agrees. While she is gone the Achaeans hold a new meeting, at which Achilles calls for immediate attack, countering sensible proposals to let the men rest and fill their bellies so that they will be able to fight properly. It is clear from all this that a new principle of behavior has come to Achilles: his life has a new purpose which will make it meaningful. That is revenge. In his attempt to navigate the sea of life, he is about to embark upon a new ship. First he had dedicated his life to the traditional ideal: the glory which came to the warrior justified his existence and rewarded his efforts and pains by the repute which would last after his death. Then anger, because of Agamemnon, an anger which was in itself an adequate reason for existence. But the anger abated, concern for his friends returned, and he was prepared to share again the ordeals and values of the Achaean warrior. That too failed, and with the death of his dearest companion, Patroclus, a new ideal emerged to dominate his life. Achilles' quest for revenge, and his relentless pursuit of Hector, thwarted at first by the intervention of Apollo, is again a matter of anger, as Achilles' words tell us: "The man is near who has particularly touched my anger."[3] Four times Achilles charges futilely into the mist in which Apollo has enclosed Hector, until he leaves off the pursuit for the moment and turns to scatter destruction among the Trojans. The song of slaughter continues, and the gods mix in and dispute with one another, until finally, in Book XXII, Achilles at last encounters Hector and kills him. The monumental quality of his wrath bursts out in his response to Hector's last pleas to Achilles to return his body to the Trojans for decent burial. There will be no ransom for the body, and Achilles only wishes he had enough fury to hack away Hector's flesh and eat it raw. The corpse will be left as carrion for dogs and birds. He calls his comrades now to return to the ships for a proper funeral for Patroclus; meanwhile he turns from despoiling Hector's body to even more ferocious treatment of the remains of his enemy. Graphically the epic details how holes are made in Hector's feet for the thongs Achilles draws through them and ties to his chariot. Then, in front of the walls of the city, in full view of the Trojans who mourned from the battlements, Achilles drags Hector's mutilated corpse in the dust of the battlefield.

But the epic does not end with the killing of Hector; the goddess has not yet finished with singing of the wrath of Achilles. He is to undergo one more transformation, and we are prepared for it, indeed led to it as, in a way, Achilles is too, in the next-to-last book of the epic. The funeral of Patroclus recalls the sorrow of Achilles which is combined with his anger, as he calls to his dead companion, killing and putting on the pyre some Trojan captives. Even here, there is divine intervention as Apollo protects the body of Hector so that it does not putrefy, and Achilles must remember to offer a prayer to the North Wind and the West Wind so that they come to kindle the fire which then mounts into a great blaze. Thus finally, Achilles, exhausted, could close his eyes in a sleep. But even then his rest is interrupted and he rises and arranges the burial of the ashes of Patroclus, with funeral games to be held in his honor. Then, for the more than 600 lines which detail the various contests of the games, we have almost a review of the leaders of the Achaean host and in microcosm the rivalry and reward for honor which was at the core of that wrath of Achilles which put all these events in motion. And the wrath is still not satisfied, for, as the final book of the *Iliad* begins, Achilles, unable to sleep for sorrow the whole night through, as dawn is breaking once again outrages the body of Hector by dragging it around Patroclus' tomb three times – dragging a body still fresh the twelfth day after death, protected still by Apollo.

The epic tale is close to its end. The bards and their audiences would have known that, as certainly did generations of Greek readers as they came to the last in the bundle of papyrus rolls that made up the *Iliad*. Now too, the gods intervene strongly again, not, this time, in protecting or smiting in the heat of combat, but in telling Achilles explicitly what they want him to do. Thetis comes to tell her son of Zeus' desire that he allow Hector's father Priam to ransom Hector's body, and Achilles shows no hesitation in obeying the command. He accepts Zeus' order with a terseness that emphasizes the readiness of his obedience and his complete trust in his mother's words. So when, on the advice of the gods, Priam appears at his tent, Achilles receives him graciously, shares sorrow with him, and, apart from a single warning to Priam not to stir him up, treats him with full respect and gives him Hector's body for proper burial. There is only a hint of anger left in Achilles; he is even willing to share his sorrow – his own sorrow for Patroclus and for his father who, like Priam, will survive his magnificent son – with Priam who is mourning for Achilles' bitter enemy, Hector. Achilles even goes so far as to offer Priam a truce to make it possible for the Trojans to conduct an appropriate burial, and grants the full eleven days proposed by Priam for the ceremonies. This magnanimity goes beyond the respect to the body commanded by Zeus; it is Achilles' own idea and it is a measure of the generosity now possible for him. With this we have come to the end of his wrath, and he has come to a new spiritual point, so that after the short description of the funeral games for Hector and his burial, the epic can end.

The goddess has sung the wrath of Achilles. However much else has informed the song, that theme and the full compass of its inception and final quietus has been the beginning and end of the epic. But what that wrath meant to Achilles, to the audiences, and to later Greek readers cannot really take on much meaning apart from the context of Achilles' whole being and psyche, and in turn, these must be seen in their relationship with the actions of the gods and their effect on his life. These gods, the so-called "Olympian" deities of Homer, shared the veneration of Greeks with other more obscure powers, unnamed daemons, family gods, spirits, ghosts, and all the other mysterious forces and agents which recur in so many religions. Yet, for all the respect in which the mysteries of various cults were held, and for all the awe in which most held the unknown forces who along with the Olympians influenced human life, the perception of the Olympians and the worship portrayed by Homer remained a distinct aspect of the tradition long after the epics passed from oral poetry into writing, and long after many new approaches to religion and the influence of philosophy developed to offer distinct alternative or supplemental beliefs.

These gods do not "personify the forces of nature so that man can understand them," nor are they merely human beings writ large with the extra dividend of immortality. In Homer they are beings of enormous power who are portrayed and viewed as having human attributes, characteristics, and even foibles, and humans are part – the lower and weaker part – of the tapestry of existence which the gods both weave and decorate. There is a continuum from Zeus to the lowly Thersites, from the top of Olympus to the back halls of Priam's palace. The gods move over the earth, directly and indirectly affecting human actions, and flit from sea to heaven to accomplish their wills. They are pleased with men's sacrifices, worship, and services, and usually reward such attentions although what people want is not always granted, or granted quite in the way hoped. Nor, except in such a rare instance as the matter of the yielding of Hector's body, is there any question of justice in the relationship of the gods with each other or with men, and there is absolutely no corollary between what men might see as just or ethical conduct and the approval or assistance of the gods. What happens to men depends on what the gods want, and it is often affected by the gods acting at cross purposes with one another. And there is no rationale to what the gods want. It is in such a universe that Achilles must work out his destiny. We would describe it as a universe of moral chaos. People are expected to respect the gods, but with a service entirely of ritual and sacrifice rather than adherence to an ethical code. The worship of the Olympian deities offered no principles of human social interaction which were commanded or in any way at all endorsed by religion. Achilles had no external standard on which to base his actions, and no rules which he could follow to assure him some form of happiness.

I do not suggest that his intellectual problem was posed as a literary theme by some philosophical bard who then proceeded to work out an answer in the epic, or that the narrative emerges as an expression of unconscious mythic thought or human psychological depths.[4] Rather, philosophical or religious problems and their solutions mold the language and legends which make up the poetry, and the bards tell their tales and make their characters behave according to norms comprehensible to themselves and their audiences, presenting the events of a man's life in a pattern understandable and believable to an audience familiar at least in part with the experiences portrayed. Nonetheless, there is no reason to suppose that singer and audience must be unaware of the intellectual content of a tale: the tale may not be devised as a vehicle for a concept, as the plot of a modern novel might be, but a bard may impose on a tale his particular view of the world – so long as that view would be comprehensible to his audience. In a series of incidents to which the subjects react, the reactions can leave us with the sense of meaning. Thus Achilles reacts to the choice he must make between a long life or a glorious one; he reacts to the insulting behavior of

Agamemnon; he reacts to the message of reconciliation; he reacts to the dire predicament of the army and Patroclus' plea; he reacts to Patroclus' death; he reacts to his success over Hector, to the orders from the gods, and finally to the presence of Priam in his camp. How he reacts tells us something about him, and how a Greek audience would construe his situation. He consistently acts to restructure the principle on which he bases his life. In this human condition which we have already described, in which there is no divine instruction or pattern of behavior imposed by religion, Achilles continually attempts to assert his own view and his own will in the interpretation of what kind of life is best for him. At the start, he accepts and is ready to follow the standard view that the life of valor to create eternal glory is the one to be chosen. But this view of life does not work out satisfactorily; he is insulted, his glory impaired, and there is grief rather than satisfaction as reward. He tries something different, withdrawal from the army, and, as becomes clear from his reply to the embassy in Book IX, he plans to base his life on a new principle: *carpe diem*, as the Latin has it, "seize the day," or "eat, drink, and be merry," the enjoyment of his possessions while he lived.

That too, in its outcome, fails him, for it brings about the death of his friend. However one interprets the ambivalence apparent in his last conversation with Patroclus, whether he is moving toward returning to battle, or his anger is gone, the death of Patroclus dashes any satisfaction with the course he has been following, and forces him into a completely new emotion and a complete turnaround in action. Neither the prolongation of his life nor the increase of his glory interests him in the least in his sorrow for Patroclus, and he is now wholly dedicated to revenge. But that too leaves him unsatisfied, for even after he has killed Hector and violated his body, the sorrow for the loss of Patroclus remains, as we might expect it would. So revenge is not an adequate principle upon which to base one's life. Achilles comes to the end of this episode in his life still sorrowing, but now for more than himself in his loss of Patroclus, as he includes his father and even bereaved Priam. And, just as the sorrow has persisted with the revenge achieved, so too his anger lurks near; it is not really gone and threatens to burst forth. We leave him, as does Priam, exhibiting a generosity and greathearted kindness which we had not suspected he could show, a humanity which might seem foreign to the society in which he lived.

It appears that nothing works, or that nothing has worked for Achilles. However he tries to order his life, whatever principles of conduct he selects to guide him, his efforts come to an unsuccessful conclusion and leave him unhappy. And yet we do not think of Achilles as a failure, or, if this aspect of his life is noticed at all, he appears as a noble failure. It is his nobility rather than his failure that distinguishes him, his larger-than-life emotions and actions, rather than his dissatisfaction with results, that make him a figure to be reckoned with by the ages. Achilles, in short, refuses to quit. He will not allow reverses, adversity, misfortune, or even the actions of the gods to overthrow his insistence on imposing his will on his surroundings. Achilles demands his way;

*he* will choose. He will turn about at every defeat or setback to seek out and pursue another line of conduct on which to base his life, a different means of chasing the elusive goal of happiness and satisfaction in human life. The absence of some universal rule may make inevitable his failure, but it does not deter him from trying to reach that goal.

In the context of a society over which the Olympian gods rule, Achilles is pursuing an almost hopeless task. Because human happiness is almost negligible in the cosmos, humans are defeated before they start any attempt to order their lives. There is no rhyme or reason to success or failure, death or life, sickness or health, victory or defeat, riches or poverty. There is no justice to reward virtue or penalty for vice, indeed, there is not even such a thing as virtue in the sense that we, or later Greeks, use the word. With no virtue, no code, no punishment by the gods for crimes committed, human success or failure can only be attributed to the whims or wills of the gods, fate, or both. In face of this there is hardly any hope for a person to achieve success. The magnificence of Achilles lies not in his achievement in face of these odds, but in his indomitable will and his refusal to give up.

# 5

# The problem of morals
## Archaic Greece and
## private and social ethics

The Athens of the mid-sixth century BC, which saw the recording of the Homeric epics at the behest of the tyrant Peisistratus, was just emerging from a period of fundamental social change. The community was no longer completely dominated by a small clique of wealthy, landowning aristocrats who maintained the power and safety of the city by individual martial prowess cultivated over years of training and practice. In Athens, as in many other Greek centers, the noble warrior, with his brilliant armor, fine horses, and magnificent chariot, was losing or had lost his dominance on the battlefield, and with that went some of his authority over his society. The pre-eminence in war of the aristocratic warrior was giving way to the need for larger numbers of combatants, heavy-armed citizens who stood together in ranks facing the equally disciplined lines of the enemy, battalions made up of troops from a much broader class of citizens, men who could afford the heavy armor but who would not have had the riches to permit them the lavish arms of single combat or the leisure for training enjoyed by the small noble class.

The change in style of warfare has been seen as the catalyst which triggered wholesale changes in Greek society, not only the shift from aristocracy to a broader democracy in governing Greek cities, but the development of that unique ideology of democracy which can be traced so notably in the development of Athens. The Greek city-state – *polis*, as the Greeks called it – and particularly the democratic *polis*, is such an exceptional structure among human institutions that historians and philosophers alike have sought evidence of some exceptional circumstances which might serve to explain its genesis. The current trend, impressed by the obvious importance of materialist factors to the evolution of society, understands the emergence of democracy as a response to the demands of the newly important military class for a greater role in directing the state. As time went on, after the collapse of the great palace centers of the Bronze Age, populations grew, this reasoning supposes, and escalating struggles for the few good agricultural plains of Greece generated more and more warfare amongst neighboring communities. Military necessity called

46

more and more on the prosperous, if not noble, farmers to defend their lands, and battles were fought less by warrior champions for fame and more as a response to material needs, for possession of valued lands. More was at stake, more men were involved, and eventually as the state came to depend on these newly militarized citizens, the nobles were less able to resist their political claims.

Changing institutions reflected this shift. Kings and their coteries of aristocratic advisers found themselves supplemented and eventually supplanted by elected magistrates and councils. Law emerged from its background of tradition and paternalistic dispensation to become more formal, publicly known, and even in some instance publicly established. The settlement of disputes by private means yielded to the votes of popularly constituted courts, and even the definition of what was a public, rather than a private, matter expanded greatly. Family and clan loyalties, although never, of course, entirely eliminated, bowed before a strengthening sense of civil loyalty, and the sense of community which extended to the entire city-state eventually dominated the Greek social ethos.

The basic character of the Greek *polis* had been established by the time of the great colonizing movements of the eighth to sixth centuries BC. This explosion of Hellenism, which many have attributed to the same population increase and land hunger which generated the impulse creating the *polis* itself, spread Greeks and their institutions across the world. From Spain to the Levant, all along the Mediterranean coast of France, Spain, Anatolia, and south to Cyrene in modern Libya, Greeks established new cities. They reached up to the Black Sea, along the coasts of Bulgaria, Romania, and south Russia. There were to be prosperous Greek centers in the Crimea and along the northern coast of Turkey. The foundations of what was to become Marseilles were laid. With the encouragement of the Egyptian pharaoh Greeks from a number of cities joined to found Naucratis in Egypt. Miletus, on the west coast of Turkey, together with her own colonies was responsible for upward of a hundred new cities in the Black Sea area. Italy and Sicily saw the establishment of many of their most famous cities – Neapolis (Naples), Taras (Taranto), Syracuse.

This period of colonization was utterly unlike anything the world had ever seen before or would ever see again, for the colonization itself was carried on in a manner unique to the Greeks. The new cities were not, as colonies have been in modern times, outposts of empire for economic or political expansion, nor even, in the Roman fashion, urban centers conceived as still part of the founding state. They were new, independent, cities, tied to their founders by bonds of culture or religion, but in no political sense. When a city planned to send out a colony it planned an act of separation, in which a group of citizens would leave the city to create a wholly new and independent entity, a physically new city and citizen body. The deliberate act was taken in the context of the ethos of the *polis* which made a city the physical expression of the social, familial, and religious bonds which unified its citizen body, and a decision to send out a colony was as much a religious matter as a practical move to meet material needs. Oracles were consulted, and when the replies were affirmative colonies would be sent out, or, on occasion, oracles initiated the foundation of colonies. Despite the great diversity of founding cities and the wide expanse over which they were scattered, these colonies shared the basic characteristics of the Greek city-state. And in many ways, the colonizing movement is another expression of that particular Greek attitude toward social structure and government of which the most outstanding expression is the city-state itself.

It was, in fact, in the period immediately before the colonizing age that the institutions of the *polis* were beginning to take form. Some later Greeks reconstructed the process, and Aristotle's projection of organic development from family to village to city is at least a conceptually clear account, and fits the shift from monarchy through oligarchy and aristocracy to a broader-based citizen government which occurred in a number of important cities. At Athens, for which we have the most information, power passed from kings to magistrates, called archons, who were first elected for life, then for ten-year periods, and finally annually. At Corinth a family known as the Bacchiadae initially provided the kings of Corinth and then later formed a ruling group to make up a very close oligarchy. At Sparta, the royal institution carried on through two kings whose constitutional authority was curtailed by magistrates and councils over the years but whose real power could be increased by individuals with military or political talents.

The nature of society in the eighth and seventh centuries BC, when these aristocracies were prevelant in domination, is difficult to assess. I do not think that it is safe to generalize from the limited evidence which bears on one characteristic at one place, a different one at another. In a few cities the body of aristocrats holding control seems to have come through the turbulent early centuries down into the historical period of written evidence, while in others their formal power was gone long before we have any real information about political life. Some cities met changing conditions by modifying institutions, and the very existence of formal lawgivers shows some relaxing of the tightest form of aristocratic control. To promulgate law, however limited its application, is to limit the authority and arbitrariness of clan leaders who earlier might have exercised their judicial power with no consistency or fairness whatever. We have some indication of such injustice in Hesiod's *Works and Days*, where the poet complains about the "crooked judgements of the corrupt rulers."[1]

These were the times when some of the basic Greek attitudes toward the relationship of family and clan with city were forming, ideas which eventually developed in their fullest form in the flowering of Athenian democracy in the fifth century BC. Because the Greek *polis* was such an unusual political structure in the Mediterranean region, moderns have looked for particular phenomena which might have caused it to occur, seeking in the collocation of events and social conditions a matrix from which to comprehend the development of such structures. Not only can we see how the needs of war might call for increased political power on the part of a more widely based military class, we can see how the continual military and political strife among neighboring cities could generate the fierce patriotism and local loyalty which mark the *polis* ethos. The citizen body, emerging from interrelated families and clans, was a community more of blood than politics in the first instance. Membership in the group not only entailed obligation to the group, it answered all the social and spiritual needs most people feel. Only a member of the group had legal standing, could own property in the territory which the group controlled, could share in the worship of the group's gods, and, in general only through marriage with another member of the group could children's status be assured. By the fifth century BC this Greek concept of the "citizen" as an individual constitutive of and with "rights" in the state had developed fully. It had come through a difficult period, one of severe internal strife in many different cities, as some members of society, perhaps adversely affected by the land hunger and concomitant strife of the times, sought to take a greater share in civic wealth from the dominant aristocracies and oligarchies. At the beginning of the sixth century the Athenians called upon Solon to implement measures which would alleviate the strife, and the lawgiver left us some of his poetry in which he not only describes the trouble but expresses some of his principles of reform. To the west, the Boeotian Hesiod earlier sang of the injustices suffered by the peasant famer. The aristocrats found voice in the work of the Megarian Theognis, who deplored the rising power of the un-noble new rich who were demanding and gaining greater power in the state.

In some cities the aristocrats' dominion was eventually taken by a single man, called in Greek *tyrannos*, which designates a man who held monarchical power by force or unconstitutional means rather than by the inheritance of royal position. In later times most of the tyrants acquired a bad reputation, probably due to the eagerness of their opponents to denigrate the activities of the governments which had been supplanted, although there is really not much detail about these activities. Thucydides of Athens, one of the few who attempted a general understanding, explained that tyrannies rose as Greece "acquired more wealth than before,"[2] and Alcaeus of Mytilene, with remarks like "Money is the man, and no poor man is noble or good,"[3] or Theognis' complaint about the base marrying their betters, "money mingles family,"[4] shows that the increase in wealth was not always the accomplishment of the aristocrats or welcome to them. Thucydides' remark implies that growing wealth generated stresses which opportunists could use for the seizure of power, and Aristotle certainly blamed the pursuit of wealth for those animosities which unsettled the stability of ruling oligarchies. Herodotus, observing the earlier period from the vantage point of south-west Anatolia, across the Aegean from the Greek peninsula, thought that factionalism was endemic to oligarchies, and that this strife generated bloodshed which then issued in tyranny. Solon saw the overturning of the state as the effect of the destruction wrought by the great men of the state, from whom the people in ignorance turn to the tyrant, while at Megara Theognis wrote that when leaders turn to wrong, then come "factions, and kindred slaughters of men, and sole rulers."[5] All the causes identified or hinted at by Greek authors were probably relevant at one place or time or another. Whatever the cause or causes, the phenomenon was common from the seventh century BC on, but, while widespread, tyranny was not an inevitable stage in the development of the Greek *polis*, and many cities survived these early centuries without it.

But few came through these years without being touched by the concept of "justice" which appears in so many places, and was finding expression in poetry. Its appearance in literature with a meaning like that of the modern "justice" may have as much to do with the concept winning its way to the center of Greek thought as to the background which generated it, but it emerged in a number of places far apart in time and character. This concept of justice marched hand and hand with the advance of the *polis* organization, expanding with the numbers of those who sought an increase in their authority and in their share of the state's benefits. "Justice" and "injustice" came more and more to express a sense of political and even economic relationships, but always, of course, in the family context of the *polis* and the interrelationships among its citizens. Although attempts to explain and understand the nature of justice would become one of the driving forces behind the development of Greek philosophy and would inspire some of the most far-reaching explorations of the nature of humanity and its place in the cosmos, the earliest uses of the term relate as much to practical and social issues as to philosophical or intellectual ones. But in a century or two of usage it showed an importance to Hellenism's view of people and society which made it a fundamental influence on the development of values which would ultimately define the nature of western society.

Just about when the era of epic poetry was coming to a close in Ionia, a different kind of composition was being put down in central Greece. The eighth-century Boeotian Hesiod, writing in the traditional dialect of the Homeric epic, was a representative of the burgeoning development of the Dorian-speaking Greeks who had been infiltrating most of Greece in the centuries after the collapse of the Mycenaean centers. He is the first Greek poet of whose life and character we have any real knowledge, and he has left us two long works of supreme importance to understanding the Greek mind in the early period. Of the *Theogony – The Generation of the Gods* – much has been written, for, with the *Eoiae* and the *Catalogues* which explain the genealogy of the Greeks, it presents a coherent history of the generations of the gods and the evolution of the ages of man. In the *Theogony*'s account of the formation and development of the cosmos, the natural forces of Chaos separated into Earth and Tartarus, and these in turn ultimately gave rise to the cosmos in its material form. Earth and Heaven produced the gods, who were first ruled by Cronus

6 This bronze bust, found in the Villa dei Pisoni in 1754, with even its inlaid eyes preserved by the eruption of Vesuvius, is now considered to represent Hesiod, although this identification of the many copies of the representation of this personnage cannot be considered secure. It is based on a Greek representation of the second century BC. (National Museum, Naples)

and then by Zeus. Men were created by the gods, and before Hesiod's time four races of man had been born and passed away, each inferior to the preceding, with the fifth, the men of iron, the worst of all and suffering the worst existence. In all this structure and evolution, which is more simplistic than that which can be derived from the Homeric epics, and seems to have been a rationalizing of diverse traditions from different parts of Greece, Zeus is the giver of justice, and as such, will eventually destroy humanity for failure to follow the strictures of justice. These strictures, in turn, are no different from what people ordinarily understand as justice, and Zeus in his power and wisdom ensures that just behavior is rewarded and wickedness punished.

These principles are set out in truly mundane detail in Hesiod's *Works and Days*, a poem which combines homely peasant moralizing addressed to Hesiod's rapacious brother Perses with an agricultural calendar based on numerological superstition. The advice to Perses is the kind of simple thought one might expect from the rural inhabitant of Boeotia, and the adaptation of the sophisticated Homeric language does not influence it very much. Whatever sort of person Hesiod might actually have been, he writes in the guise of a peasant quite effectively, and evokes a harsh marginal existence with great conviction. Hard work, honest dealing, truth-telling – these and similar virtues he recommends to his brother, promising him prosperity and happiness if he follows justice. Just as *Theogony* assumes that the rule of the gods enforces and rewards the kind of justice which Hesiod understands, so too in *Works and Days* he assumes that hard, honest labor will be rewarded by the gods.

*Works and Days* is clearly the writing of an individual, prescribing for a life lived mostly in isolation from other people, certainly one not part of the city life with which we associate so much Greek literary activity. It is the earliest surviving example of the poetry which wends its way through the personal and love lyrics which are so characteristic of this period, and for which such names as Archilochus, Alcaeus, and Sappho still hold their fame. The theme of individual happiness and satisfaction remained dominant, and even when the strain of ethical conduct was strong, as it had been in Hesiod, it was orientated toward individual virtue, not toward the problems of justice and lawfulness which arise in social contexts. This orientation found its continuance in the poetry of Theognis of Megara, a Dorian aristocrat, and was carried to its highest exposition by another Boeotian, Pindar, who, however splendidly he might sing of aristocratic *arete* – "virtue" – had in common with Hesiod and Theognis the unquestioned acceptance that his ethic was endorsed by Zeus. And to all of these the definition of virtue could be relatively easy and clear, for they were not involved in fitting it into the complexities of urban life.

Quite a different matter was the thought of Solon. Living as he did in the Athens of the first part of the sixth century, and deeply embroiled in political life, his ethical and political thought received the full impact of the changes coming about as Athens moved from domination by a traditional aristocracy toward a more formal and impersonal set of civic institutions. Solon is certainly the most famous of all the lawgivers of Greece, even outside Athens, and his activity and the acts attributed to him border on legend. While we have some of his poetry to provide insight into his thought, our knowledge of the period before him and even of his own time is so limited that it is very difficult to be precise about the details or significance and effect of everything he did. Later Athenians attributed many aspects of their legislative tradition to Solon without any real evidence that he was involved with this or that detail, and the scope of the Solonian reform is illustrated by the myriad acts and rules listed in Plutarch's *Life of Solon*. He carried out a thoroughgoing reform of the Athenian political system, as Plutarch tells us, and this, according to Aristotle's *Constitution of Athens*, was the foundation of Athenian democratic institutions.

Solon is remembered today for great economic reforms like the "shaking off of debts" and the prohibition of debt slavery, more than for the political reforms like the division of the citizens into property classes, the establishment of councils and regulation of their size, the recognition of certain legal rights in suits, and the creation of courts. Beyond these, however, a whole series of individual measures attributed to Solon deal with testamentary procedure, marriage and family affairs, commerce, agriculture, funeral and sexual matters. All these regulations, which later Athenians credited to Solon but which probably came into being over the years before Solon himself enacted some of them, represented a far-reaching change in the relationship between individual and state at Athens. Before this legislation, almost all social and economic activities in Athens had been unregulated. But, as Solon himself tells us in his poems, there was great unrest and pressure for the satisfaction of grievances, and although these complaints were in all likelihood primarily economic, there were probably some purely social and political complaints as well. In any case, to make some provision for the alleviation of distress, it was necessary for the first time in the history of Athens to interfere rather extensively into the life of the citizens, and to regulate the conduct of private economic and social affairs as well as political activities.

Solon's poetry and political ideas must be seen against this background of reform and its effect on Athens, and against the whole panorama of the shift at Athens from a clan- and family-dominated society to a structure based on a political state. So much is clear from Plutarch's account and even more from Aristotle's history of the Athenian Constitution. For a long time after the so-called *synoikismos*, "living together" or unification of Attica attributed to Theseus by the Athenians and dated to the post-Mycenaean period by moderns, Athens was more like a great extended family than it was a political state. The leaders disposed of matters according to their views of what was right and what was best, ideas influenced heavily by religion, tradition, and, presumably, to a significant extent by their own self-interest.

Thus, at least, do moderns see the state of affairs in the Athens dominated by an aristocracy which arrogated to itself the powers of the kings who no longer ruled in Attica. This modern view, impressed by the evidence of increasing trade activity in the Aegean and influenced by the economic interpretation of history which has been current for most of this century, interprets the Solonian reform as a response to a serious economic crisis at the end of the seventh century. The quarrels among the inhabitants of the plains around the city, those who lived along the coast, and those distant from the city and beyond the nearby hills, attested quite firmly in middle of the sixth century, are projected back to the century's beginning. Then they may be explained as economics-based disputes between the new – as they are assumed to be – merchants who are interpreted as the leaders of the inhabitants of the coast, and the long-dominant aristocrats who made up the heads of the clans of the inhabitants of the plains around the city and Athens itself. It makes a nice, neat picture to fill out the vague allusions to strife in Solon's poems. One can develop an exciting account of honest farmers losing their land, becoming bound to the rich and powerful as near slaves, obligated to farm now mortgaged land for the benefit of the moneylenders, while at the same time the increasing commercial activity and trading undertaken by a growing merchant class had serious disruptive effects on the patterns of economic activity in the more urban areas of the state. Exciting, but largely guesswork.

The guesswork may be correct, but whatever the actual events which led to the changes in the early part of the sixth century, Solon's poetry gives us something definite to go on in assessing their effects not only on the social and political structure, but on the intellectual outlook of at least one Athenian – Solon himself. One can see much from his political poetry, where for example, in one lyric he refers to some of his specific acts, eliminating the mortgages on the land, and the freeing of those who had been enslaved for debt, actions for which he was famed in later times. He also focuses in his writing on his creation of law, "fitting together," as he says, "force and dikē" – justice.[6] The laws which he made, he further claims, apply to all citizens, both well-born and lower-class, which is what he means by the Greek words which can translate merely as "good" and "bad." We have the concept of universal law, without which a political state cannot exist, and a law which admits the legitimacy of claims of the underclasses and provides to some extent for their needs in order to avoid civil war. Inherent in this is the concept of political government, something explicit for the first time in Greek literature, as Solon writes of good government as neat and orderly, often required to chain those who would break the laws.

Controlling this process is the force of Justice, which Solon also makes explicit, rebuking the excesses of greedy and rapacious evil leaders, who steal from the people and from the gods, until Justice comes to exact her penalty, often bringing disaster on an entire city.[7] Justice is not a metaphysical abstraction; she is a real power, and she acts upon humans. Two things are important here. First, misfortune is not just the whim of the gods, imposed on people for some divine purpose but serving no human good, or just the accidental by-product of divine action, but rather comes as the result of human behavior. Justice brings retribution for human wickedness, and – the second important aspect of Solon's ethical thought – a whole society may be made to suffer for the actions of a part. In ethical terms as well as social, political, and geographical, a *polis* is a unit, an organic whole, and the retribution which justice brings does not merely single out the individual wrongdoers, as does

Hesiod's justice-bringing Zeus, she imposes her punishment on the whole society. It helps to explain why the innocent suffer misfortune.

Solon's poems also show some evidence of his more general political and ethical ideas, even though these poems were written as much or more as justification of his actions than as explication of ideals in the abstract. Some of this poetry is quoted by Aristotle, in *Constitution of Athens*; like us, he uses it as evidence for Solon's activity, and there are repetitions and supplements in Plutarch's *Life of Solon* and elsewhere. Aristotle quotes material of particular interest to him, such as Solon's claim that "I gave the populace just so much privilege as was fitting,"[8] and he uses the poetry as evidence for Solon's decision not to redistribute land, his cancellation of debts, and his freeing of the debt slaves. The best evidence for Solon's attitudes in these matters remains these poems, particularly those quoted by Aristotle, but there is in addition poetry of a less political nature which is very enlightening.

In a long prayer to the Muses, Solon reveals his views on human prosperity, on wrongdoing and retribution, and on human misfortune; he acknowledges his desire for wealth, but forbears to gain it unjustly, for fear of the retribution which would come as a result. The attitude is very like Hesiod's when he warns his brother Perses to avoid wickedness, and Solon waxes eloquent on the advantage and solidity of wealth when it comes from the gods. When produced by violence or crime, however, it initiates disaster, which, however, does not always come immediately or in the same way. Zeus watches, and strikes suddenly; "One man pays immediately, another in the future," while in other cases the blow falls on innocent later generations.[9] This is an attitude which we find commonly expressed in later Greek thought, and it expresses an idea of divine justice on which much Greek tragedy turns. The disasters which overtake Agamemnon and his house, while immediately attributable to Agamemnon's own actions, are ultimately caused by the crime of the family ancestor Thyestes, and the misfortune of Oedipus and his children is retribution for the crimes of the house of Laius. However this idea of the "inheritability" of retribution, or looking at it another way, pollution, developed, we can be sure that it was in the corpus of Greek ethics and morality by the time of Solon, and it is at least interesting to see that it accompanies the concept of pollution of a whole society. As is clear from the treatment of killing, for example, in Greek tragedy, Greek religious and ethical thought accepted the notion that a crime of such a serious nature polluted the whole city which then required cleansing. While it is certainly true that many human societies require ritual cleansing of religious crime, it is also reasonably clear that such a procedure was not part of the world view represented in Homeric epic. To the moral thought of the epics, the poems of Solon add the concept of crime in the fifth-century sense, and they broaden greatly the scope of ethical thought which we must accept as part of Hellenism at the time of Solon at the latest. While wrongdoing might not be immediately punished by the gods, it adhered to the doer and to his innocent descendants, who, regardless of their

55

own blameless lives, might be forced to pay the penalty of their forebear's crimes. In the same way, crime and the retribution therefor might not be limited to the single individual who perpetrated crime, but might spread as a miasma to infect and ruin the whole extended family, or city, of the guilty. This latter concept, as we have seen, appears clearly in the political poetry as well as here.

In the final part of the lyric which deals with divine punishment, Solon introduces the action of fate, in a way that, to me at least, is not completely clear and does not seem to fit quite with the other concepts of justice and punishment treated by the poet. After contrasts between the desirable and undesirable gifts which man might enjoy – health and sickness, cowardice and heroism, ugliness and beauty, poverty and wealth, and so on, Solon concludes that it is fate which brings good and evil. Doing brings risk, and outcomes are uncertain. Good intentions may be unrewarded, while the evildoer may get everything he wants from the gods by pure luck. Over a century later, Athenian audiences would hear very similar sentiments from one of Euripides' characters, but not in a context which holds the contradictions which appear here. In this passage, Solon seems to state that misfortune and good fortune are matters of luck or at best, fate, and have little or nothing to do with the intention behind actions, and, therefore, nothing to do with morality. Not only is intention irrelevant, actual bad acts may go unpunished. One thinks in this connection of today's cynical Murphy's law, which reads "No good deed goes unpunished." In this, Solon is not finding inherited guilt as an explanation for the misfortune which falls on the apparently innocent, but assigns the cause to blind luck. It does not seem that Solon has worked out a consistent system of ethics or morality, but these poems do show that his legislative activity was based on some serious ethical considerations, and that he was formulating concepts of justice and morality which add significantly to our earlier extant texts. At the least, the Solonian poems have given us the earliest texts in which some of the main lines of later Greek investigation of moral problems are laid out.

There are, as we have seen, no real moral issues in the *Iliad*. There is general agreement as to what characteristics and what kind of behavior can be expected of a "noble" man, and the ideal of conduct, insofar as there is one at all, aims at the greatest renown for the performance of the deeds expected of nobility. The gods conduct themselves independently of humans and have no code of conduct to which they expect people to conform. There is no praise of justice in the *Iliad*, no complaint of its lack, no notion that one's deserts should be in some measure conform to one's standard of behavior. That idea, that the gods do expect people to behave in certain ways, appears in Hesiod, but even there, in a very simple, *quid pro quo* formulation: the gods give good to those who conform to righteousness, and deal out punishment to the wicked. Hesiod seems to have no question about the reliability of the punishment imposed for evil acts, or, in turn, of his own (and therefore the human) ability to make assessment of what in fact constitutes crime deserving punishment by the gods. Hesiod's approach may seem simplistic, but it is no more so than many clear-cut moral and ethical systems in service in the world today, which have clear and unambiguous answers to many questions of right and wrong – not just the easy ones, like murder, theft, and falsehood, but complex and debated issues, like abortion, blasphemy, drinking, drugs, cigarette smoking, and extending even to dancing and card-playing. Hesiod's morality, then, need not be taken as either simplistic or primitive, and it persisted, in one form or another, for a long time in Greek thought. Hesiod's writing can be thought of as presenting wrongdoing and punishment in a manner by which the idea of morals can be conceived.

In Solon's poetry, the problems of morality are explored, in terms of a society much more complex than that envisioned in Hesiod's poetry. Human justice, reward and punishment, the role of the gods and the nature of their activity, all these were no longer disposed of in a simple series of occurrences. There were obvious anomalies, and Solon's approach to these was the first on record in which a Greek thinker attempted to make some kind of moral order out of the observed disparities of justice on earth. It is interesting that the context in which this is written is that of the developing city state. Unlike the writing of Theognis, where the right and wrong of social behavior are seen and evaluated against the backdrop of the aristocratic code of *arete* more than political justice, Solon's ethics are intimately tied to the interaction of people in a society. It is, in all probability, the fact that justice was becoming a catchword, a concept, a demand, in the emerging political state of Athens that pushed a thinker, Solon, if not people before him, to deal with it in social and political, and not just personal, terms. That is, it was reasonable to explain action by the idea that there was some Justice – and I capitalize it here – beyond and outside what the powerful figures in a clan or in the city said was right, and that there was some standard beyond raw power or family custom which ought to regulate human behavior in the increasing complexity of life in a growing urban center. Commerce, with gifts, marriages, sales, loans, contracts, manufacture – all the myriad arrangements people make with one another for livelihood and profit – was producing everyday instances of trickery and deceit on the mundane level, while in the broader realm of political power and structure the weak had no guarantee of fair treatment and were without recourse. "The wicked prosper as the green bay tree" would describe the situation, which demonstrated both the inefficacy of the Hesiodic analysis of crime yielding punishment, and the inadequacy of the political system in which "the rich got richer and the poor got children" – and had to sell them. It was in this context that we find, in Athens at least, state and morals intertwined, and both, probably not fortuitously, carried forward under the name of Solon.

## Part Two

# Hellenism in
# the fifth century

# 6

# Fifth-century Athenians
## *Politicians, philosophers, and poets in imperial Athens*

When in 404 BC the Spartans began dismantling the walls of Athens, they were ending more than the threat of a dangerous rival. The Spartans and their allies felt that they were removing the last strength of the power that had shadowed Greece for almost a century; the pipes and flutes which sang to the workers pulling down the battlements celebrated a return to the state of affairs which they had been fighting for. They had, in fact, ended much more than the threat of the domination of Greece by the Athenian Empire, for with the end of the Peloponnesian War came also the end of three-quarters of a century of rampant imperial democracy. It had been a unique period, one in which the expansion of political control over other states, military adventure, and imperial economic arrangements had been directed by assemblies of citizens of Athens, or at the very least by officials elected by these assemblies, officials who followed the policies which these assemblies had debated and decided by vote.

It was the end of an era in more than political terms. In the fifth century BC, Athens had created tragedy, indeed the dramatic form itself, out of the performances at the Dionysiac festival. The first of the great playwrights, Aeschylus, fought at Salamis and lived to see the growth of the Athenian Empire, the empire which ended in 404. Sophocles, whose life was almost co-terminous with the whole period, and whose works seem best to express the spirit of the age, had died just two years before that fateful date. Euripides' death, probably in the same year as Sophocles', brought to an end the flow of tragedies which mark for many the heyday of Greek literature. There would be only a few more comedies from Aristophanes, and most of these were comedies of manners or private life, middle comedy, rather than the political or social commentary of the most vigorous of his work. The period of great building on the Acropolis was over, and the streak of inspiration in Attic black-figure and red-figure vase painting which had begun in the sixth century was almost exhausted by the end of the fifth. And in 404 Socrates, at 65, had done most of his teaching, and was a scant five years away from execution by a nervous and weak democracy.

While 404 BC certainly did not bring to a close all forms of cultural activity at Athens, it marked a major transition in the arts. Just as Athenian political power was not ended, but would see a resurgence, albeit of a different kind, so too, in cultural activities. Athenians would be noted for different achievements from those which brought them fame in the fifth century. To many who lived after, the fifth century marked the high point in Athenian or Greek cultural activity; the drama has had such a great influence on later literature that, even more than the epic poems which evolved over centuries in a number of places, tragedy has been taken as the great achievement of Greek letters, an evaluation which has influenced the precedence accorded the fifth century. And the Athenians produced so much more in the fifth century. Many people consider the historical work of Thucydides the "best" historical writing of antiquity, and the Athenian Thucydides has been elevated over the Ionian "father of history," Herodotus, as an accurate or "scientific" historian. The fifth was the century of the Athenian Phidias, the one Greek sculptor whose name comes to mind even if one knows no other. These and other achievements of the Athenians have so engrossed our attention that they have become almost synonymous with Greek culture. We speak of Greek tragedy when we mean Athenian tragedy. Greek comedy when we refer to Athenian, while Greek philosophy is in large part the creation of Plato and the Olynthian immigrant to Athens, Aristotle. In using the term "Greek" for what is more specifically Athenian, we distort history by obscuring the uniqueness of Athens, and by overlooking many aspects of the Athenian experience which separate it from the rest of Greece.

Athens was certainly not the norm of fifth-century Greece. It had many exceptional qualities even beyond the literary and artistic efflorescence which assures its fame. Above all, it was the richest city in Greece.[1] And it was, doubtless, the wealth flowing in from empire that made it possible for Athens to attract and support the rhetoricians, musicians, metaphysicians, logicians – in short, the Sophists – from all parts of the Greek world. The effect, combined with the encouragement of the plastic arts and literature which the new wealth allowed, was even more marked on the intellectual front than on the economic, drawing the greatest talents of all the cities of Greece to one city, to create for the first time in the Greek world what we call a cosmopolitan center.

It was in this international center, probably, that the experiences, ideologies, and knowledge worked out in individual places for the first time impinged upon each other and began to form what would later be, in fact, truly Greek, rather than Corinthian, Spartan, Milesian, Samian, Theban, Athenian. The epic poetry of Homer had been common to all, and had travelled through dialect and region. For hundreds of years, perhaps a millennium, the epics had both transmitted and fashioned the thought of most Greeks into commonly understood perceptions of man achieving greatness not through success but by the mere struggle to succeed in a universe dimly understood and not at all under control. Attitudes and ideology found in Homer can be found in the literature of many different centers, in that of Herodotus of Halicarnassus, Sophocles of Athens, Tyrtaeus of Sparta, and in all the literature of later Greece one can find a common bond provided by Homer.

Not much else appears as a common Hellenic heritage at the beginning of the fifth century. There are occasional references to Hesiod by fifth-century Athenian writers, but this is, after all, the cultural center Athens, and they are in no way comparable in extent with the treatment of Homer there and elsewhere in that century.[2] The early stirrings of philosophy, geography, physics, and the like among the Ionian Greeks did not cross the Aegean, and remained a relatively narrow tradition until the century was well under way. Early lyric in general shows a particularism not only in its focus on individual personality but in the repeated localism of its references, suggesting that its audiences were not expected to have been abroad. Overall, indeed, apart from Homer, Hesiod, and some lyric, little survives of Greek writing prior to the fifth century. Although we know the names of many authors, we have little connected text, and if that fact cannot be taken to show the narrowness of the early tradition, then the virtual absence of citation except by specialists – philosophers by philosophers, historians by historians – certainly suggests that the work of writers before the beginning – or even middle – of the fifth century was not widely known. Indeed, all this should hardly come as a surprise, since it is a commonplace to put in the fifth century the first common "Greek" effort since the Trojan War: the alliance of the Hellenes, or most of them, against the Persians, and even that is acknowledged as an unusual phenomenon in the face of Greek particularism.

There were, of course, some centripetal forces, like the games at Olympia, the oracle at Delphi, and a few other common shrines and enterprises. The Greeks were aware that they were Greek – different from the *barbaroi* whom they encountered as they sailed, traveled, and settled throughout the Mediterranean basin. They had common bonds of language and religion, but language was fragmented by dialects, and common religion was often less forcefully felt than the very important local cults in which different cities placed their trust. Even so influential a matter as the calendar was particular to each city, with different month names, or similar names in different positions in the year; calendars might be shared between mother city and colony, hundreds of miles apart, while neighbors would differ enormously.

The breakdown of this particularism had begun before the end of Athenian supremacy in 404 BC. Indeed, Athens and Sparta together had been responsible for the first great common political expression of Hellenism, the alliance against Persia first struck in 490, and subsequently extended to meet Xerxes' invasion a decade later. Although Athens boasted its own individual glory in the great victory over the Persian landing force at Marathon, Spartan aid had, in fact, been requested and was forthcoming, and this a scant twenty years after a Spartan invasion of Athens and Spartan collusion in a late sixth-century attempt to nip Athenian strength in the bud after the fall of the tyrants. Against the Persian threat, however, the Athenian–Spartan alliance held, and the allied

Greek land and sea force which met the Persian invasions of 481 to 479 established a precedent which would be recalled again and again.

The success of the allies against the Persians was a Greek accomplishment in which many shared, rather than the triumph of a single city or group of cities. It was the first of its kind, a Hellenic effort, and it would be rare ever to have so many Greek states acting in concert. Old ways die hard, and cooperation was not to triumph, even with the evidence of its obvious success. Athens, which by now had developed a political as well as an economic need for expansion, was committed to filling any vacuum which the Persian defeat might leave. The Spartans, however, were not about to change their ways and, initially at least, were willing to let the Athenians go their own way, so they withdrew from active participation in the alliance.

The sources tell the story in a way that illustrates the personalities of the two cities. When faced with the problem of support for the Ionians, former possessions of the Persians, the Athenians offered to move their power into the area, while the Spartans suggested withdrawal from potential conflict by resettling the Ionians in the safety of old Greece. Whether this is the way things really happened, or whether this is the kind of contrast Greek historians liked to impose on events in order to make their meaning clear, the fact is that the Athenians did find themselves the main counter to the Persians along the coast of the Aegean, and the effects of this would be momentous, in both political and cultural terms.

The alliance devised to protect the Ionians was formulated to recognize the autonomy and individualism of each of the participating states. There was no sacrifice of any sovereignty for the common good; cooperative action was limited to defence (as any action was seen) against Persia, in the usual alliance phraseology in which the Athenians and Ionians agreed to have the same enemies and friends. But events soon moved toward producing Greece's first permanent inter-state structure, pressing toward union of economic as well as military activities, with institutions devised more for permanence than for defence against the enemy of the moment. The alliance was quickly converted from what might have been seen as a generous effort by Athens into an instrument for expanding its power and wealth, and the interests of the League, rather than of the individual members, were soon made paramount by the Athenians. By the end of the 470s, the city of Carystos was forced into the alliance, and Naxos, after an attempt to leave it, was forced by siege and campaign to return – the first "enslavement," as Thucydides called it, presumably indicating that the intent of the signatories to the alliance did not include the use of force to maintain it. Within the next decade, more revolts needed putting down, and Sparta was antagonized and grew more suspicious. The Athenians responded, probably in 461, by the ostracism of the major advocate of accommodation with Athens' former friend and close ally. The direction of events was clear for all to see. The first territorial state in Greece, created centuries before by the union of the cities and towns of the peninsula of Attica, was well on the way to the permanent establishment of a Hellenic empire.

By 454 BC the nature and goals of the new regime would be comprehensible to anyone. Joining the Egyptians in their revolt from Persia almost brought success, and the Athenians might have controlled the wealth and fecundity of the land of the Nile. Skirmishes and full-scale war with Sparta demonstrated Athens' determination and ability to stand up to Sparta's vaunted army. Success in Boeotia secured Athens' western borders. The island of Euboea, along the east coast, was pacified after revolts, as the fast-rising Pericles showed the flag in a series of lightning moves across the straits, back again to discourage a Spartan invasion, and then across to the island once again, in his campaigns of 446 BC.

There was an economic as well as a military aspect to policy. In 454, after the failure of the Athenian expedition to Egypt, and with consequent exposure to the Persians cited as a reason, the treasury of the League was transferred from the island of Delos to Athens itself. Whether the security thus gained was necessary or not, the move gave Athens even more complete control over the funds, which were enormous. Soon after[3] came a currency decree, which aimed at far-reaching economic effects. All the cities of the League were thereby required to use Athenian coinage, weights, and measures; local mints were closed, and local currency was to be brought to the mint at Athens, where at least half was to be converted to Athens at a fee thought to be 3 drachmas per mina. By requiring that Athenian currency alone be used in the cities of the League, and banning all local issues of silver, the Athenians took complete control of monetary policy, and the fee for re-coining represented a *de facto* tax of 3 per cent.[4] Most of all, the decree went a long way towards centralizing economic activity and the formulation of economic policy in Athens.

In the course of the subsequent years, more and more capital built up in Athens. Thucydides indicates that 6000 talents[5] of coined money had accumulated by the beginning of the Peloponnesian War, a significant sum measured against the 1200 talents or so which had been expended on the Samian War. The 6000 talents remained after war expense, and after disbursements for the building on the Acropolis, a construction program of great expense for which Pericles' patronage can be praised in terms of art, if not of fair use of the money of the League. In the end, Athens' grip on the economy of the Aegean was so tight that economic reprisals could substitute for military action. For example, displeased with Megarian assistance to Corinth, with whom Athens had just fought in the west of Greece, in 432 the Athenians excluded Megara from all the harbors of the League. The decree meant ruin for Megara, and was a major factor in the subsequent Peloponnesian decision for war. But arms were the resort of the economically weaker; Athens' economic power had grown so much that, left alone, it might regularly have chosen economic warfare as the preferred instrument.

7 Roman copy of a contemporary portrait of Pericles which was found in a villa near Tivoli, Italy, and is now in the Vatican Museum.

The effect of all this accreting military, political, and economic power was a qualitative change in the life of the city of Athens. The officials and assemblies, which in earlier times had had enough difficulty in defining policy amidst the conflicting interests and opinions of citizens, now had to contend with lobbyists from abroad, and Athenians were forced more and more to become familiar with the concerns and problems of other cities, in order to determine

the effects and benefits of their decisions. There was money to pay those who
would bring information and skills, and no dearth of those who would travel to
Athens to earn those rewards. Hippodamus came from Miletus to redesign the
Piraeus for Pericles, and then to plan the town grid for Thurii when Pericles
established that pan-Hellenic colony in south Italy in the mid-440s. And,
according to one tradition, it was Protagoras, from Abdera in Thrace, who
came first to Athens in mid-century, who drew up the laws for the colony.

In the mid-fifth century, Pericles was the political leader of Athens. The city
which he led was small by modern standards, and for all its activity and
domination, boasted an upper class which was very small in number. There
could not have been more than about 2000 men,[6] at the most, whom we could
call prosperous, or who would have had the leisure and means to involve
themselves either in political or cultural activities. In the circumstances, all must
have been acquainted with one another, social and cultural circles would
undoubtedly have overlapped, and the effect of the influences from overseas
would have been general and intense.

We know something of the circle of Pericles himself. Much of our information comes from Plutarch's *Life of Pericles*, which tells us not only that the great
statesman was not very convivial, but gives us the names of some of his close
associates. It was an international group, the most memorable of whom,
perhaps, was the Milesian native Aspasia, Axiochus' brilliant daughter, to
whom Pericles was devoted. The person who saw most of Pericles, according
to Plutarch, and who influenced his character particularly, was the resident
alien Anaxagoras, originally of Clazomenae, who came to Athens in mid-
century and remained there for thirty years.[7] Another foreigner in the circle
was Protagoras of Abdera, close enough to be influential,[8] who was perhaps
selected as lawgiver for Thurii. How well Pericles knew the Milesian Hippodamus, planner of both Piraeus and Thurii, remains uncertain, but he was
aware enough of his work to choose him, and the two could hardly have
escaped communications over the port.

Sophocles the tragedian, who served as general with Pericles and as a
treasurer of the Delian League, Phidias the sculptor, elevated by Pericles to
supervise the sculptures of the Parthenon, indeed most of the leadership of
Athens at the acme of Pericles' power, came to know the foreigners who so
interested the "first citizen" of the democracy. Although some of Pericles'
friends – Damon his teacher of music, Phidias, Anaxagoras, Aspasia herself –
would face legal onslaughts from those who would not challenge Pericles
directly, the cosmopolitan flavor of his associations had its effects. The city
which had for some time attracted merchants, traders, artisans, and bankers to
set up residence and establish commercial enterprises was now becoming
attractive to purveyors of ideas as well. The last half of the fifth century brought
the Sophists there, a movement which neither the death of Pericles in 429 BC
nor the long war which had begun two years before would do anything to
slow.

We have met some of these philosophers already. They include Protagoras, perhaps the most noted, and Damon, the statesman's teacher. Pericles seems to have attracted them, and it is likely that it was Pericles' own encouragement which brought so many of them to Athens and made the city their focus of activity.[9] A few of them were natives of Athens, like Damon, Critias, and Antiphon. But the Athenians do not seem to have reached the first rank in importance, unless we include Socrates among them. The really influential figures were all foreigners, like Protagoras, Hippias from Elis in the Peloponnesus, or Gorgias from Leontini in Sicily. They came from much of the Greek world, from cities which varied greatly in their cultural and political importance. Many also traveled extensively, and brought to Athens news and familiarity with cities which hitherto had only been names, if indeed Athenians had even been aware of them at all. While the Sophists did not have the scope of Herodotus, with his interest in and awareness of the histories and customs of so many barbarian peoples of the east, they could bring to Athens profound knowledge of many Greek cities and peoples.

How all these ideas and all this information were disseminated amongst the Athenians is clear from the writings of Plato, in whose dialogues so many of the Sophists appear. While Sophists might offer public lectures for a fee, they also stayed and taught at the houses of Athenians, and discussions took place there. For example, at the beginning of the *Republic* Socrates is induced to go to the house of Polemarchus to have dinner and then view a night festival. There he found Polemarchus' father and two brothers, along with some other Athenians, notably the Sophist Thrasymachus, and the group launched into a discussion of justice which ultimately produced the very long *Republic*. A similar scene served another dialogue, the *Protagoras*. The famous visitor was lodging at the house of Callias, and there took place the discussion of the teaching of virtue, a dialogue in which other well-known Sophists, Prodicus and Hippias, are represented as having participated. Whether these, and other, particular groups actually gathered in the houses mentioned to discuss the specific subjects treated in the respective dialogues is quite irrelevant; it is enough for us to know that such meetings took place in private houses. The informality of the sessions, often taking place over dinner and prolonged into the late hours, assured the opportunity of milking the visitors of their information and experience as well as their specialized teaching, not only by the eager young but by the more mature heads in the group, who could make practical use of the intelligence from abroad either in the Assembly or on campaign.

Athens thus became a clearing-house of Greek thought, a city in which the eclecticism of ideas was even more pronounced than that of the more visible work of architects, sculptors, artists, and planners like Hippodamus. It was the first such in the Greek world. Today we speak of the "Ionian" or "Milesian" or "Eleatic" school of philosophy, or of the "school of Cos" in medicine. No one has ever thought to use the term "Athenian school" for anything. Too much was going on at Athens, too many disciplines were brought there, too many different views found followers. There, in fact, all the "schools" could be found. If the Sophists can be said to have "no real nationality,"[10] Athens could be said to have provided them with their intellectual home.

By the year 431 BC, when the Peloponnesian War broke out, Athens' position as a cultural and intellectual center was secure. She was the only such center in Greece in the fifth century, since the breadth of activity there far outstripped that at such specialized centers as the medical school of Cos. Even in the important realm of religion Athens had much to offer. Although Delphi remained a prime pilgrimage center, Delos was close behind, and Athens' domination of that island brought all the activity of the Apollonian cult there into the Athenian orbit. Eleusis with her mysteries was another magnet, of a different sort but equally strong. Athens now exercised a pull which was felt all across the Greek-speaking world from southern Gaul to Egypt. It was now an international city, with the ability not only to incorporate but also to influence ideas and attitudes in many parts of the world, often tying together many divergent threads from distinct and different communities. As it turned out, this characteristic of Athens was to be permanent.

The Peloponnesian War, with all its disasters, in no way impeded or slowed this activity. The dramatic time of the Socratic-Sophistic dialogues must have been the war years, for Socrates was under 40 at the outbreak, and Plato himself had not yet been born. Socrates is certainly not portrayed as a man in his thirties. In any case, we know of specific visits to Athens by a number of Sophists during this period.[11] Prodicus for one, we are told by Plato, came frequently as an ambassador from his native city of Ceos, and used the occasions to teach, as did Gorgias, when he came as ambassador from Leontini. Their activity in Athens during this period shows in the pupils whom they taught in the city, among them the orator Isocrates, the later Sophist Antisthenes, who lived on at least until 366, and of course Plato himself. At least one foreigner, Eucleides of Megara, took some risks to visit Socrates while war divided their cities. The three aspects of the evidence converge to demonstrate the persistence of Sophist activity even while the war was being fought.

For all their diversity of origin and experience, the Sophists had much in common with the political leadership of Athens, even with Pericles himself. Hippias and Prodicus served their native states repeatedly as ambassadors. They were chosen for their remarkable rhetorical skills, we are told, and whether or not their qualifications also extended to the high financial and social status which we are accustomed to find in the background of most Greek statesmen of the period, their political activity alone would give them common ground with Athenian leaders. Gorgias of Leontini too served his native city at least once in this capacity, but the indications of his itinerant life and the fact that his brother was a physician, as Plato tells us in the *Gorgias*, rather suggest a background quite different from that of the traditional leisured aristocratic class. Protagoras, on the other hand, came from great wealth. His father

Maiandros was called the richest of the Thracians, but he was no Greek aristocrat, for he hobnobbed with Xerxes and the Persians and persuaded the Great King to allow the young Protagoras to study with the Magi.[12] We know less of the other non-Athenian Sophists, so that information about their backgrounds has been lost, but for those who were natives of Athens, the tradition seems to confirm an upper-class origin in some cases. Critias, for example, who engaged in all the Sophistic activities by teaching for hire, was from a family of wealth and aristocratic lineage of great antiquity, reaching back to one Dropides who was eponymous archon after Solon. Others seem to have been of a significantly lower class, such as Antiphon or Antisthenes, but we do not hear of those two in the exalted Periclean circles, and in any case they certainly do not seem to have been poor.

At Athens, all these Sophists were well known, and not just to those who had been members of Pericles' group. For the aristocratic Aristophanes, they were useful as butts of comedy, and whether or not his representation of their behavior and their ragged, dirty, and unkempt appearance has much basis in reality, the individuals who turn up in the plays were personalities known to the audience.[13] Prodicus, Gorgias, and Thrasymachus were all slipped into one or another of his comedies, while Damon, the teacher of Pericles, and Protagoras were derided in the works of other comic playwrights. The Sophists as a group frequently came in for mockery at the hands of Aristophanes and other late fifth-century writers, and the attacks were not limited to the stage. Plato makes Protagoras, in the dialogue named after him, allude to hostility toward the Sophists and the fact that the profession entailed some risk. Plato wrote, of course, in full awareness that Protagoras ended his career at Athens banished or condemned to death; that Damon, the teacher of Pericles, had been ostracized; that Anaxagoras had been tried; and, of course, that Socrates had become the most prominent victim of the hostility towards the philosophers. The reasons went deeper than political harassment of Pericles, for the trials continued after his death. The Sophists represented a new strain in Athenian life, bringing not only new ideas from abroad, but generating what was becoming a native Athenian spirit of scientific enquiry, logic, impiety, and challenge to traditional law. To ordinary people as well as aristocrats, they brought an unsettling political influence, while to those trusting in the traditional religious practices, their ideas were anathema and their actions downright dangerous.

Into this group came Socrates, and without the advantage of aristocratic forebears, for his mother was a professional midwife and his father was a *lithourgos*, a 'stone worker', to translate the Greek literally (a term which has often been taken to indicate tasks no more exalted than those of a stonemason, but which could also be applied to Phidias). We know remarkably little of Socrates' life, even with works by three contemporaries: one a philosopher, one a general and later a historian who wrote reminiscences about Socrates, and the third a comic dramatist who wrote a whole play about him. But Plato has few occasions on which to reveal much about his teacher's life, and Xenophon, who, like Plato, was a great deal younger than Socrates, was more concerned to describe the man he admired, to explain his behavior, and defend him from the accusations which brought about his condemnation and death in in 399 BC. Aristophanes, the comic poet, took a completely different line. He was satirizing Socrates, or the Sophists, or both. There is no certainty which aspects of his portrait apply specifically to Socrates, and which are generalizing. Finally, Aristotle, who never knew Socrates directly, but wrote of him from information which he obtained, presumably, from Plato and others, dealt with Socrates' philosophy rather than his life.

The reconciliation of all these sources constitutes what is often called the "Socratic Problem," the determination, insofar as is possible, of the philosophic concepts held and taught by Socrates. There are a few facts.[14] He gave respectable service during the Peloponnesian War, was notable in opposition both to the democracy when he refused to go along with the public demand for trial *en masse* of the generals who lost many of their sailors in a storm after a victory at Arginusae, and he opposed the tyranny of the Thirty when ordered to participate in an arrest of one Leon of Salamis. He was executed in 399 after trial and conviction for "not acknowledging the gods which the city acknowledges, but introducing other new divinities . . . and corrupting the young."

We know something of his associations during the last decades of the century, if we can trust the testimony of Xenophon and Plato. They both report his discourses with many of the young aristocrats of the day, men like Alcibiades and Plato himself, and also with mature men, some of whom made their mark in politics, such as Critias, whose activities, to be sure, reflected discredit both on himself and on Socrates. There is a little independent testimony on the circle, for such a figure as Chaerephon, memorably reported by both Xenophon and Plato to have obtained from Delphi the oracle which stated that there was no man wiser than Socrates, also turns up in the *Clouds* of Aristophanes in which he is the only member of Socrates' group of students to be specifically named. And perhaps most interesting is the tradition that Socrates was, with some of his associates, at least an occasional visitor to Aspasia.

It is clear that Socrates was an important figure in Athens in the latter part of the fifth century, and it is doubtless for this reason that he was singled out for attention by more than one comic dramatist. He himself, as we shall see, was familiar with the developments in philosophy of his own time and before, and was part of that development himself. He and his fellows moved among influential politicians and statesmen as much as among philosophers, and he was as well or better known to the Athenians at large as Protagoras, the most famous foreign Sophist. In this way Socrates was a major participant in the activity in which the Sophists also played an important part, making Athens the most active intellectual center in all Greece. Socrates, like the Sophists, must be credited (or blamed) for his share in bringing new ideas to Athens and focusing

71

the interest of influential citizens on new concepts in science, ethics, and politics.

Much of this activity of Socrates, like that of many of the Sophists, took place in that last third of the century during which Athens was fighting out her fate in the Peloponnesian War. It was also, in fact, to this period that we owe the great majority of Greek plays which have been preserved. Only Aeschylus, who died in 456, gives a dramatic ideology of an earlier period, for of Sophocles' seven extant plays, only two, the *Antigone* (c. 441) and the *Ajax* (perhaps a bit earlier), can be dated to years before the outbreak of war. The *Oedipus Tyrannus* is placed soon after 430, along with, perhaps, the *Trachinians*, while the remaining three fall after the first decade of war. As one might expect, the grouping of Euripides' work is even later. There are nineteen plays which have come down to us, and only one, *Alcestis*, was produced before the war, in 438. The *Medea* followed in 431, and the rest appeared during the years of plague, battle, truce, and disaster.

Much that we have of tragedy, then, had an impact on Athenians during these war years, and these plays of Sophocles and Euripides took part in the interplay of ideas both native and foreign which were making Athens so cosmopolitan an intellectual center. We tend to think of Sophocles as a figure of mid-century, a contemporary of Pericles, a spokesman for Athenian ideals at the peak of empire. His lifetime certainly justifies that idea, for he reached his prime as Athens grasped at power, and won his first victory with a tragedy produced in 468, while his official activity in Athens also coincided with that of Pericles.[15] He served as *hellenotamias* – treasurer of the Delian League – for the important term of 443/2, and was elected general for 441/0, concurrently with Pericles, and then again when he was much older. Sophocles' most important office, however, fell later, if we accept the evidence[16] that he acted as *proboulos* on a board appointed to deal with the crisis precipitated by the Sicilian disaster of 413. His public service thus continued well after Pericles' death, and was concurrent with the years in which most of his extant plays were produced. In a sense, Sophocles was the one major figure in Athens to provide continuity from the period of the growth of empire through the dominance of Pericles down to the close of the Peloponnesian War. Through his association, however casual, with all the major political figures of his time, he provided a point of contact between literature and life, and was one of the major participants in the mutual interaction and influence of experience and art which made imperial Athens so important in the development of Greek culture and ideology.

Euripides played a different role. He was little involved in public activities, having served once as a local priest of Zeus at Phyla and once as a member of an embassy to Syracuse. That he was well known as well as popular among Athenian audiences is obvious on a number of counts: the number of plays preserved and references to his work, the allusions to his life and plays by the comic poets, and his actual representation on stage. He appears in Aristophanes' *Thesmophoriazusae*, where he is singled out for attack, and his dramatic activity is also the target of Aristophanes' comic literary criticism in *Frogs*, where he again appears, this time in a competition of dramaturgy with Aeschylus. He is portrayed in comedy as an associate of the Sophists, and the picture we have of him from antiquity in general helps to confirm this representation. In this sense, both his life and his work can be said to have been closely entwined with the intellectual developments of the latter part of the century.

All these people, politicians, philosophers, and poets, knew each other, contributed to and drew ideas from each other, and generated the intellectual ferment which marked Athenian life in the late fifth century. The war with Sparta did not interrupt this activity, and in some ways may even have promoted it. The war, which came after, and in fact because of, Athens' great success in expanding to empire, was the background for the greater part of the philosophical and literary activity which makes up the contribution which Athens made in the fifth century to western culture. That so much of this work came so "late" in the century is often forgotten, and too often it is all attributed, along with the art of Phidias, to the period of Pericles' dominance, to make up what is so frequently called the "Periclean age." That there was an age which could be so called is not in doubt; it encompassed the ultimate elaboration of the Delian League into an assembly of states dominated by Athens, and it saw the arrival and encouragement of foreign philosophy at Athens. But we do not today have much Athenian writing from this period, for Aeschylus had produced the *Oresteia* in 458 and died two years later, just when Pericles was first coming to real prominence. Only three of the plays of the other two dramatists appeared before the very end of Pericles' life, when war had already broken out, and the writing and activities of the two other major writers of the century, Aristophanes and Thucydides, fall outside the period of Pericles' lifetime.

Much, therefore, of what we know of Athenian thought in the century came later than Athens' growth to empire, and is a reaction to, or was at least affected by, the events of mid-century. But it is a reaction given some time for formulation, influenced by the knowledge of what that empire was to cause – the great war. It is with an awareness of this relation of events to thought that we must assess the state of mind of philosophers and poets at Athens in this period. Apart from the plays of Aeschylus and a very few others, our knowledge of the Athenian mind in the fifth century is almost exclusively based on ideas formulated at the time when Athens was fighting for her survival, and the issue was in doubt.

# 7

# Divine and human justice in fifth-century Hellenism

## *Religious and ethical ideology in drama, history, and other literature*

The fifth century, when writing had a diversity of locales and genres, is the first period in which we can trace developments in Greek thought amongst writers who knew the work of their contemporaries, and it is the first time that we have a sense of the ideas and ideology current in a particular city. This is not to say, of course, that we have anything like a complete picture of the writing of the fifth century, and from Athens, for example, the city best represented in our extant literature, we can estimate something of the enormousness of our losses: 97 per cent of the tragedies produced, let alone written; we have the work of only one Athenian historian, but there were many working before the end of the century; there were many writers of Old Comedy, but complete plays by only one, Aristophanes, have been preserved. Outside Athens the situation is the same or worse. Only Herodotus' histories survive from the extensive writings in the historico-geographical tradition of the coast of Asia Minor, and not a single complete work – or even sizeable fragment – exists to elucidate the thought of the Ionian philosophers or other writers of physical or metaphysical speculation native to east Greece in the fifth century. Any writings by the Sophists are lost, and our knowledge of their ideas depends on tentative reconstructions from comments of later philosophers. In the west, there are some large pieces of the work of the philosopher Parmenides, but we have nothing from the school of the Pythagoreans except a collection of fragments the authenticity of many of which is dubious.

Despite these losses, there is a great deal we can re-create from the texts which we do have, for an extensive body of literature has survived. While it is true that we have only seven of the eighty or ninety plays that Aeschylus wrote, they are all fine plays, and they certainly give us clear statements of some of his thought. From Sophocles and Euripides too, we have enough work to judge their views. The historian Thucydides provides further insights into that period, and the works of Attic orators of the late fifth century, such as Lysias, Antiphon, Andocides, and others, yield a more pragmatic outlook on political, moral, and religious matters of their time. We can thus gain some perception of what sorts of ideas might have been current among fifth-century Athenians, or at least what might have been acceptable. While we may not be able to develop a perfect composite, we can at least find out what was common ground for Athenians, and can compare that with the writings of other Greeks. Thus, while we may only rarely be able to say that any one idea or concept found in the fifth century represents beliefs which we can find common or current among Greeks in a number of centers, we can sometimes determine what is "Athenian," or can identify particular ideas in the work of individual writers. And we can certainly be confident that, whether an idea was common or unusual among Greeks of the fifth century, if we can find it in our texts, so too could readers in antiquity, and we can be sure that it was available to influence subsequent thinkers and writers.

The earliest extant Athenian tragedy is Aeschylus' *The Persians*, produced in 472. Thus tragic drama, after an unknown number of years of competitions and performances at the annual rites of Dionysus in spring, and through an imperfectly understood evolution, comes to us in a fully developed form, a play, rather than the ritual choric song which most agree was the origin and predecessor of tragic drama. The play depicts the great Greek victory at Salamis through its effects on the defeated, the anxious wives, families, and fellows who waited in Persia for news of the great expedition. The action, which unfolds in the palace of Xerxes where the king's mother has inklings of the bad news to come, is primarily a report of the battle itself. The Persians, who behave in the play like Greeks and even call their own people "the barbarians," react with grief and lamentation, naturally, to the reports of destruction and the naming of the dead. They also make continual reference to the gods of Hellas, and their judgments, comments, and prayers are couched in terms of the Greek pantheon and Greek theodicy.

By the time *The Persians* appeared, Aeschylus had been writing tragedies for a quarter of a century or more; the work and thought is not that of a beginner. He had won his first victory in 484, twelve years before that production. The philosophical observations, the concepts of the gods, and the views of divine justice which emerge from the text have the benefit of the experience of a man in his fifties, with a full life already affecting his attitudes, and some ideas we find in Aeschylus' other work turn up in comments of the chorus or actors in *The Persians*. One of these themes, the idea that the gods are in some way the enemies of humanity, appears early in the play, in the words of the chorus which refer to divine deceptiveness (ll. 107–8): "Will any mortal man escape the cunningly conceived deceit of god?" The concept is not pressed very hard, not beyond the observation that even the swiftest are caught, that "*ate* [a sort of blindness or ruin[1]] beguiles mortal man into the net, from which he cannot emerge unharmed." It is not a very happy or comforting concept of divinity, and the chorus moves quickly on to other matters.

That the misfortunes of the Persians are just retribution for evil deeds is a much more suitable view of the divine order, at least for this play. The

8 A fourth-century BC Apulian crater from Italy, in the National Museum, Naples. The painting depicts King Darius on his throne, in council with his officials before the embarkation of the first Persian expedition against Greece. Greeks carried their historical themes as well as pottery styles to their overseas colonies.

audience, after all, is Athenian, and unlikely to approve of the notion that its victory was due to malignant demons. So the Persian queen would be expressing a good Greek idea in lines 753–8 when she says that King Xerxes conceived his expedition by consorting with wicked men whose taunts he listened to. The ghost of the former King Darius carries the theme further, asserting that the Persians suffer for their sacrilegious destruction of temples, altars, and statues of gods, and because they had done evil they suffer evil. Zeus, says the ghost, brings extravagant thoughts into line. The Greek word *euthunos*, "corrector, straightener, rectifier," used here for this activity is important. It brings all the connotations of law and human justice to bear on the evaluation of divine action, for it is the title of an Athenian official who judges the acts of magistrates, applied now in the divine sphere to Zeus. That the divine order is known suffuses Darius' judgments, in the sense that the crimes for which retribution comes are crimes well known and commonly agreed to be sacrilege among the Greeks: profanation of temples, altars, and statues; binding the sacred Hellespont as if it were a slave, "thinking to rule the gods, even Poseidon." For one doing this, any Athenian would expect trouble.

The other concept of divine activity, that of the universe as malign and the gods as enemies, is the theme of *Prometheus Bound*. The play deals with Zeus' punishment of Prometheus, one of the Titans who ruled the cosmos before the lately victorious Zeus came to power. The authenticity of the *Prometheus* as a play of Aeschylus has been challenged,[2] but whether the play is in fact by him or by a different poet of mid-century it is enough to know that the concept of Zeus expressed in it existed. Zeus is the enemy of humankind and seeks its destruction, as Prometheus says specifically early in the play (ll. 233–5). Only Prometheus opposed this, and it is to him alone that mankind owes the knowledge of all the arts which mitigate the wretchedness of human existence. Prometheus cites again and again his concern for humanity and the benefits he has brought, and most of all, the benefit of fire, for the theft of which he is riveted in suffering to his crag in Scythia. Although Prometheus is accused of, and acknowledges himself, wilfulness in opposing Zeus, his wilfulness is in aid of humans: it is thus made clear that human interests are in opposition to those of Zeus. The god himself is called a tyrant again and again, and with recollections still current that it was the last of Peisistratus' sons, the expelled tyrant Hippias, who guided the Persians to their landing place at Marathon in 490, the repetition of "tyrant" and "tyranny" can only have clothed Zeus with an aura of resentment and hostility.

If there is any doubt that we are to perceive Zeus' behavior as arbitrary, harsh, unmindful, and even hostile to humans, the long Io episode removes it. Io, sought by Zeus but unyielding to his passion, is nevertheless the object of Hera's resentment. The goddess sends a gadfly to sting her painfully, pursuing her across the world in unceasing agony. But even though Hera is the immediate agent of Io's torture, it is to Zeus that Io, Prometheus, and the chorus alike look as the cause of her misfortune. Prometheus blames him specifically (ll. 735–8), calling him *tyrannos* and violent. Io too says (l. 759) that she suffers her woe because of Zeus. While there may be some rationale behind the punishment of Prometheus, however hostile to humankind that rationale may be, there is none at all to the wretchedness of Io. She is presented as blameless, the pure victim, suffering because of a tyrant-god with yet worse in store for her. This is the harshest representation of Zeus the enemy of man, displaying violence and hostility without the slightest justification. The moral order, if one can call it that, within which this Zeus works can have no parallel to that of humanity or any meaning to human beings. And here one can hardly apply the justification of Zeus that is sometimes used to explain his violent treatment of Prometheus, that since he is a god only newly in power, political exigencies force him to put down ruthlessly any rebelliousness on the part of a Titan. Io represents no danger to Zeus, however newly enthroned. The length and force of the Io scene rather represent the unalleviated cruelty of this divinity.

Many believe that *Prometheus Bound* was part of an Aeschylean trilogy, so that the representation of Zeus may be incomplete without the other plays. But we do not know enough about a putative trilogy to guess what sort of "change" may have affected Zeus' representation – if in fact there was any change at all.[3] We are, in the end, left with the text, as was any ancient audience or reader, to interpret as encountered regardless of any subsequent modification in any plays which followed. Thus divinity as hostile was there to be considered.

There remains Aeschylus' other conception of divine morality, that it exists, that its nature is intelligible, and that it serves to mete out justice. That kind of justice is at least punishment for crime, and may even show itself as a caring concern for humanity, such as that assumed in all the invocations and characterizations of Zeus in *The Suppliant Women*. There he is the god of suppliants, and it was he who stopped Io's torture; he is called father, and it is to him that all appeal for mercy and help. This is the Zeus that most see as the Aeschylean god, the ruler of gods and men, stern in his judgments but fair, a dispenser of justice to mortal and immortal alike. This is the Zeus envisaged by Darius' ghost, and this is the Zeus of Aeschylus' masterly trilogy, the only trilogy which has come down to us intact from antiquity.

The *Oresteia* is not only the subject of a vast literature in modern times, it is also the source of an enormous amount of what we know or think we know about the Greek mentality. Into it Aeschylus has woven so many themes of human experience – the value to be assigned to male and female prerogatives; conflict of loyalties to family and state; obligations amongst people in the roles of husband, wife, father, mother, daughter, son; and finally the dominant theme of the role of the state in the administration of a justice which is not only suitable to humans but is divinely sanctioned. All this and more is explicit in the texts of one or other of the three plays of the trilogy, *Agamemnon, Choephoroe, Eumenides*. These themes, although couched in terms of Athenian religion, custom, and social behavior, have such universal application to human experience that we still respond to them today. The issues raised by the *Oresteia* are still the concern of philosophy, religion, and politics, and Aeschylus' treatment of them is so direct and so profound that it has influenced approaches ever since it was produced. In fact, the *Oresteia* has so influenced western ideas on these matters that it has created the parameters of thought, so dominating subsequent writers and thinkers as to preserve a Hellenism that ensures we still have an understanding of the Greek mind in a way that leaves other cultures alien to us.

The *Oresteia* treats justice in both universal and specific terms, as a force of nature, an unseen agent of the cosmos that lies behind the events of history and the motives of gods and men who are the causes and actors in history. The trilogy develops the application of this justice to human affairs as the transfer of the power over judgment and retribution from divine to human hands, to lay to rest the need for vengeance and murder. Through the first two plays vengeance follows murder follows vengeance, as each character in turn interprets divine law and exacts retribution for a killing deemed unjust. In *Agamemnon*, Clytemnestra, whatever her parallel motivations of jealousy and lust, uses Agamemnon's sacrifice of their daughter Iphigeneia as her justification for killing him. That sacrifice, to pacify the goddess Artemis and thus to permit the sailing of the Greek fleet to Troy, Clytemnestra sees as a butchery. She alludes to it repeatedly in her triumphant announcement of her killing of Agamemnon at the conclusion of the play, and she uses it to justify her statement that she has fulfilled divine law in punishing him.

The problem of punishment remains, however, as we learn in the second play, *Choephoroe*, or *Libation Bearers*. Apollo demands vengeance on Clytemnestra for her killing of Agamemnon, and calls on her son Orestes as the instrument of that retribution. Now grown up and returning to Argos to exact retribution for his father's murder and to claim his throne, Orestes is reluctant to take vengeance so far as to kill his own mother. The act is demanded by Apollo, and is ultimately carried out by Orestes, who forces himself to it. Immediately the Furies sweep down upon him; avenging his mother's blood they pursue him screaming off the stage.

In the final play Orestes flees first to Delphi to seek Apollo's protection, and then to Athens, where his fate is to be decided. The ambiguity of justice is demonstrated by the support he has from Apollo, on the one hand, against the pursuit by the Furies on the other. Athena is to decide which of the other two divine forces has the greater right, and she creates a human tribunal, the Athenian Areopagus, with whom she shares the judgment. The issues are presented to the court, and they include such fundamental values as male or female dominance as well as murder itself. Ultimately the judgment goes in favor of Orestes, to the outrage of the Furies, who are at length conciliated by a transformation into kindly tutelary deities of the Athenians, and are given a place of honor forever in Athenian ground. The establishment of the Areopagus as the means for all time thereafter to adjudicate such matters[4] thus transfers jurisdiction and administration of divine law from gods to humanity; in the voting itself, both share equally in the decision, to provide the link between gods and humans. The right to judge killing and assign punishment, hitherto the prerogative of the gods and the unseen forces of retribution like the Furies, is now given to human beings. Beyond the adjudication of this specific case and the implications therein for the future is an elucidation of cosmic justice itself. Aeschylus' sense of the nature of that justice permeates the entire play. It is a moral order in which retribution serves to hold the fabric of the social structure – divine and human – together in the same way that civic law preserves order in the *polis*, restricting the freedom of individual action in pursuit of the collective good, prohibiting aggression or abuse of power on the part of the strong. To Aeschylus, divine law was the same, and throughout the *Oresteia*, Zeus and the other gods act to uphold this kind of order and law. People see it and gods express it alike. Agamemnon himself, immediately on his return from Troy in his first announcement of victory, presents his success as a retribution (ll. 823–4) caused by Troy's original act. It is not to any particular virtue or ability of his own that Agamemnon attributes his victory; success only comes from Troy's punishment for transgression.

Again and again it is vengeance for crime which justifies action. Clytemnestra's triumph is her imposition of vengeance, and she defends her action against the reproaches of a stunned and baffled chorus by concurring in their statement of retribution (ll. 1562–4). The chorus understands the principle; the application is more difficult. The punishment of Agamemnon fits; the murder of the King by his wife does not. The chorus, which has questioned whether Clytemnestra could find absolution even though she has vengeance as an accomplice, has also seen that the events could not have occurred without the concurrence of Zeus.

Each event arises from the workings of the law of retribution, which is understood as equally divine and human. When Electra asks what penalty she is to ask for the murderers of Agamemnon, the chorus instructs her that human understanding of death in requital fits the divine order (ll. 118–23). So Apollo tells Orestes, and Orestes finds in the end that he has not been misled. For in the *Oresteia*, the gods do not lie. There is no deceitful god or beguiling *ate* to mislead man into error and destruction. The principles of divine law are known, and divine revelation of them is accurate. The gods themselves, far from being hostile or uncaring like the Zeus of *Prometheus Bound*, care for humans and help them.

Divine help is both plot and theme of *The Eumenides*. Apollo, who earlier was Orestes' adviser, even commander, is now his defender. Athena too exhibits concern for humanity; not only does she strive for fairness and justice to Orestes, she also acts to ensure that her people will not suffer as a result of the outcome of the trial, and finds a means of reconciling the Furies to turn their wrath aside from Athens. The Furies themselves, bringers of retribution, horrible and grim bearers of the misfortune which comes to those who break divine law, now find a softer side to their part of the divine plan. They are to bring victory without evil, and safety to the citizens. Athena and the Furies – now the Eumenides, Kindly Ones – recite the blessings which they will bring to the Athenians. All this emerges as the will of Zeus. Zeus rules all (l. 759) and even the gods depend upon him, just as Athena says that there is nothing more to say than that she trusts in him (l. 826). Humankind has a place in the universe of this Zeus and conduct is regulated by the divine order which he administers. Zeus' thunderbolt punishes and protects, but the thunderbolt is not random nor is humanity helpless. While Zeus rules and the other gods share that rule, they are all trusty guides to anyone who seeks their advice. The rules of conduct and law which humans know and apply to themselves are the same rules which gods apply to people, and divine law is human law. Zeus has made sure that humanity knows this law, and Athena can thus set up the Areopagus as an agency of judgment.

This Zeus is far from the tyrant of *Prometheus Bound*, and this perception of humanity's place in the universe is far more optimistic than that presented there or in the portrayal of trickery and *ate* set out in *The Persians*. But while the two perceptions may be mutually exclusive in logic, one may see truth in each. There is validity in the sense of helplessness before the forces of the cosmos, of people as victims of an inscrutable and ineluctable divinity. But the description of humanity as part of the cosmos, knowing its laws and with the duty of obedience, also has force as an interpretation of life.

Far removed as we are from the days when the living Aeschylus might have sat sipping wine and discussing such concepts with his friends, so far too are we from conceiving the course of conversations which he might have had with his much younger contemporary, Sophocles. But so long as we remember that the two men were fellow citizens and were both writing during the last dozen years of Aeschylus' life, we may be able to have some feeling for the force of his ideas on Sophocles and other Athenians of his day. In the years in which Aeschylus was posing the questions and offering some answers, they were relevant not only to individuals pursuing the eternal search for some understanding of the human place in the universe, but also to Athenians seeking to lay down an acceptable rule of law for the cities and people over whom their rapidly growing power was giving them authority. Aeschylus' treatment of these matters would have been laid before politicians such as Pericles, who was choregus for the production of *The Persians* in 472 and was about thirty years Aeschylus' junior, as well as Pericles' coeval Sophocles, who became involved in both drama and politics. Euripides would have been in his late twenties and early thirties at the time of the production of the *Oresteia* and *Prometheus Bound*, Sophocles around 40, with ten years of his own productions at the Dionysia under his belt.

It is a commonplace to remark the generation gap between Aeschylus and Sophocles, to note that Aeschylus came to his maturity amidst the tensions and glory of the victories of the Persian Wars in which he himself fought, and died before the great empire which he knew in his old age fell upon evil days, while Sophocles on the other hand matured with the empire, was active not only at its peak but through the long years of its fight for survival, and had, as so many have sententiously said, the good fortune to die just before Athens' final defeat. But the events of history or the oft-blamed emerging Sophistic philosophy and

9 The portrait on this standing figure of Sophocles is one of many copies of the original Greek type made around 340 BC. This one, found at Tarracina, Italy in 1839, is now in the Vatican Museum.

teaching do not exhaust the reasons for the differences between the two. The difference between the work of Sophocles and that of Euripides was as great or greater, although these two were almost exact contemporaries, their extant work overlapping almost completely, with only two of the former's seven extant plays dated outside the period covered by the latter's nineteen, and these by a mere three or four years. Yet the two dealt in very different ways with the historical experiences of Athens and the intellectual currents which affected Athenians during their lifetimes.

Even Aeschylus, in his later years, would not have been immune to some of these influences. Many have seen the traces of the teachings of the Sophists in his last plays, and there is certainly ample evidence of them in *Prometheus Bound*, in which Prometheus not only speaks of the education he has brought mankind, but willingly takes on the appellation of *sophistes*.[5] And in their own activity the Sophists dealt with some of the concerns which Aeschylus voiced, whether the gods are just, whether man's fate is a concern to them, and whether human justice is the earthly paradigm of the divine. By and large Greek – or at least Athenian – disputants opted for analysis in these terms rather than those of the contemporary, but foreign solution, Persian dualism.[6] Rather than explain misfortune in the face of virtuous action by the existence of an independent force in the cosmos which sought and generated evil, Athenian thinkers tended to attribute human experience of evil either to a misperception of the divine order or, in the worst circumstances, to the irrelevance of humanity to the workings of the universe. This is true even of Protagoras, who might well have known the Persian approach to ethics and the alternation between good and evil in human experience. Rather than dualism, Protagoras pursued the definition of virtue and its perception in human activity which, from Aeschylus' time on, dominated ethical speculation, at least in Athens. Protagoras could deal with the issues within the parameters of thought established by his famous statement, "Of all things, a man is the measure; of things that are, how they are; of things that are not, how they are not."[7] In this, at least as Plato presents him, Protagoras is arguing that an individual's perception of phenomena is accurate for that individual, so that, to whom a wind seems cool, it is cool, and for whom it seems warm, it is warm. The relativism of this position extended to morality, but with important modifications. First, as is made clear in Plato's *Theatetus*, in which Socrates answers for the now dead Protagoras, the Sophists' own doctrine and activity require enough modification of the relativism in order to allow for the existence of some people who are wiser in perceiving the advantages of different courses of action. Secondly, if the views put in the mouth of Protagoras in Plato's *Protagoras* are genuine reflections of his thought, not all humans are equally able to make moral judgments. The argument takes the position that this ability is passed on by the teaching of many in the society, and that they are better learned by some and better taught by some. Behavior is thus unequal, and the observed disparity between good parents and bad offspring, *inter alia*, can be explained.

These Protagorean doctrines were recorded by Plato fifty years after their enunciation, and there is every likelihood that his formulation reflected the needs of his dialogues as much or more than they did the language of Protagoras. We can, however, understand the nature of the problem which generated Protagoras' answer. Simply put, it is that regardless of which of

Aeschylus' two formulations of cosmic justice is correct, a person can only work within the framework of the "Oresteian," that human knowledge is adequate for the perception of the divine order. One cannot understand the cosmos except in human terms, and divine justice can be conceived only within a human context. This sentiment, explicit in some of the tragic plays of the later fifth century and implicit in others, is also inherent in the so-called "*nomos–physis* controversy" in which, we are told, the fifth-century Sophists found themselves embroiled. Briefly put, the dispute represents the antithesis between social norms and the pursuit of "natural" inclinations. An individual – and it is important to remember here that it is individual conduct, as for Protagoras it was individual perception, that is at stake – chooses between the *nomoi*, "rules, customs, laws, norms," set up by society, thus choosing *nomos* as supreme, or chooses instead what is perceived to be personal self-interest and advantage. There is no question of an overriding divine law to which, understood either partially, fully, or not at all, human conduct should conform. "Man is the measure of all things" because "man" is the measurer of all things.

Throughout Athenian literature of the latter part of the fifth century, one can see all sorts of responses to this formulation of the problem of establishing norms for individual and political behavior. One of these is Protagoras' relativism modified in the sphere of morality by a well-based practical perception of the different degrees of acuity arising from differences in natural endowment and training. In other instances, the inability to go beyond human values and the relativism of these almost becomes a mere excuse for the exercise of raw power in the pursuit of political ends, a pattern which frequently emerges from speeches and actions described by Thucydides. In the works of Sophocles and Euripides the characters display widely varying views on the matter, with attitudes expressed philosophically or in religious terms, so that statements about the gods range from a pious statement of their moral supremacy to a flat denial of their virtue. As far as the drama is concerned, all of this makes for very great difficulty in establishing the moral stance of the playwrights, but if that question is set aside, the texts themselves provide an invaluable testimony to the range of moral positions which could be voiced in Athens at this time.

One of the simplest positions is that which accords no special insight, just behavior, or enforcement of law to the gods. It is not a matter of the gods being uncaring; they are unable to bring justice. Thus in Euripides' *Heracles*, Amphitryon says of Zeus (l. 347), "If you are a god you are ignorant,[8] or in your nature you are not just." Elsewhere in the play (ll. 655 ff.) the chorus challenges: "If the gods had understanding or wisdom as men do, they would give people a second life as a distinction between good and evil, but there is no clear landmark for the worthy or the wicked."[9] It is not very far from this to the assertion that a god is directly responsible for a specific evil human action in *Orestes*, first by Electra (ll. 162–3), then by Orestes (l. 285). The god is only exonerated by what may be the most remarkable epiphany in Euripidean tragedy. The play closes with Apollo putting an end to the on-stage shambles of murder and destruction by assigning a future to each participant in which each will fulfill the standard mythic role, imposing a solution which makes no sense at all.[10] The god is either evil in fact, or, at best, disregarding or ignorant of justice. In these texts, injustice comes from the gods, who are either unjust themselves or ignorant of justice. People are perfectly capable of judging right from wrong, but choice for wrong is imposed upon them, so that human moral judgment is correct but human will is not supreme.

There are, of course, those who would not accept this, and hold to the view that the gods are good and enforce justice, a position often taken up to defend an action or opinion. An example might be the frequent invocation of divine law in defense of Antigone, such as her own initial defense of her burial of her brother Polyneices as according with divine, not human law (*Antigone*, ll. 450 ff.), and there are many other instances of a supplicant calling on the gods in aid of his or her just cause. It is a common characteristic of religiosity in all times to assume divine endorsement of human actions, but the Greek position is more specific than this general tendency, and presumes to know the right, assumes it to accord with divine law, and finally, expects to see divine enforcement. This can be carried almost to the point of seeing the gods as agents for the imposition of human justice and will, as in the *Heracleidae*, when, as the Athenians brace for an Argive attack, Iolaus predicts victory because of the power of Athens' tutelary deity (ll. 347 ff.). It is almost a reorientation of the very old standard that justice is helping one's friends and hurting one's enemies, whereby the gods as allies meet their obligations. Again, divinity is predictable, and justice is expressed in that predictable relationship between humans and gods.

Thus far, the views emerging from the impact of accepting human values of justice have been simple: evil exists because the gods are evil or stupid; the gods are just and make things come out all right. But Sophocles and Euripides both show us some more complex treatments of the issue. There is, for example, a recognition that the citation of the will of the gods can be almost a charade, as Philoctetes (in l. 992 of the play named after him) accuses Odysseus of making the gods liars in order to use them as cover for his own actions. Furthermore, both tragedians often present the theme that human beings do not know what the gods intend, or why they do what they do. The heroes of Sophocles' plays suffer almost unspeakable abuse from above, almost always unmerited in human terms, and rarely understood by anyone.[11] Although there is the occasional commonplace that the gods bring down those who would exalt themselves too high, there is in fact remarkably little in Sophocles' texts to justify the observation common from Aristotle on, that the hero fails because of his hubris – arrogance. Moral understanding is more difficult to achieve than this suggests. Though Oedipus in the *Tyrannus*, Philoctetes, Antigone, and even Creon act in the conviction of doing right, and we agree that they are right, neither our approval nor their conviction is worth much. It is perhaps in *Antigone* that Sophocles best constructs a drama to show that being right in human terms – whether correct in asserting the rule of law or in interpreting the will of gods – does not bring human success, so disjunctive are human and cosmic moralities. This is not to say the the gods are not moral, or are immoral enemies of humanity, or even that their will cannot sometimes be perceived by humans. There is a divine order to the cosmos, and we can sometimes see some of its attributes, as does Antigone, but human understanding is at best incomplete. While human concepts of justice are in general correct, there seem to be other principles at work which override them, in the sense that adherence to human justice is not a reliable means of achieving human prosperity.

This is central to the *Antigone*, in which Sophocles presents his most explicit examination of these issues. As in so many dramas, there are many themes in the play – the antagonism between male force and female will, the antithesis between the law of the state and the so-called "unwritten laws" of the gods, questions of filial obedience and the like – but they are all subsidiary to the question of the determination of true justice and the human cost of reaching knowledge of justice. In *Antigone* there is no question but that there is some conflict between human perceptions of justice and the truth about justice in the cosmic order, for, as the play reaches its denouement, it becomes clear that it is Antigone's view of the right which conforms to that of the gods. Nevertheless, Antigone does not come out well, and neither does Haemon, who took her side. Both die as a result of their actions, and no Greek would think that such a death was a good thing, at least at this stage in Greek thought. Thus they are not rewarded for their right perceptions, either by mortal prosperity or even some indication of divine favor, and if there is any satisfaction, it would be the meager posthumous reward of the destruction of the happiness of their opponent. The perception of divine justice or the cosmic order on the part of Antigone is thus imperfect; she is right that the burial of her brother, carried out in accordance with the laws of the gods, is a moral imperative superseding the requirement of conformity to human law and the need for the preservation of order among men, but something has still gone wrong. What it is we do not know, nor does Sophocles tell us or even suggest an answer. The notion of hubris is, as many have seen, either simplistic or entirely inappropriate.

The answer must lie in the limitation of man's ability to understand the divine. It is part of the problem of almost every Sophoclean hero. The Sophoclean hero is dedicated to justice, and divine justice at that, but is precluded by the nature of his or her humanity from reaching full knowledge of the course to be followed, and the normal goal of human prosperity. The hero may reach an immediate goal, but ultimate failure is inevitable. Thus the divine will brings the universe to a divine order humans cannot perceive.

There may be something of this theme in Euripides' *Hippolytus*, although that hero is not so satisfied with the result of his adherence to his ideals as are the Sophoclean characters, and says bitterly as he dies that his virtue has done

*10* A portrait of Euripides, a Roman copy of a Greek work of about 340–330 BC. Aristophanes, the fifth-century BC comic playwright and opponent of Euripides, depicted him as an intellectual, and something of that may come through this copy of a work made over a half-century after the tragedian's death. (National Museum, Naples)

him no good. Even more chaotic is the sense of moral purpose in other plays. The brutality of the sacrifice to Artemis in *Iphigeneia in Tauris*, the purpose-lessness of the madness and slaughter of the children in *Heracles*, the socio-pathic crimes of Orestes illustrate no apparent intervention or interest by divinity. Often, as in *Orestes* and *Iphigeneia in Tauris*, the action has plunged ahead into such a morass of personal disaster and moral confusion that no reasonable way out can be imagined, and none in fact is, for some god, some hero, or some human figure plunges in to stop the action and bring resolution to the plot. Defenders of Euripides have often found difficulty with a number of the plays which use so blatant a device for their dramaturgy, and whatever they show, they do illustrate an attitude toward the relationship between the gods and human conduct. That attitude, among other things, credits the human with an enormous capacity for evil, a capacity little restrained either by divine intervention or by human fear or respect for divine law. There are forces at work in the world and they affect human beings, but there is no calculating their effect, no means of assessing the probable outcome of good or bad actions.

It is safe, therefore, to indulge one's worst impulses – as safe, at least, as it is to hold to a perception of virtue. A play like *Medea* rolls forward like a juggernaut without impediment from the divine, and practically without a mention of the gods. Medea plans and executes the murders of the king of Corinth, his daughter, and her own children without a hint of apprehension that the gods will somehow wreak vengeance of her. She is concerned with human retribution, and when an escape route is opened, she proceeds with her plans. Even the chorus, so often the voice of orthodoxy, fails in this play to threaten Medea with divinity in attempting to restrain her, but finds only human law (*nomoi*) to cite (ll. 812–13) in support of its position. Although at times Euripidean characters sense that there is some absolute quality to some aspects of human law, some concept of right and wrong apart from the *nomoi* of a particular community, the idea is only vaguely broached and in any case remains on the mortal level, in a human sense of rectitude rather than a divine prescription. This may be the most characteristic Euripidean concept of evil and justice, that there is some universal law which determines what is right, but this universality is operative only in the human sphere, as there is a morality which applies to humankind and which humankind knows, but which may be overridden or obscured by the workings of non-human cosmic forces the rationale of which is unknown. This Euripidean position is different from the Sophoclean in that it posits morality beginning and ending with humanity, rather than seeing human morality as an imperfectly conceived representation of cosmic justice. And cosmic forces are not, as they seem to be in the Sophoclean perception, beneficial but imperfectly understood; there is no order and the cosmos is disruptive of human attempts to create order.

These are abstruse concepts, more usually found in the realm of philosophy or theology than of drama. It is not likely that Athenian audiences were much concerned about evaluating performances in terms of their presentation of one or another of these ideas, or, in fact, were any more patient with long discourses on such subjects than are modern churchgoers. But it is likely that in any audience, there would have been some people who recognized these concepts. Certainly the educated Athenians – those who had studied with the Sophists and had heard them dispute and discuss different views of justice, of *nomos* and *physis* and their importance as determinants of human conduct – would have had no trouble at all in following even the more complex and subtle present-ations of the relationship of human justice to the cosmic order. Indeed, the repetition of many of these concepts by Sophocles and Euripides must have made a fairly large number of Athenians familiar with them. If Plato's dialogues and Xenophon's Socratic discourses have any validity as indicators of the intellectual concerns of Socrates' younger companions in the latter years of the fifth century, then the elucidation of the nature of justice and the framing of attitudes toward it must have stood high on the list. The drama itself, with its constant reference to such themes, played a very large part in heightening Athenian consciousness and interest in these issues.

These concerns showed themselves in other areas. The claim of justice was a very important part of advocacy in the assembly and in the law courts, although historical texts often portray speakers emphasizing advantage over justice. There were, we are told, some decades of training behind this, during which young men were instructed in the techniques of oral persuasion. It was a skill in which some of the Sophists specialized, a skill which, according to their enemies, was nothing other than making the worse – wickeder – argument appear the better. There is no doubt that some of the politicians of the day did just that, and Thucydides portrays a number of them using their rhetorical training in pursuit of their own political ends with little or no regard for any abstract principles of justice.

Sophistic rhetoric as it was taught in Athens by Gorgias and others in the latter part of the century was treated essentially as a skill, a technique for fashioning *logoi* – spoken arguments – as convincingly as possible, although Gorgias, and probably other teachers of rhetoric took the position that the skill they taught should only be used in the pursuit of virtue. By the time Aristophanes produced his *Clouds* in 423 (or revised it in 421), the popular conception of the rhetoric taught by the Sophists included the concept that they "made the worse argument appear the better," for that accusation is at the heart of the play. The plot turns, in fact, on the Sophistic training of the old rascal Strepsiades, who seeks to use the new techniques to turn the tables on his creditors and by argument avoid paying his just debts. The rhetoric which he wants taught to his son "so that he will be able to argue down all the just cases," (l. 898) is parodied in the long debate between the Just Argument and the Unjust Argument which immediately follows. The debate, which the Unjust Argument wins after the introduction of a number of debaters' tricks, is not only an attack on the general concept of bringing success to an unjust cause by rhetorical skill, it also parodies the very devices which the teachers of rhetoric profess. Aristophanes' dramatic and comic debate is also not very far in form and technique from that which Thucydides constructs to elucidate the moral and political principles behind the actions of the Athenian democracy during the Peloponnesian War.

Thucydides uses two extensive debates to illustrate Athenian attitudes at different stages in the war, the speeches being a kind of free invention to display opposing policies and illustrate different moral positions. In the debate over the fate of Mytilene, a city which had revolted against Athenian control and had been reconquered, the leading democratic politician Cleon advocated punishment by executing the entire male population and enslaving the women and children. No abstract principles of justice were presented; Cleon took the view that the Athenian Empire was maintained by force and fear, and that ruthless punishment was necessary to deter future revolts by others. An opposing position, which ultimately prevailed, argued that so severe a retribution was contrary to Athenian self-interest, for, since executions and the fear thereof had not eliminated crime in the past, future revolt could not thus be precluded. The only effect of such punishment would be to discourage future rebels - and rebellions were inevitable – from ever giving up and making terms. Rebellions would thus become much more difficult and expensive to suppress. This argument, like Cleon's, was devoid of anything but self-interest, and both speeches, using rhetorical turns and techniques to intensify the force of the argument, illustrate the setting of policy at Athens without concern for justice or morality, making advantage the determinant for decision.

A much more explicit presentation of morality is the so-called *Melian Dialogue*, in which the inhabitants of the island of Melos argue against the Athenian order to join the Athenian side, and the Athenians try to persuade them to surrender themselves to Athens. The two parties put their cases forth in a kind of mini-drama which occupies the last 20 per cent of Book V. To the dismay of the Melians, the Athenians exclude justice as a consideration, so the argument again turns on self-interest. The Melians try to show that it is to the Athenians' advantage to let them remain neutral, while the Athenians in turn try to convince the Melians that their self-interest should permit them to surrender. The discussion is most instructive at the one point where it touches on the gods. To the Melian statement that they will trust the gods to support them, the Athenians respond that they behave consistently with human opinion about the gods and the principles which the gods take for their own behavior, and they "hold, in opinion of the divine sphere but in knowledge of the human, that in every respect it is necessary by nature [*physis*] to rule where there is power to do so." Some may be reminded here of Antigone's claim for the eternal quality of divine law, but the Athenians have something rather different in mind. It is the exercise of *physis*, natural self-interest and desire, that is the immutable rule of conduct, an argument which would be familiar to many of Thucydides' Athenian readers from the *nomos–physis* controversies of the philosophers. In the end, the Melians do not accept the Athenian view, and go off to resistance and destruction, trusting, as Thucydides has the Athenians point out almost sardonically, in vain hopes and mistaken self-respect.

Self-interest and practicality, the necessity to act ruthlessly to maintain an empire however unjustly acquired, are the hallmark of the Athenians' rhetoric throughout Thucydides' work.[12] That Athenian behavior and motives should be presented as so little concerned with morality is scarcely surprising, in view of Thucydides' own view of human character. In one of his rare expressions of personal judgment, in Book III, Chapters 82 and 83, he comments about the Corcyraean democrats' slaughter of their opponents in 427, the first example of the savage civil strife which occurred in city after city as the war proceeded and pushed men into ever greater violence and civil crime. The love of power, greed, and personal ambition drove men on to all sorts of injustices and dishonorable acts, investing their actions with fine-sounding catchwords and descriptions, but bringing every sort of evil to the cities of Greece. Thus Thucydides saw the political character of the Greeks deteriorating abysmally under the impact of the war.

The justice and misbehavior with which Thucydides is concerned here are entirely at the human level. Although there are occasional references to the gods as potential support – usually made by victims attempting to alleviate their suffering – neither Thucydides himself nor any of those to whom he attributes speeches propose or formulate any concepts of justice or fair behavior for which divine endorsement is alleged. There is, in fact, very little reference to the gods at all, apart from occasional invocations of divine support in general terms, or the infrequent mention of divine service of the sort that is usual before battle or embarkation on a major project. By and large, Thucydides deliberately underplays divine service: for example, when reporting the extensive religious activity of the Athenians in carrying out the purification of Delos, he says vaguely that it was done "because of some oracle." Even the Spartans, who are presented more often as pious, make no references to the gods in their negotiations with Athens. And in his passing references to justice, human justice is never made an important consideration, and even admitted injustice is subordinated to the needs of policy. Pericles himself does this, in his famous remark about the moral quality of the empire, in Book II, Chapter 63: "You hold your empire as a *tyrannis*, which on the one hand seems unjust to obtain, but on the other is dangerous to let go." And Pericles never invokes divine justice, or refers to the support of the gods, or in fact even mentions them at all in justification of his policies.

There is in Thucydides' account of the Peloponnesian War no moving force other than that emanating from the human actors. Insofar as there is any sort of justice at all, it is a justice which conforms to human perceptions and human needs, and is imposed, if at all, for convenience or by the necessity generated from the interaction of two parties who are more or less equal in power. Justice, in a sense, is a substitute for power, and comes into play when one's power is not equal to one's will. This attitude toward the relationship between justice and power is one extreme of the *nomos–physis* controversy of the Sophists, and Thucydides may be introducing it so baldly and repeating it so often to suggest the implications of this kind of morality for human behavior. Whether or not Thucydides himself believed in the irrelevance or non-existence of cosmic

*11* Portraits of Thucydides show a man as different in visage from that of the representations of Herodotus (see Plate 13) as the works of the two historians differ in style and content. This bust in the National Museum, Naples shares with other heads the characteristics of a short, cropped beard and a receding forehead, and perhaps even the appearance of a man of action as well as of literature.

justice, he certainly portrays the political world thus, and the force of his prose has ensured that to this day Athenian politicians of the late fifth century are seen as amoral or immoral. Thucydides' history has created an evaluation of the Athenian political and legal process as moved by Sophistic argument and motivated purely by perceptions of advantage, devoid of any sense of what is right and proper either in divine or in human terms.

It is startling to see how different a picture emerges from the work of the orators. The Athenians who listened to the speeches of Pericles, Cleon, Nicias, and Alcibiades, secular and coldly rational in approach according to the account of Thucydides, with hardly a mention of divine matters, were the same Athenians who heard the gods called on repeatedly in the courtroom pleadings of Antiphon, Lysias, and Andocides. Here we are much closer to the Athens of the tragedies than to the society which the politicians seemed to be dealing with in the pages of Thucydides. In all the court speeches which deal with murder, for example, the fundamentally religious attitude toward pollution is prominent; the prohibition against association with the accused, who is presumed to carry the miasma of impurity created by killing, is unchallenged. All parties agree on the necessity to satisfy the spirit of the dead and cleanse the city by the identification and punishment of anyone responsible for killing. Justice is part of this, and is often cited in the speeches, but even more important are the religious significance and catharsis achieved by this punishment, and in its aid, the gods below are invoked in ways reminiscent of tragedy.[13]

Antiphon the orator, or Antiphon of Rhamnous as he is called by Thucydides, was born soon after the Persian Wars, and died in 411. Some moderns identify him with the man called Antiphon the Sophist, who was born and died at about the same time. The orator was a man of strong oligarchic views. He was one of the extremists among the 400 who seized power in 411 and established a short-lived oligarchy. When the oligarchy was overthrown, Antiphon was executed for his part in it. He died leaving a number of court speeches and set pieces which illustrate the part religion played in this form of rhetoric.

In one of his speeches, *On the Choreutes*, probably written in the last decade of his life, Antiphon presents the defense against a murder charge which had been laid against an official. One of the points Antiphon makes in this very complex presentation of procedural matters bears on the failure of the prosecution to follow up immediately on the charge, thus allowing the accused to carry on his public and religious duties, when, had he been charged promptly, he would have been excluded from public places as polluted by the charge of murder. The passage not only illustrates how important religious matters were in the conduct of public affairs, it also shows, coming as it does at the close of the oration as the final item of evidence, how powerfully religious matters might be introduced into forensic composition.

Another defense speech, *On the Murder of Herodes*, brings in divine and human law, as the calmness of a voyage made by the defendant and the consistent success of his sacrifices are presented as evidence of his unpolluted, i.e. innocent, state. This again is the final item of evidence, and witnesses are brought forward to prove the truth of the statements. This speech, like that of *On the Choreutes*, belongs to the last quarter of the fifth century, when Sophistic teaching had had ample time to penetrate the society, and should be compared with another, made before the Assembly, not a law court, by one

*12* One of the relatively few Greek works known from the original rather than the Roman copy, this bronze statue of a charioteer was set up at Delphi in around 475 BC as a votive offering after a race, a reminder in a visual way of what Pinder presented in verse.

Andocides, who had been exiled for having had something to do with the mutilations of the herms in 415. Pleading to return to Athens in section 15 of his *On his Return*, the orator attributes to the gods his earlier preservation when he was in Athens in 411.

# Divine and human justice in fifth-century Hellenism

The orators repeatedly trot out interpretations of justice in support of their arguments: this in itself might not be taken as so great a contrast with the speeches in Thucydides, for the forensic speeches are, after all, presented in a court of "justice" and would naturally focus on what conclusion to a trial would be just. However, the repeated citation of divine matters both for support and as actual evidence, an approach completely alien to the speakers in the pages of Thucydides, produces a very different impression. Although like the speeches which Thucydides offers, these are constructed with all the rhetorical devices and turns which had been developed by the Sophistic teachers of oratory from the middle of the century on, they part company on the use of the divine as well as of abstract principles of justice. The rhetoricians consistently include divine evidence as part of their cases, and they present divine law as if it were not only knowable but congruent with the *nomoi* of human society. There is no hesitation in assuming that human law is valid and good, and Antiphon even remarks on the durability of the Athenian law on homicide as evidence of its excellence. Human law is assumed to accord with abstract principles of justice, and in fact this is even stated on occasion. Divine law, and the will of the gods, whenever they are mentioned, are presented as obvious and known supports of human justice, so that evidence like that of safety at sea and success in sacrifice is acceptable precisely because of the assumption that the gods act against those who are unjust and guilty of those crimes understood to be such by human society. The gods are presumed to endorse and support human principles of law, and the absence of that support would destroy the only moral principles or rule of justice available to mankind. The suppositions apparent in the texts of jurisprudence as well as in drama and philosophy in the fifth century indicate that many thinkers, at least, were prepared to elaborate and accept a morality which, though it might be limited by human knowledge and understanding, was nevertheless valid for human action. This approach to divine and human justice took its place in Athens alongside those perceptions which saw divine will as either antithetical or uncognizant of human life, or saw human morality as an imperfect attempt to pattern behavior on a divine order which mankind cannot understand, and which could be and frequently was overridden by that dimly perceived superior morality.

Just to the west of Attica lies Thebes, the largest city of Boeotia. In distance, it lies no more than a good day's journey from Athens; in spirit and temperament, its society was far apart from the Athenian. Boeotia had been home to Hesiod, whose *Works and Days* had elaborated peasant morality and philosophy, and whose *Theogony* presented an organized and consistent account of the genealogy and interconnections of the gods. In the fifth century Thebes held a writer of choral lyric whose accomplishments gained the highest admiration and respect in all parts of the Hellenic world. Pindar, who was born in the last quarter of the sixth century and survived and worked past the middle of the fifth, was one of the most, if not the most, prominent of the poets who sang the accomplishments of the aristocrats who contended and won victories at the games held for the Greek national religious festivals, the quadrennial games at Olympia in Elis, and the Pythian games at Delphi, as well as the biennial Isthmian games near Corinth and the Nemean games in the Peloponnesus. Participation was mostly an aristocratic pastime, although any genuine Hellene who was able to afford the time, travel, and training could compete. A victor could expect to hear, when he returned to his city, a choral ode composed to honor his success. Pindar was probably the most noted composer of these odes, and four books of his epinician, or victory, odes survive, preserving forty-five complete odes, while only fragments of the work of his rivals remain.

Pindar is often understood as a voice of the old aristocratic class which was losing its dominance at the end of the sixth and beginning of the fifth centuries. He is portrayed as promulgating the qualities – the *arete* – valued by that class, an amalgam of personal honor, physical prowess, courage, mutual courtesy and hospitality, modesty, respect for the gods, and loyalty to family. *Arete* is seen essentially as the standard of clan values, rather than civic virtues, and Pindar is thus an advocate of the tradition which was becoming obsolete at the beginning of the fifth century. Nevertheless something in his work caught the imagination of later Greeks as well as his contemporaries, and the qualities of *arete* hymned by Pindar, much as they might have been the particular pride of an earlier aristocracy, remained admirable qualities in themselves, constantly called to mind by the Homeric poems which were at the center of Greek education.

Pindar's thought is very different from that of Aeschylus, his slightly older Athenian contemporary.[14] The sense of divine hostility or deceptive *ate* which can be perceived in Aeschylus makes a striking contrast to Pindar's perceptions of the gods as suffused with radiance and glory.[15] To him, what there is of success in human life comes from the gods, who brighten the inferior existence of mortals, and it is the gift of the gods to make human life transcend the ordinary state.[16] What there is of moral judgment in the odes expresses reservations about human behavior,[17] while fragments deriving from his other works present a few clearer statements about morality and religion which help to fill out our understanding of Pindar's thought. He thinks that even superior human wisdom is a small thing when confronted by the impenetrable plans of god,[18] and one of his clearest statements about human and divine justice is a remark quoted by Herodotus which asserts that law or custom is king of all gods and men, and brings the strongest punishment.[19] Here, in one of Pindar's relatively rare uses of a word with the *dike* – justice – root, the *dikaia* or justices are the punishments imposed by the rule of law which is superior to both men and gods. It is a position consistent with whatever else we can deduce of Pindar's thought, wherein human activity is carried on at a level far below that of the gods, only here, the gods seem to conform to rather than impose the moral order of the universe.

# Divine and human justice in fifth-century Hellenism

There are, to be sure, only the merest hints of Pindar's attitudes toward the relationship between divine and human morality and justice.[20] So far as we can see, to Pindar, human and cosmic justice seem to be related to each other in the same way as humans and gods, and that relationship is a kind of simulacrum on a universal scale of the appropriate relationships between the different levels of human society. As in human society each class and people within it had its place, so in the cosmos humankind had its place; inferior to the gods though that place might be, it was humanity's decreed and proper place, and so long as each human "kept in place," the universe would work best for each. It was a rule which could be applied to the individual as to the species, and it was a sense of the place of humankind in the universe which could be and was expressed in terms of the *arete* so valued by Pindar's aristocrats. In the context of this vision, "justice" in the Athenian sense presented no problem, because there could be no conflict between a divine and a human "justice." There might be an overarching and almost ineffable law which regulated the universe, and an order which was best undisturbed if trouble was to be avoided, but that law and that order, rather than some humanly reasoned justice, provided the touchstone for human behavior, and so long as people kept to the appropriate place for humans, they could more likely than not avoid the worst troubles which the gods and fates might have at their disposal.

A different personality with a very different set of ideas came from across the Aegean. Herodotus, whose working life spanned the middle of the fifth century, came from Halicarnassus, on the southern coast of Anatolia. Many find in his writings evidence of a rationalism which is supposed to owe something to the more pragmatic investigations of natural phenomena by the pre-Socratic philosophers of Ionia, while on the other hand, the magisterial Felix Jacoby can dispose of this supposed rationalism by seeing in Herodotus what he calls "the old completely naïve belief,"[21] which can be classed with that of Homeric thought. There are certainly contradictions apparent in Herodotus' writing, contradictions which may attest shifting and insecure conclusions about the role of the gods and their oracles in human affairs, and they may be, as some have supposed, instances of Herodotus' willingness to lay alternate interpretations before his readers.[22] The historian's restless curiosity and dedicated investigation certainly produced a vast wealth of data on oracles, predictions, omens, and dreams, and he usually deals quite carefully with the manner in which they influenced their recipients.

Herodotus was intensely aware of the relativism at work in establishing norms for human behavior, and in a famous passage, which argues that each nation thinks its own customs best, he tells the story of Darius' confrontation of the Greeks with the Indians, the former refusing to eat their deceased parents as did an Indian tribe, the Indians on the other hand horrified by the Greek practice of cremation. Herodotus is inclined to regard human law as relative, determined by custom and not by any superior force, and that is the way he understands Pindar's phrase, "Nomos (Law) is king of all," which he quotes

*13* Like so many of later Greek portraits of famous figures of the past, this representation of Herodotus portrays the historian in vigorous middle age. (National Museum, Naples)

here.[23] His account of Persian religion, in which lying is an abomination as Herodotus puts it, not quite understanding the Persian ideas, demonstrates the ethical efficacy of other traditions, and, when contrasted with the Greek acceptance of lying in many circumstances, is a more than satisfactory illustration of the relativity of moral law. Herodotus shows the effects of this demonstrable relativism in values, for he deals with morality in terms that are congruent with this experience. Justice, when it appears at all in his work, is conceived of only in human terms, as a practical matter and not as an abstraction, to be dispensed by humans. An example is the story of Deioces

(l. 96 ff.) who sought to become king of the Medes. This people, beset by lawlessness (*anomia*) and finding both that Deioces was the only one among them who judged rightly and that they could not conduct their affairs without his services, chose him as king. Similarly, it was Lycurgus who was responsible for changing the laws of Sparta (l. 65), and although Delphi greeted Lycurgus as perhaps a god, the oracle had nothing to do with the laws themselves.

Oracles, however important they might be, had nothing to do with the establishment or maintenance of justice on earth. They, along with portents like dreams, revealed what was to happen, and the historical personages of Herodotus' narrative behaved toward them much as did the figures of Athenian tragedy. Some people impugned their reliability but most believed them. Recipients of adverse portents tried to evade them, but those attempts failed. Oracles could be misunderstood, their interpreters could even be bribed, but they had to be reckoned with. Herodotus declares himself quite categorically a believer in the veracity of oracles, and consistently reflects that attitude in his treatment of them, although this also quite clearly demonstrates the difficulty of accurate interpretations, as in the case of Croesus' famous misunderstanding of the oracle that "if he campaigned against the Persians, he would destroy a great dominion."

Apart from his anthropological interest in the gods of the Greeks and of other peoples, and their connections with each other, Herodotus' interest in divine activity focuses more on their practice of revelation[24] or their specific acts, rather than on a consideration of the workings of a hypothetical divine justice. Thus he reports Apollo's saving of Croesus on his funeral pyre by sending a rainstorm, and his deferring by three years the end of Croesus' rule. Gods predict, and they do things, in Herodotus' story, but the narrative does not, as tragedy so often does, present the problem of human understanding of divine practice.[25] The oracles and portents should be seen rather in the context of a much broader concept of human history, a concept in which justice, human or divine, plays little or no part.

Herodotus' view of the impermanent nature of human history is well known. He alludes to it frequently, after setting out the concept of rise and fall clearly at the beginning of the work. The alternating quality of human experience is the point of the lesson which Solon gave Croesus, that a man's good fortune cannot be asserted until his life is over, for his happiness may be overturned by disaster before he dies. Croesus learned it well, and summed it up for Cyrus: "Learn this first, that there is a wheel for the affairs of men, and as it turns it does not allow always the same people to be fortunate."[26] There is no moral significance to events in this view of history, neither in the context of cosmic justice nor in terms of human assessments of right and wrong. Good and bad fortune are not due to human action in any way, but are simply part of the nature of things. There is no need to attempt to explain the apparent contradiction which arises when just behavior on someone's part is rewarded with evil instead of the expected good, and no need to have resort to a hypothesis that man's fault lies in the inability or unwillingness to perceive the divine order. The divine order, if it can even be called that, consists of the alternation of good and bad, the unstable quality of human prosperity with its random appearance and endurance.

Even at the strictly human level, human justice and the perception of it are of minor importance. While the motives for almost all human actions lie in the perceived self-interest of individual actors, that self-interest is almost never evaluated in terms of law or justice. And the troubles which flow from these actions are not represented by Herodotus or any of the personalities involved as arising from the infraction of any law. Even the notorious Herodotean concept of limit, which imposes restraints on human activity by the ruin which comes when natural boundaries are exceeded, is more a characteristic of the natural world, just like the cyclical nature of prosperity, than it is an absolute principle of justice and morality. For, as a man's fortune can only be judged when life is complete, so limit can only be determined retrospectively. The exceeding of limit can only be discovered after excess has brought its disaster, for not every apparent boundary is a limit in this sense, and the boundaries which do create limit are personal, not general. For Croesus, crossing the Halys River was exceeding the limit; it was not so for Cyrus.

All this makes for a highly rational sense of history and historical causation. Although Herodotus' view of divine action has been called "naïve" on a number of occasions for its trust in omens and oracles and ready acceptance of simplistic belief in gods, this too quick dismissal overlooks the almost complete dissociation between divine beings, their actions and their portents, on the one hand, and the effects of their activity as causation for historical events on the other. Oracles and portents there are, and many, but they are announcements, not causes, of what is going to happen, and they express less the will of the gods than their knowledge.[27] Even when the gods threaten, as Xerxes is threatened for abandoning the expedition against Greece, and Artabanus for so advising,[28] people are warned not for doing or planning evil, but for thinking to stand in the way of inevitability. What the gods know and command in portents is not divine, is not morality or justice, but merely the state of affairs. Any historical necessity which might exist was not an arbitrary rule established by supernatural power, but rather part of the nature of humanity and the world.[29] Unlike the different and varied presentations of Athenian tragedy, where the gods act to punish, deceive, enforce law, or deal with humans completely arbitrarily, they do not usually[30] impel events in Herodotus' history. People do that, and in this sense the historian's approach to his story is completely rational.

Thus history is for Herodotus, as for Thucydides, essentially a human affair. He had a quite different view of the workings of the gods from that of Pindar, whose work he quotes. His view of morality and justice also differs from any of those explored by the Athenian tragedians, and thus represents yet another option in the arsenal of philosophy. Herodotus, for all his equipage of gods and oracles, is closest to Thucydides in his evaluation of human motives and the causes of historical events, for he, like Thucydides, was prepared to accept an interpretation of human life in which morality and justice, either divine or human, played either a very small part or no part at all.

A study of Herodotus, Thucydides, Pindar, the orators, and the Athenian tragedians shows that there were in Athens and in Greek literature generally, a number of different interpretations of human and divine justice during the fifth century, and that these ranged from a view of humanity as a helpless victim of forces unknown and unknowable, to one which attributed to humankind complete knowledge and control over ethical and moral behavior. Given such a wide range of opinions, none of which was demonstrably correct and any of which could be true, it was, perhaps, inevitable that thought would turn from speculation to action, away from principles to programs for behavior.

# 8

# Socrates

## *The beginning of ethics as a discipline*

In the *Apology*, the speech which Plato wrote as an exposition of the defense which Socrates made at his trial in 399, Socrates is made to say:

> As long as I breathe, and am able to do it, I will not stop acting as a philosopher, exhorting you and pointing out to any of you I happen to meet, saying what I usually say, "O best of men, being an Athenian, of a city that is the greatest and most reputed for wisdom and strength, are you not ashamed of your concern for money, that you may have as much as possible, and of reputation and honor too, but of wisdom and truth and the soul, that it become as good as it can be, you neither care nor occupy your mind?"[1]

It is a passage long a favorite of professors, who, luxuries of their societies as was Socrates, in a way, are able to spend much of their lives caring for wisdom, truth, and the cultivation of their souls, without worrying very much about how the world's work might get done. The concept would hardly attract, and would probably puzzle, many pragmatic Athenians.

If Socrates really said what Plato put in his mouth, and if he really lived in the manner depicted by Plato and Xenophon and accepted by most modern students, he was making a revolutionary break with the norms of his society. All the Greek writing which comes down to us from the years before and during Socrates' lifetime takes a completely different point of view in the examination of ethics, morality, and the life appropriate for humanity. Its questioning of the nature of justice and of the relationship between human and divine justice assumes that what I might call "public goods" – wealth, reputation, honor – are those which are important, to be used in the reckoning of reward and punishment for just and unjust behavior. The poets expect to find honor, and historians prosperity as well, as the outcome of just action, and when they portray an outcome which is the reverse, as we so often find in real life, they – and we – are forced to reconsider our understanding of what justice must be. The evidence with which to evaluate our understanding of divine or human justice, the wages of moral behavior, so to speak, are precisely the coin which Socrates dismisses as dross. And his true coin, the state of one's soul or spirit, a completely private matter, had never before been part of the equation. If, then, Socrates really used the intensely personal matter of spirit and its quality as the appropriate aspiration for humanity and the measure of the good and successful life, he was changing completely the standards of behavior and the approach to the evaluation of justice.

*14* The fourth-century bronze head of Socrates in the National Museum, Naples, moves away from ideal representation to depict the snub nose for which the philosopher was famous.

This representation of Socrates' philosophy, although based primarily on a statement in Plato's *Apology*, is consistent with much of the rest of Plato's portrait of him as a teacher, and with a large part of the representations of Socratic teaching by other contemporaries and by that most important secondary source, Aristotle, who wrote in the century after Socrates lived. But there are variant traditions, and the discrepancies between the sources for the thought of Socrates create the so-called "Socratic problem," that is, the problem of determining what Socrates actually did think and teach. That problem has been tackled by many, many writers, and their different solutions have been generated by the different approaches to the sources which they have used, for there is no touchstone of actual Socratic writing which can be used to control what the different sources report that he said.

There is no need to recite again here the sources' contributions to our knowledge of Socrates, or the differences among them that lead to such disagreement about Socrates himself and about the purposes and veracity of those who wrote about him. That has been done well frequently and recently.[2] It seems to me that most people today still depend most heavily on Plato for their interpretation of Socrates' teaching, and then supplement, refine, and perhaps even alter that picture on the basis of the evidence of Xenophon, Aristophanes, and Aristotle. Modern writers admit their subjectivity in this, but most are inclined to believe that the philosopher Plato was better fitted than Xenophon both by intellect and interest to record sensitively and perceptively the beliefs and teachings of their master. Thus, in full awareness of the potential pitfalls of accepting the evidence of a writer who uses Socrates as a speaker in his dialogues to elucidate his own ideas, many moderns take Plato as the best source for genuine Socratic thought.[3] Xenophon's evidence, on the other hand, is taken as contributing less to our understanding of Socrates, partly because Xenophon himself simply does not report as much information, possibly because, as is often thought, this gentleman-general was neither inclined toward nor capable of following the subtler aspects of Socratic thought, and as an advocate and not a philosopher himself, he is thought either to suppress or be ignorant of the more revolutionary aspects of Socrates' teaching which might have led to his trial and condemnation. Then Aristophanes, with his portrait of Socrates in *Clouds*, introduces a great variety of considerations only hinted at by Plato or Xenophon: questions of Socrates' involvement in the study or teaching of natural science, of the possible evolution in his thought and behavior in the years between the 420s, at the end of which the *Clouds* was produced and revised, and the last years of the century when Plato would have known him. Finally, the comments of Aristotle are usually accorded respect by moderns, even though the philosopher himself never knew Socrates; that he is the only secondary ancient source to be treated with such deference is due both to his own stature as an original thinker and historian of philosophy, and to the possibility which he had, and most assume he used, of ascertaining from Plato a great deal of detail about the teachings of Socrates.

Aristotle provides the earliest texts we have which explicate any of Socrates' thought or contrast it with that of other thinkers rather than portraying the master in dialectic, as Plato does. Commenting on Socrates, Aristotle sets out what he thought marked off Socrates' thought from his predecessors and from his great successor, Plato. Aristotle's comments may not be right, of course, and make only a summary statement of the significance of Socrates' activity, but they do present a specific, coherent statement in philosophical terms with which to begin.

The most important passage is *Metaphysics* 1078 B 17–32:

> Socrates, dealing with ethical virtues and first seeking definition by universals for these . . . reasonably enquired into the essence. He sought to infer syllogistically, and the start of syllogistic inference is the essence. . . . One might fairly attribute two things to Socrates, inductive reasoning and definition by universals. Both of these relate to the beginning of scientific knowledge. But Socrates did not make the universal or the definition separate in existence. It was others who separated them, and denominated them the Ideas [Forms] of whatever exists.

Another passage, *Metaphysics* 971 B 1ff., repeats the description of Socrates as seeking the universal and concentrating on definitions, but distinguishes Plato's approach which places the universal in a world other than that of sense perception.

A number of considerations affect the evaluation of these statements. First, they are presented in the context of Aristotle's discussion of the history of philosophy, to show Socrates' position in that history, rather than in a discussion focused on Socrates and intended to describe his philosophy, so there is a fragmentary aspect to this presentation of Socratic thought. Secondly, Aristotle is here concerned only to note the *subject* of Socratic investigation, and tells us nothing of the fruit of those investigations nor any of the content of his thought. And, perhaps most important, he treats Socrates' thought and enquiries within a discipline of philosophy, not as part of the overall development of Greek or Athenian thought expressed in a number of media; this excludes from comparison that large body of thought in Athens which falls outside the realm of what Aristotle would properly call philosophy.

This last point calls for some elaboration, for it has not received its due since Nietzsche. Its significance can be shown most clearly by pointing out that before Plato or, perhaps stretching the time, before Socrates – there was no such thing as a philosopher, no such organized discipline as philosophy. The Ionian thinkers who investigated the physical universe in the sixth and early fifth centuries were called, if they were given any general appellation, *sophoi*, "wise men," and not "philosophers." The fifth-century professional teachers in Athens and elsewhere, if they were not identified by their discipline – rhetoric, music, mathematics, politics, grammar, and the like – were given a generic name, *Sophistes*, and that is how the immediate predecessors of Socrates, and perhaps Socrates himself, were known. Not only were those concerned with the usual matters of philosophy not yet identified as practitioners of a particular and discrete discipline, some of the subjects which were in Aristotle's time identified as the proper concern of philosophers were the focus of attention of writers who at no time in history could have remotely been considered "philosophers." Ethics, which according to Aristotle had been the concern of Socrates, earlier was important to the work of tragedians and historians and was by no means thought to call for study by specialists or demand specialized techniques of investigation. Insofar as Socrates was concerned with ethics, and dealt with definitions, and searched for the essence of virtue and justice, as Aristotle says or implies, he was following immediately the concerns of the tragedians and pursuing the same questions; if he did so by inductive reasoning and the definition by universals, he differed primarily in technique from the dramatists, who, when they were dealing with these matters, raised and sometimes answered these questions in dialogue and chorus rather than through dialectic. Aristotle's statement, then, is of inestimable value in revealing to us just what it is that the successors to Socrates actually thought he did: he reformed the treatment of morality and justice and fashioned formal methods for investigation, and so took the discussion of justice out of the realm of the amateur and dilettante and made it into a formal discipline.

This, of course, is completely consistent with any number of statements which Plato attributes to Socrates on this very matter. The idea that there should be some especial qualification for the teaching of virtue or of political knowledge as attributed to Socrates will be familiar to every reader of the *Protagoras*, and the very issue relates to the controversy over the possibility of teaching *arete* and the fact that the Sophists were the first professional teachers in the experience of the Greeks. Socrates alludes to the professional teachers in *Apology* 20, admiring, with his customary irony, one Euenus for teaching the qualities of good citizenship for a fee of 5 minas, when he himself would have disported himself with great pride if he had had such capability. It is also in the *Apology* that Socrates emphasized frequently his dedication to the pursuit of virtue and the rejection of the quest of things customarily thought good, "saying that not from possessions does virtue arise but that from virtue possessions and all the other good things, both private and public, exist for men."[4] Socrates' insistence that he acted in this matter in obedience to the gods, guided by his divine sign, rather than for any pay, certainly marks him out as different from the paid Sophists. The same is true of his repeated disclaimer of knowledge, and his statement that he has only enough wisdom to make him aware of his own ignorance. Furthermore, his repeated assertion of his pursuit of virtue, with his constant urging of the same pursuit on other Athenians, is a clear acknowledgment that he behaved differently from other men. In this broadest sense, this unswerving attachment to the promulgation of the pursuit of virtue was a professional pursuit, in that it was all that Socrates did, and it was something done in a particular manner.

The particular manner appears in a number of early dialogues of Plato as well as in some of Xenophon's writing; Socrates' famous method, called in Greek *elenchos*, is a procedure which can be described in English as a kind of cross-examination and refutation of a position taken. Socrates asks some general question, usually a question of definition, such as "What is courage?" and manages to obtain an answer from one of the participants. This first question and answer are then immediately followed by a series of new questions, some of which may not seem to relate at all to the first question, but as the dialogue proceeds the answers to the subsidiary questions either directly conflict with or lead to a contradiction to the answer to the first. At the conclusion, Socrates calls on the participants in the discussion to pull together all the answers to the questions, and the contradiction becomes clear. The conclusion reached from all this is that the knowledge which had been presumed in the answer to the first general question was in fact erroneous and that the respondent did not know, although he thought he did, the answer to the question, and the discussion terminates. It all fits, of course, the situation which Socrates describes in the *Apology*, when, baffled by the reply of the Delphic Oracle that there was no one wiser than he, Socrates proceeded to question all sorts of people, to prove that there were those who were wiser than he. The whole procedure, described in detail in the *Apology*, was in itself *elenchos*, and Socrates admits that it was this sort of investigation which generated people's hostility toward him. He first questioned a statesman – a famous one whom he chooses not to name – and when he tried to convince him that he thought that he knew wise things but did not, he incurred his hatred and that of many of those who were present at the discussion. He then went to other statesmen, then to the poets, and finally to the artisans, and accumulated a great deal of hostility from all quarters. He gave the artisans credit for what they knew how to do, but because they wrongly thought that they knew higher things on the basis of what they did know, he decided he would rather do without their knowledge than take both their knowledge and their ignorance. He came to the same conclusion in connection with the poets, including the tragedians, but here, although he found them able to write poetry, they were unable to explain what they had written as well as the bystanders could, so he concluded that their poetry came as a kind of inspiration rather than by knowledge or wisdom.

The critical issue is knowledge, and the *elenchos* is a vital step in the acquisition of knowledge, for it is the method by which error is purged. A more positive method of achieving knowledge, of understanding the nature of things, is that of definition. Justice, temperance, courage – each was the subject of the question, "What is it?" Socrates always claims to be ignorant of the answer, the famous "Socratic ignorance," and he does not, in fact, provide an answer, choosing instead to query and refute in the *elenchos* the initial answer proffered. In this Socrates compared himself to a midwife, saying that he himself could not give birth to wisdom, but that by conversing with others, he helps them to give birth to it while actually teaching nothing himself. But the end of the conversations, even though reached when an original definition is overturned, is not so barren. Though "justice," "temperance," "courage," and "virtue" themselves remain undefined, much has been learned about each subject. Some aspects may have been defined; the common opinions, which the proffered definition usually reflects, have been evaluated and any truth they contain understood; and the relationship between the subject and many aspects of everyday activity have been considered and sometimes clarified. It is because whatever could be learned from the *elenchos* of Socrates, pursued in this so-called "*maieutic*" or midwife-like method, was learned through the search for definitions, that Aristotle found this search important. Socrates' innovation, as it appears in the dialogues and was noted by Aristotle, was the application of method to the study of ethics, and fundamental to the method was the orderly search for definitions, even if these were not achieved and the investigator was compelled again and again to report himself ignorant.

This ignorance, however, it should be noted, was philosophical and not behavioral. That Socrates had a conception of virtue – or at least its opposite – which he could use to regulate his own conduct is clear from a number of statements about actions which he took, or decisions which he made on the basis of his own understanding of what made for virtuous or wicked behavior. In *Apology* 32, Socrates tells the now well-known story of his opposition to the illegal action of trying in a single trial the generals who were charged with not picking up the men after a battle at Arginusae, on the grounds that he felt compelled, despite the high feelings against him and consequent possible danger, to act "with law and justice on my side." So too, in his next instance of his limited public activity, when ordered by the thirty tyrants to participate in an execution, he simply went home, desiring most of all not to "do anything which was unjust or unholy." That these decisions or actions were based on Socrates' own sense of right and wrong comes clear from his comment which introduces both these stories, that he would not, even out of fear for his own life, obey any order "contrary to justice." The most memorable demonstration of this attitude of Socrates' comes in the *Crito*, when he refuses to escape from prison and avoid his sentence on the grounds that in this case disobedience to the *nomoi*, or laws, of the state would represent injustice. Although Socrates affects willingness to be argued out of this view, Crito makes no serious attempt to do this nor does Socrates really seem to be in much doubt about the rectitude of his position. In a hypothetical dialogue between himself and the laws,[5] the laws are presented as arguing convincingly that Socrates in escaping would be acting to destroy them and the whole state. The laws provided for the marriage of his parents and his rearing; he had been free to leave Athens but chose to remain an Athenian; finally, he had stated that he preferred to die than be an exile; after all this, since he accepts both the laws and the judgments of trials (which Socrates is careful to do in the dialogue), it would be more than absurd to reject the requirements of the laws at this stage in his life: it would be wrong.[6] And, as he made clear in *Apology*, Plato presents Socrates as consistently refusing to do anything which he perceived as unjust.

Xenophon made the same point at the beginning of his version of what Socrates said at his trial: that his whole life had been spent in preparation for his trial, in that he had always tried not to do anything unjust. And the four books of his *Memorabilia of Socrates* gather the evidence to justify Xenophon's final quotation of Socrates, that "I never did wrong to any man ever, nor made anyone worse,"[7] and Xenophon's own final summation in praise of his virtue, wisdom, and character. On the evidence of Plato and Xenophon, therefore, and because of the impact which Socrates so clearly had on the minds and hearts of many of his contemporaries, it is safe to believe that Socrates did live his life according to some conception of what made for just behavior, and that he was consistent in his adherence to some principles while at the same time focusing his entire existence on the search for just such principles. But, since there remains a necessary doubt about the philosophy and beliefs of the "historical" Socrates because we have no statements which can be attributed to him with certainty, the "probably historical" Socrates or the "literary"[8] Socrates will do as well to provide evidence of the development of Athenian thought on matters of ethics and justice. It is this figure of whose influence Aristotle wrote, and it is this figure to whom Xenophon relates his account, and some of whose ideas Plato propounds.

There is, then, a Socrates to which Aristotle's statements can apply, the image of a man whose sole concern was the elucidation of ethical concepts. Taking for his field of effort those aspects of morality which were the subject of current intellectual discussion and which were referred to constantly in everyday life, he sought by pursuit of definition to determine their true nature, or essence. Whereas many Sophists, caught up as they were in the elucidation of the dichotomy between *physis*, the inherent nature of any creature – human, animal, natural, or constructed thing – which is properly sought and fulfilled by its possessor, and, on the other hand, *nomos*, an imposed and unnatural regulation or restriction imposed on beings in the interests of communal living, Socrates evaded that debate by rejecting old definitions and seeking new ones. According to Aristotle, his search was regulated by a much more stringent adherence to principles of argument which could be called scientific method; it thus became the first application of scientific method to the study of ethics. Socrates' predecessors then, while perhaps dealing with matters of ethics, did so without proper methodology.

In a sense, Socrates did not evade the *physis–nomos* controversy, but destroyed it, by uniting the two antitheses in redefinition. Socrates repeatedly took the position that none intentionally injured themselves; that virtue was knowledge whereby this self-inflicted injury could be avoided; that the state of the soul was the most important consideration; that injury to others harmed the soul of the doer; and again, that knowledge of this precluded the wise person from harming others. An important consequence of this reasoning

eliminates the *physis–nomos* dichotomy, because it makes it inherent in the *physis* or nature of the human to seek to do good and avoid harm to one's fellow man, precisely the object of the *nomoi* as those involved in the controversy see them. The difference between the two views lies in this definition of *physis*, for those who proceed with discussion of the conflict see the *nomoi* in opposition to a *physis* which is purely selfish, seeking self-aggrandizement at the expense

110

15 The life of Socrates has gripped the imagination from the time of his death to the present. This representation of the scene during the philosopher's last moments by Jacques Louis David (1748–1825) also shows the interest in classical styles which marks the eighteenth and early nineteenth centuries. (The Metropolitan Museum of Art, Wolfe Fund, 1931. Catharine Lorillard Wolfe Collection. (31.45))

of others, while Socrates would see no conflict between the *nomoi* and a *physis* the selfishness of which is expressed entirely in terms of improvement of the soul and which would seek to avoid any material gain achieved unjustly at the expense of others.

This rejection of material gain accruing at the expense of the excellence of the soul is both a consequence of Socrates' reasoning and a significant distinction between his views and those of the Sophists, so far as we can determine them. When Socrates argues, as he does in *Crito* 47 and 48, that the part of the person which is improved by adherence to justice and deteriorates through lapsing into injustice is a more important part than the body, he is stating an article of faith, for he does not reach this point by a series of steps. The concept that this part of the person, the psyche or soul, is more important than the body, rests on the even more fundamental idea that there exists at all a portion of the human which is improved by justice and made worse by injustice. It is not, so far as we can tell, part of the system of any of the Sophists, although again it is well to remember that our information on all of them is extremely fragmentary. But it is so characteristically "Socratic" in the works of Plato, who never attributes a doctrine anything like this to any Sophist, that we are probably safe in accepting this concept as a fundamental difference between the ethical teachings of the Sophists and the ethical position of Socrates, as well as a characteristic difference between the treatment of ethics by the tragedians and that by Socrates.

The position which posits the primacy of the soul and the improvement thereof by virtuous action helps to resolve the apparent contradiction between Socrates' regular insistence that he does not know anything, and his equally regular acceptance of the general evaluation of benefit and harm, at least insofar as they apply to the body. For, while one may inflict greater harm on one's soul by unjustly harming another, that bodily harm is nevertheless accepted as such. Killing is harm; deceiving is harm; calumniating another is harm. Extending this to broader areas of action, Socrates generally accepts the norms of his society in defining just and unjust action,[9] and has no hesitation in using those norms as stepping stones to a more fundamental definition of virtue as knowledge. Courage, for example, in being defined as knowledge, presupposes the justice of general condemnation of a man for cowardice, a condition which the knowing man will avoid even at the expense of his life, as a certain evil contrasted with the uncertain quality of death. Similarly, Socrates purports to accept the view that belief in, respect for, and obedience to the gods is right.[10] And, as I have pointed out, he accepts the authority of the laws, a social norm of importance in Athens, and deems it just that he accept and execute upon himself a judgment which he believes to be in error. In all this acceptance of conventional morality as relevant to his behavior, Socrates is at no time impeded by the advice of the god which he calls his *daimonion*, a *daimonion* which he felt opposed him even in small matters if he was about to go wrong, a phenomenon which he takes to establish the validity of the *nomoi* for members of society.

In accepting as valid these social norms, Socrates might seem to be pretending to a knowledge which he does not have. But he is not, in fact, proposing a definition of virtue or stabilizing an objective system for determining just behavior. Rather, as the *Crito* shows, he is accepting a kind of social contract[11] as valid for the guidance of individuals within a society. One can generally use social norms to regulate behavior among people in society because the issues involved are less significant than making the soul paramount.[12] In fact, it is precisely because Socrates does not have any better guide to conduct than the *nomoi* of his society that he must use them as the basis for a life in which he protects his soul by avoiding injustice.

In his reliance on the norms of his society, Socrates has apparently accepted most of the ethical conceptualization of the late fifth century. For him, furthermore, there is no conflict between divine and human morality and justice because he makes no suppositions about divine law nor does he propose any of its details. Even the *daimonion*, which prevents Socrates from proceeding in a manner wrong for him, never gave him positive precepts for action, as he makes clear in *Apology* 31. The idea of "divine law" in opposition to human is inherently contradictory to Socrates' approach to virtue as knowledge. It is only right that it should be so, for he depends on human reason alone as the means to knowledge, not only for the evaluation of everyday issues but for the determination and definition of the essence of virtue and morality. In accepting human law, however, Socrates was able to avoid the dilemma which had plagued so many earlier ethical thinkers, who saw that the just were often visited by injustice, and therefore sought explanations in a higher law.

By positing the primacy of the soul and its improvement by observing justice, Socrates was able to avoid this whole contradiction. Just behavior always benefited the doer in the most important aspect, and unjust behavior could not seriously wound the victim, certainly not nearly as much as it harmed the perpetrator. Success and failure or reward and punishment in this life could only be measured by the individual in terms of the condition of the soul, and the outward trappings of wealth, reputation, and even family were of no consequence in comparison with this fundamental gauge. Socrates thus proposed a value system quite different from anything we have seen attested before his time, in accepting conventional norms but rejecting conventional assessments of advantage. So doing, he also gave the study of ethics a twist. After Socrates, theoretical and professional study might proceed on a course quite different from and not intelligible to the kind of discussion which approached ethics on the basis of a conventional value system and on the acceptance of the usual interpretation of what makes reward and what makes punishment. This was really the beginning of moral philosophy.

# Part Three

# Idealism and reality
# in Plato and Aristotle

# 9

# Socrates, Plato, and Athens before the "Forms"

## *The missed potential of philosophical egalitarianism*

Philosophy might, of course, have taken a different course from that which Plato gave it, and Athens might have left us a different tradition and history if Socrates' lead had been more closely followed. There was a point in time – a period of a few years – when human thought might have plunged forward to justify and glorify the equality of individuals, and to demand that every potential be granted its right of fulfillment. Such a result would have been the development of the ideas of the man whom I call "Socrates," a man who might in fact have been that son of the stone worker, but also might have been Plato before he took refuge in the world of the Forms.

Athens had been moving quite quickly during the last quarter of the fifth century toward a kind of equality among citizens which later Greek writers condemned and moderns often deplore. Finally, after the disappearance of Pericles from the scene, it was no longer essential that a political leader have credentials of family and clan to achieve office or prominence in civic affairs. Pericles' claim for Athenian insouciance for good family or wealth if only a man could serve the state was becoming real. I have mentioned the career of Cleon, the rich tanner's son, to illustrate the point: he not only could sway the assembly in a new, cruder style, assuming the most prominent position after Pericles died, he could also successfully take command of troops and lead them in battle. While many of the politicians and military leaders who came after Cleon still came from the old families of wealth and reputation, there were others who did not. One such was Hyperbolus, the politician of alleged low origin who in fact succeeded Cleon as leader of those Athenians favoring continued war with Sparta, and who would doubtless have continued in prominence had he not been ostracized in 417 BC in a secret deal between the two rivals Nicias and Alcibiades. These latter two represent the best that the old aristocracy could put forward, and in view of the serious failings exhibited by each when in leadership, it is small wonder that members of the "lower classes" found their way to power. And even for the sober and conservative Nicias we cannot trace an ancestry further back than his father, so that it may be that he

117

was a relative newcomer on the scene, like that Theramenes active during the last ten years of the war, whose family arrived in politics with Theramenes' father Hagnon, and passed away quickly with Theramenes himself. Participation in the ruling group even extended to a man who could be called poor, like Cleophon, whose reputation for honesty was joined in tradition by a claim that he died in poverty. That such men would have risen to major office, let along supreme prominence in the state, and in any numbers at all, demonstrates the great diminution in the efficacy of class at this time, for the bars certainly no longer served to exclude those whose presence would not have been tolerated a generation or two before.

Into this scene comes the figure of Socrates, with an ancestry, status, and activity perfectly acceptable to the Athens of his time, but with a personality and ideas which had not hitherto been a force to be reckoned with in the city. As a teacher of the young aristocrats, Socrates' lineage, perhaps not exalted but not by any means despicable, was as acceptable as that of some of the Sophists who visited the city at the time. While many of them may have come from more distinguished families in their own cities, there were some who did not, and in any case, none was a citizen at Athens. At least Socrates was that, and indeed one who could and did shoulder the duties of warfare and the lesser tasks of government on occasion. He, perhaps like his father too, could be seen as the "good burgher," concerned primarily with his own private life, but fulfilling his duties in junior offices under the lead of the great politicians and statesmen – a life not unlike that we know of Euripides. He, like Euripides whom he admired, was dealing with ideas at a time when the ferment of Sophistic education was at its greatest and, perhaps also like Euripides, because of his non-aristocratic background, he was more willing to explore the implications of these new ideas insofar as they led away from the ethic of the old family codes.

The Sophists themselves did not do this. Not only did many of them come from families imbued with the aristocratic traditions, the reputation and livelihoods of all of them were tied up with their acceptance and support by the noble and wealthy Athenians who were their hosts, patrons, and clients. There was thus every reason for them to fulfill the needs of these clients, to teach aspiring youth the skills they would need to climb the political ladder to the glory and prominence which would acknowledge the *arete* inherent in them as nobles. Thus the rhetoric taught was expected to develop the forensic skills needed in the Assembly, and the verbal analysis and techniques of some of the Sophists aided in the development of abilities in disputation. Even the *physis-nomos* controversy, opposing natural impulse and social restraint, with which we associate the Sophistic movement so closely, was a natural outgrowth of the preoccupation of these thinkers with the problems of the upper class. Those aristocrats, whose freedom to act and exercise their will had come under increasing restraint as the century advanced and the desires or needs of the poorer classes cut away more and more from their resources, were in full

118

sympathy with the relativism aroused by the controversy and with the categorization as artificial of the social restraints imposed by *nomos*. Cleophon's introduction after 410 of the diobelia, an allotment of 2 obols a day to assure needy citizens of a guaranteed living income, was only a further progression in the practices which more and more directed the resources of the state to the consumption of the masses and away from the discretion of the upper class. However much Sophistic discussions might have engendered notions of political equality such as those propounded by Pericles in his funeral oration, they did not extend to what we would call "radical share-the-wealth" propositions, and the fundamental assumptions of the Sophists accepted the position of wealth and respect which the aristocrats were so anxious to defend.

Sophistic ethical and political thought, then, while dealing with problems of justice, virtue, and equality, was oriented toward analysis from the point of view of the powerful rather than the weak, and may even be said to represent a secular formulation of aristocratic ideology. In this, Sophistic thought stood in stark opposition to that which might be called Socratic, the first major expression of Greek thought which did not see and evaluate society from the point of view of those at the top. The difference of orientation, which is today very often neglected, is precisely that which set Nietzsche on the track of Socrates as enemy. However, even though the Sophists were so closely tied to the society and the values of the traditional aristocracy, they were able to effect very significant changes in the focus and arena of thought at Athens. In focus, they shifted the activity of professional thinkers away from investigations which seem to have been centered on the external world, to deal increasingly with human nature and with the modalities of human interrelationships in society. So far as the arena of activity is concerned, they took over these very topics of human and social nature from the poets and tragedians, and exposed them to ordinary discourse.

Thus, even though questions about the nature of humankind and human society and their interrelationships were being approached from the traditional point of view, great strides were being made in defining terms, establishing areas of agreement and dispute, and in identifying questions to be resolved, so that it would be possible for Socrates to pull together decades of discussion to create one, coherent methodology which could approach all these problems in a single manner and aim at a hypothesis of human behavior and nature which would solve the moral and political problems inherent in the *physis-nomos* antithesis. At the same time, others approached the human from an entirely different standpoint, that of the physical, as Hippocrates and his colleagues attempted, often very successfully, to establish how the physical entity worked. It is true there is a great deal of uncertainty as to how much, if any, of the so-called Hippocratic Corpus may be attributed to the doctor from Cos who was a contemporary of Socrates, but it is equally true that Plato's *Timaeus* cannot fail to impress any reader by the depth and scope of its anatomical and medical detail. There is no doubt that the location, configuration, and structure of many internal organs were known in detail, and for many of them, their function and interrelationship with other organs were known as well. Some of this information could only have come from dissection. There were errors, of course, particularly in the physiology of some of the less obvious systems, but overall the work of the fifth-century Hippocratic school had been done well. Available to Plato – and of course to any other Athenian of the late fifth century – was a vast body of new knowledge about the workings of the human organism. A person could feel that he understood something about human parts and organs, what they did and how they functioned, and that such understanding depended not only on the efficacy of reason or speculation, but on the conclusion of experts who had actually looked into the body and handled its constituent parts. In a sense, the new knowledge of physical makeup could be felt to complement the new knowledge of the social and spiritual human being.

These intellectual developments coincided with the political to offer a rare – very rare – opportunity to alter radically human institutions and the fundamental assumptions on which those institutions were built. The ideas which had been accumulating in Athens and other Greek centers for two centuries were compounded in a rush, lines of research and thought suddenly came to fruition. As a new understanding of the human body had been made possible by the physicians, so the new philosophers might produce a new definition of human nature, both individual and in relation to other people. Socrates attempted the first of these, and thus inevitably the second as well. By asserting the primacy of a person's soul and the possibility of improving it, he was defining human nature both in the individual and in the collective: it was not only the case that, as we have seen, a man is in error in pursuing the traditional goals of wealth, power, prestige, and reputation admired by nobles since the time of the Homeric epic, a person is also in error in thinking that a successful life lies in the power of anything external. The human creature is such as to possess a soul which at all times and in all circumstances is far more important than either the body or the physical conditions and surroundings on which the body subsists and depends. Proper attention to the soul and its improvement will assure the good life, for the satisfactions attendant on the soul in good condition far outweigh any pleasures accruing from the more conventional "goods."

That much established, a person's relations with others are relatively easy to define. If one's own benefit is provided by attention to the soul, the urge for rivalry with others in practical affairs falls away, and it becomes easy to yield to conventional morality and abandon any desire to arrogate to oneself anything coveted by others or deemed by others to be their property. The convention, or *nomos*, invented by society to permit social living and protect the weak becomes an easy principle to respect, for it is in no way contrary to the true *physis* or nature of the individual, which is pursuing objectives quite different from anything treated by *nomos* and in no way in conflict with any of the interests of others.

This conception of the nature of humanity is not only quite egalitarian in character as offering to anyone the possibility of achievement in the arena of the appropriate concern for humankind; it also offers a rationale for a quite different distribution of wealth and the world's goods. If Socrates' position convinced and became generally accepted, the wealthy and powerful would no longer be concerned to protect at all costs their advantage, but might be induced to turn over much or all of their surplus to those whose property failed to provide the minimum needs of family survival, let alone the proper cultivation of the soul. In so small a society as the citizen body of Athens, such a redistribution might even provide enough for all. In any case, the will of the many, clamoring for subsistence, would find easy acquiescence on the part of those who now felt that harm to others was of far greater harm to themselves than the damage done to them by any appropriation of their goods. Indeed, the 2-obol dole of Cleophon was a step in this direction, although all the comments by aristocratically minded writers suggest that the wealthy hardly treated the matter with Socratic altruism, even though the money was coming out of the public purse and not their own.

I am not suggesting that this sort of economic social democracy was in any way a Socratic idea or even a part of his conception of the human individual or human society. It is, rather, that it makes a logical, perhaps *the* logical, next step in the moral philosophy of Socratic type. By that I mean moral philosophy which treats of human affairs in terms of the human intellect, working in terms of the objects of sense perception unidealized. "What you see is what you get," my Socrates would have said of the world outside himself, and everything we can reconstruct about Socrates seems to confirm the view that even in moral and ethical matters, he trusted the objects of sense perception to be sufficiently real, and sense perception itself to provide the mind with adequately clear and reliable information for the application of reason. When he argued for the primacy of the soul over the body, he meant the soul which each individual actually had, and the body he actually perceived, not some idealization or form existing on another plane. If possessions, prestige, and reputation were to be given a lower order of preference than the qualities of truth and justice which improved the soul, it was not because these possessions, prestige, and reputation were poor representations of the form of good, but because they, as real objects, just didn't do the soul much good.

Any furthering of Socratic thought must take this practical aspect into consideration, and any social ordering based on Socrates' ideas must deal with the distribution of real goods in the society. This of course did not happen, for many reasons. In the first place, anyone would naturally back away from pursuing an approach which must lead to such a revolutionary upheaval in the society as this would bring, and so the Socratic treatment of morality and sense perception came to a dead end. Secondly, there were, in Socrates' dicta about the human, about "virtue as knowledge," and the natural inability of the human knowingly to do wrong, some flaws which common experience indicated. Aristotle, for example, wrote that our ordinary experience of the world shows that these ideas simply are not true, and many contemporaries of Socrates must have felt the same way. The reason why they are not true has become clear only in the present century, with the development of our new understanding of human psychology and of the existence and effects of the unconscious, so that until now, the Socratic argument could always be pursued by a logic which might stand up as a specimen of reasoning but fail to overcome the resistance of intuition.

It would have been possible, given the state of knowledge about humanity and human behavior current in the Athens of the time, to have taken that next step in moral and social theory. The Socratic sense of the equality of the individual which was taken over by Plato in an ideal sense could have been carried into the realm of political structure if it had been taken in its Socratic sense, and Athens might have thus been impelled to carry forward the ideals of social justice exemplified by the step it had already taken with the diobelia. The political will was there, the sense of the populace was there, the resources were there, and the philosophical justification was in readiness. Athens was on the threshold of a great human experience, looking only for the guide to beckon her through, when Plato closed the door.

# 10

# The pursuit of power
## *City rivalries, Philip II, and Aristotle in Macedon*

Behind the philosophical and ethical speculations of the Athenian dramatists and Socrates lay the political experience of Athens in the fifth century and the traditions of *polis* society which had so far provided a reasonably successful social arrangement for most of Greece. Traditional heavy-armed citizen soldiers of the Spartan army had apparently prevailed, and the implications of the great Persian financial support of Sparta which had made possible the creation and maintenance of the new Spartan fleet had not yet become apparent to most Greeks. It was, therefore, business as usual for most of the Greek states, as they set about establishing their competition with one another in the wake of Athenian defeat. Sparta's victorious impetus gave it the impulse and wherewithal to establish supremacy, and after a poor start on control of the states of Asia Minor and over a decade of see-saw fighting in Greece itself it could look at its situation in 379 BC with satisfaction, seeing itself dominant in the Peloponnese with even Thebes under the thumb of a Spartan garrison. To this, other Greeks were reacting predictably. The resurgent Athenians were casting about for allies, and when they re-established a league they found even their old enemies the Thebans, who had managed to expel the Spartan garrison in the course of 379, ready to join. At the same time the Persians, whose money and interest in Greece kept the pot boiling, played an increasing part in peninsular politics, with the Great King from time to time proclaiming and endorsing peace agreements. The location of power for control or maneuvering of events shifted from city to city, with Sparta downed by Thebes in 371 and the subsequent Theban supremacy ended with the death of its great leader Epaminondas in the course of a victory in the Peloponnesus in 362. Even the small state of Phocis in central Greece flared briefly in the 350s and 340s until its ambitions were ended by Philip of Macedon, who ultimately established his dominance in Greece by a resounding victory over the allied Athenians and Thebans in 338.

The period was a wearing one for Greeks, economically as well as militarily. The ethos of the city-state, which had reached its apogee in Athens in the fifth century, was under increasing strain as new social, economic, and even military developments made it more and more difficult for these small political units to maintain themselves. The massive Persian subsidies which had begun to flow into the Greek world at the end of the fifth century disrupted civic finances in the fourth, and state after state found itself severely financially strained to pay the mercenary armies which increasingly carried the brunt of war. The almost continual combat which continued even after the Athenian defeat precluded a significant recovery from the costs of that war, while raids, devastation, looting, and pillage sent the basically agricultural economy into a downward spiral. Under the circumstances, it is small wonder that an enterprising figure like Philip of Macedon capitalized on the potential of his territorial state and the gains his army could bring him to achieve domination of Greece in twenty years.

The changed situation did not go unnoticed. The Athenian Isocrates, a student of Socrates who ran a school and gained a great reputation as a rhetorician in the half-century after his master's death, repeatedly called for an end to inter-city strife, appealing first to Athens and then Philip to unify the Greeks in a great campaign against Persia. In political pamphlets urging this scheme, he cited the growing civic debility attributable to the constant wars. Athens, even with a new league of some seventy cities in the second quarter of the century, was unable to rebuild to anything like its earlier level, and a general rebellion of the allies in the mid-350s ended that league in a short time. Demosthenes, the dogged Athenian opponent of Philip, spoke as if Athens could really resist Macedon, but the hard facts of war and the outcome of the Battle of Chaeronea in 338 BC proved him wrong.

Events were proving that a determined leader with an army at his back could prevail, and the evidence came not only from peninsular Greece but from the power which Dionysius, the tyrant of Syracuse in Sicily, could demonstrate. To Isocrates, Dionysius, who fought often and sometimes successfully against Carthage, was the champion of Hellenism in the west. He left a powerful state in the hands of his son, and the younger Dionysius, who evinced some interest in rule by wisdom rather than brute force, seemed a possible prospect to Plato, who answered a call to the Syracusan court by Dionysius' adviser Dion in 367 BC. In less than a year the failure of the attempt was evident, and another visit by Plato to the court a few years later made it even more obvious that the philosopher's sense of obligation to try to make his ideas work in the hot kitchen of real government would lead to failure. Later tradition emphasized how much damage the philosophers did at Syracuse, reporting the subsequent excesses of Plato's friend Dion, and claiming that later short-lived tyrants who committed notable barbarities had emerged from the group around Plato. The episode was, in any case, a lesson for Plato, and it showed others in Greece how dangerous and ruthless military tyranny could be.

Inevitably, the interdependency between citizen and state suffered in all this. As the nature of warfare changed, and light-armed mercenaries from all over the Greek world took on a steadily increasing role in the struggles among the Greek states, the importance of the heavy-armed citizen hoplite soldier declined. The potential of well-trained standing armies was demonstrated by the effectiveness of such a group as the Theban "Sacred Band," but the cost of maintaining such forces was another factor undermining the financial stability of states. Citizens sought means of avoiding civic expenses, and the growing reluctance to leave trades and farms is illustrated by the fact that at Chaeronea, the line-up of Athenian citizens was not only a rare sight; it put in the field men who had little training or experience in war.

If the exigencies of war and the need for a solid body of citizen-soldiers provided the impulse behind the creation of the city-state with the political participation and civic rights which marked the earlier Greek society, then economic stress and the change in warfare can be assigned a role in the disintegration of these structures. This interpretation of history sees some of the values of fifth-century Athenian tragedy, for example, of the egalitarianism developing at Athens at the end of the century, crumbling with the collapse of the city-state ethos, under a number of blows: the undermining of traditional civic spirit with Persian gold; the expansion of mercenary activity as a result of spreading economic distress; the determination and success of the monarchy of Philip of Macedon. This "decline of the *polis*" accompanies a greater respect for autocracy like that of Alexander the Great and his successors, or even the city-based tyrants like Dionysius of Syracuse and his son to whose court Plato traveled. This spread of monarchy furthered even more the tendency of the ordinary citizen to turn away from civic affairs to find fulfillment in personal development. Some of Plato's political ideas, in fact, are seen to reflect not only his own direct experiences in Syracuse, but also to respond to the general political conditions of his time, and his proposals for civic reform have even been described as an attempt to "save the *polis*."

Such explanations help to conceptualize what was going on in Greece in this period, and may even help to clarify ideas by placing them in their social matrix. Whether or not Plato was responding to his perception of a serious alteration in the condition of the Greek city-states of his own time, there is no doubt that great changes were overtaking the Greek world in the first half of the fourth century, and that the emergence of Platonic philosophy can be understood in the light of events of the times. No state in Greece seemed to be able to sustain the long period of domination Athens had managed over its maritime league in the fifth century, and even Sparta's land dominion was shaken by periodic defections and was open to attack by what had been the much lesser power of Thebes. From a political structure dominated by the two powerful states of Athens and Sparta, Greece had moved into the fourth century as the scene of the rivalries between more or less equally balanced states, and there were a half-dozen or more at the top – Athens and Sparta still, with Corinth, Argos, Thebes, and Phocis able to muster a great deal of strength at one time or another. It might be clear to an astute observer that the changing times gave the advantage to the monarch, who could muster his power and apply it as needed without the interference of the machinations of city politics. Plato's experience in Syracuse would show him at first hand how even unconstitutional tyrants like Dionysius and his son could hold power over long periods, and could contrast that with the great volatility of "free" politics which the later Philip would often exploit.

Plato lived long enough to see the political turmoil in Greece which was reacting to the changed situation in which the cities found themselves. In Athens, for example, there was conflict between those who favored accommodation with Philip of Macedon and those like Demosthenes who saw the northern king as the gravest threat to the city's position. Class and financial interests exacerbated tensions, and Philip, with his well-known use of bribery, exploited any opportunity to use money to accomplish his political ends. Before Plato died in 348/7 BC, he had seen Athens' impotence to preserve its new league, and had observed Philip's relentless expansion across the north shore of the Aegean, his descent into southern Greece as the quarreling states called him into a war with Phocis over control of the Delphic Oracle, and the manner in which one Greek city after another became the scene of savage internal strife as governments were overthrown and control shifted back and forth in almost continual class warfare.

The influences on Aristotle were somewhat different from those which affected his teacher. Plato had been an Athenian aristocrat, one of the young men who followed Socrates around, a young adult at the time of Athens' defeat in the Peloponnesian War and a witness to the excesses of the Thirty and then to Socrates' prosecution by the re-established democracy. Aristotle, on the other hand, was born in the relatively obscure northern city of Stagira, the son of Nicomachus, the court physician of the Macedonian king, Philip's father, Amyntas III. He was two years old in 382 BC, the year that Amyntas' youngest son Philip was born, and he spent his youth as a playmate of the future king. He did not go to Athens until he was 17, and although he remained there for about twenty years, until Plato's death in 348/7, his Macedonian connections remained strong enough for him to accept an appointment as teacher to Alexander, Philip's son, in 343 or early 342. He was in Athens long enough, of course, to see Athenian power dwindle under the impact of the loss of its allies, and to note the futility of the long war with Macedon in which the Athenians were, ultimately, unable to prevent Philip from taking their allies and possessions in the north. Aristotle took no part in politics of course, as a non-citizen, and was just an observer of the struggles between Philip's supporters in Athens and his leading opponent, Demosthenes.

From 343 on, during the years before Philip's final defeat of Athens and Thebes at Chaeronea, Aristotle had been at the center of the action, in Macedonia, responsible for the education of the crown prince, Alexander. Whether he was the only teacher of the future king, as most of the ancient sources imply, or whether he was only one of a group putting together a

*16* In the early sixteenth century, Raphael was commissioned to decorate some rooms in the papal palace in Rome. In the Stanza della Segnatura he created the monumental fresco depicting the School of Athens. Here, as he gathered philosophers from many different times, he placed Plato and Aristotle in conversation as centerpiece, showing his own attitude toward the two philosophers, making the aged Plato point his finger to the sky, while the younger Aristotle has his palm turned toward the earth and mundane matters. (Vatican, Rome)

complex curriculum, as is stated by one often fanciful source, appropriately enough dubbed "The Alexander Romance," he was certainly at the court until 339, when he left and returned to his familial property at Stagira. Those three years of Philip's climb to supremacy Aristotle spent with Alexander and the royal pages at Mieza, a pleasant town a short distance from the capital, where he was closely involved with the crown prince's maturing from a boy of 13 to the youth of 16 who could command troops effectively against rebellions. It is difficult to know anything of Aristotle's political and metaphysical thought at this stage of his career, because the organizing instincts of his ancient editors disregarded chronology and integrated notes and writings from all periods of his life under titles based on themes. But, by the time he reached Macedon, his interest had expanded from concern with theoretical, mathematical, and astronomical matters to include the content of what we would call the biological sciences, botany and zoology. By then too he may have been moving away from the Platonic conception of the soul as an entity independent of the rest of the human organism, to integrate the soul with body as the form inherent which dictates, along with matter, the nature of the individual. His political ideas may be judged from his approach to human institutions, reasonably consistent in his writings wherever they touch on politics or the political life. He regards the human being in the first instance as what we would call a "social animal," and classes humankind with animals like ants and bees which live in communities, an observation which emerges even in so non-political a work as the *Historia Animalium*, or "Account of Animals." He goes further in his examination of political arrangements to accept the notion that the human being is a "political animal," in that it accords with human nature to live in cities, meaning most fundamentally that human social institutions are based on cities and that human nature can be fulfilled only in a context which includes cities – cities of the *polis* or city-state type with which Aristotle was familiar. It is difficult to imagine that such concepts did not represent the basis of Aristotle's teaching of Alexander and the young Macedonian nobles, just as it would be hard not to believe that the philosopher's own ideas about monarchy and kingship were not affected by his life-long observation of the success of Philip and the loyal support accorded him by the Macedonians. By the time he left the court in 339, Aristotle had established himself in familiarity with Alexander and his young fellows like Perdiccas, Ptolemy, and Lysima-chus, who would become his generals and later, in some cases, kings in their own right. He was also on familiar terms with at least one of the senior Macedonians, Antipater, who would act as Alexander's viceroy in Greece during his long expedition to the east. Aristotle was also fortunate in the time of his leaving the court, for he missed the turmoil there during Philip's last years.

Trouble started soon after the great victory at Chaeronea in 338 BC. In the midst of the preparations for the expedition against Persia, for which Philip had been appointed maximum leader by the assembled Greeks at a congress in Corinth, he determined on a new marriage, to the young Macedonian girl Cleopatra, a ward of his general, Attalus. It was one of Philip's many marriages, and did not necessarily dissolve the union with Olympias, Alexander's mother, but the marriage feast in 337 was the occasion of a violent quarrel between Alexander and his father. Alexander fled the court, and even though he was brought back again, there were suspicions between father and son, fueled by the latter's interference in Philip's plans to ally himself with a Persian governor in south-west Anatolia through a marriage between Alexander's half-brother and the daughter of the governor. Once again father and son quarreled, and the king banished some of Alexander's closest companions from the court. He then moved to consolidate his relationships west of Macedonia by marrying off a daughter to the king of Epirus, Olympias' brother. The new relationship would provide a tie with Epirus which was different from and stronger than that of the slightly tarnished marriage with Olympias, and thus would protect Philip against trouble from Epirus, from Olympias, or from Alexander, so the king had every reason to celebrate. He invited droves of Greeks to the lavish festivities, and instructed his courtiers to bring as many as possible from abroad. Musical contests, magnificent banquets, and the spectacle of Philip receiving gold crowns from individuals and cities alike entertained the guests, and Aristotle was doubtless among those who watched the procession with Philip's statue included among those of the twelve gods. Then, suddenly, with a stroke from the bodyguard Pausanias who rushed forward and stabbed the king, the reign ended.

An amazing life was over, one which restructured the Greek world. In the fifty years since Aristotle had been born in Stagira, power over Greek affairs had passed from city-states – Athens, Sparta, Thebes, Phocis – and had been seized by a monarch leading a fiercely loyal army of fellow Macedonians. Athens and Sparta, for almost two centuries the major powers who had vied for leadership of Greece, were now secondary compared with the Macedonia whose king had been formally elected leader. In this same period, the entire generation which had known the world of the fifth century had passed away. All who had known Socrates and had picked up from him the cause of philosophy, either to carry it forward or to distort it, had died, Plato some ten years before, and Isocrates at 98, a few days after Philip's final victory at Chaeronea. In this completely changed world, it was the lot of Alexander to wrestle with the maintenance of what Philip had won and the completion of the grand dream of the conquest of Persia; and of Aristotle to continue his struggle with Plato's legacy and impose his own views of the world on Greek thought. The success of both would also be their failure.

# 11

# Plato

## *Implications of the improvement of the soul as the prime human goal*

Socrates proposed a good that was in almost every respect different from that of the aristocratic Athenian society of the fifth century. The noble virtues of physical prowess, wealth, reputation, and bodily beauty, mostly available only to the aristocrats with whom Socrates actually worked, were replaced by therapy of the soul, a process potentially open to the lowest and poorest members of society. The turnabout in ideals which this represented was permanent, for the impact of Socrates' thought on Greek ideology was a lasting one. Even the aristocratic Plato accepted the fundamental tenets and implications of Socrates' teaching, and, however sympathetic he might have been toward conservative and aristocratic societies like those of Sparta and Crete, he remained faithful to the concept of private virtue which was not really consistent with the practical requirements of such states.

Thus Plato was forced to step away from the world around him to seek a more fundamental and absolute reality, and concluded that understanding and right conduct only became possible with perception of truths higher than those of human experience and society. Furthermore, the ideals which Plato developed for society, particularly as exemplified by his later thought in *Laws*, were far closer to the ideals of *liberté, fraternité, égalité* of the French Revolution than they were to the noble ambitions of power and eternal fame enunciated by Pericles virtually in Plato's own time. In Plato's view, society approaches perfection – unattainable though that may be – to the extent that possessions, such as wives and children as well as property, are truly held in common and all members of the society are unified in community. It is not an aristocratic ideal. Nor is Plato's next best, also admitted as an unreachable goal, that every member of a society be equal in wealth, and failing that equality, that disparities be limited in their extent.

The trend in ethical thought set in motion by Socrates, a fundamental shift in values whereby virtue was no longer defined by, and education for virtue no longer aimed at, the achievement of the goals admired by the aristocratic mind, inevitably set a different value on the members of the lower orders. A person's worth might no longer be measured by family, wealth, or prowess, or even by Pericles' standard of one's worth to the state, but by the extent to which the self, and particularly the soul, was perfected. This was the revolution which Nietzsche perceived and condemned as the triumph of the slave mentality of the weak over the ideals of the noble and strong.

The world in which the aristocratic ideal had set the standards of virtue served well enough for that purpose. For all the uncertainties of life, whims of the gods, or will of fate or chance, the world was well enough suited to imperfect and imperfectible humanity. To many, following Hesiod, the human was a late development deteriorated from what had gone before, or was merely one of the creatures with whom the gods sported; many people saw no merit in the new anthropology's proposition for change or improvement in human nature. People were what they were, the world was what it was, and the noblest nature was that which did the best job of making the best of it. Persistence, strength, the stubbornness to try to dominate were humanity's noblest effort and highest object. It was the stuff of tragedy, and the best minds of the fifth century were at one with statesmen whose policies reflected this view, and with poets whose treatment of the human condition was based on it.

Plato saw quite clearly how, following Socrates, he proposed to overturn all this, and his perception of his role in the history of Greek thought played an important part in calling forth his prohibition of the works of the poets in his ideal society. While the principled dismissal of their work as imitative and deceptive gave him an intellectual justification for the elimination of their seductive charm, the ideals of epic and tragedy ran so counter to his own that he found those works objectionable on practical and moral, as well as theoretical and philosophical, grounds. Plato's and Socrates' philosophical principles attributed independence to each human soul, and assigned different values in the scale of worth on the basis of each individual's potential for and actual pursuit of the soul's improvement. Socrates shared the earlier willingness to accept the imperfectibility of human beings, so that he was satisfied with attempting to gain virtue and knowledge, just as noble values accepted the effort, however, unsuccessful, to impose the human will, but Plato sought a means by which perfection could be established at least as a principle, if not an attainable goal.[1] Plato could not compromise on his concept of improving the soul in a world which was accepted as the senses perceived it, and there was no ideology current like that of the later Christian thinkers, who posited perfection for divinity, but accepted the reality of the imperfect world and imperfect humanity created thus for the divinity's own unknown purpose. For Plato, perfection must exist. The occurrence of imperfect phenomena and concepts in the world around us required the notion of their perfection in form, and such a concept as good, or virtue, must have a perfect form. That perfect form was objectively real, perceptible to the mind, and the exemplar for the multifaceted, different, imperfect, and changing concepts and phenomena which we call "good" among the perceptions in the world of the senses.

131

*17* Bust of Plato, in the Vatican Museum, Rome.

The Socratic–Platonic view of humanity also called for a definition of the role of the state in society, and of the relationship required of each individual within the state to society as a whole. Athenians had for a long time been witnessing the political institutionalization of a community effort, and that fundamental attitude toward political institutions remained part of the Platonic vision. Throughout the *Republic*, all the complex argumentation developing the particular structures which would create a society most conducive to harmony and justice is predicated on an understanding of the state as an organic entity, on an analogy with the organism of the human soul. The discussion attempting to define Justice, after several false starts wherein "vulgar" definitions are examined and discarded, moves to use a hypothetical state as a structure which may, when properly constructed, exemplify Justice. The idea is that if Justice can be identified and understood in the macrocosm of the state, then it can equally be delineated in the miniature model of the soul. The analogical construction can only work and be informative if the state is the same kind of phenomenon as the soul, and the entire treatment of the state in the *Republic* makes it obvious that Plato takes the state as a no less vital and living organism than the soul.

It is, however, important to remember that the *Republic* was not written to describe an ideal state, but rather uses an ideal state to describe the state of harmonious interrelationships of the human spirit which would make for a just soul. The carefully structured class system, with the philosopher king at the top and the working population educated to perform their necessary tasks, is not necessarily Plato's final word on perfection in human social organization. The structure is put together for the argument, not the argument for the structure, and we have quite a different, albeit general, proposal for the ideal society in *Laws*, in which everything is held in common and everything works in common, as eyes, ears, and hands function in common. The unity of such a city is expressed by a proverb, "the things of friends are truly common."[2] Such a constitution is far above and beyond what can exist, however much it is the ideal to emulate, for the constitution created intellectually in pursuit of these goals, with its laws framed so that the citizens "will be happiest and as much as possible friends of one another,"[3] lies beyond the realm of practicality and possibility.

The ideals of *Laws*, with stress on the political goal of providing the environment for the individual soul,[4] are not in conflict with those of the *Republic*, even if the approach in the earlier work is different. The *Republic* sets out to discover the nature of Justice by examining it as it appears in a city, and Socrates and his companions meet success in their quest: in this virtuous city, wisdom, courage, moderation, and justice dominate. The rulers have wisdom, the army courage, and moderation produces agreement and satisfaction in every segment. Justice is another word for the harmony of the state which prevails when each member of the society fulfills his or her own role and does not resent or interfere with others fulfilling theirs. In finding this harmony we have identified Justice. This Justice in the state can be demonstrated to be the same thing in the individual, with a correspondence between the three divisions of the city and three parts of the soul. The same virtues apply to the soul as well, and are used by the appropriate parts: wisdom by the reasoning part, courage by the spirited part, which imposes moderation in controlling the appetites, the third part. When the parts fulfill their functions the soul is in harmony with itself; this parallels the Justice which we saw working in the larger entity of the state.

Plato has generally been portrayed as a philosopher of conservative and aristocratic attitudes and opinions. One or another dictum of the *Republic* is often trotted out to support this representation, as are favorable remarks about the so-called "aristocratic" Constitutions of Crete and Sparta. This description of the philosopher makes a nice, rounded picture, particularly when into it is fitted a Platonic resentment of the democracy which was responsible for the execution of his beloved teacher Socrates. But a characterization of Plato as "conservative" or "aristocratic," although it suits his class background and the general orientation of his social attitudes, is not a completely comprehensive description of his political views, which do not always accord with such a neat classification. For example, Plato quite clearly approves, in *Laws* 698ff., of the Athenian Constitution as it stood at the time of the Persian Wars, a hundred years before his own time. It was not like the permissive democracy attacked in Book VIII of the *Republic*, but a state which provided a liberty which the authority of respect for the laws served to restrain. This respect, as Plato saw it, was a kind of fear which gripped the Athenians and united them against the Persian threat, but they were none the less a free people, with the political institutions associated with democracy – the elections, the magistrates, the people serving on law courts, and the openness of political life which we associate with fifth-century Athens. But if fear and obedience are dissipated, first in audacious neglect of the laws of music, then with refusal to obey magistrates, society deteriorates, with the rejection of submission to parents and elders; citizens then avoid subjection to the laws and ultimately even to the gods. It is this, the reckless exploitation of liberty, which we might call licence, that Plato condemns in *Laws*; he praises the Constitutions of Sparta and Crete because they have proceeded less far to this licence.

It is interesting that Plato fastens on to the pursuit of personal taste in music as the first stage of licence. In view of the importance he attaches to the work of the poets in the *Republic* and *Laws*, arguing in both works for the need for censorship because of the vigor with which poetry influences the mind, it is hardly surprising that he should see a collapse of appropriate respect for the canons of taste as a direct precursor of the collapse of political propriety. But in none of this does he question the propriety for a citizenry to be free, autonomous, and at liberty to administer itself. In fact, in the immediately preceding passage in *Laws* he attributes the degeneracy in power of the Persian monarchy to a failure to maintain the freedom and openness available to the Persian subjects under Cyrus. With the accession of the poorly educated and tyrannical successors of Cyrus and Darius, the Persians became more and more enslaved and thus less able to maintain the power of the kingdom.

While Plato may be considered a conservative insofar as he thought the Athenians governed themselves better, or at least were more successful, before the Peloponnesian War, it is difficult to imagine anyone, then or today, not agreeing with his assessment. It has been traditional for almost all historians to join Thucydides and Aristophanes in sneering at the social backgrounds of the politicians – forgoing the term statesman – who followed Pericles. Cleon was the son of a tanner, and Cleophon was of no family and died poor. (We may pass over Nicias and Alcibiades, aristocrats who gained leadership but made no success with it.) This degeneration in the quality of leadership (let's forget that Cleon was successful against the Spartans at Pylos) – must be part of what Plato had in mind when he wrote of the deterioration of Athenian society and government. It is an easy assumption to make, particularly for the gentlemen who have made up the body of classicists until the last decade or so. It is comfortable to think that the loss of control by the well-born and well-brought-up is accompanied by a loss of national power as well as gentility, and that Plato endorses the view, but that smug assumption won't jibe – not with history, not with Plato, and not, so far as we can tell, with anything of the Socratic tradition.

A stunning implication of the Socratic definition of virtue seriously undermined the traditional position accorded the aristocratic notion of *arete* – "goodness," "nobility," "prowess," or however one might translate the Greek. If virtue is knowledge, it is teachable, and teachable to anyone with the wit to learn. Worse, if no one knows anything, and Socrates' wisdom consists in his awareness of his own ignorance, then all the vaunted *arete* of the nobles is worth nothing, and the stone-worker's son is better than the lot of them. Then too, if Socrates' daemon is a guide to virtuous action, the nobles would have no monopoly on that. And finally, if one's duty is first and foremost the service of one's soul and the pursuit of that knowledge which is virtue, all the activities on which the nobles prided themselves had no value and little importance. However much political democrats might have disliked Socrates for his associates and his presumed oligarchical predilections, well-bred aristocrats like his accuser Anytus would have hated his ideas if they knew and understood them.

Plato did understand them and he accepted the basic theme as well. Indeed he stresses this particular aspect of Socrates' thought over and over again in the dialogues, and has Socrates – and not only Socrates but others – carry the concept that virtue is knowledge forward to the implication of the obligation to pursue that knowledge. Even more destructive of the aristocratic ideal, the attributes of nobility, athletic or military prowess, good family, comeliness, wealth, and political position, are all rejected as criteria either of a good man or of a good citizen. Only excellence of soul makes a good citizen, and the idea is expressed not only in *Laws* 770D, but underlies a large part of the *Republic* as well. Indeed, the *Republic* is explicit that neither family, nor background, nor any characteristic other than potential for training in virtue qualifies a person for the education which ultimately leads to the duty of philosophical kingship. While Plato admits that it is not likely that parents of the lower orders will produce offspring suitable for higher things, it is not impossible, and the system must acknowledge and provide for this possibility. This is a fundamentally egalitarian position, one with which no one of the traditional aristocracy would be likely to have much sympathy, and the egalitarianism is even more noticeable and contrary to traditional Greek thought in that it posits equal treatment for and equal potential of women. All this fits with the hints of egalitarianism which begin to appear in tragedy at the end of the fifth century, a major change in literary treatments of the lower classes which, from the time of Homer on, were portrayed negatively.

The very word "aristocratic," from the Greek *aristoi*, the "best," shows the attitude at the very basic level of language, and all the words for "lower classes," like *kakoi*, *phauloi*, and the like, carry a moral as well as a social derogation. This attitude is clear in all early writing and in tragedy down to that of Euripides. Even in the works of this poet – whom Socrates admired, we are told – the claims of the lower classes are proclaimed only on some occasions, and the presentation can often be compared with that of the aristocratic comedy writer Aristophanes. His lower-class characters, even when they learn something or come to good conclusions, even when they are on the "right" side of peace, have nothing admirable about them. They show no courage, no honor, no virtue, no generosity – in short, no *arete* – and none of these qualities or the class that thinks itself their possessor is burlesqued by Aristophanes.

It is difficult for us to appreciate, after a century of militant climbing by the working classes, how revolutionary might be the idea that those who worked with their hands might be as good as those with clean fingernails. The idea that education might be constructed on the principle of equality, and aimed at developing in anyone that virtue of soul which Plato predicated as the proper concern of every man, was just as startling if not more so. Hitherto education had consisted in developing and propagating those skills, talents, and arts in which the aristocrats took the greatest pleasure or for which they felt the greatest need: rhetoric, music, gymnastics, military techniques, and such improvers of the mind as mathematics. None of the "profitable" crafts was pursued by aristocrats, not even those which are today prestigious, such as medicine, architecture, sculpture, or painting, and still less carpentry, pottery, or the manifold everyday tasks of fitting out the house and person.

Now Plato proposed an education which would subordinate all the traditional aspects of Greek culture to the goal of improvement of the soul. The proposition entailed the exclusion of most of the literary treasures which represented Hellenism to the Athenians, such noble works as the great epics of Homer and much of the lyric and even tragic tradition. They were to be eliminated because they offered misleading guides to conduct, encouraging belief in gods who were anything but perfect and offering examples of behavior which distracted from rather than promoted right thought and right conduct. Plato's whole conception of social organization and conduct, education as well as family life, political life, and participation in the artistic life of Greek culture, was based on an interpretation of virtue and the techniques for enhancing it stemming from the original Socratic notion that virtue of any sort eventually came down to knowledge. As an essentially rational matter, the pursuit of virtue could be carried on by reason, and reason as supreme could decide what was pertinent and what counterproductive. The dependence on reason alone also meant that any person pursuing virtue could follow a course which did not in any way depend upon familiarity with the traditional skills or arts of the nobility.

This was, beyond question, the first truly revolutionary human ethic in the history of western thought. All earlier intellectual activity, whether of the Sophists, the physical philosophers, the poets, or religious writers, was concentrated on improving and refining the traditional virtues of Hellenic life, the virtue of participation in a *polis*, the aristocratic family virtues of clan and class, the values of warriors, patriarchs, politicians, and citizen-soldiers. Plato's ethic swept all of this away. These ideas were attractive, for example, to members of the newly rich mercantile class, who were more than glad to see an ethical ideal which put them on a par with the snob-ridden older aristocracy. By the end of the fifth century there were many Athenian citizens of no noble background who had managed to achieve prominence in politics or culture. Cleon the tanner's son had been one; Socrates himself another; even Euripides the tragedian, according to some reports, came from a family of lowly shopkeepers, and even the best that was said about him made his family no better than "respectable." People other than citizens in Athens, too, looked for a self-image of worth. Wealthy foreigners, "metics," had established themselves so firmly that their families continued on in Athens. The prosperity which commerce had brought these foreign traders also gave them the leisure to seek some form of self-improvement, if not for themselves then for their sons and descendants. By the middle of the fourth century, one Pasion could leave the ranks of slavery and climb, via a fortune made as a banker, into Athenian citizenship itself.

Platonic thought might have attracted some because it offered a moral stance to this emerging wealthy middle class which was despised by the aristocrats, particularly since it never pushed people's minds to the logical extreme of including the unfree. Just as the argument for "life, liberty and the pursuit of happiness" could comfortably ignore the slaves of eighteenth-century America, so the implications of Plato's thought could be ignored by the readers of the fourth century or later. No one, dealing with and evaluating Plato's prescriptions for a society which would allow the souls of the members to be developed best, worried at all about the souls of slaves or even the very poor, any more than the middle-class socialist-inclined university students of today campaign very actively for the execution of Marx's threat: "You reproach us with intending to do away with your property. Precisely so: that is just what we intend."[5] If the fourth-century intellectuals in the Academy under Plato's tutelage thought that their body-servants had as much potential as themselves to reach the heights of virtue, we have heard nothing of it, and the social comedy of Menander points us in quite the other direction.

Nevertheless, the implications were there, and they would persist to disturb

Plato's most famous student, Aristotle. For the time being, however, the analysis of ethical conduct and the method of political organization most conducive to it left aside the social questions relating to the vast majority of society who could not afford the leisure to study or think about the matter. That the effects of Plato's revolution might have spread beyond the philosophical circles of the Academy is suggested by the growing tendency to accept more readily the notion that metics and freedmen could contribute importantly to the social body in which hitherto only the participation of citizens had been considered of importance. Perhaps the most striking evidence of this comes from the pen of Plato's contemporary Xenophon, who had also been a student of Socrates, in *Poroi*, or *Ways and Means*, an economic essay proposing methods of increasing Athenian revenues. Among the propositions was the suggestion that Athens attract more and more aliens to reside with the citizens as metics, on the grounds that their presence increased economic activity and thereby brought in more and more funds through the tax levied on them, port duties, and the like. To encourage this settlement, Xenophon proposed that the metics be relieved of the obligation to serve in the infantry, and be allowed some privileges and the right to serve in the cavalry. Perhaps most revolutionary of all, he suggested that the metics be allowed to build houses on vacant sites within the walls, thus knocking down the age-old distinction between citizens and foreigners whereby only the former could own land, the resource which had been for so long the sole reliable source and measure of wealth. That such a proposal could be put forward seriously, and especially by an author with a reputation for conservatism, suggests a much wider advance in egalitarianism than constitutional history reports, and it is particularly significant that the source of the ideas and the evidence was, like Plato, a member of the Socratic tradition.

While Socrates may have provided, perhaps not entirely deliberately, the genesis of the idea of broadening the bases for respect, Plato provided the reasoned arguments to produce a full theory. That theory even included a hypothesis – some would say a demonstration – of the soul's possession of knowledge unbeknownst to the individual. The *Meno* presents this hypothesis: a slave boy is used in an experiment to demonstrate that, though totally unaware of the fact, he knew propositions of mathematics. That the theory of knowledge will work with a slave suggests that the theory of universal potential for improvement of the soul would do so as well, and, if these implications of his thought were lost on his contemporaries, they were not lost on Plato. That any human, free or slave, could and should attend to his life, making the improvement of his soul his main concern, had the broadest implications for human society. Had the idea spread beyond the few members of the classes wealthy and leisured enough for philosophical contemplation, the revolution would have been disseminated beyond philosophy to overturn society.

But it did not, and Plato knew that it could not. He was perfectly aware that in Athenian society of his time there was absolutely no possibility that the poor and the unfree would have any opportunity at all to develop their souls, or be allowed in any way at all to participate in educational or any other activities which would make such development possible. And so, in order to keep his theory honest, he was forced to abandon any attempt to impose it on the world around him, and sought a higher reality in which the theory could be valid.[6] The search generated an exotic fantasy proposing the independent existence of another, more genuine reality, in which the ideals he proposed could exist, and of which this world of the senses was only an imperfect and inaccurate imitation. The search and the theory saved his egalitarianism, and made it, for all time, both interesting and safe.

# 12

# The real world of city politics

## *Humanity and society in Plato's "higher reality"*

The implications of Socrates' conversations were left for his associates and students to explore. Of those whom we know best, only Xenophon and Plato are represented by complete works or even a significant quantity of text, and only Plato carried on the philosophical analyses of his teacher. In an outpouring of writings which range from fairly straightforward accounts of Socrates' conversations to the most abstruse doctrines of metaphysics, Plato covered not only Socrates' ideas but broke new ground for himself. Perhaps both are blended most smoothly in his *Republic*, which many have described as Plato's masterpiece. It has something for everyone: political theory for the political scientist and statesman; the theory of reality and the Forms for the philosopher; myths like that of the Cave and of Er for the poet; educational theory for the psychologist and the teacher; proposals for the role of women and for the family for the sociologist and proponent of women's rights; discussion of Homer and the tragedians for the literary critic – and the civil rights advocate. All this and much more has made the *Republic* central to the discussion of ancient thought in all of its aspects, and a massively influential text in its effects on the development of western thought.

Cognizant of the egalitarianism implicit in his elaboration of Socrates' delineation of the nature of the soul and its supervening importance for the guidance of all human conduct, Plato proceeded to the formulation of his ideal state on the basis of participation in and service to it to the maximum potential of each member of the society. The theory, in short, did away with all preferment and distinction on the basis of family, wealth, or inherited position, proposing, instead, a structure whereby each person was to be trained to his (or her) maximum inherent potential. Aware also that his readers would find it difficult to believe that the state proposed in the *Republic* could ever come to pass, Plato allowed Socrates to be pressed on this very point in the course of the dialogue, and the old dialectician was able to get agreement from his interlocutors that the scheme, though very difficult to implement, was at least possible, and on that account, to be pursued as the best state. Plato knew, however, that the seductiveness of his prose would be insufficient to induce large numbers of pragmatic Athenians to rush to implement his ideas, and it was equally difficult for him to believe that the egalitarianism implicit in his and Socrates' idea of the nature of humanity and the soul could ever be realized in a society anything like that of the Athens of his day.

It has been said that the ideal state proposed in the *Republic* was Plato's answer to the need to save the Athenian *polis* from the disintegration he saw around him. That might be so, although many, like Xenophon, Isocrates, Demosthenes, and others would be rather surprised at this modern assessment of the vigorous military and political activity of their times. Whether or not Plato was making any truly political proposals in the *Republic*, he was certainly using some hypothesis of a much more fundamental nature, and this related directly to an assessment of the validity of Socrates' ideas about the soul and the possibility of their realization. For the *Republic* contains allusions to Plato's theory of the Forms as if they had already been promulgated. The proposition that the philosopher king who will be educated to rule the state must be a lover of the Forms is a clear indication that the formulations of the *Republic* benefited from the existence of that theory.

There is not very much discussion of the Forms in the *Republic*, but what there is helps from the clarity of its presentation to show what Plato meant by the Forms and how he expected people to relate to them. At this point in the argument, Plato, having asserted that the rulers of his state must be philosophers, characterizes the true philosopher as a lover of the Forms. He mentions the Forms without explaining them, and every editor of the *Republic* must insert at this point some explanation of what he means by them: there are Forms of Justice, Beauty, Courage, and the like, the only true realities, and, as objects of the knowledge of philosophers, the only ones which really exist. The world perceived by the senses is the world of appearance in which objects are inconstant and subject to change, without the eternal stability or quality of permanence enjoyed by the Forms. Any intellectual treatment of objects in the world of appearances can only be opinion, while that of the Forms is true knowledge. And although, at the end of Book V, Plato's argument aims primarily at the distinction between knowledge and opinion, the implication involves the acceptance of these Forms as separate entities of existence, not merely as an idealized class concept. For he concludes that, agreed that there are things that exist and things that do not exist, knowledge deals with those that do exist, that is, the perfect and immutable Forms. Floating between that which exists, the Forms, and non-existence, is a whole assembly of intermediate entities which partake of the Forms but are unstable and of differing aspects, such as the many so-called beautiful things which seem so to some but not to others, which thus only partake of Beauty which, if known, would be agreed to be beautiful by all. These intermediate entities, phenomena, and objects of sense perception, are the objects of opinion, just as the Forms perceived by reason are the objects of knowledge.

The *Republic* does not deal in detail with or develop the theory of Forms, satisfied to use it as a given, with the Forms acknowledged as "real" entities existing separately from the objects of opinion. Discussions of the theory and various treatments of parts of it or of its implications recur in many other dialogues. In the crucial *Meno*, for example, as part of the investigation of the possibility of the teaching of virtue, it emerges in the attack on the dilemma that knowledge is either present in the seeker, making the search after knowledge unnecessary, or if not present renders learning impossible because the object if found will not be recognized. The rejection of this verbal contradiction ultimately makes an argument for the Forms possible. The *anamnesis*, or "remembering" the items of knowledge, all of which is held in the immortal soul which learnt it in previous existence, is perfectly consonant with the assertion of the independent existence of the Forms, which exist somewhere for the wandering soul to meet in one of its passages. The *Meno* warns us of what is to come.

What comes can show some striking intellectual and verbal pyrotechnics. In the *Timaeus*, for example, a dialogue dealing with natural science, Plato offers an explanation of the creation of the universe, humanity, and the animals, as the eternal creator fashioned the world as a spherical body modeled on the perfection in shape of a being which is to comprehend all else. And before he gets down to business with a long description of the human organism and its afflictions, with an anatomy and perception often surprising in their validity, he deals briefly with the Forms, since the concept is relevant to the discussions, and asserts that they are existent on their own, not perceptible by sense but by true reason. The dialogue provides a fascinating insight into Plato's use of imagination and abstraction to mythologize and write in a manner that leaves his intention obscured by some ambiguities, for he ranges from medical discussions which are clearly based on the most recent practical researches to the hypothesis of a creator who is prior to and responsible for the generation of even the most primal deities of Greek tradition, as well as the elements of earth, air, fire, and water. Nowhere in the dialogue does he give any hint as to whether we are to have more faith in his statement of one proposition than another.[1]

That kind of problem is even more acute in the *Parmenides*, a dialogue which divides into two almost equally baffling parts. The first is a telling critique of Plato's own theory of the Forms, using the young Socrates as an unsuccessful defender of the concept against an effective attack by Parmenides. No one has proposed a completely convincing explanation of Plato's reasons for presenting such damaging arguments against the Forms as he described them elsewhere without at least attempting a better defense than that allowed to Socrates here, although some see this part of the dialogue as evidence of the older Plato's own doubts about his theory. The second part of the dialogue, given over to Parmenides to set out his own concept of the unchanging One in a series of confusing and self-contradictory arguments, has produced equally contradictory assessments by those who have tried to follow it. Some see in it a kind of transcendent reality, while others regard it as a parody of the kind of reasoning used by Parmenides and his followers.

Then there is the *Phaedo*, in which the drama of Socrates' last hours and death makes the dialogue seductive and renders us unusually sympathetic to any ideas propounded by him. Here Socrates aims at the demonstration of the immortality of the soul, approaching that demonstration from a number of points of view and using a number of lines of argument. He does depend in this on the conclusions reached in the *Meno*, where he obtained agreement that all knowledge was a matter or recollection of what the soul had learned in earlier incarnations. In the *Phaedo*, the Forms are discussed a number of times, as, for example, when Socrates alludes to the absolutes of Beauty, Goodness, and the like in opposition to the imperfect copies of such concepts perceived by the senses. In fact, as part of the argument of the soul's immortality, he makes a very neat summary of the independent existence of the Forms and the imitative nature of perceived objects: as the Forms have existence, so souls exist before people are born; the Forms are apprehensible only by the intellect, for they are formless and invisible, and imperfect copies take their names from the Forms in that they partake of their characteristics.[2] The Forms exist. They are unchanging, the models for the objects of sense perception, and are only amenable to perception by reason. Their presentation is intricately tied in with the development of the argument for the immortality of the soul. Here Socrates has changed his original concern with the improvement of the soul and his pragmatic insistence on the primacy of the soul over the body in terms of everyday attention. Instead of a soul which must take attention to gain improvement, there is a new conception of a soul which has wandered, immortal, through an untold number of existences, developing through its association with the Forms of absolute reality an acquaintance with them which calls on recollection to provide humans with the knowledge they seek.

There is a contradiction here, even if it is not pointed out by Plato or any of the interlocutors of Socrates. The contradiction cannot be lightly resolved by asserting that the therapy of the soul is precisely that kind of reasoning which makes it possible for the immortal soul to recollect what is known already, so that the "Socratic" notion of attending to one's soul as a matter of primary importance is a matter of pursuing the calculations which will yield up the knowledge already held. However one squirms between Socrates, "Socrates," and Plato, there is a qualitative difference between the approach to the soul when it is treated as part of the human makeup which is more important than the body and requires preferential treatment, and those approaches which argue for its immortality, its perception of the Forms in a different existence, and as a determinative which can move into forms of life other than human while at the same time preserving a record of all its experience. In all of this, Plato uses the theory of the immortality of the soul in a particular way that obviates the problems generated by Socrates' initial proposal for the primacy of the soul.

What problems, and what particular way? The problems, of course, are those engendered by the egalitarianism inherent in a life and a society predicated on the doctrine of the primacy of the soul. As I have already said, Plato was either unwilling or unable to follow the doctrine to its proper conclusion of calling for a radical extension of some Athenian practices to a point which would result in an almost complete overhaul of Athenian society. Thus the doctrine had to be understood and followed in a different way, and this is the way indicated by Plato's application of the doctrine of the immortality of the soul and his development of the theory of Forms. The way, in effect, reinterpreted human experience and redefined human nature to make it conform to Socratic notions in a higher reality, and to make possible the understanding of humanity and society in the manner of their representation in the *Republic*. By "higher reality" I mean the reality of the Forms, a reality which had a separate but nonetheless genuine – indeed more genuine – existence on a different plane from that of the objects of sense perception. The existence of the Forms, the soul's communication and familiarity with them, and the immortality of that soul itself made the world of sense perception a matter of secondary and imitative character, of lesser importance to the world of Forms just as the body was to the soul in the first discussion. Thus any egalitarianism in the world of sense perception was essentially an irrelevent consideration, and any egalitarianism which might seem to be called for could be ignored as against the true equality afforded souls in the world of absolute reality.

In this world of absolute reality, there existed all the qualities in their absolute and unchanging Form – absolute Good, absolute Beauty, absolute Justice, absolute Truth, and the like. It is extremely important to the understanding of this portrayal of the nature of existence to recognize that it is essentially dualistic – not unlike the separation by Descartes into the *res cognitans* and the *res cognita*, different only in that the *res cognita* of Plato is in no circumstance susceptible to apprehension through the senses. But there is, in Plato as in Descartes, the sense that the "me" exists and has some relation with the "out there." However Socrates may have dealt with that dualism, and have relied upon the faculties of the "me" to deal with the "out there" of sense perception, Plato abandoned reliance on the senses and reified the absolutes. Thus, whatever treatment earlier thinkers gave these matters, Plato established the arena in which the game was to be played. In so doing, he completely redefined the game, and so firmly established the parameters of approach to the definition of reality, the concept of humankind, and the nature and validity of ethics that, as classics professors often observe, "all Philosophy since Plato is an argument with Plato." The approach has so dominated western thought that even for those who have never read Plato and have not the slightest interest in doing so, the problems posed for solution and the methodology of thought used in attempting solutions have been framed in reaction or response to the fundamental hypotheses offered by Plato. And even those who have developed convincing (to themselves) refutations of these assumptions or representations are unable to free themselves from a treatment of the question of the nature of "reality" even if they reject Plato's concept.

In the development of this world view, Plato was of enormous influence, and it is in this sense that Shorey's description of philosophy as an argument with Plato applies. So influential was the concept of an absolute apprehensible only through reason or thought rather than sense perception, that it was taken up in religious as well as purely philosophic constructions, and divinities were seen as imbued with the characteristics of the absolutes. One or another of the traditional Greek divinities, as well as immigrants from other lands, could be understood as reified absolutes, and religious activities were often suffused with a search for means to transcend the world of the senses and approach the absolute. It has been said that as time went on philosophy became more religious, and religion more philosophical, and if true, such was the bequest of Plato.

But this was the effect in the long term, and we shall see it in detail later. For the moment, Plato's immediate successor in the Academy, Speusippus, and Plato's best pupil, Aristotle, wrestled with the question of the validity of the theory of the Forms and with the implications of that theory, as did many other philosophers of the age. Thinkers of the generation after Plato were caught up in the intellectual ferment which his writings generated, and his theories were evaluated, supported, and attacked by a number of thinkers and from a number of points of view. The fundamental assumptions, however, attributing all authority to consciousness and the inclusion of all existence in a single mode of being, persisted through the work of his followers, none of whom even noticed, let alone challenged, these assumptions, so strong were the patterns of thought which Plato had laid down for them. The limits which Plato had set and the definition of the area of investigation which he had established were so clear and so firm that no work would be undertaken which might reveal evidence that the basic assumptions were wrong. Thus even the generation after him, the generation which might have challenged him the most strongly, before he had become a "sacred cow," was too constrained by the nature of the problem which he had set and the manner in which he had posed it to search for flaws in his approach. His writings obsessed that whole generation, so much so that nothing he wrote was lost, and the complete body of Platonic writing was preserved (even added to) and handed down to later generations.

# 13

# Aristotle and
# the middle world
## A philosophy of reason, sense perception, nature, ethics, and physics

It is abundantly clear that Aristotle found much of Plato's philosophical speculation uncongenial, and the system which it produced downright disagreeable. It is also obvious, however, that Aristotle was reluctant to attack Plato and his writings directly, probably because of his own affection and respect for the man. From time to time, however, Aristotle does find it necessary to explain the thought of his predecessors, and when he does that he shows his rejection of Plato's conclusions. For example, in a criticism of Plato's theory of the Forms, Aristotle allies himself firmly with Socrates, making clear not only that the Forms theory itself should be blamed on Plato, but that Socrates would have none of it. Rejecting the idea that the Forms as universal substances are separable and distinguishable individually, Aristotle explains that:

> the people who state that the substances are universal did not make them amenable to sense perception. They considered that the individual items perceived by the senses are in flux, and none of them are stable, but that the universal stands beside them and is something other. This, as we said early, Socrates proposed, because of his definitions, but he did not make them [the particulars and the universals] distinct from one another; and he understood rightly in not making the separation.[1]

Having dealt here and there with the Platonic idea that the Forms of which the world of sense perception produces mere replication are independent, separate in existence, and subsisting in themselves, Aristotle treats subject after subject without reference to such notions, basing his discussion instead on his own views of the nature of form. All of his writing, from that on natural history, motion, and astronomy, to that on the nature of the human spirit, logic, politics, and ethics, is permeated with the effects of his view that the form which determines or controls the development of the particular is structurally integrated with the particular, and forms an inseparable unit with it. The Form

*18* A millennium after the creation of the head of Aristotle now in the Bibliothéque Mazarine in Paris, one of the sculptors of Chartres Cathedral presented his sense of the appearance of the man whose writings were the most influential on medieval thought.

is basic to the very existence of the entity, for the entity can neither be what it is without the Form, nor can the Form exist without the entity to express it. This fundamental disagreement with Plato determined the development of Aristotle's thought, and created his very different approach not only to science but to political and moral philosophy as well.

Aristotle's writing is truly astounding for its range, its depth, and its originality. Much of what he wrote established opinion on its subject for two millennia after his death, and even where that was not the case, his work was the foundation of the methodology by which people approached a subject. His work encompassed theories and rationale of the relationship of bodies in space, in such a work as the misleadingly (for moderns) titled *Physics*, dealing with the nature, effects, and causes of motion. He dealt in his *Metaphysics* with the nature, causes, and substance of phenomena, while among the works we call the *Organon* he presented a fully developed system of reasoning, not only with analysis of definition and the explanation of valid syllogisms and fallacies, but also careful explication of the building of arguments and the refutations thereto.[2] Elsewhere, in a long work, *On the Heavens*, he argued on the basis of both reason and observation that the cosmos was spherical and its motion circular, illustrating again and again how the observations available to us through sense perception can be used to extrapolate from that which can be immediately comprehended to that which is quite remote from direct perception.[3] An even more extensive example of the utility of observation and the scope of conclusions which can be reached from it is the massive compendium *Historia Animalia*, with explications and analyses of animal life not merely classifying but also analyzing life functions. Rather than merely describing distinctions in the appearance and structure of different species Aristotle, starting with the concept that the requirements of animal life relate fundamentally to feeding and breeding, compares and relates the different forms of life in terms of the different manners in which these fundamental functions and their subsidiaries are accomplished. The process produces a much deeper understanding of the nature of animal life than would be achieved by mere description, and it is a process of analysis which arises from Aristotle's fundamental view of the relationship between the particular and the form which determines its development. The significance of this kind of scientific analysis is perhaps most striking in his works *On the Soul* and the so-called *Parva Naturalia*, a collection of short essays on sense perception. Here, in attempting to understand the "form," as it were, of the human individual, in Aristotelian terms, as the determining but integral aspect of the human being rather than as Plato's separate entity, Aristotle proceeds in much the way modern analysis does, trying to square observation with economy of hypothesis. Although his attempt to understand and explain how sense perception actually works frequently reaches erroneous conclusions because observation does not always reveal basic function, his method is consistent and legitimate in depending upon what seems to be observably true.[4]

A good deal of Aristotle's scientific writing, based as it was on careful observation, is still valid today, especially in the biological and zoological sciences, where observation could generally be applied. It is limited, however, to what I call the "middle world," that part of the cosmos in which our sense perceptions seem to give us reliable data, in which "common sense" in the Einsteinian sense of the prejudices which we have acquired by the age of 18 is a good guide to reason. It is the universe in which the distinction between the observer and objective reality seems valid, and for which the treatment of external objects as objective, independent, and unaffected in their nature either by our perceptions or our understanding of these perceptions produces predicted and useful results. Although this does not always work in the domain of sub-microscopic particles and the huge domain of super-space and super-speed, where ordinary concepts of matter, motion, time, and mass do not apply as they do in the world of ordinary perception, this middle world is the one in which we live most of the time, and to which we have been completely limited until very recently, and the concepts which we have used in it and have applied to matter have produced remarkable results in the manipulation of matter. It was Aristotle who founded these basic approaches, and who used them for science, or "physical" reality.

Aristotle readily admitted that the application of his method to ethics would produce results and conclusions less precise than those he found for science.[5] Still, he attempted to use the principles of observation and comparison to establish an ethical and political system which would have a working validity, presented in two major works on the subject, *Nicomachean Ethics* and *Politics*, which form a connected whole. Aristotle saw the work, essentially, as an essay on the governance of humanity, with political systems predicated on an analysis of the nature of the human, and of the behavior which conduces to the highest human good, which is, pragmatically, happiness. That good, of course, must not only be identified, but, within the parameters of general proof proposed by Aristotle, its nature must be demonstrated. Thus the very long discussion of Justice in *Nicomachean Ethics* Book V, as well as the often lengthy treatments of the mean in defining such virtues as Courage, Temperance, Liberality, and the like in Books III and IV, are all elicited by Aristotle's attempt to establish the Good in human terms, reachable, definable, and accessible to human reason in the face of and in rejection of Plato's Ideal Good. What are to some truisms, frequently introduced and often banal, as well as the prolixity of the writing, proceed from the desire to establish, define, and create agreement about the nature of the Good and miscellaneous goods and virtues as practical guides and not as abstract definitions. Aristotle repeats and even overwrites to ensure that his statements are understood and accepted. He deals in this manner with moral or character virtues, which are different from those intellectual virtues of Wisdom and Good Sense and the like which make for the particular quality of happiness for man which is the life of contemplation. It is all, in short, an attempt to provide a specific and practical guide to the regulation of conduct to achieve happiness, much as descriptions from observation are offered to explain the nature of external phenomena and objects.

The *Politics* carries forward the investigation of the manner of achieving happiness by examining the social and civic structures most conducive to the fulfillment of this goal for individual citizens. Like everything else which Aristotle wrote or stated, his conclusions were reached after taking into account a great body of empirical evidence; what made for "good" Constitutions could only be determined from the experience of the outcomes of many different constitutional arrangements. Certainly the research on and compilation of the Constitutions of 158 states which Aristotle is reputed to have carried on, with one extant as the Constitution of Athens, was undertaken for the purpose of application of data to political theory, even if we cannot be sure that all this work had in fact been completed before the drafting of the *Politics*. There is certainly no doubt that the frequent allusions to one Constitution or constitutional experience after another in the *Politics* demonstrates that a great deal of detail about many Constitutions and a large body of historical data were at hand as a guide to the statements in the work.

There are certain basic assumptions about the phenomena which are advantageous to human institutions underlying the statements and recommendations in the *Politics*. Perhaps the most important of these is that to Aristotle, as to Plato, stability is the major social good at which to aim, and for which institutions should be designed. A great deal of the discussion to which Aristotle addresses himself involves explanation of change and overthrow of Constitutions, "destabilization," as we would call it today, an examination necessary from the point of view which sees change as essentially undesirable and antithetical to the development of a society in which the individual good of happiness can be achieved. As against the evaluation of the causes of change, the examination and classification of the different types of Constitution aim at an explication of how each type works best, what advantages for citizens each type offers, and what drawbacks will be found by the residents of states governed by each of the various types of systems. The utility of presenting all this information is related to what Aristotle sees as the obligation of the statesman or politician to look after the material well-being of that constituency which is sovereign under a particular Constitution,[6] and justifies the establishment of overall requirements for holding office, like loyalty to the Constitution, competence, and appropriate goodness and justice.[7] Requisite for meeting these requirements is a thorough understanding of the type of Constitution to which one is to be devoted, and for which one is to be able to exercise suitable justice. It is to provide for that understanding that Aristotle has presented so much constitutional detail in the *Politics*.

Aristotle not only looks at the question of what structures make for the best state, he also faces the realities of the world in which a number of different kinds of Constitutions exist, both in their proper forms of monarchy, aristocracy, and constitutional democracy and in their degenerate forms of tyranny, oligarchy, and excessive democracy. He addresses the question of the means of administering for stability each type of Constitution when it is framed and functions according to its proper form, and the avoidance of upset, and the means of achieving the best reform when "destabilization" has already taken place. While Aristotle obviously had his own preference for the "constitutional" state, or limited democracy, in this discussion (in some ways he preferred monarchy), this preference is not based on any abstract notion of what is best, but rather on the belief that in that kind of structure the greatest stability is most easily achieved.

In his political and social inclinations Aristotle was, like most Greek writers whose works have survived, an aristocrat, sympathetic to the ideals and values of the small upper class of birth and wealth. Thus in his preference for a mixed kind of Constitution, wherein the broad citizen class shared power at least in law, he rated the potential quality of the state on the basis of the manner in which that citizen body earned its livelihood, which affected, in fact, just how much involvement in the affairs of state the mass of citizens actually could have. For that democracy in which the citizen body at its lowest level consisted of the

150

poor but hardworking free farmers, the state worked well because the mass of the citizens were just too busy to involve themselves in day-to-day government, and were forced to leave the administration of the state to their betters. Implicit again and again in the discussion of different forms of Constitution in the *Politics* is the notion that the "better class" of people comprises those who have the larger portion of wealth, and not those engaged in daily trade or the litigation and activities of the law courts and the assemblies. The best people are those whose property represents in aggregate the greater part of the wealth of the state, the "few" whose riches match all those of the "many." Indeed, an aspect of some of Aristotle's doubts on democracy relates to what is to him the inequality inherent in a situation wherein those exercising greater power, the "many," represent a smaller portion of the total wealth of the state.

This is, of course, a standard attitude among Greeks; it prevailed among the Athenians, even at a time when the democracy at Athens had reached the greatest extent of power, that stage which Aristotle describes as the one in which the people have power even over the laws. His treatment of royal government is consistent with this approach, since he assesses suitability for this kind of Constitution in terms of the quality of the ruler or ruling family: when a person or a family surpasses in virtue all other members of the state, it is right that the individual or family should rule because of that merit.[8] The important quality for Aristotle, therefore, is virtue, and although he falls into the common assumption that virtue is most likely to be found among the propertied class, he is careful to make clear in his treatment of the different Constitutions – monarchy, aristocracy, democracy – that they work satisfactorily only when that group which is *kurios*, "sovereign," is also that group in the state which is most virtuous. He is, therefore, quite comfortable with the tradition of Socrates and Plato, seeing virtue as the requirement of rule, and the virtue which emerges from the discussion in *Nicomachean Ethics* is treated as the sum of those ordinary good qualities of character so often discussed by Socrates, not some highly refined, perhaps transcendent, perception of ideal forms demanded of the philosopher king of the *Republic*.

In this sense Aristotle must have seen himself as the intellectual descendant of Socrates. Inasmuch as Socrates neither proposed any external, divine or non-human, or superior form of knowledge by which to regulate human conduct, nor went beyond his experience of his own personal daemon which only guided him away from error, evaluation of conduct and definition of virtue could be expressed in human terms, and could be understood at the human level of functioning. Aristotle not only made no challenge to this basic attitude, but implicit in everything which he says about public and private virtue is a rejection of almost every aspect of Plato's reasoning about the development of knowledge of the Forms of Good or any other absolute. Aristotle, in fact, directly denies the interpretation of knowledge as innate or developed from some higher state. Rather, scientific knowledge – or, perhaps, "intelligized" knowledge – arises from sense perception, which passes into

151

memory, and frequently repeated memory is the phenomenon which we understand as experience; that experience then becomes the universal as knowledge stabilized in the soul.[9] The only kind of valid thinking other than scientific is that which apprehends the primary premises directly and is the originative source of scientific knowledge.[10] This view of knowledge makes possible the assertion of the nature of virtue which underlies everything in *Nicomachean Ethics* and *Politics*. Sense perception provides information about the effects of actions, and memory of these effects frequently repeated provides experience, which in turn becomes stabilized in the soul as the standard against which to measure future actions. With these standards established in the soul, evaluation of good requires only the fixing of the objective, the end, or aim of human life, in order to determine as good those actions which, experience shows, serve to advance that end.

The establishment of that end is the task of *Nicomachean Ethics*. It is essential, in Aristotelian thought, to determine that end, for it is not only the inherent form which controls and orders the development of behavior, but knowledge of it is essential to make possible the proposing of any code of ethics or behavior. He starts with proposing three types of lives, the Life of Enjoyment, the Life of Politics, and the Life of Contemplation. Men of quality eschew the first as beneath them. In general, and as men of action, they pursue the Life of Politics with its end as virtue, allowing, however, that an end of happiness must be part of the equation.[11] Aristotle then attacks Plato's conception of a universal Good as a foundation for Ethics, and, in seeking a working definition of the Good which will serve in all fields, proposes that the Good must be self-sufficient, not a good serving the pursuit of some further end. That final end he established as Happiness, on the grounds that no one aims at Happiness as a means of achieving something else, but that there are many subsidiary ends which are sought as a means of ultimately achieving happiness. This Happiness or Good is defined for man as the *energeia*, or occupation and activity, of the soul in conformity to virtue, and if more than one virtue must be admitted, then it is the best and most final virtue. This Happiness, as activity of the soul, while requiring some minimum level of physical provisioning, is relatively independent of the vicissitudes of fortune. From this point on, in a very long and exhaustive analysis of Happiness and the manner of its achievement, Aristotle surveys the aspects of the soul and the virtues which pertain to it. These will include intellectual virtues, like Wisdom and Good Sense, and moral virtues, like Liberality (the common translation) and Soundness of Mind or Moderation.

All that follows in his examination of these various virtues is profoundly practical, as is his citation of the common opinion of mankind as a support of his definition of the final human Good as Happiness.[12] The virtues result from action, or, better, correct action, for they are not inherent in people but are developed by repetition of proper behavior as a matter of habit. The situation regarding the senses is reversed, since there we see because we have eyes,

*19* When Rembrandt painted Aristotle he broke with classical representations of the philosopher, and made him a contemporary. The Greek world is brought to mind, however, by the bust of Homer on which Aristotle rests his hand. (The Metropolitan Museum of Art. Purchased with special funds and gifts of friends of the Museum, 1961. (61.198))

whereas in the matter of moral virtue, we do not act rightly because we have a virtue. We develop that virtue in the soul by consistent right action. By Aristotle's definition, "Virtue is a deliberately chosen permanent state, representing the mean between two extremes in regard to ourselves and which is ascertained by calculation, and in the manner in which a man of good sense would determine it."[13]

Having asserted that moral virtue is a mean, Aristotle offers practical advice on the manner of finding that mean, and then argues the case to show that the acquisition of the virtues lies within our power and depends on our voluntary choice. A large part of the work is then given over to discussion of specific virtues, such as Courage, Soundness of Mind or Moderation, Liberality,

Magnificence, Greatness of Soul, Proper Concern for Honor, Easiness of Temper, and a number of other assets of character, as well as an exploration at great length of the virtue of Justice, so that the manner of achieving it by an individual can be understood.

Turning from the virtues of the character to the intellectual virtues, Aristotle relates these to the nature and aspects of the soul. Of the two parts of the soul, the rational and the irrational, the rational is adapted to address itself to first principles, which do not change, by a capability which can be called scientific, and deals with subjects which admit of change by an ability termed deliberative. The intellectual virtues, among which Aristotle numbers five which can produce truth, namely Technical Skill, Knowledge, Good Sense, Wisdom, and Mental Capability, include a broad range of what we would include under the designation of intellectual ability. All these intellectual virtues, as well as the moral virtues and then a wide range of character flaws and praiseworthy features of character, are all treated as attributes of the soul, so that when Aristotle comes to his final assessment of and repeated argument for Happiness as the End, he can deal with Happiness in terms of the soul in order to present that Happiness which is the most perfect. That Happiness must accord with the highest virtue, and it is the Happiness which Aristotle calls the *theoretike*, usually translated "contemplation." The Happiness of Contemplation suits the best in us, and it provides among its benefits a pleasure which is most steady, sweetest, and self-sustaining, and it suits the aspect of humanity which partakes of the divine. Thus, returning to the concept of the types of life treated earlier, the Life of Politics, which Aristotle allowed as acceptable and virtuous, is nevertheless inferior to that highest life, the Life of Contemplation, which, he claims, provides the highest and most permanent happiness. It is, of course, a judgment which we should expect of a philosopher, but there are probably many people active in the Life of Politics who would readily admit that he might be right.

The conclusion will only work, however, so long as virtues are regarded as attributes of the soul and Happiness its condition or activity. There are some parallels between Aristotle's conclusion that the highest happiness is to be evaluated in terms of the activity of the soul and the Socratic view that the most important human concern is the improvement of and concern for the quality of the soul. Both points of view assign to the soul the most important place in the makeup of the human being, and both concur that in this makeup in which the soul plays so important a role, soul is present in the total being, and can be dealt with in terms of the perceptions available to the senses and the intellect. In this sense, Aristotle might be seen to have continued on from the discussions of Socrates, and he might have explored further the implications of the egalitarianism implicit in Socrates' position, particularly in view of the fact that such issues, exposed by the difficulty of defining "natural" states such as slavery and freedom, present him with difficulties. But to Aristotle, the difficulty presented by slavery was not the problem of defining a condition in which any participant might pursue the proper activity of the soul with a clearer vision than many a free person, but rather the fact that it could not be said that some people were by nature slaves, others free: a free individual might be enslaved, even by a just act such as war. How was one to treat such a situation, particularly in view of the fact that a so-called "free" person, required to earn a living by menial labor, might live a much more constrained and illiberal life than a slave who, well treated or in a more liberal occupation, could pursue most of the occupations ordinarily associated with freedom?[14] The issue was certainly less vital than that which flowed from the assumption that the soul was the proper concern, and that the activity of the soul was that which, when pursued in accordance with justice and goodness, ultimately produced the highest happiness.

Aristotle's orientation in determining the quality of highest happiness as the Life of Contemplation had been strongly affected by Plato. However much he accepted the Socratic notion that the goodness to which the soul must conform to achieve happiness is human goodness, and the kind of human goodness which is related to the soul and not the body, he has still taken over the idea of perfection, as he indicates by remarking in *Nicomachean Ethics* that "happiness is a certain activity of the soul pursued in accord with perfect goodness."[15] Thus the service of the soul, which in Socratic terms is the highest human activity and which can be seen to offset any potential benefit of other activities, is carried on not as an end in itself but as the process which best leads to the final end of the human, the most perfect happiness. This happiness must fulfill defined conditions which include not only character traits and intellectual attributes, but some modicum of bodily comfort as well. Rejecting the position that the Good, or any of the goods, were independent of phenomena, he accepted that they were recognizable through experience, and thus definable. And at the same time, choosing to accept a certain validity of human consensus to establish knowledge in a scientific manner rather than by a "memory" of an immortal soul, as Plato proposed, Aristotle was forced to include among the goods and the virtues a whole galaxy of subsidiary characteristics which were accepted as good not only by thinkers and the upper class of educated Greeks of his own day, but which had come down as a legacy from preceding generations. Once Plato had muddied the water, so to speak, Aristotle could not be the free agent that Socrates had been, unfettered by a system which had proposed the hypothesis of an ideal Good. He was forced to do, in a different sense, what he had credited Socrates with doing, "bringing philosophy down from the heavens," to place it among people and propose principles of scientific enquiry according to which knowledge of the Good, like anything else, could be achieved.

There was one other attribute to Aristotelian happiness in the Life of Contemplation, probably also elicited in response to Plato. This is the assertion that contemplation is not only the highest activity of humanity, but is also the activity of that part of man most like the gods, that is, the intellect. For, Aristotle says, the activity of the gods in their blessedness is also contemplation, and it is thus the Life of Contemplation which is most like the life of the gods.[16]

Thus dealing with the divine, Aristotle seems to have accepted without much comment the common conceptions of the multiplicity of gods, but he also proposed a divine force of unity and priority to all else in the cosmos. For Aristotle, this was essential, not so much in the areas of ethics or moral philosophy, but to his system of explaining the physical universe. The motions of the objects in that universe, motions which Aristotle accepted as genuine, required some ultimate generator of activity, since in his conception of the cosmos, nothing began out of nothing, the universe was eternal and had always existed, and within that system, all phenomena were moving or changing (the two, motion and change, were equivalent processes). Since nothing can move of its own stimulus, or cause its own change, every motion or change in the cosmos must be caused by something else, something external to itself, generating the process of change, which moves everything in the universe from its actuality at a given time to the realization of its potential. In terms of the universe itself, for the universe to experience motion, that impulse must be external, and come from outside the universe, a mover which must also be, as the universe itself is, immortal. This is Aristotle's Prime or Unmoved Mover, god.

Aristotle's god is also related to the explanation of the functioning of the celestial sphere as the necessary and primary impulse to the eternal revolving motion of the celestial bodies.[17] At the center of a spherical cosmos is the earth, also a globe; working outwards are spheres, each carrying one of the moon, the sun, and the planets, in succession, until the furthest sphere is reached, the one which carries fixed stars. All these spheres rotate on axes, but axes of different polarities and with different speeds, so that the motions are different. The motion of each sphere affects and combines with the motions of the adjacent spheres, and those compound motions account for the apparent orbits of the bodies in the heavens. All the motion originates with god, the perfect being, which by mere existence imparts *energeia* – activity – to the entire universe.

The characteristics and the life which the Prime Mover enjoys are defined in accordance with the principles which Aristotle has perceived and demonstrated in other researches; it moves other things, for example, by its quality as an object of desire, for being itself the Good, it can cause movement as the object of desire, for the Good is desired,[18] and so it can cause movement without moving itself, and in the manner consistent with Aristotle's view of motion overall. In other regards, it is actuality rather than potentiality, and the life which it leads is of necessity the best life, and permanently the best or even better than any experience with which we are familiar. That best life is the life of thought, so that the Prime Mover spends its eternity in the sole function of thought, with itself as the object of that thought. This god, this being separate from the universe, the life of which is eternal thought, is the only perfection which exists, as a perfection which exists only of itself and for its own activity, forever happy, the best immortal living being.[19] It does not act on the world, but by its nature impassive and uninterested, it indirectly inspires and attracts all activity and all motion in the universe.

After all his pragmatism, after all his insistence on knowledge deriving in the first instance from the information provided by sense perception, and despite his frequent attacks on Plato's conception of ideal and separate perfect forms which in some way inform the phenomena of the world of perception and change, Aristotle ultimately yields to the seductive force of the Platonic hypothesis of some separate existence of a kind of perfection. It is true that he does not follow Plato in his challenge to the world of the senses, and it is true also that his perfect god is not an idea which our sense objects imitate or partake of in some way in the manner of Plato's "world of becoming." His system also allows for process in the world, which impels phenomena to move from potentiality to actuality, ultimately moved by attraction of the distant and separate god. Nevertheless, the system preserves some of Plato's quality of transcendence by positing a being of perfection which is outside nature, and which, however impassively, is the fundamental influence on the natural processes which cannot be explained totally in themselves. Indeed, the very term "metaphysical" which was used of Aristotle's work only to designate it as coming in logical sequence "after the Physics" as the Greek is properly translated, now comes to designate philosophical speculation or concepts which transcend nature and physical reality.

In Aristotle's system, each thing has its form, the form of the actualization which determines its ultimate nature, and all natural processes, impelled by the relationship with the *energeia* of the Prime Mover, operate to move each object toward the actualization of its form. Just as Plato could conceptualize an ideal state for which he proposed at least the possibility of realization, so Aristotle's system conceives of the actualization of Constitutions in their perfected form. There are states which are better by their nature and states which have better realized their nature. So too there are people who are better by nature, whose inherent forms qualify them for a life and a role in the world higher than that suitable to those of inferior nature. Not everyone, in other words, is suited for the Life of Contemplation, nor are most people, by their natures, even inclined toward the political life. This is a different orientation from that of Socrates, for whom everyone could at least attempt to improve the soul.

Aristotle's basic interpretation of the world would not be likely to lead to any revolutionary assessment of the position of the individual in society, or rejection of the essential Hellenic values with which he and most upper-class Greeks were familiar. Indeed, this concept of the distant, separate, and impassive deity could serve to enforce values and attitudes, for it might be seen to follow that if god does not care, then this "middle world" of our perceptions is pretty much as it is supposed to be, with the different features of living beings and of social structure merely working toward the fulfillment of their essential nature in a process which people cannot really affect. It is an attitude which, in fact, will surface again in the centuries which followed. In a sense, Aristotle's system is an attempt to strike a compromise between what was to him the necessary connection between sense perception and scientific knowledge, and Plato's proposal of the existence of a world of Forms. His writing, though it changed the scientific world and wrought a fundamental change in the history of western thought, nevertheless left intact a set of concepts about form, about actualization, and about perfection. Much as Aristotle liked to cite the reasonable and limited propositions of Socrates, he did not carry on from Socrates' fundamental insight into human life and society which so undermined both trappings of power and rewards for its service. There were, to Aristotle, constraints of nature which made it impossible for him even to conceive of the realization of the vision of Socratic humanity.

# Part Four

# The expansion of Hellenism

# 14

# Point of departure

## *The orientation and impact of Alexander the Great*

More than any other figure in our history, Alexander the Great shows us success on the grand scale. His accomplishments seem almost beyond comprehension, with a scope so extensive that its physical dimensions cannot be grasped easily, and with effects so broad and so durable that we are still evaluating them. He is, as everyday language might put it, "too much." Too much campaigning and marching over too much territory, too much force of personality and character for even his contemporaries to grasp, so that he lies beyond the pale of ordinary understanding, so much done by a man so little understood that it is small wonder that of all great figures of antiquity, Alexander stands outside the perception of our literature. There are no great plays about him, poems to depict him, novels to follow him. He defeats even the imagination.

This young man, succeeding to his father's mighty kingdom at only 20, took an army of Macedonians and Greeks with their experienced generals more than twice his age along a campaign trail of 10,000 miles or more, conquered a vast empire before his death at 33 and left us an inheritance of questions as well as accomplishments. That he changed the world there is no doubt, but beyond the narrower questions of how he did it and what his intentions were, lies the overriding problem of understanding what the nature of that change was, what long-range effects arose from his conquest of the Persian Empire and the establishment of Greek kingdoms throughout the east.

The geography is easy enough. After his succession in 336 BC, Alexander fought a series of rapid campaigns to demonstrate that Philip's sudden death left Macedonia in no less able hands. Border troubles were quelled, and a revolt in Greece came to a devastating end, as Alexander demonstrated his ruthlessness with a defeat of Thebes and a sack of the city so complete that only the house of Pindar was left standing, acts symbolic of Alexander's devotion both to Greek literature and his own security. By 334 he was ready to set off on the expedition against Persia for which his father had been preparing. Toward the end of the next year he stood at Issus, in north-west Syria, where he

20 Tradition represented the ferocious Alexander as a man thoughtful, almost gentle, with his head inclined and his eyes turned skyward, as Plutarch noted and as this bust shows him. It is a Roman copy of a Greek original and now is in the Capitoline Museum, Rome.

administered a shattering defeat to the Great King, Darius III of Persia. Then, after a seven-month seige of Tyre, Alexander arrived in Egypt, and spent the rest of 332 and on into 331 dealing with Egyptian affairs. During this time he visited the famed oracle of Ammon at Siwah, where he received a revelation which confirmed or implied that Zeus, and not Philip, was his father. He also spent some time founding a city on the Egyptian coast, a city he called

Alexandria, which was to become his greatest foundation, and he was crowned in Memphis as a legitimate Egyptian pharaoh.

It was now 331, and Alexander was back in Syria. Darius now made diplomatic attempts to turn the attack aside, but Alexander would have nothing of compromise nor share the rule. He was right, as it turned out, for he defeated Darius again, in September, at Gaugamela, in the battle which was to be the Persian's last. Darius fled before Alexander, as the young king proceeded to Babylon and onward into Persia itself by early 330. Alexander caught up with him only after he had been murdered by one of his governors. In late spring of 330, with Darius dead, Alexander could claim himself to be the Great King, and the march might seem to be over.

It was only the beginning. Alexander hurried the army on to Parthia and Aria, what is today north-east Iran, and then, after dealing with trouble in his rear, marched south into the wild mountainous country of eastern Iran. The army was far from home, in the wild and remote mountains of the east, and Alexander showed no intention of returning to enjoy the spoils of victory. For three years he and his forces moved back and forth across what is today Afghanistan, up into south Russia as far as Tashkent, eastwards into the Hindu Kush, fighting a series of guerrilla wars with local leaders. Finally, with the most important of his enemies defeated or killed, in the late spring of 327 he took the army across the mountains into India, descending into the Punjabi region of northern Pakistan. Another year and a half would pass, filled with campaigning and victories, before the soldiers, now at an eastern tributary of the Indus River and heading for the Ganges, had had enough. They refused to go on, and despite Alexander's dramatic attempts to persuade them to follow him, they remained obdurate; it was the king who yielded. In the spring of 325 he moved out, marching south and fighting campaigns as he went, until finally, after moving up and down the Indus, he went westwards through the desert, with the army suffering dreadful thirst and privation on the way, until finally they all reached Carmania in southern Iran early in 324.

Here they rested and celebrated with a Dionysiac comus, a religious revel dedicated to Dionysus. Alexander then proceeded further west, back to Persepolis and Susa, where he recognized the relations of his officers with native women and performed a mass marriage of eighty officers. Alexander himself married two native women, although he had already married the half-Greek Barsine after Issus, and in Sogdiana the Princess Roxane. In the summer of 324 the Greeks heard from him. At the Olympic Games of that year, Alexander's decree regarding exiles was read out: all the cities were to take back their exiles. It was a convenient manner of solving the problem of the mercenaries whom Alexander wanted settled somewhere for safety's sake, and it was also a clear demonstration that Alexander was alive, well, and perfectly willing to intervene in the affairs of the Greeks. The year ended with a campaign in Media, and Alexander's descent in spring down to Babylon where, overriding prophecies with some hesitation, he brought the army inside the walls. There, after a sickness of several days which followed a drinking party, he died on 10 June 323 BC. The troops were devastated, but the generals were ready to act.

During Alexander's sickness, as the mourning soldiers filed past the sickbed on which the feverish and speechless Alexander lay, the leading officers had time to agree upon a course of action if the king should die. When he did, Perdiccas, perhaps the most senior on the scene, was made guardian of the man who was to act as king, Alexander's half-brother Arrhidaeus, now renamed Philip Arrhidaeus. At the same time the right of inheritance was ratified for Alexander's son, should Roxane, now pregnant, bear a son. Other generals were given provinces to administer as satraps, a title taken over from Persian practice. Antipater, Philip's old general, received Greece and Macedonia. Craterus, a veteran leader of the foot-companions, having been named "protector" of the kingdom, was in Cilicia, and he remained there for a while. Of the younger generals, Ptolemy received Egypt, Lysimachus Thrace. Antigonus was assigned western Turkey, while the secretary Eumenes was sent to take over Cappadocia and Pamphylia on the southern coast of Turkey, and lesser appointments went to others. All these decisions and arrangements took about a week to complete, and then, as Ptolemy first left hurriedly to the security of Egypt, the satraps scattered to their posts. For better or worse, the world was in the hands of Alexander's generals.

Who were these men, and what was their experience? What had they thought they were achieving when Alexander was alive, and what would their goals be now that he was dead? What, indeed, had Alexander thought he was doing when he started out? How much can be explained by the early experience of Alexander and his friends at Philip's court, with the association of Ptolemy, Perdiccas, and Leonnatus of the pages? They all must have felt the effects of Aristotle's teaching, if they did not in fact join him and Alexander at Mieza, possibly along with the sons of Antipater, who was a friend and admirer of the philosopher. There have been many attempts to relate Alexander's activities to some texts of Aristotle, but there is no direct evidence for the influence, and Alexander's behavior can be explained as easily as that of a pragmatic politician and general as that of an idealistic world reformer impelled to his task by philosophy. The teaching of Aristotle was certainly not the only Hellenic influence on the youth[1] and we can hardly make it precise or related to specific doctrine, but, perhaps more pervasive and permanent, affecting not only Alexander's view of politics and the world but that of the successors who were educated with him – their fundamental assumptions about the nature of society and government, even about humankind itself. They were part of Aristotle's own inheritance of Hellenism, as it was understood by him, and as they framed the specifics of his views about ethics and politics. As transmitted to his students they provided the intellectual framework within which they thought, and the basis for their own rationale of behavior and actions.[2]

Aristotle's Hellenism would have been particularly attractive and influential among these young Macedonians, a prince and his nobles who saw themselves as men of action. Aristotle's long struggle with Plato had forced him to examine the seductive notion that there was another, higher reality beyond the reach of sense perception, and which in fact beggared the physical world of the senses. An idea which would always attract sedentary professors and theologians had not been very convincing to Dionysius of Syracuse in Plato's own time, and it would probably have irritated Alexander and amused Philip. Fortunately for both, Aristotle had rejected it, and although Platonism would return in later centuries to control the parameters of thought, in Aristotle's and Alexander's time, at least, the willingness to wrestle with perceived phenomena as the only data with which to deal could be an unchallenged principle of thought and investigation. "What you see is what you get," might be a byword, or perhaps, "what you see is what you must deal with." Just as the subjection of observations about animals and plants to hypothesis and analysis could produce understanding and conclusions of greater or lesser probability, so too, with perhaps less precision, observations of a different sort could produce guides and conclusions about ethics and politics which were valid not for some other world but for this one, and thus valuable for its occupants here and now. To this end all the teachings of Aristotle, discernible from his lecture notes on logic and language, on the characteristics and behavior of animals, on motion and the causes of existence, both in the world and in the heavens, would have trained Alexander and his pages in the proper manner of investigating things and understanding them.

There is no doubt that this basic philosophical stance established the patterns of thought for Alexander and his immediate successors. With nothing contradictory between Aristotle's concept of a divine prime mover and the concepts and practices of conventional Greek religion, even so theoleptic or "god-taken" a person as Alexander has been thought to be could blend Aristotelian pragmatism and rationalism with service to any deities he might encounter in his lifetime. Indeed, the Aristotelian concept that the opinions of intelligent men were an acceptable guide to truth justified his – and his successors' – endorsement and propagation in Hellenized form of the cults of the territories they conquered and controlled. And Aristotle's deep interest in the collection and interpretation of data would be carried on with the support, if not of Alexander himself, as has often been alleged, at least of several of his successors. The famous library and museion of Alexandria, so much part of the conception of royal patronage for the Ptolemies, owes its conceptualization to Aristotelian interests,[3] with the attention to literary and philological matters, to natural history, mathematics, astronomy, and measurements and study of the earth, to anatomy and medicine.

Of the after-effects of Aristotle's teaching through its influence on others of Alexander's young friends, there is much less to say. Some died before Alexander himself; others passed quickly from the scene in the struggles over the succession, while still others disappear from our ken by their obscurity after the passing of the leader. After Ptolemy, the one whose intellectual interests we know best is Lysimachus, who managed to live on until 281 BC, when he was defeated and killed by Seleucus. We are told specifically that he was interested in philosophy,[4] and even, as the story goes, had been a pupil of the Indian philosopher Calanus.[5] Then there is the case of Cassander, the son of Antipater, another contemporary of Alexander who, when struggling for control of Macedonia and Greece toward the end of the fourth century, chose to install a student of Theophrastus, Aristotle's successor, to rule Athens for him. Demetrius of Phalerum, who ruled Athens absolutely for ten years, from 317 until he was expelled in 307, was himself a writer and rhetorician who laid claim to the title of philosopher with moral treatises and an extensive body of writing.

Whether Aristotle's ethical teachings had any impact on Alexander and his peers or not – or, indeed, whether we need even bother with a question so framed – the fundamental outlook on human nature which Aristotle's teachings presumed would have permeated the atmosphere of youthful thought. That happiness was a state to be sought in the here and now, that the rules for the conduct of government as well as the laws of physics were discoverable by study were concepts eminently suited to the needs of men who were to attempt to create for Greeks new societies in the lands of the autocratic empires of the east. So too, Aristotle's fundamental Hellenic orientation, accepting as the supreme political good the stability of state and society, would certainly have served as a basic guide for the formulation of social goals by the new king or kings-to-be. And finally, the Aristotelian conception of the relationship between the manner in which the citizen mass of a society earned their living and the ultimate nature of that society would not have been lost on Alexander or any who might have had discussions on the matter with either the king or the philosopher.[6] The notion may have been a sort of tacit underpinning of much Greek political and social thought, but it was Aristotle who first broached it openly and presented a clear statement of the idea.

I am not suggesting that such ideas were put before the young Macedonian nobles as a kind of programmatic outline of a new world to be created. Rather, that such fundamental notions of humanity and society would have been part of the intellectual atmosphere which the teenaged future kings breathed. Whether, in fact, they even attended all or any of the sessions which Aristotle provided to Alexander for two years, these ideas provided the fundamental lines of Alexander's own intellectual development, and they could hardly have failed to affect or infect his peers. The future leaders of Hellenism thus stood at the end of a long tradition of Athenian political and ethical thought, stretching from Solon at the beginning down throught the tragedians, and passing under the influence of the Sophists and Socrates before its reformulation by Plato and then Aristotle.

Of course, the influences on the leaders of the succeeding generations were by no means exclusively Athenian. Many of the leaders of the expedition,

Alexander's close associates for the ten years of marching, were neither Athenians nor Macedonians who would have benefited from Aristotle's teaching. Nearchus came from Crete; he joined the inner circle quite early, was one of those whom Philip banished from Alexander's circle along with Ptolemy, and ended his career as admiral of the fleet and a writer on India after Alexander died. Like him, there were other non-Macedonians close to Alexander and exiled with Nearchus and Ptolemy, who were appointed as Companions to high position when Alexander was king; for example, Laomedon, who knew a barbarian language and was early given charge of barbarian captives, and, surviving Alexander, became Satrap of Syria. There were over a dozen Greeks among Alexander's officers with the title Companion, and in addition to these personages of rank, there were, apparently, a number of Greeks of perhaps poor talent who made up a literary coterie which joined Alexander's closest circle, not to mention some very distinguished Greeks, like the seer Aristander from Telmessus, and the philosopher Anaxarchus from Abdera. Above all there was Callisthenes from Olynthus, a nephew of Aristotle and the most notable of the intellectuals to accompany the expedition. Greek writers like Aristobulus and Onesicritus accompanied the expedition to write histories of the campaign, and the sources present a picture of busy activity for all these men. Alexander listened to readings by Aristobulus and Onesicritus from their histories, Onesicritus himself serving as envoy to and consultant with the Indian gymnosophists. Callisthenes spoke at banquets to regale the Macedonians with demonstrations of eloquence and was detailed at Babylon to gather up the data from an alleged 31,000 years of astronomical observations by the Babylonians. During the ten years of marching, the influence of these men and many others like them must have been felt in the development of the characters and ideas of the generals at headquarters who would rule the world after Alexander's death, compounding and probably widening the effects of the Hellenism which Aristotle brought to many of them when they were young.

There was, however, more to their formation than that brought by the Greeks; there was another, enormously powerful influence, that of Alexander himself. One could hardly overstate the effect on others of that wild, brilliant, crafty, and emotional personality. Through the centuries writers about Alexander have emphasized the extraordinary power of his character which, combined with unrestrained energy, courage, and tactical sense, made him as irresistible a man as he was a general. He gathered up in one all the Hellenic civilization and rationalism which Aristotle and the other Greeks could give him, but did not lose a demonic quality which his willingness to live and appear larger than life exploited. A terror to his friends, in all probability, throughout his reign, he came to the end of his life as fearful of them and their plots as they were of his intentions. If there is any validity to the picture presented by our sources, he was overwhelmingly proud, fearless in battle almost to foolhardiness, ambitious in totality and unable to compromise, a heavy and moody drinker, subject to violent fits of anger and emotion, demanding of complete loyalty, and suspicious almost beyond conception. Could such a personality fail to have a great impact on his companions and successors? The impact would be particularly strong in view of his intense and continual involvement with religious matters,[7] a characteristic sometimes laid at the door of his mother by moderns, who are quick to take ancient hints to find the cause in Olympias. Scholars, being, in general, male, are delighted to find an explanation for what they see as irrationality in the dire influence of a woman. While there is little doubt that Alexander was strongly devoted to and influenced by his mother, and may well have felt the effects of being raised by a strong-willed woman, particularly since his father was away on campaign for much of his childhood, we need hardly go so far as to imagine that Olympias was some kind of exceptionally god-struck devotee of Dionysus, swept up in a frenzy of cult,[8] transmitting to an impressionable youth a permanent distortion of character which made him incline to a superstitious religiosity.

As I have written elsewhere, Alexander was a Greek and a Macedonian; as such he could be expected to show respect for the gods of Hellas in general, of his own people in particular, and of foreigners in any circumstances where they might hold some power. Nothing of the account of his life or his expedition shows him behaving in any manner not suitable to his station or his culture. He attended to the special divinities of the Macedonians and the gods of the Greeks, and observed the cults of the gods of the places he visited. Belief is hardly to the point, although there is no reason at all for us to suppose hypocrisy in anything religious which Alexander did, and the important thing is action. If at least one ancient writer, Arrian, saw Alexander as the most religious of men,[9] the comment was approving, not challenging to his intelligence or honesty. His generals saw him consult oracles – Delphi and Siwah most memorably – and many seers to discern the will of the gods. They would witness again and again how careful he was always to propitiate local gods, in religious customs which regularly observed, as Greek religion always did, the connections between specific divinities and specific places. But they never saw him relax his attention to what the sources call variously his "usual gods," his "customary gods," and his "national gods." And they could also see the manner in which he attended to the cults of the gods in the new places which fell under his sway, how he made sure that he and the Hellenes and Macedonians with him paid proper service to Isis, Ammon, Osor-Hapi in Egypt, Marduk of Tyre, Bel of Babylon.

The patterns of religion which Alexander set were carried on with little change by his successors. Where we can follow developments at all closely, as in the religious practices of the first two Ptolemies, there seems to be no doubt at all about this. Item after item of procedure and practice attested in the time of Alexander recur under his Egyptian-based successor. Temples to traditional Greek gods appear throughout the land, and traditional Greek practice was followed by the Greeks who settled in the countryside. At the same time, the king dutifully and obviously served the cults of local gods, offering donations to the Egyptian priests and temples and carrying on major hieratic construction in the traditional Egyptian manner. The Greeks were introduced to the local divinities, and Hellenized versions of cults of Egyptian deities were provided, even to the extent of importing a statue of Serapis from abroad so that the Greeks and Macedonians could serve and feel comfortable with the gods of the place. Even the characteristic Ptolemaic dynastic cult, with its extensive and complex establishment of priests to attend to the worship of Alexander and then later sovereigns, built on practices which Alexander had used, and even these, going back as they did at least to Alexander's father Philip, were not original with the conqueror.

When Alexander left his generals and companions on their own as heirs of his empire, he left them with the heritage of their joint Hellenic upbringing and experience together with the memory of his own personality. What they would do with their own armies and their own bureaucracies in the lands which they came to rule was enormously affected, perhaps even controlled, by the twenty-year experience in the court of Philip and then Alexander which was common to most of them. They themselves would carry the imprint of two kinds of Hellenic stamp, and they would find themselves comfortable with and would encourage in their own time and among their followers two characteristics of Hellenism which would come to particularly signify what we call Hellenistic culture. The scientific spirit exemplified and concentrated by Aristotelian rationalism continued, with its results expanded and its product specialized, attracting first-rate minds like those of Euclid, Archimedes, Apollonius of Perga, Eratosthenes, Theophrastus, and many, many others. Advances of knowledge and skill in physics, mechanics, botany, zoology, astronomy, and mathematics were stunning, establishing a floor under scientific knowledge for all future generations, and providing in most fields a body of knowledge beyond which there were few advances until the Renaissance. None of this, however, permeated much of popular culture, which rather was marked by that other aspect of Hellenism, traditional religiosity, which saw the world as controlled by forces which, if not irrational, were far more powerful than humans or anything which humans could bring to bear, and which must be dealt with not by science or reason but by cult and prayer. If Alexander feared the gods and felt the need to propitiate them, his successors would do no less, and if all these kings with all their power ultimately depended on the divine goodwill for their well-being, ordinary folk would hardly dare to differ.

The expansion of cults and so-called "mystery" religions across the Mediterranean basin during the period after Alexander has often been noted, sometimes even called the hallmark of the times. Worship of Isis, of Serapis, of Syrian goddesses, and even the expansion of the Hebrew faith can be found from Syria in the east all the way west to Italy and Spain. Yet it has not so often been noted that these cults were essentially Hellenic in character, however foreign the origin of the deities might have been, and that the efflorescence of religious activity in the period followed the noble precedent of Alexander and fitted quite comfortably into the established patterns of Greek religion. Indeed, the cults of more traditional Greek gods prospered as well, with the Eleusinian mysteries flourishing, and cult centers to Zeus under many guises, to Hermes Trismegistus, and to the healing god Asclepius planted and expanding at center after center in the Mediterranean. Many of these cults, served devoutly by the successors to Alexander for 300 years after his death, provided the major religious outlet for millions of Greeks and Hellenized natives in the cities and countryside of the lands that surrounded the Mediterranean Sea, and the religious literature which emanated from priests and laymen alike generated a blend of religious and philosophical teaching which owed a great deal to the religious and philosophical literature which had been firmly established as Hellenic before Alexander was born.

The career and expedition of Alexander the Great have often been called a watershed in human history. The conquests are meant by this notion, of course, conquests which as "watershed" are seen to have spread Hellenes and Hellenism across thousands of miles of the east, to mix with and learn from many different peoples and thereby to create a new Hellenism, modified and enriched by oriental ideas, to be passed on to the future. The "blending" of cultures is exaggerated, often drastically, as we have come to realize after 150 years of scholarship, and the age of Alexander is today seen much less as a turning-point in the history of Hellenism. The "Hellenistic" world is now understood much more as building upon what had gone before, and so the idea of the watershed loses force. On the other hand, the advent of royal patronage and the support of the kings for cultural, intellectual, and religious efforts gave a great impetus to the expansion of Hellenism, so that it spread with new vigor. And, in a way, Alexander and his generals had the effect not so much of creating something new in the history of Hellenism than of returning to more traditional modes of thought. Apart from the impact of Aristotelianism in the narrow and perhaps more pragmatic natural and physical sciences, the orientation of the kings was felt more in its endorsement of long-standing Greek attitudes towards gods and the divine. Aristotle's concern to deal with the world in terms of the information achieved through sense perception, which was in the first instance philosophically grounded and intended to influence philosophy, was focused and narrowed into science, perhaps at the behest of kings who understood it that way, while philosophy was allowed to return to the earlier habits of pure speculation which had ultimately produced Platonism.

Thus Alexander and his generals did far more than conquer the Persian Empire, and their effects went much beyond the establishment of a group of Hellenic kingdoms in the territories of the old oriental autocracies. They provided a kind of "point of departure" for all the Greeks and Macedonians who went out into the far-flung reaches of the Persian Empire to establish new centers of Hellenism. Alexander and his generals were from youth all bene-ficiaries of a "state of mind" which was generated at the Macedonian court while Philip was still alive, and was preserved and expanded as the young men grew in age and experience along the long route to the east. This state of mind was, of course, royal and aristocratic, neither supportive of nor congenial to the faint flickerings of egalitarianism implicit in the ideals of Socrates in the century before, nor to the reality of the expanded democracy of Athens in the late fifth century. And if there had been any possibility that the pragmatism and political realism of Aristotle might have returned political philosophy back to the days of Socrates and away from the authoritarianism and idealism of Plato, that opportunity was lost with the advent of Alexander and his generals. By the time the kings and their successors had sat on their thrones for 300 years, they had destroyed any vestiges of that impulse to individual freedom and equality which Socrates had brought to a Hellenic environment which was in any case hostile to such ideas. This, I fear, is the true legacy of Alexander.

# 15

# A world of kings

*Kingship, political history, and
literary and scientific developments
after Alexander*

Like a flower which leaves behind its blossoming a pod of seeds which will scatter a multitude of future generations, Alexander left his empire with generals and officers who would grow in power and ambition until they burst the pod to become kings in their own right. The generals, of course, had not been totally unprepared when the flower fell from the stalk. During the long march east they had doubtless discussed what would be done if Alexander should die – certainly when he lay gravely wounded, or in his tent threatening to starve himself to death after he had killed his friend Cleitus. His ten-day final illness gave them the opportunity to plan, and they had come to a basic agreement by the time he died. Interests differed, notably between the foot-soldiers and the more exalted cavalry forces, but the disagreements which must have been violently expressed during those ten days are obscured by the settlement which was forced by the fatal outcome of the king's illness.

The agreement which emerged was conditioned by the fundamental nature of Macedonian kingship. It was not a territorial rule, but personal, based upon the relationship between the king and the nobles who accepted his leadership. It was, therefore, the same kind of kingship which had been accorded Philip when Macedonia was weak that had to be taken up now that the Macedonians had conquered vast tracts of the east. Basically hereditary, the kingship nevertheless must devolve with the consent of the Macedonian nobles or generals, and if there were no clear heir, as was the case at this time, they could and did take charge for the time being. As a compromise between opposing views, two kings were chosen, a grown man and an embryo. Arrhidaeus, the half-brother of Alexander, choice of the infantry despite his reputed feeble-mindedness, was made king immediately; this decision overruled the proposal by the cavalry of waiting to see if the pregnant Roxane would produce a boy; but it was agreed that if a boy was actually born Arrhidaeus would rule jointly with him. Roxane did produce a boy, who ruled as Alexander IV, along with the now renamed Philip Arrhidaeus.

All this was form, at least for the moment, as the generals surely knew, and the reality of power would be expressed through the governorships or satrapies which were parcelled out, notably, Egypt to Ptolemy, Greece to Antipater, Thrace to Lysimachus, western Asia Minor to Antigonus. Although the generals agreed that the kingship would continue *pro tem*, for some that also meant *pro forma*, and the first years after Alexander's death were filled with conflict over the issue of the independence of the governors, most of whom refused to bow to centralized authority. By 320, a conference at Triparadeisus in North Syria ratified the original assignment of provinces. The conference, which tacitly disavowed a central control, still brought no peace, but ten years of war and the stalemate which followed wrought no real change in the structure. The next conference, in 311, brought another treaty agreeing to the usual division of zones – Egypt to Ptolemy, Thrace to Lysimachus, Asia to Antigonus, and Macedonia to Antipater's son Cassander until the young son of Alexander, Alexander IV, reached maturity. To secure his position, Cassander killed the child, but that fact was ignored, deliberately, for more than five years by the generals, who continued to rule as governors for the dead king, for they were not yet ready to claim the title for themselves.

The conflicts which had led to a compromise settlement in 311 did not stop with that treaty. The earlier position of Antigonus as "odd man out" continued for ten more years of war, in which he was regarded as the enemy for most of the political and military alliances of the period, but the shifts in loyalties among his enemies prevented either a unified onslaught which could dispose of him or a stable defense which might be impregnable to his attack. Many Greek cities found themselves drawn into the conflicts, as the warring generals waved an "independence" at them which in reality was limited to selection of sides. Ptolemy remained secure in Egypt, as did Cassander in Macedonia and Greece for the most part, controlling Athens as well through his loyal supporter, Demetrius of Phalerum. In Syria, Seleucus gained Babylon, while in Cyprus, Ptolemy's overseas forces brought him mastery of the island. None of this was very stable, for in 307, Demetrius, son of Antigonus, suddenly grasped control of Athens. Next he engaged Ptolemy's naval forces off Cyprus, demolished the Egyptian fleet and took control of the island, but then tried a follow-up attack on Egypt itself, which ended in disaster. In the end, the issue was decided at Ipsus in 301, where the combined forces of Seleucus, Lysimachus, and Cassander destroyed the army of Antigonus and Demetrius. Antigonus died in the battle and Demetrius survived only by fleeing the field.

The domains could now be called kingdoms, because in the course of all this, the generals had begun to call themselves kings. After Demetrius' victory over Ptolemy's fleet at Cyprus in 306, Antigonus, exhilarated by the victory, we are told, "assumed the diadem and from then on used the title king."[1] He granted Demetrius the same honor and form of address. According to Plutarch, the masses first addressed Antigonus as king, and he was given the diadem by his friends; he then himself accorded the title to Demetrius. However it actually happened, it did not stop with these two. Ptolemy soon took the same title, probably after his successful defense of Egypt and defeat of Demetrius' attack in the next year; and Seleucus, Lysimachus, and Cassander too soon called themselves kings. Thus the last years of the fourth century saw the conflict not of generals, satraps, or governors but of kings, and when Antigonus was carried off the field of Ipsus, or when Demetrius fled, the troops were watching the conduct of kings. So too the victors – Ptolemy, Seleucus, Lysimachus, Cassander – wore their triumphs in diadems.

What it meant for them to be kings is not so clear. They were not kings quite as Philip or Alexander had been, and they were certainly not kings like those of Sparta or of more modern nations. They were not, in fact, kings of anything, or of specific domains, but were kings by virtue of some quality which they attributed to themselves, a quality of kingship quite separate from any territories which they might control. An indication of the nature of the attributes of kingship comes from a later royal letter which alludes to best wishes for the welfare of the king, the king's friends, and his pragmata, or "affairs, concerns,"[2] with no sense that a territorial kingdom is involved at all; the new kings depended rather on the institutions and emblems of royalty patterned on Alexander, at least for their Macedonian and Greek followers, while perhaps taking on local coloration for the other peoples whom they ruled, as Ptolemy did in Egypt. Thus the courts had the official Macedonian ranks of "Friends" and "Companions" of the king, as had Alexander's court, and room was made for a coterie of intellectuals to present the image of an Alexander.

Kingship obviously also carried a religious role. Where the culture was suitable or the institutions required, the new king might fit into an established religious pattern, as did Ptolemy and his successors in Egypt. There, the native population required the traditional position of pharaoh to be filled, and thus Ptolemy became pharaoh, and so a part of Egyptian religion. As a leader of Greeks, however, he must fill different needs, and in his sense of those needs he followed the example of Alexander, so far as we can see, showing a scrupulous concern for divinity. As a result of a dream, he procured a statue of the newly discovered divinity Serapis all the way from Sinope on the Black Sea, and constructed a new temple to house it. The statue, as we can tell from the representations of it, showed the god in Hellenic form despite his Egyptian origin. For the Egyptians themselves, Ptolemy's service to Serapis was matched by his devotion to Horus, Buto, and the Apis bull, while elsewhere and outside of Egypt, we find at many sites evidence of dedications by him, his family, and his *philoi* – "friends."[3]

Ptolemy also claimed a divine ancestry, following Alexander who had emphasized his descent from Heracles. Ptolemy, we find, had that same hero as origin,[4] and he was not the only king to find that he had such a distinguished genealogy. Apollo was the ancestor of Seleucus,[5] and Demetrius was hymned with the statement that he was a son of Poseidon and Aphrodite.[6] This divine aspect of kingship advanced quickly and prominently as each of the kings received divine honors and formal cults, not only in the areas which they dominated, but in the cities of Greece and the Aegean as well. By 307 BC, Athens had established a cult of Antigonus and Demetrius, addressing them as *Soteres*, "Saviors,"[7] and Rhodes also gave Ptolemy the same title.[8] In Egypt, Ptolemy set up a cult of Alexander, establishing an institution which was to evolve into a complex religious structure with priests and ceremonies dedicated to the living kings and queens and all their royal ancestors.

In all this religious activity, there was nothing which could not be traced back to Alexander, or even Philip, although much of the earlier development is still obscure to us in the few references to Philip's activity, and for Alexander, it is only at the end of his life that we see cities reaching out to dedicate cults to him. So in religion as in so much else, the successors, although introducing nothing specifically new to Hellensim, considerably widened the scope of these concepts of kingship and applied them with greater intensity over a much greater territory.

Some of the kings who contended at Ipsus had another two decades of conflict before them, but by 280 BC all the first generation of successors to Alexander were dead. To each of the kings there was a successor, but in all the twenty years of war after Ipsus, the only changes were brought about by the son of Antigonus. Demetrius, left with only a few thousand troops after the defeat at Ipsus, basing himself on possession of coastal cities in the Levant and Asia Minor as well as a number of islands, returned to the arena of conflict and alliances with the other kings, and after a series of events which made it possible for him to gain control of Athens and restore its democracy, he was able to take advantage of weakness in Macedonia to seize power there. He was now king in Macedonia, establishing a dynasty of kings most of whom were named Demetrius or Antigonus, and despite his own later misfortunes, effectively transferring the house of Antigonus to the throne of Macedonia. This was the only shift after Ipsus, for Lysimachus had maintained control of Thrace, Seleucus of Syria, and Ptolemy of Egypt.

The accession of the next generation ushered in a new period, both politically and socially. The world might be no more at peace, but the wars would be fought for territory or reputation more than in any expectation of domination over Alexander's old empire, and there would be as much or more strife issuing from struggles over dynastic successions as between the kings of separate dynasties. A more important cause of disturbance was the eruption into Greece in 279 BC of disorderly bands of Gauls, who swept south in the next year, stopped only by heavy snows which Apollo threw in their way as they tried to reach Delphi. The Gauls turned back, yielding victory to the Greeks who had been harassing and trying to stop them, and their departure from Greece was seen as such a triumph that as far away as Cos a decree was passed congratulating the Greeks and offering thanks to Apollo for his epiphany.[9]

175

With the departure of the Gauls, Macedonia had a chance to find some peace, and for the most part, did so under the rule of Antigonus Gonatas, the son of Demetrius. He was able to maintain control of Macedonia after an uncertain start to his reign and despite the emergence of important leagues among Greek states and cities, first the Aetolian League in central Greece, and then later, the Achaean League in the Peloponnesus. Antigonus himself had the reputation of being a philhellene and something of a philosopher, a king who maintained a court in the best traditions of Alexander. He interested himself in the philosophers, invited the noted Stoic, Zeno, to Macedonia, and actually appointed a Stoic philosopher, Persaeus (a disciple of Zeno, who had come to Macedonia in his master's stead), as his governor in Corinth – where the philosopher committed suicide after losing the city in 243. Besides philosophers there were literary figures, such as the notable Aratus of Soli, composer of a long astronomical poem based on the writings of Eudemus, and Antigonus counted the respected historian Hieronymus of Cardia as a friend. While Athens remained the paramount center for philosophical study and investigation in Greece – indeed the whole world – Antigonus' court also became a comfortable place of resort for many of lesser rank who could not hope to compete with the great names of Athens for leadership in any of the schools there. It was, in fact, the only royal court with any reputation at all for philosophy, and Antigonus' reign went a long way toward bringing Macedonia back to something like the state it had known under Philip II. Northern Greece, at least, remained submissive to a king who showed himself effective, and the Greek cities could hardly fail to recognize the solidity of a leader whose behavior exemplified at least some of the philosophical ideals of the day.

Another court, famous for literary figures, scientists, and scholars rather than philosophers, was that of Ptolemy II in Alexandria. The atmosphere, safely remote from the turmoils of Greece and Macedonia, was quite different from Philip's capital of Pella in Macedonia, and Ptolemy Philadelphus was able to attract some of the most noted Greeks from all over the Mediterranean to the security of his capital, which was peaceful and secure despite the king's involvement in war in Syria, Asian Minor, and the Aegean, as he used both naval and land forces to maintain an extensive network of overseas allies and possessions. Eventually the defeat of the Egyptian fleet in the Aegean ended Ptolemy's ambitions for naval supremacy, and the general peace which followed led to a dynastic reconciliation between Egypt and Syria, whereby the Seleucid king, now Antiochus II, married Philadelphus' daughter Berenice. This settlement in Syria, and his drastically reduced involvement in the Aegean, eliminated most occasions for conflict with Antiochus. The last years of Philadelphus' reign were tranquil, and his kingdom was at peace when he died early in 245 BC.

Even such wars as he fought were no distraction from the development of Egypt for which Philadelphus is remembered. How this was done emerges from a large quantity of papyri, public and private documents, which the dry sands of Egypt have preserved, giving us one of our rare direct documentary views into everyday life in antiquity. Macedonians, Thracians, Greeks, and others were settling in Egypt in the employ of the king, obtaining allotments of land which they would farm themselves in peacetime or maintain in one way or another when off on military service with the king. Men from most major cities of the Hellenic world turn up in the royal bureaucracy, as district governors, finance officials, and military and police officers, based not only in Alexandria but fanning out over the countryside to ensure the most thorough collection of taxes. The society was confined in a tight economic structure whereby the king maintained monopolies over commodities like oil and salt and the products of mines and quarries, with prices set for some commodities, but allowed to vary from district to district as need might require.

The isolation of Egypt made this kind of economy possible, and the familiarity of the native Egyptians with this kind of tight royal control made it possible for the Ptolemies to impose the system. However unfamiliar this kind of "storehouse" economy might have been to the Greeks, who were, like us, more used to the market economy in which goods were traded and exchanged either in barter or for money, it was acceptable to the vast majority of the peasants, who probably saw little change from earlier times. The Greeks who came to Egypt, moreover, were given the opportunity to obtain land and profits, and however closely the royal officials might try to contain the goods and taxes which were to flow into the royal coffers, it is clear that Greeks and officials had the opportunity to make money in extra- and para-legal ways. Doubtless the king knew this perfectly well, but the system was so profitable anyway that a little leakage could easily be endured – so long as the control was tight enough to ensure that the losses remained small.

By and large the country remained predominantly rural, as in fact was most of the world throughout antiquity, but the settlement of the Hellenes in the little villages and towns of the countryside made the Egyptian experience quite different from that in the territories under the domination of the other kings. Whereas elsewhere the Greeks and Macedonians tended to settle in cities, either the old Greek cities of an area or in new foundations established for them by the kings, in Egypt they found it profitable to do otherwise. Although there was the great city of Alexandria, along with the old Greek city of Naucratis, and Ptolemy's new and only foundation, Ptolemais in southern Egypt, intended as a counterweight to the old Egyptian center of Thebes, none of them had much free land available from which new settlers might make livelihoods. So the countryside was the only place to settle, and the great majority of immigrants from the Greek world settled there. The king used the land to attract settlers who could serve in his army, and to establish them with stability in Egypt once they had come. Soldiers received allotments, while officials might obtain gift estates which could be so large as to encompass whole villages and their surrounding farms. Most agriculture took place on "royal land," which "royal" farmers cultivated, paying a rent beyond the usual taxes. To some extent, the king even regulated land belonging to temples, although for the most part the Ptolemies avoided the trouble which might have come from too much interference with these tracts, which were often extensive. The grip on the lands shows how the king was, as the Greek expresses it, *autokrator*, "complete master," a ruler whose authority was absolute and who could manage everything in his realm as he wished. The land was his, cultivable at his discretion and by whom he pleased; office and rank were his to grant or to take away; even the rights, privileges, and institutions of the free cities in his domain were subject to his will, to be extended or contracted as his will or power might require. There seemed, in the third century BC, to be less restriction on kings – less, even, than that to which Philip and Alexander had been subject. Only the Antigonids in Macedonia felt anything of the influence which Macedonian nobles had traditionally exercised over their kings, and even they felt free to use Greeks rather than Macedonians in positions of power both at court and in their administration of their subject cities. In general, the kings were now seen to have an authority which was limited not by principle but only by power. Theirs was the fulfilment of Aristotle's fifth kind of kingship, which exists "whenever one person is lord over all in the way that each tribe and each city is lord over the community, a kingship drawn up according to the patterns of household management."[10] Such a king one might oppose, go to war against, or call upon for aid, even plot against, or try to overthrow, but one would not deny the nature of the power even while trying to bar an individual from it.

While it is a matter of some uncertainty just how much the elaborate bureaucracy of Ptolemaic Egypt was duplicated in the dominions of the other kings, the underlying assumptions about the nature of royalty which served the Ptolemies underlay kingship elsewhere. There were gifts of land and estates to individuals attested throughout Asia Minor and the Levant at the hands of many kings,[11] and royal control over revenues could approach the detail and extent which the Ptolemies enjoyed, with peasants attached to the land in Asia Minor and Syria and soldiers given allotments in Pergamum and elsewhere. The titles, thank-offerings, and honors voted Seleucids and Antigonids took the same form as those voted the Ptolemies who were honored by free cities, while inscriptions calling upon kings to arbitrate between disputing cities illustrate the importance they had now assumed.

By the time the third Ptolemy, Euergetes, came to the throne in 246 BC, all these patterns were firmly established in Egypt, a strong kingdom which was to escape for a little while longer the troubles which were beginning to close in on the other kings. The successors of Seleucus probably faced the greatest difficulties and the most complex problems, for the regions which they controlled were the most diverse in population and tradition, and stretched over by far the greatest amount of territory which any of the kings tried to govern. From the start, the extent of the empire made its maintenance difficult, and each succeeding generation often found itself with a smaller realm, passing on a yet smaller to the next king. By the time Seleucus III succeeded in 226 BC, much important territory was gone. A series of wars with Ptolemaic Egypt, as well as dynastic quarrels and a partition of the realm, had been responsible for these losses, and even though Antiochus III, "the Great," who took the throne in 223, was to recover a great deal of the lost dominions, the dynasty had been seriously weakened by the events of the third century and would never be able to overcome some of the problems which had arisen. It always remained a much more heterogeneous realm than those of any of the other kings, founded as it was on the ruins of the old Persian domain, and within the empire were the remnants of many earlier kingdoms, peoples who could look back on earlier glory – Babylonians, Medes, Persians, Phoenicians, Hebrews, to mention just a few – and the Seleucids had to find administrators to govern them. Aside from a very few natives – 3 per cent of officials known – the Seleucids used Hellenes: Macedonians, Peloponnesians, Ionians, Athenians, citizens of any city whatsoever, so long as they were willing to come – and they used any enticements they could devise to bring them in. And instead of the Ptolemaic practice of giving the Hellenes land and holdings in the small villages and towns to live alongside the natives, Seleucid cultural and social policy was based on gathering the Greeks into cities, using some of the older settlements of the area to serve some, and founding entirely new urban centers or garrison towns to accommodate others. The Seleucids were *ktistoi* – "founders" – *par excellence*, and the first three kings of the dynasty were responsible for literally dozens of foundations from the Iranian plateau westwards through Mesopotamia, Syria, and into Asia Minor. Many were named after the kings or members of his family, so that we have a confusing number of cities with the same name of Seleuceia, Antiocheia (Antioch), Apamea (named after the mother of Seleucus I), and Laodicea (after Laodice, the wife of Antiochus II).

The Seleucid cities varied widely in their character and size. Antioch, 15 miles inland on the Orontes River, grew rapidly after Seleucus I transferred over 5000 Athenians and Macedonians from the nearby city founded by Antigonus, Antigoneia. To this group, settled in one quarter, was added a native quarter, and the numbers of Greek traders, artisans, and merchants necessitated expansion of the city later in the century. The city held a large Jewish population, who were given privileges – citizenship, according to the later Jewish writer Josephus[12] – and administrators making an important, if small, element of the population. The city itself was famed for its beauty, but apparently did not develop the kind of scientific and literary activity which Ptolemy promoted in Alexandria. Antioch and the other cities like it – Apamea, Seleuceia-in-Pieria, Laodicea-on-the-Sea, Seleuceia-on-the-Tigris, and so many others which served as administrative centers – were in fact capitals of satrapies, for the Seleucids divided their empire in somewhat the same way as had the Persian kings when they ruled these areas. They also had their own "countryside," lands controlled by the cities themselves and the officials who served civic roles. These lands were allocated to Greeks and Macedonians, perhaps some native people as well, and they formed the territory of the city much as older Greek cities had their own agricultural land surrounding the built-up, walled, and heavily populated portion of the state. Many of these cities were accorded the normal institutions of Greek *polis* life – with the Constitutions, laws, and civic and religious buildings characteristic of Hellenism for centuries. The intention on the part of the Seleucid kings seems to have been to provide their Greeks and Macedonians with a replica of the kind of life which they had left behind them in Greece, a concept quite different from that which Hellenes would find in Egypt, and one which created a social situation almost entirely different from that of the Ptolemaic realm. The concentration of the Hellenes into cities meant that any possibility of homogeneity in the empire – already by the very nature of the realm infinitely more difficult to achieve than had long been the case in the land of the Nile – was eliminated. Outside the city walls the thousands of square miles of inhabited tracts, sprinkled with native villages and farmed by locals who might rarely come into contact with Greeks, remained much as they had been for centuries. Iranian, Babylonian, Semitic customs, institutions, religion, even law and political and social structure remained largely untouched by Hellenism in most parts of the empire. Although occasionally natives might serve their Seleucid lords in an official capacity in essentially non-Hellenic centers, the upper echelon and potential leadership of many peoples of the empire seem to have receded into the countryside for a while, safely away from the cities, nursing their resources against the time when Seleucid weakness would give them the opportunity to wrest their territories away from the central government. Even in cities, in the old urban centers of the east, where the Seleucids and settled Greeks and Macedonians – the Hellenic element – were not numerous enough to provide more than an enclave within an essentially foreign environment much like the "Hellenion" of Greeks in the Memphis of the pharaohs and Persians, and there were many non-Greeks whom the Hellenic tradition never touched.

More, however, was possible in the Greek cities of long-standing traditions, those in Seleucid areas and those in the areas controlled by other kings. They had carried on an independent existence long before the advent of Alexander the Great and were not prepared to relinquish their autonomy or their pride now that kings were more powerful than city-states or even leagues of cities. Under the protection of the kings, the Hellenism of such cities often prospered, and with royal patronage, literary figures, scientists, and philosophers emerged from many cities not hitherto associated with important cultural activities. While they often did not remain in the place of their birth, their very existence as well as the contents of their writings and teachings show that their cultural background was based on a thoroughgoing Hellenism. Such was Zeno, of Citium of Cyprus, who came to Athens to study philosophy at the end of the fourth century, and remained to teach his own ideas. There was Aratus of Soli, a city in Cilicia in south-east Turkey, who accepted the patronage of two courts in his lifetime. Callimachus came to Alexandria from Cyrene, an old Greek city on the coast of Africa west of Egypt, as did the great scientist Eratosthenes. None of these cities was noted for any important literary or philosophical tradition of their own, but they contributed noted individuals who, in concert with others of literary or philosophical interests, were responsible for the creation of vital traditions in both new and old cities.

The most important literary and scientific activity of the period took place in Alexandria. Here Ptolemy II built the mouseion and library, the first a center for study and research, the second a collection of books which required cataloging, editing, and the attention of a group of learned scholars. The institutions and patronage attracted the most notable literary figures of the Greek world to Alexandria, either as permanent settlers or visitors who worked there for long periods of time. Callimachus emigrated to Alexandria while quite young, and after his arrival came to the notice of Philadelphus, who appointed him cataloguer of the library. Theocritus, who must have spent a good deal of time there before returning to Cos, was an accomplished poet before he came to Egypt. The third best-known member of the Alexandrian literary circle was Apollonius, so-called "of Rhodes" because of his later retirement there, but who in fact was a native of Alexandria itself (or, possibly, of Naucratis), a younger member of the group who studied with Callimachus.

The literary output of the Alexandrian circle in the fourth century BC exemplifies one of the strongest aspects of Hellenism in general and in its literary manifestation in particular – the conservatism in ideas and in form which honored faithful following of valued models as much as or more than the development of the novel or different. The popular taste of the Greeks in Egypt shows this clearly in the dominance of Homer, tragedy, and early Greek literature in general among the papyrus remains from Egyptian sites. As readers preferred the traditional great books of Hellenism, so the writers in Alexandria drew heavily on some of the earliest writing in Greek. The "Hymns" of Callimachus, for example, to Zeus, to Apollo, Artemis, the Island of Delos, to Athena, and to Demeter, are all patterned in form and content on the Homeric hymns, and although two use the Doric dialect, only one forsakes the traditional epic meter for elegiac couplets. The myths of gods presented in these hymns bear resemblance to the early Homeric hymns or to the myths included in the odes of Pindar, and where there are any references to matters contemporary, they are fitted into the hymns in such a way that very traditional Hellenic ideas apply to them. For example, the reference to Ptolemy Philadelphus in the "Hymn to Zeus," praising the king in that he stands before all others, comes in the context of a treatment of kings in terms of their relationship to Zeus and to justice: "From Zeus kings, for nothing is more divine than the kings of Zeus."[13] A few lines later the thought is presented that Zeus looks over those who rule the people with "crooked justice" and those who do so with straight justice, the Greek for "crooked justice" being precisely the words used by Hesiod in *Works and Days* for the crooked justices which the immortals take note of. The context into which Callimachus puts his own king and patron is that of earliest Hellenic tradition, and any morality which applies to him is that of the tradition of Hesiod.

The same conservatism can be found in the work of Callimachus' contemporary, Theocritus, who joined the literary circle of Alexandria for a time. Although he concentrated a good deal of his attention on bucolic verse, a genre which, so far as our surviving texts go, is hardly represented at all in Greek literature before him, his noted *Encomium* to Ptolemy II Philadelphus is a traditional panegyric, and the attributes of Ptolemy mentioned and praised are those which are as suitable to praises of Homeric kings as they are for a Ptolemy: Philadelphus' father is "equal in honor to the gods, and he has a golden house in the abode of Zeus, with Alexander seated by his side."[14] Theocritus praises the ancestry of Ptolemy – Heracles – and rejoices that Ptolemy Soter, the warrior, had a warrior son, and that Philadelphus is clever at wielding the spear. He praises the king's land of Egypt and his other dominions, his fleet, his armies, his wealth, and his generous use of his gold for service to gods, cities, and friends. Ptolemy, so eulogizes Theocritus, for his good actions gets a noble fame, and is one of the semi-divine beings.[15] Details differ, but Theocritus and Callimachus have a common attitude toward the content of their poetry.

Whether or not the genre is traditional, as it so often is, the ideas are traditional, almost trite, never reaching beyond conventional wisdom or morality. In this they are quite like the third great member of the Alexandrian triad, Apollonius, called the Rhodian. This poet's long epic on the search for the golden fleece by Jason and the Argonauts follows Homeric meter and vocabulary, and is Homeric in length, but apart from a reorientation of Homeric language to focus on romantic love, it introduces nothing of importance in terms of ideas. In short, Alexandrian poetry went a separate way from philosophy, selecting as its ideological content ideas and concepts seen as suitable for literary work, rather than philosophical. The professionalization of philosophy which began a century before with the Socratic method and scientific approach to enquiry, as Aristotle put it, evolved to remove intellectual, ethical, and religious speculation or investigation from the realm of literature. Neither drama, lyric or epic probed the individual's relation to self, to fellow beings, or to the universe as had earlier Greek literature. Specialized writing in philosophy, as begun by Plato and continued by Aristotle, took up these themes, and poets did not seem anxious to reclaim them. The Alexandrians were content to leave such problems aside, occupied with "pure" literature, with literary criticism, or with scholarship.

But even if literary men stayed away from philosophy, Alexandria in these years certainly did not lack for original ideas, which came, however, from science. Starting with the mathematician Euclid, who lived in Alexandria during the reign of Ptolemy I, mathematicians and astronomers made Ptolemy's capital the scene of such dramatic advances in knowledge as to create the revolution in science which marks for many the importance of this period. It was Alexandrian science, for example, which produced Aristarchus' revolutionary theory that the earth orbited the sun.[16] In the mid-third century, Eratosthenes of Cyrene added to the fame of the Alexandrian group with outstanding achievements in geography. It is clear that he was something of a polymath, his career illustrating the breadth and range of the interests of the scholars in Alexandria in mid-century.

The activity of the denizens of the Alexandrian library and museum was a phenomenon made possible largely by the patronage, interest, and support of the Ptolemies. So long as the kings continued to fund the institutions and invite the famous from abroad to visit or to remain, literature, science, and scholarship flourished in their capital. The whole movement was grounded in the first instance in the self-image of Ptolemy I as king, and the object of the exercise was image, so to speak, rather than practical achievement. The king could be seen to provide a focus for the cultural and intellectual activity of his day, to attract, as it were, the bright lights of the world by his own brilliance. What Ptolemy I began his successors continued, so that the court of Alexandria offered in the third century BC the greatest concentration of Hellenic talent the contemporary world knew. Other kings in other places would imitate, for the idea of kingship came to comprehend this kind of promotion of Hellenic literature, art, and science, and even though they did not, as it turned out, match the achievement of the Ptolemies, the very fact that they engaged in the enterprise was enough to establish it as a means of demonstrating royal accomplishment. To success in war, service to gods, generosity to friends and Greek cities was added the promotion of culture as an attribute of kingship. None of it needed to be practical, and Archimedes might come bearing the techniques of raising water, potentially so useful for agriculture along the Nile, to have his inventions admired but unused by Greeks who were more concerned to observe the values and techniques of traditional Hellenism, and who were conservative in practical as well as intellectual matters. The kings were expected to present the trappings of power and the characteristics of leadership, and to enhance the traditional aspects of Hellenic life, not, to use a modern expression, to increase the gross national product.

Such was the world of kings which followed the short reign of Alexander. Within two generations of Alexander's death Greeks expected that leadership and power would focus on kings, that government would emanate from royal personages who would rule through royal appointees and retainers. Although individual cities might retain the ability to administer their own affairs and, exceptionally, play a role in the large world, men were now making different adjustments to the exercise of power. Even the city-state, now so reduced in power in comparison to the kings, could flourish if it adjusted to the new circumstances. That adjustment worked best for those who could accommodate the nature of kingship, who accepted the kings as the embodiment of Hellenic power and the expression of Hellenic political ideals. For many Greeks, it was easy to do this, as the kings promoted Hellenic culture, encouraged Hellenic education in cities and towns all over the east, and, for most of the time, wielded power in quest of political stability rather than in pursuit of revolutionary change. The realities of power and human nature were there, of course, to influence and often disturb what might otherwise have been a better expression of ideal monarchy, but the concept of what this kingship could be remained. Kingship became a legitimate form of government, that form, in fact, which was expected to provide security, stability, relief from misfortune, protection to cities, and justice to individuals, duties which, as Callimachus writes in his "Hymn to Zeus," they fulfill under the aegis of Zeus. An individual king might execute his role well or badly, but kingship as a concept now comprehended much more than the mere exercise of political power. It comprehended an intellectual, cultural, moral, and religious nature as well, and not in the age-old Homeric fashion of tribal leader, but as an expression of the most advanced philosophical ideas of Hellenism. This new kingship would also have a most profound effect on ideas in the years to come.

# 16

# The connecting of east and west

## *Sicily, Carthage, and the rise of Rome*

The Hellenism that was spreading eastward in the generations after the death of Alexander the Great confronted different cultures in the west as well. There, in south Italy and Sicily in particular, there had been an old and concentrated settlement by Greeks from many cities in the Aegean area, and by the time Alexander made his great march to India, the Greeks in the west could look back on a long history. They had been responsible for some important influences on intellectual development in old Greece, but there was never a close political or even social bond between the Aegean area and the west, and interventions like the Athenian expedition in the fifth century or a rescue operation by Timoleon in the fourth were relatively rare. And apart from their own colonies. Greek involvement with the west was almost non-existent, hardly noticeable apart from connections between mother cities and colonies. All this was to change in the century after Alexander, as the connections between old Greece and the colonized cities in the west progressed toward long-term alliances between dynasts, and, ultimately, involvements which would being Greek kingdoms into conflict with the rising tide of Roman power.

The first close relationship between a western Greek leader and kings of the eastern Mediterranean was established by Agathocles, an autocrat at Syracuse at the end of the fourth century. Syracuse had been in turmoil for decades, with conflicts between oligarchs and democrats and civic strife necessitating the intervention of Timoleon of Corinth, who had brought peace to the city for about ten years after the middle of the century. Agathocles took advantage of the strife which recurred after Timoleon's retirement in 337 BC, and by 317 he was firmly established as autocrat of the city, by 304 as king. Agathocles' glance east came as a result of a war he was fighting with Carthage. In summer of 310 he escaped a Carthaginian blockade of Syracuse, landed with a small force in North Africa, and by the end of the year had gained enough support from North African subjects of Carthage to put him in control of some 200 towns.

This was the point at which he moved across North Africa in diplomacy. A thousand miles to the east was the Greek city of Cyrene, at that time controlled by one of Alexander's old officers, a man named Ophellas, who had established himself there as a semi-independent agent of Ptolemy I. Agathocles invited him into the Carthaginian war, and when he brought his forces across the desert, murdered him and took over his army. All this ultimately came to nothing for Agathocles, however, as the campaign began to turn against him. He managed to extricate himself in 307, made peace with Carthage in 306, and continued his adventures from his secure base in eastern Sicily. He held the island of Corcyra for a while, campaigned in south Italy, married as a third wife a daughter of Ptolemy I, and used his own daughter Lanassa in dynastic marriage, first to Pyrrhus of Epirus and then to Demetrius, son of Antigonus. When he died in 289 he left Syracuse without a dynasty, and Sicily entered a period of trouble and confusion. Over twenty years would pass, with short-lived tyrants rising in some cities and a batch of Agathocles' mercenaries establishing themselves in the city of Messana to establish a little empire in the north-east of the island, while the Carthaginians interfered again in eastern Sicily and King Pyrrhus of Epirus responded to appeals for help against them in a brief but not permanently successful campaign. With Carthage again in control of the western and central parts of Sicily and allied to the mercenaries at Messana – Mamertines, as they now called themselves – the new Syracusan general, Hiero, intervened in Messana, and was only stopped by the arrival of a Carthaginian garrison. Hiero, proclaimed king in Syracuse in 270, thus faced enemies in Messana and more danger from Carthage, when the Mamertines precipitated a new conflict by negotiating an alliance with Rome and expelling the Carthaginian garrison.

The Rome on which the Mamertines were calling was a very different kind of state from any with which Greeks had been familiar. This central Italian city had been, at least on Roman tradition, about a half-millennium in developing its power. Events of early times, which as we know today, involved a complex evolution of relationships between a number of peoples on the peninsula once they had established themselves there, were recounted by the Romans in terms of the combination of factors which had made it possible for them to defeat one after another of these peoples: the self-sacrificing leadership of the patricians, indomitable courage of the citizens, the stability and reliability of the laws, and, not least, the support of the gods.

If anything besides war and battle comes through the Roman account of 250 years of kingship and then centuries of republican government down to the capture of the neighboring Etruscan city of Veii at the beginning of the fourth century, it is the sense of the steady development of Roman institutions in an evolution relatively free from domestic travail or internal hostilities. Although members of those families who could not claim to be members of the ruling class periodically demanded a greater role in the direction of the state, the demands were expressed without undue violence and did not beget complete revolution. And the patricians were able to tolerate the loss of their monopoly on public offices and priesthoods, because for a long time they held the reality of their power even when the forms were shared to some extent.

Like everything else in early Roman history, most of the story of the struggles between patricians and plebeians – the non-patrician mass of citizenry – mixes a great deal of tradition with fact, and is told from the Roman point of view which focuses on the importance of constitutional history and law. Among the earliest acts in this development, as the fifth century proceeded and land and new citizens were added to the state, was the formulation of Roman law in the published Twelve Tables, as well as the elimination of the prohibition against cross-class marriages. Such, at least, was Roman tradition, and in focusing on the codification and publication of law, it illustrates that Roman preoccupation with legal formality and procedure which became such an important part of western tradition. Steps in the evolution and growth of Rome – the Gallic invasion in the fourth century which demolished the city and would have taken the Capitoline fort but for the near-miraculous warning by honking geese, the evolution of the magistrates known as tribunes to protect plebeian rights, the gradual opening of senior magistracies to the plebeians, and the increasing authority of plebeian assemblies, repeated wars in the fourth century which gradually brought Roman dominion over the neighboring Etruscans, Latins, Volscians, Campanians, and Samnites, and the Greek cities even in the southernmost parts of Italy – all these and more were taken by Roman tradition as an orderly progression of events towards the fulfillment of the Roman mission which Virgil later described as the task of ruling the nations with law. Later Romans thought of these early centuries as "the better days," and idealized both institutions and citizens of earlier times, looking back, as Livy, in the first century BC, says in the preface to his Roman history, "from the prospect of the evils which our own age has seen through so many years" to the story of the glory of the Roman people which can serve as instruction in morality. Roman accounts of their past not only emphasize the devotion to duty of the patricians and the patient humility with which the plebeians followed their leaders in war after war to the glory of the state; they also exemplify certain basic attitudes which were essentially Roman.

Central to politics as well as religion was the sense of an order to the cosmos extending from the highest gods down to the lowliest humans, an order in which the Roman state had an ordained role to play. Long after the Romans came into contact with the very different and diverse Greek attitudes to the cosmos, these basic Roman attitudes persisted, and we can see the Roman reaction in writers like Lucretius, Cicero, and Virgil. Greek ideas were reworked to create a Roman philosophy to fit the Roman environment. To Romans, things were not only much as they seemed to be but much as they should be. While the will of the gods might not always be clear, signs and portents could usually be relied upon to make it so, and in any case, Romans could proceed about their business in the confidence that whatever the gods and the future might bring, their state would have a central place in that future, and that Rome, Romans, and the gods were cooperating in the building of a world in which humanity not only had a place, but a place which would be satisfactory both for people and the universe as a whole. So Romans could proceed, for example, in their conflict with the Greek cities of the south in the early third century, stubbornly refusing to accept defeat because of the losses imposed by King Pyrrhus of Epirus when he crossed to Italy to aid the Greeks, and return time and time again to battle with him, with the Greek cities, and with the Samnites in the south. By 272 they held all Italy from the Rubicon River in the North to the Straits of Messina at the end of the peninsula, and they could look across the narrow stretch of water and contemplate Sicily.

By the time they reached this position of power, the Romans had made adjustments to the new position they had in the world. Rather than exploit, they incorporated. Some latent sense of the Roman republic as comprehensive as well as dominant led the Romans to deal with the vanquished in a way not paralleled by other states either in Italy or in the east. Rather than enslave the defeated or reduce them to occupied territories, the Romans granted them rights of relationship which extended from alliance with autonomy and freedom from tribute up a ladder which included rights of intermarriage with Roman citizenship and property rights according to Roman law, citizenship without voting rights, or ultimately full citizenship in the republic. Latins, Sabines, Campanians, and others would hold one or another of these rights as they moved up to citizenship. At the same time, the establishment of coloniae and subject allied cities in varying categories of status, along with planting Roman citizens in sensitive areas, assured Rome's grip on peninsular Italy. Internally, the plebeians rose in political importance within the state, as they achieved the power to enforce the decisions of their own plebeian assemblies by the beginning of the third century, and a number of plebeian families joined the patrician families who had gained rank through achievement of the highest office. The magistracies of the state now ranged from junior offices to deal with lesser matters – these became more numerous as public affairs became more complex – extending on up through higher positions like aedile, quaestor, praetor, to deal with public works, finances, judicial matters as their respective briefs might be generally described. The Romans saw the rank and career steps, called in Latin the *cursus honorum*, "the sequence of honors," as an almost required progression to the supreme magistracy, the consulship. There were two consuls, each with full military command and full civil executive authority, and either might exercise that authority, to be restrained only by opposition from the other; ordinarily the consuls cooperated in sharing that authority which was denoted by the particular Latin term, *imperium*.

The *imperium* of the consul was a particular characteristic of Roman political thought, different from any "authority" which a Greek magistrate might have, and it contributed ultimately to a conceptualization of earthly government which could be compatible with Christian thought. It was not the power of office *qua* office, but rather all the authority, religious, secular, military, and civil, of the entire state of Rome, envisioned also in physical dimensions and in terms of the populace. Perhaps more a metaphysical than political concept, it was conveyed to an individual by virtue of his occupying the consulship, but it was separable from the office, and could be conveyed independently, so that other offices were created from time to time "with consular *imperium*," either as standing offices or as extraordinary appointments to meet a particular need. The concept illustrates that unique Roman attitude toward the state as a thing of itself, with its authority and power in the hands of men who might be its temporary agents, but in its aggregate of institutions always independent of any individual or group. Even the Senate, which was the most important single institution by the third century and served as the permanent body for the setting of policy, did not express the state, even though it was made up of former senior magistrates, and with their collective experience had enormous weight in the conduct of public affairs. The Senate dealt with matters of religion, war, finance, provincial administration, and domestic and external policy, and the government of Rome became, in fact, a cooperative enterprise for Senate and magistrates. The special position of Senators was recognized not only in Rome by such privileges as reserved seats at games and religious ceremonies, but also by foreign powers who sent their ambassadors to Rome to be received by the Senate. For example, Ptolemy II sent an embassy in 273 BC after the Roman success over Pyrrhus, and it was the Senate which the Mamertines addressed when they asked for help in 265.

The Senate recognized that the request had very serious implications for Roman relations with Carthage, which up to this time had been reasonably good, and we are told that the Senators made no decision on the matter, leaving it to an assembly of the people to tip the balance in favor of the Mamertine alliance. At all events, Rome accepted Messana into alliance, and in 264, as the Carthaginians were expelled from that city and a Roman army crossed the straits into Sicily, a war with Carthage formally opened. It lasted for twenty-four years, during which the Romans were compelled to build a fleet in order to contend with Carthage for control of the sea. Despite repeated misfortunes like their costly failures to make invasions of Africa stick, after stalemate on land in Sicily, and a series of naval disasters in which hundreds of ships were lost to battles and storms, the Romans finally defeated the Carthaginians at sea, cut off the Carthaginian army in Sicily, and forced them to a treaty in 241.

The terms of the treaty gave Sicily to the Romans, recognized the Roman ally Hiero of Syracuse as king of that city, imposed a heavy monetary indemnity on Carthage and required that it evacuate not only Sicily but the islands between Italy and Sicily. The seas around Italy were henceforth to be Roman, and in fact, a few years later, Roman demands on the exhausted Carthaginians led to their agreeing to cede Sardinia as well. Nevertheless, Carthage was allowed to keep her army and continue her domination of the North African coast. Thus the Mediterranean was divided into two zones in the west, that from Sicily northwards under control of Rome, with the southern tier left to the Carthaginians, who also maintained their trading posts ranging all along the African coast beyond the Straits of Gibraltar as well as their posts and colonies in southern Spain and the Balearic Islands. For a while, that Semitic civilization ethnically and culturally so different from the Greeks and Romans continued to share the world with them, maintaining a government different from that of Rome or the Greek cities, but nevertheless admired by Aristotle for a stability engineered by a strong oligarchy. Carthaginian society, according to the hardly friendly later Roman accounts, rested on the wealth of a noble mercantile class, rich traders and manufacturers who were able to give exclusive attention to money-making by using the services of mercenaries to maintain the state's power. Furthermore, we are told, Carthage supported herself on the backs of subject peoples in North Africa and her colonies, using conscripted troops to fight alongside hirelings; this bad reputation may owe something to its hostile origin. As time went on, Carthage developed some ties with the Greeks of the east, and received some influences from the Hellenes, although little went the other way, and Carthaginian culture made little impact on the Greek world. Overall, the Carthaginians remain quite outside the pale of our heritage, despite their obvious importance to the political picture of the Mediterranean in the third century.

That importance still remained for a while after the peace of 241. For the first years thereafter, the weakness of the state prompted a rebellion in North Africa, based on an army of discontented mercenaries, and the threat was averted only after the Romans permitted Hiero of Syracuse to send food supplies. The difficulties engendered by that war, which did not end until 238, gave the Romans the opportunity to demand and gain the cession of Sardinia. In the next year, Hamilcar landed in Spain. Carthage still had ambitions. There would be trouble again between Rome and Carthage, but the next time, it would have great implications for Rome's relations with the east.

# 17

# The bridge of Athens

## *Athenian and Greek politics, and philosophy in Athens in the third century BC*

During the first half-century after the death of Alexander, as the generals were quarreling and setting up their new kingdoms, the great city-states were adjusting to circumstances in which it was often difficult, sometimes impossible, to act with the same independence with which they had fought one another in their attempts to dominate Greece. Corinth, Sparta, Thebes, Rhodes continued to take a leading role in their own areas, and Athens, which had been left ungarrisoned and still had an appreciable naval power, was particularly important to anyone who would rule Macedon, especially when the Athenians led attacks on Macedonian rule. As a result, Athenian life during the period in which many other new and old cities settled down to a relatively peaceful existence was full of turmoil, war, and uncertainty.

Conflict in Athens between pro- and anti-Macedonian factions, which went back to the time of Philip and Demosthenes, continued through the reign of Alexander and on into the period of his successors. Athenian leadership of a coalition against Macedon, organized immediately after Alexander's death, led to the destruction of the anti-Macedonian party, the suicide of Demosthenes, and the establishment of a garrison, but did not end the pattern of conflict. There was another upheaval which put democrats in control in 318 BC and led to the execution of a number of prominent Athenian politicians who had cooperated with the Macedonians. The assault on that group extended to an attack on Theophrastus, the head of Aristotle's school, nominally for impiety but doubtless in fact for the school's Macedonian connections. The accusation failed to gain much support, however, and the threat soon passed when Macedonian rule returned with the installation of Demetrius of Phalerum to rule as the agent of the Macedonian king, Cassander.

For ten years, from 317 to 307, Athens was under the control of a man trained in philosophy, inclined to moderation in ideals, and with practical intelligence in policy. Demetrius of Phalerum had studied under Theophrastus, and could claim authorship of a wide range of literary, rhetorical, and philosophical writings. It was a time of relative prosperity for Athens, the period of the playwright Menander's social comedy which we now know so much better from the finds of papyri in Egypt. The philosophers, or at least Theophrastus and the Aristotelians, found support from Demetrius, and the school, a kind of religious club which Theophrastus headed, bought a garden in the city. There the philosopher built accommodations and a shrine to the muses to which the association was devoted, as well as some porticoes – *peripetoi* – from which the group took its name. Here there were monthly dinners, religious services to the muses, officials of administration as well as priests of the cult, and regular teaching as well as visits by distinguished foreigners. What little we can detect of the life of the Peripatos, as the group was called, reveals it as a kind of communal activity focused on learning and research, wherein younger affiliates would associate with the older and more knowledgeable in preparation for a professional life of teaching or study.

Demetrius of Phalerum's regime ended suddenly, when Demetrius the son of Antigonus fell on the city in 307, expelled the Macedonians, and restored the democracy. Almost beside themselves to show gratitude to Demetrius and his father Antigonus, the Athenians erected gold statues, established annual games to honor them, called them king, and made them the heroes of two new Athenian tribes, called Antigonis and Demetrias. All this and more far exceeded honor previously given men, to the disgust of many ancient and modern commentators, but the enthusiasm shown to the new kings indicates both the dedication of the Athenians to their democracy and the need for outsiders to support it. To the Athenians their liberators could be called gods, saviors. The hymn addressed to Demetrius reported by the later writer Athenaeus shows in part just how the populace could approach the kings: "Other gods hold themselves afar, or have no ears, or don't exist, or have no care for us. But you we see present, not wood, not stone, but real."[1]

Clinging to autonomy meant trouble for the Athenians in the decades after Demetrius the son of Antigonus restored the democracy, and the troubles which they made for themselves, combined with those that swept over them because of external events, made for a period of even greater instability than that which had preceded. There was war with the Macedonian forces while Cassander tried to regain the city, then an attempt at neutrality which failed in the 290s when Cassander's death plunged Macedonia into a struggle over the succession and Athens herself confronted domestic quarrels. Once again Demetrius the son of Antigonus was on the scene, intervening in an Athenian struggle between the democrats and the partisans of an autocrat in the city. The democrats aided Demetrius in a long and cruel siege of the city in which the populace experienced the most desperate privation; finally, in 294, after Demetrius defeated a rescue squadron from Ptolemy, the Athenians yielded. Demetrius had control of Athens again, and in the following year made his success in Macedon which brought him control there. Later the Athenians fought and then came to terms with Demetrius, and after he was taken prisoner during an ill-fated expedition to Asia Minor, they were more or less left alone while his son Antigonus Gonatas was occupied with other problems. But once Antigonus' successes against the invading Gauls put him back in control of Macedon in 276, the Athenians were plunged again into international politics. Moderates in control in the city accepted a Macedonian garrison in the harbor of Piraeus, but a few years later, when Ptolemy II was encouraging the Greek cities to oppose Macedon, the Athenians undertook yet another conflict. In the Chremonidean War, named after the proposer of the decree of war against Macedon, the Athenians fought in alliance with Sparta, but in the end they were brought to their knees by a long siege and capitulated to Antigonas Gonatas in the mid 260s. With this, Athens settled down to a long period of Macedonian rule, ending not only her attempt to act the great power in a world dominated by kings, but also closing more than a half-century of terrible internal strife and foreign conflict.

It is not surprising that the events of these years had some impact on the philosophers, particularly in view of the fact that on some occasions the schools or their leaders came under attack, as in the case of Theophrastus. Much more serious than this episode was the legislation of Sophocles of Sounion, passed after the expulsion of Demetrius of Phalerum in 307. This proposal, accepted and implemented by the *nomothetae* – "law setters" – prohibited any philosopher from operating a school without the explicit permission of the council and assembly of Athens. The law prompted Theophrastus to leave the city, but, because in restricting schools which were in form religious associations, the law came into conflict with Solonian legislation, it could be attacked on the grounds that its proposer had put forward legislation which was contrary to laws. Such a charge against Sophocles in the middle of 306 succeeded, and brought a fine of 5 talents, the cancellation of the law, and the return of Theophrastus.

At the time Sophocles thought up his measure, there were only two schools of philosophy in Athens, the Peripatos of Aristotle headed by Theophrastus, and the older school founded by Plato, the Academy. The head of the Academy during most of the period of the turmoil was Polemon, who came to the position in 314 and seems to have been a man of considerable force of personality, attractive and compelling, with a concern for ethical conduct which he transmitted to others. His pupil, Crates, took over the Academy in about 270 for a few years until his own death, and, just about the time of the Chremonidean War, passed it on to Arcesilaus, who revitalized it with his own original contributions to sceptical analysis. In Aristotle's Lyceum, in the same period, Theophrastus' contribution was by far the greatest. Although many of his works have been lost, those that survive, like his works on the classification and physiology of plants, show that in the natural sciences he was pursuing the lines of investigation laid down by Aristotle. What we have of his texts on metaphysics deals directly with matters treated by Aristotle, and his well-known set of essays, *Characters*, derives directly from Aristotle's comments about personalities in the *Nicomachean Ethics*. According to his ancient biographer, Theophrastus had over 2000 students, was accepted by Cassander as a teacher, and was invited by Ptolemy.[2] He also taught the playwright Menander and Demetrius of Phaleron. When he died around 287 he was succeeded in leadership of the Peripatos by Straton of Lampsacus, who actually came to Athens from Alexandria to take the position. All in all, however much the world outside the Academy or the garden of the Peripatos might have seemed to be falling apart, the residents of both schools seem to have been protected, or at least to have maintained themselves essentially unaffected by events.

If the old schools carried on as before through the crises of the late fourth and early third centuries, there were new foundations which did not. One of these was founded in Athens in 306, immediately after the restriction on philosophical schools was canceled. An Athenian citizen named Epicurus, who had grown up on Samos where his parents had gone earlier as colonists, finally returned permanently to Athens. While at Samos he had studied philosophy with a Platonist, and later in the city of Colophon where the family had gone when the Athenians were expelled from Samos, he continued the study of philosophy, and, according to some ancient sources, attended the teachings of a follower of the early physical philosopher Democritus, who taught that all material objects were compounded of minute particles of matter called "atoms" – *atoma*, "uncuttables." According to his biography, he started his own school when he was 32 years old, at Mytilene on the island of Lesbos, and after five years transferred himself to Athens.

For the remaining thirty-five years of his life Epicurus remained in Athens, and died there in 271 or 270. The school which he founded took its name from the Garden which he bought in Athens when he founded it, and which served as a locale for his teaching and as a peaceful refuge from the travails of the city through which he and his disciples lived. It is easy to understand that the experience of the troubles of his time impelled him to the ethical philosophy which proposed the ideal of a trouble-free existence, with pleasure – but the pleasure of meeting the most elementary needs – as the highest good. As one great Athenian politician after another fell victim to foreign dynasts or citizen enemies, the life of retreat and no ambition could easily be shown to have its attractions. It may not, however, only have been the philosophical pursuit of security in isolation which kept Epicurus in his Garden, for his biographer sees his motivations in a more favorable light, claiming that

> he did not involve himself in politics because of his overscrupulous sense of his fitness. And although those times were the most troublesome for Greece he lived his life there, apart from the two or three times when he travelled to visit his friends located in the area of Ionia.[3]

Epicurus and his school were the targets of many attacks, whether from misunderstanding of his doctrine or because of some actual characteristics of the group in the Garden and their leader. That he admitted women to his

*21* This bronze bust of Epicurus, based on a Greek original of the early third century BC, was found in 1753 in the Villa dei Pisoni, Herculaneum, and now rests in the National Museum, Naples.

school must have seemed a flouting of Athenian convention, and may have inspired the reports of his interest in erotic pleasure and of the women with whom he lived or corresponded. He is also credited with a predilection for luxurious living, a reputation which may accord with a popular understanding of Epicureanism but can hardly square with what we have of his writing. That writing itself was extremely voluminous, amounting to over 300 rolls, "written without any quotes from other authors, but all phrases of Epicurus himself."[4] He wrote thirty-seven books on nature, plus others on atoms, and a number on sensation, as well as works on ethics, behavior, and the gods.

We can reconstruct a good deal of his ethical principles from a collection of aphorisms known from antiquity as the *Principal Doctrines*, which were believed to have been the work of Epicurus himself. There is no doubt that they present a consistent picture of the practical working out of Epicurus' position which regards pleasure as the goal of human existence. Together with the *Letter to Menoecus*, and many fragments culled from various sources, like the eighty-one from a Vatican collection, the *Principal Doctrines* provide a précis of Epicurus' teaching about the nature of human life, personality, and happiness, and his prescriptions for the manner in which best to conduct oneself through life.

The fundamental characteristic of Epicurean ethical philosophy, wherein it differs from all other Greek thought, is the value which it assigns to what the Greek calls *hedone*,[5] a word usually translated as "pleasure," the greatest and most sustained pleasure as the *Letter to Menoecus* makes clear:

> And because of this we say that hedone is the beginning and the end of living happily. For we comprehend it as a good which is primary and related to our own nature, and from it we begin every choice or retreat, and we resort to it as the canon of experience for judging every good. And since it is the first good and in our nature, we do not choose every hedone, but there are circumstances when we pass over many hedonai, whenever something more vexatious to us will follow from them.[6]

The primacy of *hedone* is clear, and as Epicurus explains a few sections later in the same letter, it is a state of not being grieved in body or disturbed in mind. While there is, in the aphorisms, frank acknowledgement of the desirability of sensual pleasures in themselves, there are also arguments that the virtues are inextricably tied to the life of pleasure: "the life of pleasure is unseparable from them."[7] This view of the relationship between virtue and pleasure, which might be called the ethical position, is balanced by other aphorisms which evaluate the good solely in terms of pleasure, "the pleasures of flavours . . . the pleasures of sex . . . the pleasures of things heard . . . the pleasurable impacts of the seeing of form."[8]

Epicurus' ethical attitudes depended to a significant extent on his understanding of the physical universe. He was attracted by the earlier concept of natural phenomena promulgated by Democritus, in which things are constituted of imperishable and indivisible atoms of different natures which link up variously to create the different phenomena of the universe. The atoms have none of the qualities associated with the objects of perception, although they do have shape, weight, and size up to the point before which they would be visible, and they are incalculably numerous in the number of shapes they take, and infinite in number in each shape, so that they are in total infinite in number and occupy in that infiniteness an infinitely large universe. The gods, the soul, and sensation are seen to be made up of these atoms, and due in their nature to the kind of atoms which make them up.

All this may be found in the *Letter to Herodotus* quoted by Diogenes Laertius, or in the *Letter to Pythocles* also quoted there, and which, although possibly the work of a compiler and not Epicurus himself, probably reflects Epicurus' views about the alternative possibilities which may serve as explanations for phenomena. The overall conception of natural phenomena as owing their nature not to some inhering form but to the chance collocations of atoms removes from the value system anything beyond the advantage to the object created. There is, in other words, no form, no goal, no perfection of itself toward which phenomena grow or reach to provide some standard of behavior or development for a human or any other creature, any more than there is the Unmoved Mover which in its perfection moves the universe by the yearning which it inspires. In this sense Epicurus' thought is a complete break with Platonism, for it not only ignores in totality the possibility of perfect forms and implicitly rejects Aristotle's attempt to rescue the form by making it inherent in matter, but deliberately rejects the validity of anything which cannot be dealt with in terms of sense perception. This attitude toward sense perception itself derives from the physical theory, for sense perception is made possible not by some quality in the psyche but by the atomic emissions from the objects perceived, emissions of extreme thinness, images of the perceptible objects and made up of very few atoms. Sight, hearing, and smell are all made possible by this flowing of particles, and it is the soul, also a finely structured assemblage of atoms, which is capable of perception, so long as it is in the body. Sense perception, therefore, like everything else, is engendered through atoms, and the images of sense perception are thus corporeal in the same elementary sense as the bodies which they represent.

With this kind of thoroughgoing materialism, the ethical principle of the paramount value of pleasure is completely reasonable and consistent. With sensation based on material qualities and the soul also a corporeal entity, pain and pleasure both assume material existence. Although Epicurus' summary letters and fragmentary aphorisms do not link the natural science with the pleasure theory, apart from the statement that accurate knowledge of the reasons for phenomena will remove superstitious fear and thus eliminate one potential source of pain, the significance of the theory of materialism for the pleasure principle is inherent in that theory. It fits as well with his treatment of the question of justice as a social matter, justice being no more than the regulation of human conduct for mutual advantage – basically, no more than agreement by people not to harm one another and not to be harmed. What is just may vary from place to place according to the individual characteristics of a country, and may even change over time. If laws which initially were advantageous in regulating the relations amongst individuals lose their usefulness, they are no longer just, for the essential nature of justice is no more than its utility for making human intercourse advantageous. The idea propounded by Plato, that there is some perfect justice, or a form of Justice, or even the Aristotelian acceptance of a universal which could be called justice, is specifically denied: "There is not anything which is justice in itself (in isolation), but it exists in the dealings which men have with each other in whatever place or time as a kind of contract not to harm or be harmed."[9]

Thus we have a redefinition of justice which harks back to the fifth-century Sophistic controversy about the conflict between nature and custom, the *physis–nomos* controversy, but one which resolves the conflict in favor of *nomos*. As Socrates evaded the conflict by defining nature as served in no way by material benefit so that *nomos* could be followed without disservice to nature, Epicurus eliminated the conflict by making nature served only by material advantage, so that *nomos* or justice always changed in order to provide for that advantage. It was an ethical theory which was coherent in itself, understandable, and completely consistent with Epicurus' notions of the nature of the cosmos.

Consistent it may have been; it was not convincing to all, and not to his most notable contemporary, a Cypriot of Phoenician descent, Zeno the son of Mnasias, who founded a school in Athens not long after Epicurus himself began to teach there. Zeno had come to Athens in around 313, reportedly as an importer of purple dye from Phoenicia to the Piraeus who had met with a shipwreck. As the story goes, he was about 30 years old at the time, and in Athens, browsing in a bookstore and impressed with Xenophon's *Memorabilia of Socrates*, he asked where such men spent their time. In response, the bookseller pointed out Crates, the Cynic philosopher, who just by chance happened to be present. As a result, Zeno began to attend the philosophical sessions of Crates, and his first experience of philosophy was thus at the hands of the Cynics.

The Cynics may have reached back all the way to Antisthenes, the disciple of Socrates, and they certainly based their teachings on the life, practices, and words of Diogenes of Sinope, who lived in the last three-quarters of the fourth century and spent most of his active life at Athens. Diogenes argued that one should satisfy one's natural needs in whatever way comes best and easiest, and that conventions which inhibit this in any way falsely represent actions as wrong. He lived a life of poverty and exhibited his rejection of conventions by establishing the program of public shamelessness associated with the Cynics, who deliberately performed sexual acts in the open for their shock value, and

22 Marble head of Zeno, a Roman copy of a Greek original, now in the National Museum, Naples.

were noted for public masturbation as a particular demonstration of their disregard of convention. The Crates whom Zeno encountered in the bookstore was Diogenes' most noted disciple, and by this time Cynic positions had been well worked out. The "wise man" will do not what is conventional, but what is natural, and that is virtue; all other acts, apart from those which contravene virtue, have no moral significance. The "wise man" is free in all respects, at

199

*23* Traditions about Diogenes made him an almost perfect subject for the predilection for personalization in art which was prevalent in the centuries after Alexander. This statue in the Villa Albani of a balding, nude, aged man, holding a staff in his left hand with a dog sitting nearby, collects many of the symbols associated with Diogenes and the cynics.

liberty to engage in actions with others so long as they freely agree, a notion which extends to "free love" for both men and women so long as both parties are at liberty to accept or reject an act.

The freedom of the Cynic "wise man" extends to freedom from dependence on others in any spiritual sense, and because the "wise man" lives at the bare minimum necessary for survival – like a dog, thus "Cynic" from the Greek word "doglike" – he is free from physical dependency as well. The virtuous independence of the Cynics won them respect, and Zeno, even before he met Crates, would doubtless have heard the remark of Alexander the Great that he would choose to be Diogenes if he were not Alexander, a remark elicited when Diogenes' only request of the king was that he step aside as he was blocking the sunlight.

Zeno did not, however, remain a Cynic, although many Cynic ideals and attitudes were incorporated into his philosophy or influenced his own concepts. Ultimately, after leaving Crates and spending some time in the Academy, Plato's old foundation, he founded his own school, sometime around 300 BC. It became known as the Stoic school, from the public building called the Stoa Poikile (Colored Porch), where Zeno met his pupils and did his teaching. He lived and taught in Athens for a long time and died in 263 BC, aged 98 and still in full possession of his senses and his opinions. He had many students, and his school continued after his death. Zeno himself was highly respected by the Athenians, not only because King Antigonus encouraged them to honor him, but because of his example in demonstrating a public, honorable, and moderate style of life. He is one of the few philosophers to be credited with improving the young who associated with him, and he was honored with a gold crown and a tomb to be built at public expense not only for his own life of rectitude, but for his teaching by example and exhortation of the young to virtue.

What he actually taught, however, is not as clear as is his reputation, for nothing even near complete remains to us of writings which can be attributed to his pen. With the success of Stoicism in later times and the appearance of successors to Zeno who were able and original thinkers in their own right and may have modified his doctrines in important ways, it is often difficult to pick out of the views attributed to the earlier Stoics those particular doctrines which originated with the founder of the school. Even when some statement made about Stoicism can be safely related to Zeno himself, the fragmentary or excerpted nature of almost all such statements often makes it difficult to discern what a later writer meant, or thought Zeno meant.

The AD third-century life of Zeno by Diogenes Laertius contains a treatise summarizing Stoic philosophy. While it is in most respects a synthesizing treatment, Diogenes does devote some attention to distinguishing doctrinal differences among some of the earlier Stoics, so we know at least his view of the main lines of Zeno's writing. According to Diogenes, Zeno divided philosophy into the three traditional branches, logic, physics, and ethics, and treated them in that order in his *Exposition of Doctrine*. Diogenes' exposition of Zeno's treatment of the first branch can be supplemented by some of the comments of the Roman Cicero, who tells us that Zeno claimed that sense perception presented reliable data, although not everything apparent to the senses could automatically be accepted as reliable. Anything which could be trusted must come from the senses in the first instance, but must then be grasped in such a way that reason could not dissolve the perception. The perception could then be considered knowledge. Those perceptions accepted by the senses may be assimilated by the mind in a kind of voluntary process, which Zeno referred to as "assent."[10]

Diogenes is somewhat more informative in his summary of Zeno's second part of philosophy, physics. This aspect of philosophy is of particular importance because Stoic thought emphasized "living in accordance with nature," so that the Stoic concept required the delineation of the characteristics of the natural universe which the human being must accommodate. The fundamental doctrine of the Stoics hypothesizes two principles, or *archai*, at work in the natural universe, an active and a passive. The passive is inert matter, the active is the divine logos – "reason" or "word" – which is eternal and is the maker of everything in matter. Within the universe there are these principles of eternal nature, ungenerated, indestructible, and formless, and elements, the fundamental components into which matter can be divided. These do have form and are destroyed when the universe undergoes its periodic cycles of destruction and regeneration through the primordial fire. In this universe, there is a primary matter which makes for the existence of all things, and a god or divine force which Zeno asserts as equivalent to the entire cosmos and heavens. For humans, Zeno alleged the existence of a soul as a kind of warm breath, the immortality of which is debated by various Stoics and which is probably to be taken as one of those animal souls which are parts of the general soul of the universe, a doctrine which Diogenes gives as a general Stoic view.

All this refers to a fundamental concept in Zeno's third division of philosophy, that of ethics. In a general discussion of Stoic views on goods and evils, where he deals with the notion of things "indifferent" as to genuine good or bad for man, Diogenes refers to the division of the indifferent between things "preferred" and those "rejected." It is a difficult concept, the meaning of which is not even agreed today, since the notion of the "preferred" seems to contradict some other Stoic assertions about the "indifferent," but as Diogenes presents it, the things "preferred" are those which have some value for a harmonious life. Of these, some are preferred for their own sake because they accord with nature, a concept for which Diogenes introduces Zeno's term *kathekon*, appropriateness of behavior, which can be defended because it is suitable for life. The term is part of the attempt to deal with the frequent problems of the everyday world, relating to choice for example, rather than the theoretical delineation of perfect virtue as it will be understood and lived by the rare or unique "wise man."

Zeno, in *On the Nature of Man*, stated, "The end is living in conformity with Nature, which is to live according to virtue. For Nature leads us to this."[11] It is, essentially, a Cynic conception in its origin, although in Stoic thought the concept of nature involves physics, and it is the understanding of the physical cosmos, with the data transmitted to the senses, evaluated by reason, and accepted by the assent of the mind, which makes it possible to locate the human sphere of activity correctly in the universe. Ultimately, the "wise man", at least, having achieved the necessary knowledge, will be able to live that life of virtue which is life in conformity to nature. Zeno's attitude toward nature and virtue differed strikingly from that of Epicurus in adherence to the notion of a Platonic perfection, an absolute truth and an absolute virtue which were possible in the context of the knowledge of the "wise man." The "wise man" by exercise of reason could use the valid information afforded by the senses to inform himself about nature and thus achieve the virtue which was in conformity with it. The conceptualization differed from Plato's in that it insisted that the only route to knowledge was through the senses; but in another, perhaps more important, aspect of Plato's thought, that there was an absolute truth and knowledge and a genuine virtue which maintained constancy, Zeno ultimately drew on the tradition of Plato and Aristotle.

Zeno and Epicurus held commanding positions in Athenian intellectual life during the years before Athens' final descent into domination by the Macedonian dynasty of Antigonus. Both of them, harking back to the traditions of physical theories of Ionian speculation a hundred years before their own time, Epicurus to the atomic theories of Democritus and Zeno to the primordial fire of Heracleitus, put themselves squarely in early Hellenic philosophical traditions. The science and attitudes toward science which would come out of their schools would gain nothing from the Aristotelian revolution,[12] and the approach the two masters took meant that there would be no real challenge from their schools to the pre-eminence in science which Alexandria was already showing. Developing as they did during the period of great crisis and turmoil in Athenian life, they produced systems of ethics, psychology, and behavior which were suited to times of distress and difficulty. Neither of them lived to see the defeat of Athens by Antigonus, for Epicurus died in 271 or 270, and Zeno only seven years later. In that same decade, the leadership of the other two schools was changing also, as Crates took over the Academy from Polemon and Lycon took over the Lyceum very soon after. By the time the political leaders had fled from the city after Antigonus' victory, some even finding refuge with Antigonus' enemy, Ptolemy Philadelphus of Egypt, a new generation of intellectual leaders was also on the scene.

It is well that it was so, for Athens' role in the coming decades was to be very different from her earlier influential place among the Greek states. Saddled with Macedonian garrisons after the Chremonidean War, Athens was kept firmly under Antigonus' control until his death in 239. The focus on Athens of Antigonus' cultural policy also added to the international attraction of the Athenian philosophical schools, and contributed as well to the steadfast adherence to Antigonus which Athenian citizens showed in these years. Athens was one of the few major cities of Greece to refuse to join Aratus' expanding Achaean league which was demonstrating great success in the Peloponnesus and spreading its influence north in the 240s. Even after Antigonus' death in 239, the failure of the truce which followed it, the subsequent combination of Achaean and Aetolian leagues against Macedon, and the assaults against Macedonian allies in the Peloponnesus and central Greece, the Athenians remained faithful to Antigonus' son and successor, Demetrius II. Throughout Demetrius' war with the two leagues, Achaean and Aetolian, and in spite of Aratus' repeated ravaging of Attica and attempts to capture the Piraeus, Athens remained a supporter of Macedon, while much of the southern and central part of Greece was combining against Demetrius. After Demetrius' death in 229, leading Athenians took advantage of Macedonian difficulties to pay off a Macedonian commander to take his garrison out of Athens. By 228 payment had been made and all the forts around Attica and that in the Piraeus were yielded to the Athenians. Athens was free of foreign garrisons at last, independent again, and her leaders set about ensuring that she would remain so.

The policy was again one of neutrality in the conflicts among the kings, leagues, and cities. The Athenians sent ambassadors about the Aegean affirming their desire to be friends with all. Acceptance flowed in from everywhere. The Boeotians renewed their friendship; the Aetolians made peace; Attalus of Pergamum sent his friendship; the various cities of Crete agreed to leave the Athenians in peace; the third Ptolemy, Euergetes, maintained the friendly relations the Athenians had long enjoyed; the Seleucid city of Seleuceia on the Orontes renewed friendly relations through the agency of the nephew of Chrysippus, the current head of the Stoic school; even the regent of Macedonia, Antigonus Doson, agreed to friendship with an independent Athens. Potential trouble from the Achaeans, whose leader wanted Athens in the league, did not develop, and from far off, the Romans sent an embassy to establish friendship with Athens. A new beginning of Athenian coinage, together with the rebuilding of defensive fortifications and the re-establishment of a citizen militia with detachments under arms at all times, announced to the world the re-creation of independence for the Athenians.

The renewed city was, of course, very different in its policy and its power from what it had been in the fifth and fourth centuries, and even from what it had tried to be earlier in the third century. Athens would move more and more in the direction which it had already begun to take in the generation under Macedonian rule, that of becoming the primary educational center for the Mediterranean world. With the continuation of the schools of Plato and Aristotle reinforced by the establishment of the newer Epicurean and Stoic foundations, Athens had already been acting as a kind of bridge between traditional Hellenism and Hellenic thought and the more recent developments on the old base. It was also serving as a bridge between cities all around the Mediterranean, as citizens from all over came to Athens for the specific purpose of study in its schools. It was, in a way, a function analogous to that of Athens in the fifth century, when philosophers from all over came to Athens to teach, but in those days it had been the Athenians who benefited from the cosmopolitan effect of the visiting teachers, while from the third century on, students would travel to Athens to receive the benefits of the schools. While Alexandria could claim to be the most productive center of scientific and cultural scholarship, Athens would be the school of the world. Indeed, with the new relations established between independent Athens and the now powerful Rome which was on the point of its first intervention into the affairs of peninsular Greece, Athens was ready to serve as the bridge to Rome over which Hellenic culture would march to Italy and the west.

# 18

# Polybius and the Roman triumph

## *Roman domination of the Mediterranean and an educated Greek's reaction*

Impressed by the power and success of the Romans, the Greek Polybius sat down in the mid-second century to write an account of the manner in which they had managed to become the dominant power in the world in the short fifty-three-year period from 220 to 168 BC. Polybius himself had the advantage of experience of political affairs. His father had been a prominent politician in the Peloponnesian city of Megalopolis and Polybius himself had been designated for an embassy to Ptolemy V of Egypt which was cancelled when the king died in 180; ten years later he was a high official of the Achaean League just at the time when the Romans were about to re-enter hostilities in Greece. Then in 168, he was one of the 1000 or so important Achaeans who were transported to Rome supposedly for questioning, and then held in Italy for a long time as unofficial hostages.

At this time Polybius was in his mid-forties. When first in Rome, he made the acquaintance of the distinguished young Scipio Aemilianus, and through the friendship which quickly developed, Polybius was kept on in the city when the other Greek internees were distributed about Italy. For over sixteen years he had the benefit of close friendship with that leading Roman general and politician, and enjoyed an association with the many prominent Romans and political and intellectual figures from all over the world who associated with members of the circle of Scipio. By the time he left Rome in 150 he had learned an enormous amount about Roman institutions, customs, and character, and had traveled extensively throughout the Roman world and the regions which impinged upon it. He remained in close association with Scipio even after his return to Greece, joined him in the last war against Carthage, and stood beside the Roman general to watch the city burn in 146. And after the Achaean war, which the Romans ended successfully in 146 as well, Polybius assisted the Romans in the settlement of the affairs of the Greek cities, a number of which raised memorials to him for his services. He probably lived on at least until 118, and his death, we are told, at the age of 82, was caused by a fall from a horse.

206

## Polybius and the Roman triumph

Although only five of the forty books of Polybius' massive history survive intact, they and the fragmentary parts of the remainder provide us with invaluable insights into the events of this crucial period and into the mentality of a second-century Greek man of affairs who was in a position to interpret it. His decision to devote a detailed history to the events of the years 220 to 168 was elicited by his interpretation of history. This was the period, he thought, in which control of affairs passed to Rome, and Rome achieved the position from which her ultimate control over the entire Mediterranean was inevitable. With a new king in every major dynasty of the east, and the Romans taking their first step to the east with the establishment of a protectorate on the Illyrian coast, 219 was a critical year, as the Romans fought their second war in Illyria and faced events in Spain which precipitated the second great war between Rome and Carthage. On the Iberian peninsula, the Carthaginians had been pushing north, restricted only by an agreement with Rome which made the Ebro River their northern limit and set the most northerly 10 or 15 per cent of Spain to be a buffer between Carthaginian dominions and the area of Greek interest around Marseilles. In 219, however, the Carthaginian general attacked the city of Saguntum, a Roman ally halfway down the Spanish coast, which had the potential of serving as a Roman port behind Carthaginian lines in the event of war.

Although the Romans initially attempted to negotiate, according to their accounts of the matter, and spent months in sending embassies to Carthage, war was declared in 218. The war made Hannibal's name one of the best remembered in Roman history, as he brought his large army with its elephants suddenly across the Alps and descended into Italy, catching the Romans by surprise. After he smashed two Roman armies in 218 and annihilated another in spring 217, Rome was on the brink of defeat, but even after another great Carthaginian victory at Cannae in 216 brought some of the central Italian cities over to Hannibal's side, the Romans fought doggedly on, winning battles in Spain and holding the loyalty of critical regions in the areas south and north of Rome and eastwards across Italy to the Adriatic.

The conflict became a multi-front war in late 215 or early 214, when Hannibal achieved an alliance with Philip V, the young king of Macedonia. As the Macedonian assaults on Illyria left the Romans barely clinging to that coast, the fighting in Italy continued with vigor and the Roman–Spanish army continued its push against Carthaginian forces in Iberia. The war illustrated the determination and endurance of Rome, as it dealt with the defection of her ally Syracuse in Sicily, finally took the city of Capua in Italy despite Hannibal's attempt to relieve the siege of that city and even march on Rome, and remained undeterred even by the loss of two armies which had been cut to pieces in Spain. In Greece, during the so-called First Macedonian War, which lasted from 211 to 205, Rome was acting as an ally of one Greek people, the Aetolians, against a coalition of a large number of states led by Philip V. That war brought no conclusive disposition of Rome's relationships with Greece, but her alliance with a number of Greek states, like that of King Attalus of Pergamum, meant that Rome could deal with the threat of Philip's alliance with Hannibal without draining her resources to an eastern commitment. By 205, the year the war with Philip V ended, the Roman general Scipio was ready to carry the conflict to Carthage's home territories of North Africa. The landing which came in 204 started inauspiciously, but by 203 Scipio was in control of most of the territories around Carthage, and the Carthaginians recalled Hannibal and his army from Italy. The final battle came in 202, at Zama, inland and south-west of Carthage, and completely destroyed the Carthaginian forces. Hannibal escaped at the end to return to Carthage and advise the people to make peace, and after negotiations during a three-month truce, terms were finally settled. Carthage was to pay an indemnity of 10,000 talents to Rome over a period of fifty years, surrender to Rome her elephants and all but ten ships, cede to Rome's ally Massinissa all western territories which had ever belonged to his Numidians, and deposit 100 hostages in Rome. All this ended any possibility of the Carthaginians ever recovering their position as a great power, and its decline was reinforced by the formal establishment of Carthaginian dependency on Rome: Carthage was to fight no wars outside Africa, and even there, only with the permission of Rome.

The Romans did not need the passage of fifty years or the services of a Polybius to tell them what their defeat of Carthage meant. After Zama they had no rivals at all in the western Mediterranean, and their ships and commerce had free access everywhere. Their hold in the west would prove to be as solid as the Rock of Gibraltar, which in fact had now passed into their hands. With the west coast of Spain they had reached the Atlantic. The success not only extended their domains, it increased their financial, commercial, and mineral resources as well. Any Roman would think, in 202, that the state was the most powerful in the world, and was now fulfilling the destiny which had been laid out for it.

The war had tested every part of the Roman system – the reliability of their friends, colonies, and allies in Italy, the quality of Roman citizen soldiers, resources, military logistics, naval capability, even the walls of Rome itself. The system had held up. There were weaknesses, defections, and failures, but overall the Romans knew that their Italian base was secure in its core. The nature of the conflict also showed the Romans capable of managing successfully a new type of war. Hitherto, wars, even long wars, had been restricted in the theaters in which they were fought, and, as in the Athenian attempt to conquer Sicily, were rarely expanded successfully. Greek campaigns, even when conducted by Macedonian kings, usually came to an end each season, and forces did not encamp in large numbers in enemy territory, as Hannibal did for so long in Italy, or Scipio in North Africa. Even Alexander's march was more in the nature of an army on the move, and certainly after Issus and Gaugamela, when the Persians had been defeated, the battles fought came one at a time, were often minor, and the expedition seemed more to occupy conquered territory than to campaign against an organized and determined enemy. The Romans, on the other hand, fought in five theaters – Italy, Sicily, Spain, Greece, and North Africa, and there was always some action in at least three simultaneously. The nature of war had changed, and now required resources of far greater extent than peninsular Greece had ever been able to muster, and called for strategy of far greater scope than Greek generals had been required to develop.

With these great changes in the requirements for the imposition of policy by force, any challenge to the winner of the great conflict between Carthage and Rome would have to come from a state with resources of the scale which Rome had brought to bear. None such existed in the Mediterranean, although the Greeks did not yet realize that. The Roman neglect of Greek affairs during the conflict with Hannibal deceived Philip V into thinking that their settlement with him on relatively equal terms had some real significance. Further to the east, Antiochus III, who had succeeded to the Seleucid throne, after some unsuccessful struggles with Egypt made a name for himself – "the Great" – by a sustained and successful campaign to the east. He returned in 205/4 as a force to be reckoned with, and an alliance with Philip V seemed to solidify the political structure of the eastern Mediterranean. Greece, however, was quickly disrupted by a Roman march against the Macedonians, made for reasons which have not come down to modern times very clearly, but seem to have involved an appeal by the Roman ally Attalus of Pergamum. The application of Roman strength was curtailed by a need to put down the revolt of some Gallic tribes in North Italy in 200, but by 197, the Romans had isolated Philip diplomatically, and defeated his army by a decisive victory at Cynocephalae.

Polybius' account of the last two years of the war offers a very good indication of the approach the Romans, and particularly their general Flamininus, were taking toward the Greeks. Flamininus comes down to us in the pages of Polybius and his later biographer Plutarch as a "philhellene," with the interests of the Greeks at heart, when he demanded in 198 that Philip evacuate Greece, and announced the Senate's peace terms after his victory, that "all the rest of the Greeks, both those in Asia and those in Europe, are to be free and follow their own laws. Those controlled by Philip, and the cities which he garrisoned, Philip is to yield to the Romans before the festival of the Isthmian Games."[1] Polybius builds toward an announcement at the Isthmian Games of 196, as he tells us that all the most notable men of all the world came there to learn what the Romans would do, that the place was rife with rumors and alternate views, until the heralds announced that

The Senate of the Romans and Titus Quintius, Proconsul, having defeated King Philip and the Macedonians, leave free, ungarrisoned, without requirement of tribute, under their own ancestral laws, the Corinthians, Phocians, Locrians, Euboeans, Phthiotic Achaeans, Magnesians, Thessalians, Perrhabians.[2]

The crowd erupted in a shout of joy, so great that some did not hear, or did not believe they heard, the good news, and a second enunciation of the proclamation was greeted by the same cheering. To ensure that we appreciate the effect of the news, Polybius tells us that the volume of the noise cannot be imagined by those not there, that Flamininus was almost killed by the expressions of gratitude pressed on him, that however great the gratitude it was still exceeded by the greatness of the act. Whatever the intentions of the Senate which this proclamation reflected, Greek reactions and Polybius' treatment of the event ensured the interpretation which would be made by later Greeks and Romans; on behalf of the Greeks the Romans had fought a king who was attempting dominion, and after defeating the threat took no profit from the victory themselves. Although the Romans might see the action as entailing a permanent obligation and gratitude on the part of those who had received the benefit, the immediate Greek interpretation and its later ratification in the text of Polybius ensured that Greeks could look back on their relationship with Rome as established in freedom and equality by the act of liberation. It helped to develop the Greeks' own self-image as bearers of culture to a Rome which respected them for their age-old tradition of learning and intellectual accomplishments, and the representation of Flamininus as a philhellene who appreciated just those aspects of Hellenism reinforced that conception.

The freedom, of course, limited the right of any Greek or Greek state to control another without the permission of Rome, a position which entailed a short war against Sparta before Flamininus could repeat his declaration in 195, and in the next year sail from Greece, leaving not a single Roman soldier on the ground. He had not, in all this, disposed of Philip's ally, the Seleucid Antiochus, to whose court Hannibal had fled to urge an aggressive policy against Rome. In the war which broke out in 192, the Romans fought both Antiochus and the Aetolians, who nursed a grudge that the Romans had not adequately rewarded them for their earlier support. After inconclusive engagements, the Romans defeated Antiochus at Magnesia in Asia Minor in 189, and the king accepted the terms which required him to withdraw from Europe and Anatolia west of the Taurus Mountains, give up his fleet, and pay a huge war indemnity to Rome.

Even after this, Antiochus still had a great kingdom, which included southern Syria and Palestine, and thence reached eastward to encompass Babylonia and most of the Iranian plateau. The kingdom had the problems of heterogeneity which had plagued it from the start, but it was large and prosperous, and best of all, currently at peace with Egypt as a result of the marriage connection of Antiochus' daughter with the reigning king there, Ptolemy V. That peace lasted through the troubled succession in Syria and the early years of Ptolemy VI, until the Egyptian ambitions of Antiochus IV brought the situation to the attention of Rome. Responding to an attack by Egyptian troops, Antiochus IV himself marched into Egypt in 169, the first successful invasion since that of Alexander the Great, where he capitalized on rivalry between Ptolemy VI and his brother. He returned to Egypt in 168, but was met as he reached a suburb of Alexandria by a Roman emissary, Popilius Laenas. The scene is a famous one. Laenas informed the king that Rome ordered him to withdraw from Egypt. Upon Antiochus' responding that he would consult about the matter, Laenas drew a circle in the sand around the king, directing him not to leave the circle until he had given his response. The king, "astounded at what was happening and the authoritarian behavior," as Polybius says,[3] after a few minutes' hesitation replied that he would, indeed, depart. He returned to Syria and in the next year faced the Maccabean revolt in Palestine.

When the Senate sent Laenas off to the east with their letter to Antiochus, the Romans had just finished another Macedonian war, this time with Perseus, the son of Philip V. It had lasted from 171 until the Roman consul Lucius Aemilius Paullus ended it with one great battle in 168. The Romans then decided to settle Macedonian affairs by ending the monarchy, and they dismantled both Macedonia and Epirus, cutting the first into four separate constituent republics, the second into three. Then, turning south to the Achaean League, where they felt they had found insufficient support for their recent war, in 167 they collected 1000 hostages and sent them to Italy as surety for the good behavior of their countrymen.

One of these was Polybius, whose account of all these events to which he was so close was the dominant influence on later interpretations, not only those of ancient times but of our own. His writing betrays his sympathies for the upper-class aristocrats who led the Achaean League, and he accepted to some extent the Roman interpretation of the destiny of Rome. He saw the Roman ruling class as made up of men of almost rigid standards of honor and fair behavior, while he conceived of Greek monarchs and leaders as often irrational, savage, or venal, acting out their roles as history moved forward in its natural course.

There is, in Polybius' view, a natural sequence of events, one which can be seen in the evolution of constitutional structure, a cycle of developments and changes of government which flow one from the other. There are, he argues, in Chapter 4 of Book VI, three good forms of government and three degenerate. Government begins as monarchy, moves to its correct form of kingship, and then degenerates into tyranny, which is then abolished for aristocracy, which next degenerates into oligarchy; the anger arising from the unjust rule of oligarchy gives rise to democracy, which in turn degenerates into mob rule. Because he can use the theory for the elucidation of the evolution of the Roman Constitution, Polybius sets it out in what he admits is a summary, as the transformation of societies "according to nature,"[4] and a theory which has been proposed by "Plato and certain other philosophers."[5] In his discussion, occasional phraseology has been taken to indicate a Stoic source for his ideas, but much of this language, like other "Stoic" expressions claimed for Polybius, has parallels in Greek outside of Stoic texts. Polybius is quite specific in naming

Plato as a source for the theory, and his mention of "other philosophers" is enough of an explanation for the echoes of Aristotle or peripatetic thought in the passage. The discussion is, in fact, much more valuable for its indications of the effects of political philosophy and ethics on intelligent laymen, that is, non-philosophers, than it is useful for tracing either Polybius' own development or the sources of his views, for what we have here is an example of an intelligent man's views on the ethical and political evolution of human society Polybius' own concept, composite and eclectic.

Polybius sees society as a natural, biological phenomenon, with, as for every body, "a certain natural growth, and after that an acme, and then dissolution."[6] There is, as he points out in VI 47.3, an inevitable relationship between the character of the citizens of a state and its laws and customs, and this biological interpretation of the development of Constitutions entwines the concept of Justice with the growth of the state. With the growing sense of community the first concepts of the Good and the Just come into existence, and notions of their opposites come into being in the same way. Some of this discussion has been called Stoic, but on the other hand, the idea in VI 6.1–7.1 that the concept of Justice arises from the experience of men in their social relationships, with the Good honored because of its social advantage, is very close to the Epicurean view that Justice does not exist in itself but occurs in relationships among people as a kind of agreement to avoid mutual harm. Throughout his work one can find evocations of or allusions to earlier philosophers with the sequence of Constitutions close to that set out by Aristotle, occasional citations of Plato and direct allusion to the *Republic*,[7] as well as reminders of ideas found in the works of the Stoics and Epicureans. Polybius' writing demonstrates that he was not a philosopher, nor even, perhaps, primarily a historian, but a statesman, a political leader of a free Greek city, a man with experience of government, politics, and war, and all the practical matters these involve. History is best written by men of action, and makes for understanding, he thought, when it is written as a comprehensive account; the local or partial histories of places or wars do not lead to an understanding of the significance of events once human history has become a unit, as Mediterranean history had since 220 BC. Polybius was not trained as a philosopher or even as a historian, but as befitted the son of an important citizen of Megalopolis and leader of the Achaean League. He knew the major works of Greek literature, he was familiar with the important concepts of contemporary science, and was acquainted with the doctrines, if not the writings, of the important philosophical schools. All this probably influenced his political behavior and certainly influenced his writing. He left an interpretation of history that held a conceptualization of causation arising from the natural evolution of societies, the birth, growth, acme, and death of successions of political organizations. Individual human beings could fit into these developments, even assist and share in the causation, and, as he showed in the long discussion of Scipio's virtues in Book XXXI 28, could exemplify ideals of conduct by the manner in which they dealt with events. But whatever was virtue was such for people and human affairs, was understandable thus, and even originated from the requirements of human social interaction. No divine abstractions existed to puzzle Polybius or explain any phenomena which he might regard as evil. Vague references to gods or to Fortune never served to explain the broad direction taken by history; what happened in history came from the nature of human societies. Polybius' notions of historical necessity, however much they may have fitted his experience of Rome and his appreciation of Roman power, can still be found to have had Hellenic roots. It was not anything inherent in Rome that brought her victory, or any particular virtue, and, as was remarked by Romans themselves, that state too would someday wane.

Polybius carried his history on to recount events which took place shortly after he himself returned to Greece, including the rebellion of Macedonia under the pretender Andriscus, which was ended after a year in 148. Macedonia was subsequently made into a Roman province governed by a Roman magistrate, ending the attempt to settle affairs there by the establishment of self-governing republics. The same thing happened in southern Greece, after the Achaean League rebelled against the Roman decision to detach from it some of its constituent states. A brief war thus caused in 146 was quickly over, ending in the sack of Corinth which resulted in the city's treasures being carried off to Rome. All over Greece governments opposed to Rome were overthrown, leagues were dissolved, and Achaea, as southern Greece was called by the Romans, was made part of the responsibility of the governor of Macedonia. The peace which then settled over Greece has been called by a modern writer "the silence of the grave," but it encountered no objection from Polybius. If he had thought of this peace as death, it would in any case have been part of the natural cycle.

# 19

# The Jews in
# the Mediterranean world
## *The history and character of Judaism
## and the impact of Greek ideas*

The revolt which Antiochus IV faced when he returned to Palestine after the Roman order expelled him from Egypt in 167 came as much from resentment among Jews at increasing Hellenization among their own people as antagonism toward the Seleucid king himself. Over 1000 years of history lay behind these events, and the experience of independence in the kingdoms of Israel and Judah, of exile and return. In that millennium the Jews had developed a sense of their culture and their history as inextricably tied up with their relationship to Yahweh, as they named their God, and related directly to their fulfilment of his Law as they knew it. Their culture and religion focused on the obedience to divine law as it was recorded for them in Scripture. That Scripture gave them their history as much as their religion, made them, as has often been said, "The People of the Book," and set them apart in later times from all the peoples of the Mediterranean with whom they came into contact.

According to the tradition preserved in the Bible, the antecedents of the Jews came from Mesopotamia, and settled in Canaan, the land later known as Palestine, in the seventeenth century BC, as modern historians date the events. This was the time of Abraham, as biblical history tells the tale, and the stay in Palestine was followed in later generations by the sojourn in Egypt, the persecution by the pharaoh, the arrival of the Law and finally the struggle to regain Canaan. Over a period of 200 years the Hebrews fought their way into Palestine, under the leadership of officials called *shophetim*, which we translate as "judges" but who were in fact magistrates of much more general authority, including that of leading in war. By about 1050 BC a formal kingship had been established under Saul. His successor David, who reigned until about 975 BC, secured Israel's borders with victories over neighboring peoples, and captured Jerusalem, where his son Solomon, whose reign began around 975 and lasted for forty years, built the temple dedicated to Yahweh. The nation in Solomon's time was prosperous, with extensive foreign trade and diplomatic relations, and the king's many wives testified to his friendship with the royal families of many other peoples. Solomon's reign also saw the beginning of what the Bible portrays as the kings' faithlessness toward Yahweh, what seems to have been an openness to foreign cult and the worship of foreign gods. Solomon allowed his wives to worship their own gods, to build altars and cult centers for them, and the evidence of excavation confirms the biblical story. His reign not only began this practice; it ended the unified kingdom of Israel. Yahweh decided to allow the house of David only one tribe to rule henceforth, and accordingly on Solomon's death, the rebel Jeroboam took control of the entire north of Palestine, thereafter called Israel, leaving for the legitimate heir, Solomon's son Reheboam, only the small southern remnant which was to be the Kingdom of Judah.

From that time on the two kingdoms went their separate ways, often in hostility to one another. Their story, written from a point of view which is partial to the southern kingdom of Judah, is an account of dwindling power, encirclement, and pressure from the kingdoms and empires which surrounded Palestine. The biblical account particularly emphasizes the apostasy of the northern kingdom, Israel, repeating for each king after another that "he did what was displeasing to Yahweh." For both kingdoms the story in the two biblical books of Kings is one of Yahweh's people falling away from the Law, not only in observance and worship to the exclusion of other – empty – gods, but also failure to heed repeated calls from prophets to abandon the ways of iniquity and return to the true God. In Israel, the ninth century was marked by the introduction of foreign gods by King Ahab and his wife Jezebel, and the work of two great prophets, first Elijah and then his successor Elisha. There were more such kings and more prophets condemning them throughout the eighth century BC, while the power of Assyria steadily increased and encroached on the lands immediately to the east of Palestine. Finally, in 721 BC, the northern capital, Samaria, fell after a siege, and the Assyrian king Shalmaneser V deported the inhabitants, and settled foreign colonists who mixed the worship of their own gods with that of Yahweh. The little kingdom of Judah was left to stand alone.

The history of Judah was much like that of Israel, although the compiler of Kings was not so insistent that every single king in Judah had broken faith with Yahweh. In the last half of the eighth century the southern kingdom faced the powers pressing in on Palestine from all sides. As the kings of the beleaguered nation sought to find support against their enemies from foreign allies, Judah produced a great prophet, Isaiah, whose vision of the awesome power of God and the unworthiness of humanity called him to urge that his people place their faith only in Yahweh, not in the uncertain force of earthly alliances. His oracles against the nations and his messianic prophecies for his own people are expressed in poetry of great force, which was imitated by followers whose own work was later included in the Book of Isaiah. A century later, another prophet, Jeremiah, born about 645 BC, arose to express in an even more personal manner the exclusivity and magnificence of Yahweh's domain and Law, condemning the wickedness of the people of Judah and calling them back to the dictates of the Covenant.

In these years the so-called Neo-Babylonian Empire was becoming the dominant power in the east. By 600 BC the Assyrian Empire had been destroyed and King Nebuchadnezzar was on the throne at Babylon. Judah had sought help against Babylon from Egypt, despite Jeremiah's exhortations to yield, but when Egypt was defeated at Carchemish in 605 there was nothing for the Judaean king to do but accept the position of vassal of the Babylonian. By 598 BC, there had been a revolt, much opposed by Jeremiah, and a siege of Jerusalem which brought the surrender and deportation to Babylon of the new king, Jehoiachin, who had reigned for only three months. Another revolt in 589 BC brought another siege of Jerusalam, and in 586, in June or July, the city fell again. This time the dynasty was ended permanently. Nebuchadnezzar installed his own governor over the country, destroyed the city of Jerusalem with the Temple, and deported large numbers of its inhabitants to Babylon. The independence of Judah had lasted only 150 years longer than that of Israel to the north.

The end of the independent kingdoms and the years of captivity in Babylon marked a fundamental stage not only in the history of the Jews, but in their consciousness of the history. The destruction of the Temple and the Jerusalem which it had ornamented seemed to be Yahweh's retribution for apostasy. The promise of eternal possession of Canaan was yet to be fulfilled, and the interruption of the enjoyment of the promised land was deemed by the religious to have been a well-deserved punishment for wickedeness. Those in exile and those left in Palestine looked to their religious texts in the absence of the Temple. Old Scripture - the ninth/eighth-century BC sources for Genesis, Exodus, Numbers, and Leviticus – had been supplemented by the discovery of Deuteronomy in 621 BC, and during and after the exile in Babylon all the legal provisions of the Bible were correlated and edited to provide more cohesive texts, so that the Jews could find and follow the Law to which they had been directed by Yahweh. The historical books[1] continued the story from the time of Moses, in a narrative which demonstrated the effect on history of Yahweh's will and the failure of his people to obey it. The story of these books is essentially theological, an account of a Covenant which Yahweh's chosen people continually violated though Yahweh and his prophets repeatedly called them to return to it. Much had been promised the Israelites, on condition of their exclusive attention to Yahweh's Law. That Law was not only "cultic"; it formalized many old Near Eastern traditions into an ethical code founded on the Ten Commandments and later expanded in its meaning and application by the prophets who followed Moses. But those provisions most open to examination, the requirements that no worship or facilities for worship of pagan deities be allowed in the land which Yahweh had given Israel – those were repeatedly and obviously violated. Patterns of pagan worship, in the "high places," at altars set up even in the Temple, with golden calves and other pagan idols and symbols, were pronounced from the time of Jeroboam, Solomon's successor at the end of the tenth century who was responsible for the division of the people into two kingdoms. The people failed to take advantage of Yahweh's repeated opportunities for reconciliation and remained what he had called them from the start, "headstrong," and the kings, consistently in the northern kingdom but sadly deficient in the south as well, led the two segments of Israel inevitably into dissolution. Only the oracles of the later prophets Isaiah and Jeremiah leave any hope for the future after this tragic story of wilfulness and wickedness. While condemning the people for their sin and apostasy, both these prophets turned their vision of Yahweh's punishment of Israel into a hope of redemption and restoration, a hope which ultimately appears in the Book of Jeremiah as a promise of a new Covenant with each man individually instead of with the nation as a whole.

Thus, by the time the Jews had experienced the misery of exile and loss of their land, and had been brought back into the mainstream of Mediterranean history when Cyrus of Persia liberated and restored them in 538 BC, their particular nature as a people had been formed and confirmed. "The People of the Book" had a life and ethos fundamentally and strikingly different from their neighbors. With the Greeks, who were at the time of Cyrus just beginning to come into their own with the development of their city-states, the Hebrews had virtually nothing in common. The difference in attitude toward the nature of god or gods is obvious, as is the acceptance of pluralism by the Greeks and its vehement rejection by the Jews. Much more important, and more basic in its effect on moral, political, and social attitudes, was the Jewish perception that there was a purpose behind events, a direction which history was taking, a meaning to their lives individually and collectively which was created by their special relationship with the god Yahweh, and that they were a people "chosen" to live a life of purity and separateness. They had been selected by Yahweh to exemplify to all the nations the life of fidelity to God and his Laws, and their history unfolded in accord with their fulfilment of that destiny. Everything that happened in history, from the division of the kingdom after Solomon, through the rise and fall of the empires of Egypt, Assyria, and Babylon, was the will of Yahweh and was arranged with the apostasy of Israel and its punishment as the focus. As later Greeks might have felt that the Hellenes stood as the fount and center of culture, the Jews felt that they were, not the movers of history, but its very cause.

Such was one effect of the Book upon its people. But there was much more, for the Jews were as much the "People of the Law," and the Law had great depth and scope. While the notion of codified law was an old one in the east, it had never penetrated in its ethical and moral form to the Greeks. The Jews tied these ethical and moral regulations to the requirements of religion, blending cult and ethics into a system which was ratified as an imperative by divine command. That such was the case quite early in Jewish history is demonstrated by the embedding of the Ten Commandments in the Mosaic code. These were fundamental ethical proscriptions of murder, adultery, theft, false witness, and covetousness of one's neighbor's wife or property, mixed with the requirement of honor to father and mother, the theological regulations of exclusivity for Yahweh, proscription of images and misuse of the divine name, and the command to keep the Sabbath. Anthropologists might insist that all these ethical requirements can be found among many, if not most, early peoples in their tribal state, that they are necessary for the survival of the tribe and are therefore often given transcendent endorsement. But among the Jews, the rules very early left the sphere where only the tribe was protected, and passed the limited regulations which provided for tribal protection through such concepts as pollution for blood guilt with which we are familiar in the Greek city-states. For example, intermingled with the elaborate ritual regulations of the Book of Leviticus come prescriptions for honest behavior and commandments for kindness to the poor,[2] which are repeated often in terms of justice and protection to the poor, the weak, the widows, and orphans in Deuteronomy.[3] It is not just the tribe which is protected: Deuteronomy 10: 19 calls on Israel to befriend the stranger, "for you were strangers in the land of Egypt,"[4] and Deuteronomy 14: 29 includes the stranger amongst those who are to benefit from the triennial tithe of charity. Most striking is the phraseology of Leviticus:

When a stranger resides with you in your land, you shall not wrong him. The stranger who resides with you shall be to you as one of your citizens; you shall love him as yourself, for you were strangers in the land of Egypt: I the LORD am your god.[5]

The Law, with its rich detail of religious observance, its elaborate prescriptions for ritual behavior and code of "uncleanness," dominated the minds of the Jews from the time of its earliest formulation. Long before they went into exile in the sixth century they were being told by their leaders and prophets that the tribulations which they suffered were imposed by Yahweh in retribution for their failure to keep the Covenant. As early as David's time, however, the concept of retribution has been extended to cover violations of the social code as much as ritual regulations.[6] The eighth-century words of Isaiah[7] give ethics and the social code a central role in prophecy: there is no justice for orphans and widows; infamous laws refuse justice to the unfortunate and cheat the poor of their rights; kings reign by integrity and princes by law; and integrity will bring peace, and justice lasting security; Yahweh brings true justice, frees the captive from prison, and opens the eyes of the blind,[8] above all, the prophet begins the book with a demand for justice:

I am sated with burnt offerings of rams. . . .
Your new moons and fixed seasons Fill Me with loathing. I cannot endure them. . . .

Put your evil doings Away from My sight. Cease to do evil;
Learn to do good. Devote yourselves to justice, Aid the wronged, Uphold
the rights of the orphan; Defend the cause of the widow.[9]

Nothing in the Greek tradition remotely approaches the sense of sin, transgression, and rejection of God expressed by Isaiah; nothing in Hellenic religion, culture, or ethics acts as such a rigorous guide to the fulfilment of ethical and ritual commandments as the Law served the Jews.

The prophets return again and again to the themes of justice and divine law. The early prophetic tradition revives again and again the theme that Israel has betrayed the Covenant with Yahweh, that the fundamental prohibition against worship of other gods is being ignored, that idolatry and witchcraft are rife in the land, and that the immorality and wickedness of the people call for a cleansing of the nation. It is not only ritual that is at stake, but fundamental morality and ethics,[10] as we would say, that the prophets put forward as violated by Israel. Line after line of fulminations predict doom, ruin, and suffering, only occasionally relieved by a promise of Yahweh's eventual forgiveness or relenting.

The Law, and Yahweh as its giver and enforcer, also served to explain the existence of evil in the world long before that problem arose to plague Greek tragedy and philosophy. Evil and trouble arise directly from human failure to keep the Law, and the people are responsible:

Surely this instruction which I enjoin on you today is not too baffling for you, nor is it beyond reach. It is not in the heavens, that you should say, "Who among us can go to the heavens and get it for us and impart it to us, that we may observe it?" Neither is it beyond the sea, that you should say, "Who among us can cross to the other side of the sea and get it for us and impart it to us, that we may observe it?" No, the thing is very close to you, in your mouth and in your heart, to observe it.[11]

However much later wisdom literature might insist on the obscurity of wisdom, the sense that the Law conveyed truth to humanity and thus made humans responsible is a pervading theme of Jewish ethics.

Thus the idea that trangression and punishment therefore create a collective responsibility appears early in biblical literature. The collective is the people of Israel, whose possession of Canaan at the expense of the inhabitants comes not for its virtue, but because of the Covenant with Abraham and "because of the wickedness of those nations."[12] The Covenant made with the parents is carried forward and kept with the people for generations, and the Law stands, clear and known, for observance. Yahweh is patient with both kings and people when they fall away, but eventually, retribution comes. For the sins of the kings all the people suffer; for the sins of some, all pay. Gradually, Israel dwindles away in a collective atonement for a guilt seen as collective.

24 This image of God's transmission of life to Adam by Michelangelo combines the Hellenism of the visual image with the sense of the directness of the relationship between God and humanity which suffuses the Old Testament texts. A detail of the ceiling fresco in the Sistine chapel, Vatican.

By the time of the exile, however, this sense of collective responsibility began to erode. The theme that is repeated throughout Judges, Kings, and in the writings of the early prophets begins to yield to a sense of individual responsibility. By the end of the seventh century the potential had been carried to open expression in the personal religion of Jeremiah, as he rejects the old concept of collective responsibility, the punishment of the sons for the sins of their fathers: "In those days they shall no longer say, Parents have eaten sour grapes and children's teeth are blunted. But everyone shall die for his own sins."[13]

Jeremiah predicts a day of a new Covenant, in which the Law will be internalized with no need of external teaching, in which all will know Yahweh, and "No longer will they need to teach one another."[14] These notions of individual responsibility contrast strikingly with early Hellenic thought. Even in the fifth century, when Athenian tragedians wrestled with questions of divine and human law, they would do so not merely from the standpoint of Jeremiah's questioning the prosperity of the wicked, but from a point of view that was unable to offer any certainty at all about the nature of divine law, or even whether divinity was friendly or hostile, involved with man or detached and remote. Deuteronomy could say that Law was at hand and within reach; tragedy would ask whether it even existed as an absolute.

By the fifth century BC, the Jews had experienced exile and return. They were, however, still not masters of their own political destiny, and Palestine would be for a long time a part of one or another oriental empire, often fought over or maintained as a buffer zone between Egypt and any rival which controlled Syria. Throughout the fifth and fourth centuries the Jews of Palestine also remained relatively separate from the events which were overtaking the eastern Mediterranean, insulated from many changes by their status as part of the Persian domains, under a government which was quite tolerant of non-Iranian religion and willing to allow its subjects to keep their own cultures. The period was for the most part a peaceful one in Palestine, but the succeeding waves of returning exiles found a land not only devastated by earlier wars but suffering from drought. The country was never very prosperous at this time, and its residents received a serious setback in the mid-fourth century, as the result of a general revolt in Syria, and a rebellion in Egypt, which took the Persians three years to subdue. The Jews participated in all this, and as punishment their city of Jericho was destroyed and many were again carried off into captivity, some as far as Hyrcania on the Caspian Sea. After this they remained quiet, but their later literature shows that they regarded Alexander the Great as a liberator. After him, the Jews would reckon with Hellenism as the culture of their rulers, which had a quite different effect from that of the Persians.

These centuries also saw the beginning of the spread of Jews outside their old territorial limits of Palestine. By the last quarter of the sixth century a Jewish military colony had been established at Elephantine, an island just down river from the first cataract of the Nile. They had built a temple there, and, as we learn from sixty-two fifth-century BC Aramaic papyri found there, the religion was Yahwistic with other intrusions. They engaged in various commercial activities in the area, but still maintained contact with Palestine. This colony of mercenaries was not unique in bringing Jews into contact with the wider Mediterranean world for there was a settlement of Greeks at Acco in the mid-fourth century,[15] and there is archaeological evidence of Greek activity or Greek wares in Palestine even as early as the seventh century.

While biblical literature leaves us in a relatively poor position in regard to historical information for the post-exilic period, it contains a wealth of material of a different sort. These are the centuries which begin the tradition of so-called wisdom literature, the books of Job, Psalms, Proverbs, Wisdom, and others similar. The wisdom literature had entirely different origins from the historical literature, which in one way or another went back to very early times. Except for some of the psalms, which certainly do go back to early times and may even, in some cases, actually have been the work of David himself, the wisdom books were all written in the first instance in the post-exilic period with not many direct sources from earlier times. Job is probably a composition of the early fifth century, possibly with some later intrusions. Proverbs was also put together in the fifth century, in all probability, with the prologue written then, as some collections of very early wisdom literature, typical of a number of societies of the east, were gathered up and made into a single work. Other books, Ecclesiastes and Wisdom, for example, belong even later, to the period after Alexander.

While there are some concepts which, in their emphasis at least, seem different from earlier attitudes, the wisdom literature is more a continuation of what had gone before than a radical shift in religious views. Yahweh as founder of the earth appears again and again in Psalms.[16] The importance of the Law is re-emphasized,[17] and is central to the thought of many of the poems, and the long Psalm 78, with its survey of Jewish history to demonstrate the penalties of rebellion against Yahweh, begins with the Law as God's first requirement for obedience. The concept of God the Judge comes more to the fore,[18] and the concepts of social justice which appeared in the earliest laws remain prominent. Not only is care for the weak and poor the human duty,[19] God himself has a care for the orphan, the widow, the poor.[20] One may sense some change, whether post-exilic in origin or earlier is hard to say, in the more frequent allusions to the compassion of Yahweh, as in Psalm 103, or his everlasting love, as in 136 and 138, but there is, in fact, nothing here that cannot find strong and legitimate basis in the earliest texts of Scripture. The same situation obtains in Proverbs,[21] even with its assemblage of mundane practical advice on the pattern of so much other oriental wisdom literature.

One wisdom book which has been thought to introduce new and specifically Hellenic ideas is Job, but even here, occasional similarities of thought or expression are overwhelmed by the fundamental differences in world view between Greek writers and the composer of Job. As literature the book is one of the great masterpieces of antiquity, in its treatment of the manner in which Job is plagued by a succession of troubles sent by Yahweh as a demonstration that the man will remain steadfast in his faith even when not rewarded. The work uses a series of colloquies to deal with the question which has often bothered those with religious faith: Why should the virtuous suffer? Job's three friends approach this question and answer his complaints in various ways, all three conceiving of divine justice as perfect, and concluding that Job must have sinned in some way. The last urges on Job the conclusion that if God wished, he could reveal to him in what way he had sinned, and that his opinion of himself as blameless arises only from his lack of knowledge, not perfect virtue.

Job will have none of this. He understands the issue, and he sarcastically dismisses the counsellors: "Indeed, you are the (voice of) the people, and wisdom will die with you."[22] Job intends to contest the case directly with God, for he is convinced of his innocence, and he challenges Yahweh to reply, to show how he has broken the Law. Instead of God's answer, Job again receives moralism from his three friends, informing him of what he knows already, that rebellion against God brings ruin, that the wicked will suffer. In the face of the platitudes of his friends, who insist on his guilt in order to make sense of God's action, Job persists in maintaining his innocence, an insistence which in fact goes further to explain the workings of God than do the simplistic statements of his friends.[23] Ultimately, Job concludes with a reiteration of his misery, a catalogue of sins which he did not commit, a denial that he ever failed to be insensible to the needs of the poor, or failed to share with the widow, with the orphan or strangers. He is confident that he has met the requirements of the Law.

Parallels have been drawn between the questioning of divine justice by Job and some ideas of Athenian tragedy, but many of the resemblances are more superficial and verbal than revealing of any confluences or concurrences in moral thought. Job charging God with injustice, portraying Yahweh as his enemy, has reminded readers of the representation of Zeus as the maleficent enemy of humanity and Prometheus in Aeschylus' *Prometheus Bound*, but the god portrayed there is completely different from anything in the minds of Job or his fellows. Zeus is selfish, interested in his own ends only, hostile to Prometheus for disobedience to the will of a god whose purposes have no relationship to virtue. Yahweh on the other hand has revealed a Law to humankind; the commandments are to be obeyed because they make up the moral code according to which the creator of the universe had decreed it is to be governed. Job's problem is not that he faced God as enemy, but that he cannot understand why he is made to suffer as God's enemy when he has built his entire life on the observance of God's Law and obedience to his commandments. Like his friends, who try to save the system by proposing that Job has in some way sinned, Job believes in the system. He cannot, however, accept guilt. God exists, his Law is just, Job has obeyed, and yet his lot is worse than that of the wicked.

Readers of Sophocles have sometimes felt themselves on familiar ground as they read the Book of Job. Like so many Sophoclean heroes, Job is sure that he is right; like the Sophoclean heroes, he both is and isn't. And, as the book rises to its climax, after an interruption by the speech of Elihu which some think an interpolation and which in any case anticipates some of the themes of the concluding speeches of Yahweh, the conclusion that the human is limited in his understanding of the divine order seems almost to be a Sophoclean concept made explicit by the words of God. Yahweh thunders his awesome poetry out of the tempest:

I will ask and you will inform Me.
Where were you when I laid the earth's foundations? Speak if you have understanding. . . .
Have you ever commanded the day to break, Assigned the dawn its place,
So that it seizes the corners of the earth And shakes the wicked out of it?[24]

A sequence of questions, none of which can Job answer. Yahweh has given his explanation, and Job understands:

I know that You can do everything, That nothing you propose is impossible for You
Who is this who obscures counsel without knowledge? Indeed I spoke without understanding Of things beyond me, which I did not know.[25]

In the end of the tale, Yahweh returns Job to his happiness and material prosperity – doubling, in fact, what he had before. He has learned the lesson of the supremacy of Yahweh, and has acknowledged that learning.

Although the story deals with the question of apparent injustice in the world and thus has some parallel in concept to some Sophoclean tragedy, the basic ideology is different and the intellectual presumptions fundamentally foreign to Greek thought, even if roughly contemporary with the Athens of Sophocles. The Sophoclean hero is usually satisfied with his action, even though in his single-minded devotion to his principles he meets the disaster which is inevitable for humans in a world run by gods according to principles imperfectly understood. In contrast, Job is most emphatically not satisfied. In his world, and the world on which the book is predicated, divine justice and the principles of the cosmos are not imperfectly understood, and he is not in the Hellenic position of fumbling toward approximate and sometimes erroneous conclusions about the provisions of divine law. To Job, like other Jews, the rules are laid out in precision and detail in the Law, and at hand. They deal not only with service to God but with the correct treatment of fellow humans, and Job is conscious – insistent – that he has fulfilled not only ritual requirements but also the mandates of social justice, emphasizing this aspect of divine law that fits into the biblical tradition, but is quite alien to Hellenic. Job knows that social injustice attracts God's anger. He claims that he had always been considerate of the needs of the poor, helpful to the afflicted, the widows, the orphans, strangers, and the weak.[26] His sense of the universality of humanity is quite different from anything we read in fifth-century Athenian literature, as he acknowledges brotherhood with slave and servant: "Did not He who made me in my mother's belly make him? Did not One form us both in the womb?"[27]

It is a concept which can only emerge out of a tradition which sees the relationship between God and the human race to be that of creator–created, long established in Hebrew thought. Not only is Job's tradition fundamentally different in this regard from that of fifth-century Greek tragedy in allocating such importance to social virtue, it diverges also in its characteristic Jewish focus on the Law as the central feature ordering relations with God, the ritual behavior in Temple and home, and social intercourse. Only Yahweh and Yahweh's will direct life and give meaning to it. This is Job's discovery, and the eventual outcome of the tale, with God returning to Job all he has lost and giving him even greater prosperity, is in itself a striking difference from the outcome of tragedy, where the hero never gains practical advantage from his conduct. In this way too the overwhelmingly theocentric character of Hebrew thought and Jewish life is as strong in Job as in the earliest strands of the Yahwistic tradition of the first books of Moses, a feature of Jewish thought which continued on in the centuries which followed.

The history of Palestine in the nearly two centuries between the advent of Alexander in 332 BC and the re-establishment of an autonomous Jewish state in the latter half of the second century BC is interwoven with the conflicts and politics of the kings who followed Alexander. For about a hundred years after Alexander's death, the Ptolemies ruled Palestine, and even with the Syrian wars of the third century, there was no serious threat to Ptolemaic control until the reign of Antiochus III, and even his successes were overturned in 217 when the Ptolemaic victory at Raphia brought Palestine back firmly under Ptolemaic control. Antiochus tried again in 201, with the young Ptolemy V newly on the throne, but this time, his decisive victory at Panium in 200 brought an end to Ptolemaic rule in Palestine. From the beginning of the second century, Syria and Palestine were Seleucid.

What all this meant to the Jews, and what effects these events did or did not have on Jewish religious or political attitudes, is now very much a matter of scholarly speculation, guesswork, and controversy. We know of some events, like those of 201 and 200, when Jerusalem passed first into the hands of Antiochus, then was recovered by the forces of Ptolemy, only to pass again to Antiochus after his victory at Panium. There is no narrative treatment of the period of Ptolemaic dominion in biblical literature, and modern studies have explored late books, apocryphal material, and documentary and literary Greek sources extensively to discover some explanation of the circumstances which led up to the successful revolt of the Maccabees.[28]

For that revolt we do have narrative information, two accounts which are roughly contemporary, 1 and 2 Maccabees, uncanonical scripture so far as the Hebrew Bible is concerned, but the main historical sources, to which may be added information from Daniel and Josephus' *Jewish Antiquities*. The basic outline of events is quite clear. In 175, when the new king, Antiochus IV Epiphanes, had just succeeded to the throne, Jason, the brother of the high priest but supported by a different faction, obtained the endorsement of Antiochus to become high priest himself. With the king's agreement and decree, he had Jerusalem established as a Greek city, Antioch-in-Jerusalem, with all the institutions of a *polis*, including some which were controversial amongst the Jews, such as the gymnasium and the *ephebeion* for the education of the citizen youth in the Greek manner. Within three years Jason was ousted by one Menelaus, who, according to the account in 2 Maccabees, purchased the office for himself from Antiochus when he was supposedly on a mission to Antiochus for Jason to pay the taxes. As a result of the deposition, civil war broke out amongst the Jews – a civil war in which, as the accounts are usually interpreted, the powerful Tobiad family supported Menelaus. While all this was under way, Antiochus was involved in two expeditions to Egypt, and although there are differences in the sequences of events as told in 1 and 2 Maccabees, there was a sack of the Temple by Antiochus as well as revolutionary activity against Seleucid rule, and by the time Antiochus concluded his second expedition in 168 (on Roman orders), there had been a prolonged period of civil violence and political conspiracy. In 167 began the famous persecution of the Jews, with the installation of pagan cults in the Temple and prohibition of the observance of the Law, banning, for example, observance of the Sabbath and circumcision of boys. There were resistances and martyrdoms; one Mattathias, a respected figure in the town of Modein, killed a Jew who was on the point of obeying the king's commissioners, and then killed the king's officer as well. Mattathias and his associates then fled. Among the group were Mattathias' sons, who, starting with Judah, whom we know as Judah Maccabaeus, led the opposition to Antiochus until they gained control of Palestine and autonomy under the Seleucids.

These events, and the sources which report them, remain the subject of a great deal of historical controversy, with the central issue the question of the causes of Antiochus' persecution of the Jewish religion, not a usual act by Greeks, and the extent to which Hellenism on the part of some Jews and orthodoxy on the part of others were motive forces behind the revolt and civil commotion which preceded it. It is clear, in any case, that the writers of 1 and 2 Maccabees themselves inclined, and wrote to make us incline, to accept religious factors and Jewish Hellenizing on the part of all the power seekers as a fundamental cause of conflict among Jews and with the government. Then too, while the presentation of Antiochus' decrees ordering the persecution holds hints of political motivation, the account makes the persecution focus entirely on religious matters, and relates the outbreak of the Maccabean revolt directly to an attempt to enforce the religious legislation. In fact, 2 Maccabees interprets the whole episode in religious terms, making the persecution God's chastisement which will save his people from worse calamities.[29] While the didactic phraseology of the work, which was composed in Greek, shows a Hellenic approach in style, the concept is in every respect part of the tradition of the early prophets and of the compilers of the historical books, who wanted to show how the deterioration of the position of the nation arose from the falling away from the Law. That is, in the mind of the compiler of 2 Maccabees, exactly the position in regard to the imposition of the persecution by Antiochus.

These accounts represent Hellenization as the corrupting influence on Judaism, and this interpretation remained at the heart of later Jewish versions of these events, as it appears a century and a half later in the work of Josephus. Whatever the realities of these things are, it is what people think they are that matters in the long run. Although we will probably never have certainty about the extent to which religious motives generated the Maccabean revolt, or how much part the pursuit of personal power played, the general pattern of the cultural development of the Jews in Palestine is clear, and its significance for the evolution of religion and philosophy amongst them is unarguable. By the first half of the second century BC, there had been some Hellenization. That Hellenization was expressed in political terms, with some Jews glad to emulate the Greek political institutions with which they have become familiar in the twenty-nine Greek cities up and down the coast. Hellenism also penetrated the intellectual and religious milleux, if not immediately, then certainly before the end of the century, and its influence can be found in its imprint on religious literature.

Some of the most striking influences of Greek literature can be found in the books of Maccabees themselves. Generally speaking, the compiler of 2 Maccabees shows himself completely familiar with Greek culture as well as Greek idiom, and his references to the Seleucid king's activities, the correspondence with the Jews in Egypt which opens the work, and the easy reference to the Romans in 11: 34–8 shows that the compiler's world extended to the wider Mediterranean. The same world outlook is apparent in 1 Maccabees, even though in this case the Greek text is based on a translation of a Hebrew original. That author is familiar with the main lines of recent Roman history, knows something of Roman government, and is inclined to eulogize them, doubtless because of their support of the Jews and their hostility to the Seleucid house. Like the Greek author of 2 Maccabees he writes under the influence of the Hellenistic historians' use of documents, and is comfortable quoting the record of diplomatic relations between Jews and Spartans.[30] He lives, so to speak, in the Mediterranean world, not limited to the confines of inland Palestine. But despite this clear familiarity with Hellenism, neither of our authors has acquired a Hellenic mentality or very much in the way of Greek ideas. Both write with a strong antipathy to Hellenization of Jews, and neither sees very much in the way of the supposed benefits of Greek culture.[31]

This might be no more than one might expect on the part of authors who see and endorse the Maccabean revolt as a reaction against Hellenism. There are, however, other more or less contemporary works which demonstrate the same relative purity of Jewish thought. In the case of the Book of Daniel, for example, however much the Greek additions in Chapter 14 of the stories of Bel and the Dragon resemble contemporary Greek wonder tales like those told of Alexander the Great, the work shows only the start of the changes which were to be apparent in Judaism by the end of the first century BC.[32]

It would, however, be foolish to suppose that Judaism could completely insulate itself from outside ideas, or, once the Greeks and the Hellenized had arrived in the train of Alexander's generals and successors, that they would not feel some impact of the culture of the rulers. One need not expect changes everywhere, for the Jews were, for the most part, residents of the countryside and not the Greek cities of the coast. Nor need Hellenic ideas penetrate very deep into religious thought, certainly no deeper than the influences of Zoroastrian thought from Iran. The early emulations of political and cultural life may have been very superficial, and it could have been a long time before Greek philosophy influenced any Jew to the extent that it molded the thought of the Jewish philosopher Philo of Alexandria. Nevertheless some influences can be seen in the literature of the third and second centuries BC. If there is a lesser, or less direct influence than some modern readers think to perceive, it is nonetheless present and a factor in the evolution of religion and philosophy amongst the Jews.

There are many works in which these influences can be found. Much has been made of the wisdom book Ecclesiastes, with its pessimism reminiscent of the Egyptian *Dialogue with his Soul of the Man Tired of Life*, and its insistence on the value only of pleasure here and now as an influence of Greek Epicureanism. There certainly are similarities of expression, and the dating of Ecclesiastes in the third century BC allows for influences from the west. While it may be "Epicurean" to say, in Ecclesiastes 3: 12, "Thus I realized that the only worthwhile thing there is for them is to enjoy themselves and do what is good in their lifetime,"[33] there is a Stoic ring to another formulation of the idea that "There is nothing worthwhile for a man but to eat and drink and afford himself enjoyment with his means."[34] But while these may share an outlook we can find in the words of Zeno and Epicurus, there need not be any kind of direct influence, any more than we should posit such for the remark, "A lover of money never has his fill of money,"[35] a piece of everyday wisdom which is hardly limited to Stoic and Epicurean writing. The pessimism evident in Ecclesiastes may share the general state of mind of Zeno and Epicurus and their followers, but there is a risk of positing direct influence on the basis of what may be the expression of relatively commonplace ideas. Indeed, Ecclesiastes sees existence, however negatively, as part of the plan of God and arranged for the purposes of God; this makes it much more "Jewish" than "Hellenic" in any case. In this vein, it is interesting to contrast Ecclesiastes' assessment of death with the Homeric:

> For the same fate is in store for all: for the righteous, and for the wicked; for the good and pure, and for the impure; for him who sacrifices, and for him who does not; for him who is pleasing, and for him who is displeasing; and for him who swears, and for him who shuns oaths. That is the sad thing about all that goes on under the sun: that the same fate is in store for all.[36]

The language is evocative of Achilles' sentiments in *Iliad* ix. 318–20:

> Fate is equal for a man standing back, the same if he fights vigorously.
> In one honor we are all, the despicable and the noble.
> The man who accomplished nothing dies equally with him who has done
>  a lot.

The differences, however, are even more significant than the similarities. To Achilles, the alternatives of conduct for which reward is indifferent are bravery and cowardice, the life of nobility and the life of meanness. For the pessimistic writer of Ecclesiastes the alternatives of conduct are ethical and moral: virtue or wickedness, cleanliness or no, observance or neglect of religious requirements. But there is no escaping death, whether one follows the Law or violates it. And in Ecclesiastes, interestingly enough in view of the emergence of the idea of the resurrection of the body in Jewish writing of the next century, death is unalterable, irrevocable:

> For in respect of the fate of man and the fate of beast, they have one and the same fate: as the one dies so dies the other, and both have the same lifebreath;. . . Who knows if a man's lifebreath does rise upward and if a beast's does sink down into the earth?[37]

We are in a tradition very different from that which had the benefit of Socratic and Platonic speculation about the psyche.

Greek ideas have also been found in other later scriptural works. The sense of the universality of man in Sirach (Ecclesiasticus) 10: 19, written in around 200 BC and later translated into Greek, or the representation of the Lord as mindful even of non-Jews living in Nineveh, in Jonah 4: 11, have been taken to show that Jewish thought was sharing in the developing sense of human brotherhood which emerges in the works of some Greek philosophers. Beyond specific matters like these, the whole tenor of Jewish writing changes by the third and second centuries. The treatment of historical events shifts from the earlier focus on Palestine and Israel at the center of history and geography, as later writers move to an emphasis on the history of the Jews as a people as much as a political nation. This perception of the relationship of Israel to the rest of the world reaches its fullest expression in the account of the Maccabean revolt, after the persecution by Antiochus has been presented as the chastisement and correction of the Jews. Once the interpretation is made clear, history goes forward no longer primarily as the story of the disobedience of the Israelites and their abandonment of their obligation to Yahweh, but instead, as a human story of a nationalist rising and its success, an account based on human motives and human activities, which relates events to the context of the political history of the world in which the Jews of Palestine find themselves. Events flow from the actions of Judah, Jonathan and Simon, the Seleucid kings and their agents. The overall story is affected by events on the wider stage of the Mediterranean, so that the Romans and their relations with the Seleucids play some part in determining the outcome of the Jewish struggle. What is particular about the Jews is no longer their political relationship with Canaan, but their possession of the Law and their responsibility to follow it, even into martyrdom.

Prophetic as well as historical writing in the later period reflects this shift toward increasing reliance on the Law as the defining attribute of the Jews. From a vision of a day-to-day relationship between Yahweh and the Jewish people and its leaders as the mark of the special mission of the Jews, later prophecy evolved to represent the Law as the primary guide for Jewish behavior. Thus in the wisdom, historical and prophetic writing of the fourth, third, and second centuries BC, the representations of direct intervention by Yahweh decrease. Prophets, priests, and scribes are rarely called on directly by the voice which had spoken to Moses, Samuel, and Elijah; Jonah is an archaizing exception and the story of Job comes at the beginning of this evolution. Instead, the prophets and wise men interpret the will of God, giving their own views of his commandments. The tool for this was the Law, and although in later times it was no more fundamental an expression of Yahweh's commandments than it had always been, it assumed a greater role in life because it was almost the only means of determining the will of God. And because it could be interpreted in a way that a direct, spoken command cannot be, the interpretation of the Law gave rise to variant schools, and differences amongst the interpreters. The wisdom literature stands at the beginning of this development, and the historical experience reported in Maccabees shows something of the later stages.

Along with changes in the treatment of the Law and Yahweh's communication with his people came changes in the stories of miracles and Yahweh's demonstrations of his power. In the early history of Israel, Yahweh's miraculous upheavals or reversals of natural processes usually served either to save the Israelites in crisis or demonstrated his power to them. Each act met a current need or crisis, one which almost always affected the entire people or the future

231

of the national state. The story of Job, on the other hand, begins a change. Although the misfortunes which plague Job are by no means irregular in terms of natural phenomena, they differ from most of Yahweh's earlier direct interventions in human life in that they affect a single man, and a private person at that. Job, and also Jonah, an archaizing book in which Yahweh's remarkable acts are aimed at forcing Jonah to fulfill the role of prophet, rather than saving Israel, foreshadow the kind of demonstration which is found in the later Daniel. The miraculous preservation of Shadrach, Meshach, and Abednego from the furnace simultaneously serves as a reward to three men for their willingness to undergo martyrdom and as a demonstration to King Nebuchadnezzar of the power of their God and the validity of their faith. These three men were not leaders of Israel; on the contrary, they were high-ranking officials of the court, appointed to their position at the recommendation of Daniel, who himself was using his abilities as dream interpreter for the benefit of Nebuchadnezzar. Later when Darius, who replaced Nebuchadnezzar, produced the edict forbidding praying, which resulted in Daniel's consignment to the lions' den, God preserved him by a similar miracle. Both stories are essentially accounts of God's wonders performed for the preservation of individual men who were loyal to the faith, and have nothing to do with the story of the people as a whole.

This focus on the relationship between individual and God had parallels outside of Palestine. In the Hellenic world, while official piety took the view that the state as a whole can suffer from the pollution created by the individual, Hellenic religion always allowed for a greater particularism of religious action and effect than had early Judaism. Cures in the shrines of Asclepius, the religious experience offered by the Eleusinian mysteries, and traces of rural cult all show the importance of religious observance which related primarily to the individual self, family, and household. This aspect of Hellenism need not have influenced the Jews directly, and in fact probably did not do so, but as Jews developed this more personal approach to religion they would have found Greek worship, with its cults, sanctuaries, and mysteries, more and more comprehensible. That Jews were receptive to such ideas is amply demonstrated by the story of Tobit, which was written amongst the dispersion Jews, probably in the fifth or fourth century BC. It is a personal story, a tale of a devout man, Tobit, whose blinding gave him a wretchedness shared with his kinsman, Raguel, whose daughter Sarah had lost seven bridegrooms to the slaughtering hand of a demon. God intervenes, sends the angel Raphael, who arranges the safe marriage of Sarah with Tobit's son Tobias, and cures Tobit's blindness.

This personal moral tale is a precedent in Jewish literature for the later stories of the rewards of private virtue. The stories of Job, of Jonah, and of Tobit, the wisdom literature which seems to have burgeoned in the fifth century, all illustrate the movement of Jewish religiosity on a parallel course with that of Greece. By the third and second centuries there are many expressions of belief or interpretations of divine action in the Jewish tradition which, if not common with those of the Greek world, were at least intelligible to it, and the evolution of Greek and Jewish thought had reached the point at which Greek religious and philosophical ideas could be understandable and meaningful to Jewish sages. Whether or not there had been influence from Greece, the Jews themselves had changed their thinking about divine and human matters. The experience of the captivity and the return to Palestine under the suzerainty of a foreign dynasty may well have prompted Jewish thinkers into loosening the knot between Yahweh and the national state. Patriotism was still there, as much or more than in the Hellenic world, as the history of Judah Maccabaeus shows, but there also was an increasing emphasis on the personal fulfillment of the Law, the sense that each individual could be treated in isolation in terms of the responsibilities and the rewards of keeping the commandments.

When Antiochus Epiphanes came to the throne in 175 BC and began dealing with representatives of the different factions in Jerusalem, he was dealing with a political situation complicated by ideological as well as social and economic change. The rebellions which broke out in 169 and 168 had these ideological undertones, and because the political opposition to Antiochus identified itself with traditional Judaism, he deceived himself into thinking that the overthrow of that religion was necessary or useful to his cause. The persecution thus emphasized the identification between Antiochus' government and the corruption of Jewish life and thought, and played into the hands of Judah Maccabaeus and the other rebels. The Seleucid government, struggling under the obligation to continue the indemnity owed to Rome, and further weakened by dynastic confusion after the death of Antiochus, was not able to cope with the movement led by Judah and his brothers. The rebel forces were able to overcome those of the government-supported aristocracy and even of detachments of government troops, and eventually Judah, and then his brother Jonathan, controlled most of the country, including Jerusalem, with the "Hellenizers" cooped up in a walled portion of the city called the Akra. By 142 even the Akra and its Seleucid garrison had fallen, and Simon, now elected high priest and leader of the people, held his power as an independent dynast rather than a Seleucid appointee, and thus established the basis of a succession in which subsequent rulers would actually take the title of king.

Because Antiochus' persecution identified the king so clearly as an enemy of the religion, his opponents, the Hasmoneans, as the Maccabee brothers and their successors are called, were associated with the protection of Judaism. They were, however, no less Hellenic than had been their predecessor. Judah himself had been a militiary leader of a type common in the Hellenic world at the time, Simon's court and court protocol followed the patterns familiar from the royal behavior of many minor dynasts of the period, and later rulers even added Greek inscriptions to the Hebrew of their coinage. But all this was acceptable, and it was only at the plundering of the Temple by John Hyrcanus, Simon's son, who became high priest in 135, that any opposition was expressed. It is the very reputation of Judah, Jonathan, and Simon as protectors and restorers of Judaism that insulated them from the criticism and resentment which had plagued the earlier aristocracy at the beginning of the second century. Under the aegis of high priests who had come to power with a program of de-Hellenization, who in fact enforced Judaization of Greek cities in Palestine as a political measure, the intellectual and cultural effects of Hellenism proceeded apace. In the next century, as Palestine returned to the rule of natives as a Jewish state, Hellenism penetrated Jewish thought to a greater extent than it ever had done before.

# 20

# The Egyptian connection

## *Egypt, Rome, and*
## *the Greek east*

While the Jews of Palestine were achieving a considerable measure of success in preserving the essence of their culture in the face of Hellenism and were able to regain a great deal of political autonomy as well, their co-religionists in Egypt and the native people of that country were meeting with a completely different experience. The Hellenism of Egypt was not limited primarily to cities as it was in Palestine and Syria, and the Ptolemies, despite some difficulties, were in much firmer control of Egypt than were the Seleucids of Palestine or Syria. They were still a powerful dynasty at the end of the second century BC, and in Egypt it was the Hellenic dynasty which made friends of the Romans, unlike in Palestine, where a native Jewish kingdom could look for Roman support.

By the middle of the second century BC, the reigning Ptolemy was the only remaining eastern monarch with a sizeable territory to administer and any real future. Even the Attalids of Pergamum, though friends of the Romans too, would shortly end their line, as Attalus III was to will his kingdom to Rome in 133 BC. Rome was dominant in Greece and Asia Minor, with Pergamum supported by Rome but limited by Rome's support of her neighbors as well. There was dynastic confusion in Syria, and in Egypt, Ptolemy VI Philometor had to contend with his own brother based in Cyrene and aiming at Cyprus, and without potential allies Philometor was effectively isolated from the Aegean world. By mid-century Egypt had retired from international politics. The old ambition of the Ptolemies for an Aegean empire which had been so prominent in the third century was long dead. Equally significant, the Greeks, Macedonians, Thracians, and others who could claim or pretend to be Hellenes had stopped coming to Egypt to settle. Philometor was probably the first Ptolemy to come to the throne to rule over a population of Hellenes in Egypt almost all of whom were second or even third generation born in Egypt. A Greek culture which knew of nothing of the Aegean world first hand was coming into being in Egypt, a culture which was Greek in its essence but which was converting its Egyptian experience into something Hellenic, and which was uniting in its Hellenism not only the immigrants from different parts of the

Aegean world, but large numbers of Jews coming into Alexandria as well as native Egyptians who adopted Greek traditions.

The new focus had eroded the old Macedonian traditions of the court. The Romans had disposed of the old Macedonian dynasty of Greece, while Egypt had no family connection with the kings of Pergamum, descended – in a sense – from the eunuch Philetaerus through his brothers, and the Seleucid throne was being contested by usurpers of no relationship to the Ptolemaic dynasty. In the circumstances, it is hardly surprising that the court developed protocols and a tradition which suited Alexandrians rather than immigrants, and at lower ranks in the society the social and legal relationship which the first settlers had kept with their native cities disappeared almost completely. From the time of Ptolemy V on, there was a clear and formal court hierarchy with established ranks and titles, a system which built on the old Macedonian titles but which was particular to the Egyptian scene, and which continued to grow and develop through the subsequent reigns. The fortunes of the Greeks in Egypt were now wholly tied up with the fortunes of the crown or its challengers, for the ambitious could find no other arena for their activities.

There was also less opportunity to become rich, either by settling or taking over land in Egypt, or by sharing the profits of commerce. By this time, a great deal of the most profitable international trade had been taken over by entrepreneurs from the west. Moving into Greece in the wake of the Roman armies who had fought the wars against Philip V, against Perseus, and against the Achaeans, Greeks from south Italy set up in business to profit from the eastern trade. These were the traders called "Romans" by Greeks, and these westerners concentrated their activities on Delos, as the island served as a major transfer point for easterners from Anatolia, Syria, and Egypt on the one hand, and the Italians on the other. Now Alexandrians no longer carried on the profitable ventures which had involved them in direct communication with Italy, Sicily, Carthage, and the rest of western North Africa. By the end of the second century, Romans would look on Alexandria as a dependency, and there is a famous story of Scipio Aemilianus, on a visit to Alexandria during the reign of the very fat Ptolemy VIII Euergetes II, remarking that the Alexandrians owed him thanks because his visit gave them the opportunity to see their king walk, as he was forced to escort the great Roman about the city.

In all these circumstances, the Ptolemies were taking what steps they could to adjust to the changes. Perhaps the most important of the new dispositions was a much greater openness to the use of non-Hellenes and non-Egyptians in royal service, a change which had an important effect on the history of the Jews in Egypt. As a result of unsettled conditions in Palestine, large numbers of Jews had settled in Egypt, and Philometor had received an Onias, almost surely the high priest's son,[1] and in any case a member of the house of Onias, the focus of resistance to Philometor's enemies in Palestine. This Onias was in Egypt relatively early in Philometor's reign, not later than 160 BC, and his name turns up 200 years later in the pages of Josephus' account of the importance the Jews had in that period.[2] There was an Onias and Dositheos in command of the army, and this military Onias remained faithful to Philometor's sister-wife, Cleopatra II, after Philometor died, marching a force to Alexandria to rescue her and maintaining opposition to her other brother and enemy, Euergetes II, the eighth Ptolemy.

Philometor's reign thus brought much closer association between crown, state, and Jews of Egypt. The Jews had moved, in short, from being foreigners tolerated in Egypt to being a significant political force, the only non-Hellenes and non-Egyptians to do so. It was in this atmosphere, or very soon after, that the so-called *Letter of Aristeas* was composed.[3] This essay, which claims itself to have been composed by a non-Jewish courtier of Ptolemy II, is an account of the translation of the Hebrew Scriptures into Greek by seventy-two wise men sent to Egypt at the request of that king. Though an artifice in the sense that it pretends to issue from the pen of a third-century Alexandrian, it exhibits great familiarity with Ptolemaic court practice, and extensively exploits the literary devices developed in Alexandria and elsewhere in the Greek world. It was, however, almost surely intended for Jewish readers, not for Greeks, since its contents, both ideologically and narratively, make for a justification of the view that Jews can become Hellenized and live as part of Greek society while still remaining loyal to their Law and the best of Jewish religious tradition.

It is an optimistic narrative, one which shows great self-confidence on the part of the Jews in their relations with the non-Jewish world. Jews like the high priest of Jerusalem and the seventy-two sages write to or face the king with no sense of humility. Throughout the work, the king, his servants, and his Greek philosophers treat the Jews with deference and respect. The whole tone of the work reflects what we know of the favorable treatment of Jews in Egypt in that period, their comfortable position under Ptolemy Philometor which continued despite a short-lived persecution by Ptolemy VIII which was probably connected with Jewish support for his rival, Cleopatra II.[4] Later, after the death of Ptolemy VIII in 116 BC opened the way to dynastic struggles again, two Jewish generals served the king's wife in those internal wars. It is small wonder that in the course of this century the self-confidence of the Jews and their sense of security could rise to the levels shown by the text of *Aristeas*.

Once the text of *Aristeas* received circulation, it gave the Jews the tradition of the royal impetus behind the creation of the Greek translation of the Hebrew Scripture. It also shows a familiarity with Hellenism which made it a piece of literary art which is Hellenic in every way. As an ethical essay of a genre known to Greek literature of the period, it uses history with more attention to the truth of significance than to that of detailed fact, to convey moral, ethical, or cultural ideas; it bears resemblances to essays of Plutarch, that polymath of later times, and shows some striking parallels with the *Alexander Romance* attributed to Callisthenes. Furthermore, the language of letters quoted in *Aristeas* shows the writer fully conversant with contemporary Ptolemaic court administrative and epistolary style as well as the broader base of Greek literature.

The *Letter of Aristeas* shows how Hellenized the Jews of Egypt could be by the latter part of the second century BC. It also demonstrates a characteristic of Hellenic culture in the eastern realms which it reached. That culture, as it developed in Egypt after the arrival and settlement of the Greeks from many parts of the Greek world, remained relatively pure, and even when it was taken up by people of non-Greek cultures it did not acquire many of their characteristics; the borrower became Greek. Thus Egypt's ruling class remained, culturally at least, very much what it had been for a hundred years, and Hellenized Egyptians, Jews, and others who joined the intellectual and political leaders of the Ptolemaic kingdom in its last century continued to have more in common with the Greeks of the cities of old Greece, the Aegean, Asia Minor, and Syria than they had with the native people, who remained in their own cultural milieu. The population did, however, play an ever greater part in influencing events as time went on. Native Egyptians as well as citizens of Alexandria chose sides in the dynastic wars that shook the country in the latter part of the second century, and an amnesty decree, promulgated in 118 BC when Cleopatra II was reconciled with Ptolemy VIII, illustrates royal gestures toward the population.[5] It grants a whole series of protections, prohibiting illegal seizures, ratifying places of asylum, forbidding compulsory services for private use of officials, and granting remissions of taxes, payments, penalties, and the like. The sovereigns give crown funds for certain performances of Egyptian ritual, and perhaps most interesting, show themselves willing to continue the two legal systems, Greek and Egyptian, which had coexisted in the country since Alexander the Great took it over. This and other provisions of this decree – called a *philanthropon* to emphasize the sovereigns' love of their people – have been taken to show the desire of Ptolemy VIII to conciliate the population after the years of trouble, and overall it shows something of the ideology of the monarchy as the king presents himself as totally responsible for the country and its people, the source of benefactions as well as specific legislation.

Ptolemy VIII the "good-worker" – for such is the meaning of Euergetes, the name he took – did not live long after the promulgation of this decree. The dynastic situation returned to turmoil after his death in 116 BC, and the Alexandrian populace intervened on occasion over the next thirty-five years of often bloody struggle among members of the royal family. In 80 BC, when the young King Ptolemy XI killed his Queen, the populace dragged him to the city gymnasium and killed him there. He was the last legitimate male in the Ptolemaic line, and Rome took the view that the throne was empty, so the Alexandrians hastened to find themselves a king. They settled on an illegitimate son of Ptolemy IX, who was known informally as "the bastard," or "the flute player," and identified in documents as Ptolemy (XII) Theos Philopator Philadelphus – "the father-loving-sibling-loving god." Auletes, "flute-player," as he was and is commonly called, was entirely a dependant of Rome, and in the succeeding years various petitioners went to Rome to present their claims to be placed on the throne instead of him. The Romans did nothing, neither endorsing nor replacing him. They had other kings, big and little, to deal with.

Through these years the Seleucid kingdom had been deteriorating steadily, and by the end of the second century the Seleucid kings controlled only Syria. It was becoming more and more difficult to be a king, as Attalus III of Pergamum acknowledged by leaving his kingdom to Rome when he died in 133 BC. When Rome took up the bequest, she was firmly established in Anatolia and the only real power there apart from the kingdom of Pontus in the north. That state, in fact, would be the last of the Greek kingdoms of the east to provide any significant resistance to Rome. King Mithridates VI, recognizing that Rome was an enemy to be dealt with if he was to fulfill his expansionist ambitions, after years of preparation, struck in 88 BC, sweeping the Roman forces away. Demonstrating his hatred of Rome, he slaughtered some 80,000 Roman and Italian tax collectors and moneylenders in a single day, and presented himself as a champion of Hellenism, referring to the Romans in his correspondence as "the common enemy of all."[6] It was the last stand against Rome, executed by a monarch of great ability and nerve, but it failed. By 86 BC the Roman general Sulla had defeated Mithridates' allies in Greece, with terrible costs to the Greeks, and after Mithridates sued for peace and returned to Pontus, Sulla levied an enormous exaction on the province of Asia before departing for Rome in spring 84.

In Syria, the situation had degenerated to the point where the Seleucid line was represented by a scattering of minor kings who held either individual cities or nothing at all, since King Tigranes of Armenia had annexed all remaining Seleucid territory in Cilicia and Syria by 83 BC. In 80, the king of Bithynia, in northern Anatolia, bequeathed his kingdom to Rome, and that brought Mithridates back into action. He occupied the country, defeated a Roman army in the field in 74, but Roman victories in 72 forced him to seek asylum with King Tigranes of Armenia. The war continued for years, as Roman armies were unable to finish off either Tigranes or Mithridates, who in 66 was back in Pontus, having defeated yet another Roman army.

In that year, politics at Rome resulted in the appointment of Pompey as supreme commander to clear the sea of pirates, and in the following year his *imperium*, or right of command, was expanded to include the entire east. This action would turn out to settle the future of everything there but Egypt. Pompey's arrival in Syria effectively ended the Seleucid dynasty, and his capture of Jerusalem after a three-month siege did the same for the independent Jewish kingdom, while Mithridates' coincidental death in 63 ended the threat from that direction. Pompey was able to effect a sweeping reorganization of the entire east, making Syria, Cilcia, and Bithynia Roman provinces, and establishing Roman dependants in a series of small kingdoms all along the perimeter of the Roman provinces, running from the Crimea in the north, then east and south through Armenia, Asia Minor, and Syria. Palestine was left under the control of the son of the former king, but the title allowed to this Hyrcanus was not king, but high priest. The Greek cities of the area were left "free," which did not mean immune from taxes, but they held essentially the same status which they had enjoyed under Seleucid domination. Pompey then returned to Rome to resume the political wars there.

The last decades of the Ptolemaic dynasty were tied up with these wars. Auletes, seeking official recognition by Rome, had spent vast sums in support of Roman politicians whose political expenses kept them in constant need of money, and by 59, through the agency of Julius Caesar, he had succeeded. The enormous sums involved are suggested by the amount the king paid to Caesar when he carried the law which recognized Auletes as king and ally of Rome. That amount was 6000 talents, which, depending on which source of Egypt's revenue one accepts, was either an entire year's revenue for the king, or at least, half. Egypt, even avoiding direct conflict with Rome, was still suffering from the great cash drain which had pulled so much wealth out of the east. Later, when popular dissatisfaction expelled Auletes from the throne, he spent three more years at Rome borrowing and bribing to raise support to restore him. Finally, when the decision was made that he should be returned, it cost another 10,000 talents to bring a Roman army to Egypt to displace his opponents, and Auletes had to bring a Roman banker to Alexandria as finance minister to suck money out of his country to repay his loans.

When Auletes died in 51 BC, the eldest of his children was a princess of 17 or 18 years of age, who ruled as Cleopatra VII. The story of her reign is more part of the account of the last convulsions of the Roman civil wars than a history of Ptolemaic rule in Egypt, for she took an important part in Roman politics, first, as a paramour of Caesar at the time of his campaign in Alexandria in the winter of 48 to 47 BC. She had Caesar's support in the usual quarrel between Ptolemaic heirs, and she first co-ruled with her younger brother. Later she bore Caesar a son whom she put on the throne as a co-ruler. She followed Caesar to Rome, only to flee after his assassination in 44; then, after Caesar's assassins had been defeated, she cast her lot with Mark Antony, who for the moment was sharing the rule of the Roman world with Caesar's official heir and adopted son, Octavian. She remained loyal to Antony when he and Octavian fell out, and remained his ally until their joint defeat and death in 30 eliminated all opposition to Octavian and brought an end to the Ptolemaic dynasty. There had been no room, in the two decades of her reign, for an Egyptian monarch to strike any position independent of Rome.

To many, Egypt in the last century of Ptolemaic rule seems a kind of holdover of the past, a survival of monarchy allowed to persist for a while by the Romans who had better things to do than eliminate it, a country of negligible rulers and people who had been unable to preserve much of their great past. There is, of course, some truth in this. The Romans did control the flow of events in the eastern Mediterranean from the middle of the second century BC. They could, had they wished, have taken over Egypt at any time. And, just as political power waned, the cultural achievement of the period did not match that of the third century. Nevertheless, a good deal was going on, not only in the great metropolis of Alexandria but in the countryside as well. Although in mid-second century Ptolemy VIII had dealt a serious blow to the intellectual establishment of Alexandria by expelling many of its members, either as a deliberate measure or as a side-effect of his assault on his Greek opposition, the city still supported a few important people like the noted astronomer Hipparchus, and a poet, Moschus. In the first century BC Alexandria forged ahead to become eminent again, now in philosophy, a field for which it had never before been noted. A distinguished philosopher of that period, Antiochus of Ascalon, spent some time there, and before he returned to Athens, he established a tradition of Platonism in the Egyptian metropolis. Later one Arius Didymus, a close associate and philosophical adviser of Augustus, worked there, and was reportedly offered the opportunity to be Prefect of Egypt at the beginning of Augustus' rule. Alexandria also saw the revival of interest in the tradition of Scepticism, which insisted that judgment should be avoided because the nature of phenomena was not knowable. It was in this atmosphere of philosophical activity that Philo was born in the Jewish community of Alexandria just as Roman rule began. With Alexandria then a center of philosophical writing and teaching, it is small wonder that this Hellenized Jew could become so immersed in Greek thought.

Outside of the great city, Hellenism flourished in the small towns and cities of Egypt. The papyri, which show up in smaller quantity in these centuries, still include literary texts in sizeable numbers, suggesting that there was no significant decline in the copying of books, and the texts themselves show that same fidelity to Homer and other traditionally favored works which marked earlier times. And out in the Fayum, on the gate pillars of an Egyptian-style temple, are four Greek hymns to the goddess Isis which follow the normal Greek hymn style of later Hellenism, but which follow old Hellenic poetic traditions more than the everyday Greek spoken at the time. These and other remains of cultural activity in the countryside show that in Egypt the Hellenism of the smaller communities had succeeded in maintaining itself over a long period, an important phenomenon that meant that Hellenic ideas and attitudes were not confined to major cities, as they generally were in Syria and Palestine, but could exercise a much more pervasive influence.

Even with the political debilitation of Egypt, the great center of Alexandria remained a major fount of Hellenism during this whole period. The city felt and contributed to the intellectual currents which flowed around the Mediterranean, and Alexandrians played a large part in the dissemination of Greek philosophy to Romans, contributing to that eclectic blend of ethical thought which marked Roman ideology. Not least, the Hellenization of Egyptian deities and cults, which had established itself firmly in the third century, made it possible for these cults to sweep the Mediterranean world in the next two centuries. The very weakness of the Ptolemies in political terms meant that the cults could be taken up without any political or propaganda implications, and emerging from their Egyptian base they moved from city to city, and their adherents and devotees served their gods in Pompeii as well as in Antioch as religion became progressively less local in nature.

There was also an effect on thought, an effect not precisely definable, made by the exercise of kingship in the last two centuries before Rome controlled the entire Mediterranean, and this lasted longest in Egypt. Kings like Antiochus IV operated under the assumption of a sovereignty more comprehensive than anything exercised in the Greek world since the very beginning of *polis* society. Sovereignty was absolute, and the king expressed it all. He was total ruler of his people, a position which implied not only absolute power but absolute responsibility. His ordinances were expressed in terms of his care and concern for his people, and his *philanthropa* – the benefactions which he offered – were free gifts. All his kindness, all good works, all favor which he accorded stemmed not from obligation but his goodwill and affection for his people.

Such were the Seleucids and the Ptolemies. Their kingship expressed the attitudes of political leaders and philosophers of the time, and the idea of kingship interacted with the developing religions to create a mutual influence. Together with the vigorous state of Greek philosophy in Egypt and the rapidly spreading new religions, conceptualization of kingship also affected Roman ideas of government and political leadership in the first century BC. Egypt and Alexandria long remained a powerful disseminator of evolving Hellenism, and as Cleopatra conquered the hearts of Caesar and Antony, Alexandria and Egypt played a large part in Hellenism's overwhelming of the mind and spirit of Rome.

# Part Five

# Philosophy, religion, and the rise of Christianity

# 21

# The impact of materialism
## Epicureanism and its adherents

In the centuries after Alexander, as the kingdoms of his successors fell one by one to Roman power, Hellenism flourished and grew stronger as a culture despite its political problems. Ideas of science, religion, and philosophy which emerged at one center or another spread rapidly among the Greeks of cities all over the Mediterranean, and, inevitably, influenced one another, so that science had an impact on religion and philosophy, and these two also influenced each other. The philosophic and religious currents which were introducing people to new ideas on the human condition and the nature of the gods swept beyond the limits of the Greek cities, and as the Romans made their political impact on the Greeks, Hellenism returned the favor in cultural terms. by the time the kingdom of Cleopatra collapsed to the control of Rome, the Roman character and the Romans themselves had been heavily influenced by the ideas flowing westward from Greece.

Among the influences which acted most strongly on the Romans were the philosophies of Stoicism and Epicureanism. Of the two, the philosophy of Epicurus first received expression in Roman terms, although ultimately it did not find the acceptance which greeted many Stoic ideas. Epicurus' ideal of withdrawal from political activity, of escape from reliance on human interdependence, was uncongenial to Roman attitudes, and Epicurean physics and astronomy, however extensively treated by the Roman poet Lucretius, were not in the forefront of Roman philosophical interests. So too, Epicurus' view that there is no overriding destiny or necessity[1] which imposes itself on humanity ran counter to basic Roman attitudes, while the implicit acceptance of the individual as the entity of ultimate value did not fit the Roman view which put the state in this position. Epicurus' categorization of laws as a mere convention to protect men one from the other, his dismissal of natural and absolute justice all cohere as produced by an attitude which sees human interests and actions in community as generally inimical. The kind of life which he advocates is possible only under conditions which pertain only to a kind of non-society, a community of mutually non-dependent friends who are psychologically hermits. There is no room in the system for any concept of

245

"Good," let alone its pursuit, and certainly no dedication to the state. Despite all this, it was a Roman who took up the case a century and a half after the master's death, in a proselytizing poem which is our fullest exposition of Epicurean thought.

Little is known of the life of this Roman who has left us only his single poem. That Lucretius was a member of the upper class we can easily infer from his educated mastery of language and his association with the powerful politician Gaius Memmius, for whose edification Epicurean philosophy was put into Latin verse. The association with Memmius, among other things, helps us to date Lucretius' birth to around the year 100 BC. He died in about 55 BC, and a reference to the British climate in the poem gives rise to speculation that he might still have been alive in that year to hear reports of Julius Caesar's crossing to the island.

Lucretius' life thus stretched over the years which saw many of the bloody upheavals generated by the civil strife which brought an end to the Roman republic. His birth came scarcely a half-century after the final Roman victory in Greece in the Achaean War of 146 BC, and only a third of a century after the assassination of the populist leaders Gaius and Tiberius Gracchus. Born during the civil strife between the victorious general Marius and his junior Sulla, Lucretius' early years were those of Sulla's victory over Mithridates in the east and his subsequent domination of Rome. Throughout his life the poet witnessed savage conflicts over power, and he knew by experience the cost of the struggle between the Senate and the populist leaders, and the expense to the city of the ambitions of men like Sulla, Cinna, Pompey, Crassus, and Caesar. It is small wonder that the un-Roman philosophy of Epicurus appealed to him. The fruit of ambition was bitter not only to the seeker after power, but to all whom he affected. Lucretius found in the philosophy of the man he referred to as his master a unified approach to answers to most of the questions of life – questions of ethics, psychology, anthropology, physics, and cosmology. He made no claim to originality in his poem "On the Nature of Things," and his detailed presentation of Epicurean thought in Latin is generally accepted as a faithful version of Epicurus' own views. Where it can be checked, it is so, at least in essence, although Lucretius had his own emphases and interpretations.

Lucretius gathered the essence of Epicurus' whole philosophy into six books in a Latin which, as its author complains, was a difficult medium for the expression of many Greek philosophical concepts. The very idea of doing such a thing was Greek, and the east in this period produced many such poems on philosophical or physical subjects not unlike Lucretius' explanation of the essentials of Epicurus' physical theory of the composition of the material universe. He explains the basic concept of the cosmos, with indivisible and indestructible atoms the primary building units of matter, in an absolutely empty void. Through the infinite expanse of space move the atoms of infinite number, colliding and linking up from time to time by chance, to create in their combinations all the phenomena in the cosmos. This motion of the atoms is constantly creating, and by the assault and impingement of atoms on already created entities also constantly destructive. As a result nothing is immortal, and all entities in the universe have their births and dissolutions. Furthermore, everything which exists is material, composed of atoms in one construction or another, as, for example, the human being has both body, made up of a relatively dense collection of atoms, and spirit, which is a particularly thin and fine construction. Body contains spirit, but with death, as the body putrefies and breaks up, so the spirit, a much more delicate and thinly interwoven construction, without body to protect it, breaks into its constituent atoms that much more quickly. There is no more immortality to the spirit than there is to the body, and mind, which is present in the human along with the interconnection of spirit and body, is also composed of atoms very minute and extremely fine in texture.

Even sense perception depends on matter: in the act of seeing, for example, atoms in the form of films shed by objects actually reach the eye to create perception. Some atoms are susceptible of apprehension by sight and touch, others by smell, hearing, or taste. The streams of these films are constantly flowing from the objects emanating them, and the films conveying the different perceptible sensations can be discriminated by the senses at various distances and at varying speeds, depending on their nature and the nature of the objects from which they come. In all of this, there are apparent anomalies, like the square tower which appears round in the distance, and Lucretius is at pains to explain these apparent contradictions of the validity of sense perception, a validity which he is anxious to demonstrate. While reason may explain why a square tower looks round in the distance, ultimately the evidence of the senses has priority: "The idea of truth was created by the senses, and the senses cannot be refuted . . . whatever is perceived at any time is true."[2] Genuine truth is in the evidence of the senses, and only that evidence is valid.

The position is a direct rejection of the Platonic doctrine of the limited value of the senses and the mutability of apprehended phenomena, and excludes from validity any conclusions based on intuitive perceptions. Thus, not only Platonic reasoning to achieve knowledge of the Good but also some of the processes of thought set out by Aristotle are rejected by the Epicurean dependence on the senses. In this respect, at least, the Epicureans rejected one characteristic of Greek thought which had marked Hellenism hitherto – a tendency toward abstraction which often questioned the absolute validity of sense perception. Epicureanism carried to its limit the Aristotelian endorsement of the value of sense perception against the Platonic derogation of the senses as means of acquiring knowledge, and even denied Aristotle's conception of direct knowledge of some first principles as a means of basing solidly the superstructure of empirical knowledge. One could go no farther than Epicurus did, and the firmness with which Lucretius repeats and defends the principle shows that after Epicurus' lifetime, it remained clearly understood and its implications were well recognized. The effects on other schools of philosophy were limited, however, for most resisted the notion that their understanding of the cosmos and its workings was restricted by the very limited data available through the senses. And in the one domain in which its empiricism might have gained the day for Epicureanism, that of science, Epicurus' disdain for unifying explanations was a major obstacle to any serious interest in his philosophy.[3] From the time of Aristotle on, thinkers in astronomy, physics, cosmology, and natural history had been interested in unified explanation, much as modern scientists endorse the principle of "economy of hypothesis," and Epicurus' rejection of that principle meant that his scientific discussions remained outside the mainstream of Greek scientific thought.

The same was largely true of Epicurean assertions about the nature of the gods and the role they played in human affairs. Lucretius makes it clear that Epicurean thought did not challenge the existence of the gods, but rather stressed the point that the gods took no part in the creation, organization, or running of the cosmos. The gods had no need of or interest in humanity, the Epicureans insisted, and the world carried on without divine intervention. The gods, as people suppose them, emerged from "marvelous figures they saw in the waking imagination, and in dreams,"[4] and what humans think them to be or to do comes out of supposition. So, too, human arts were taught not by gods but by human usage and experience, and law and justice were created by "the human race exhausted by a lifetime of violence,"[5] and ready to submit to law. Lucretius accepts this position completely in his account of the development of human society, although alluding only lightly to it, and treats these moral concepts, like everything else in the Epicurean universe, as owing existence not to gods but to chance, to the collision of atoms, or to those entities developed out of the collision and linking of atoms. Thus to Lucretius, as to any other Epicurean, the study of ethics to produce a guide for moral conduct is not very productive, since the standards are mere human conventions and subject to change whenever they lose their utility. Only the direction of life toward happiness is of interest, and the life of happiness, defined as freedom from physical or mental pain, can be achieved not only by withdrawal from competition for wealth, fame, and power which occasion anxiety, but also by understanding the true nature of the workings of the cosmos. That is, when one understands that all things, even the world, are transitory, and that what happens occurs by chance and not according to some grand design, then one is freed from apprehension. Anxiety disappears for those who realize that nothing in the world but their own frame of mind is in their power.

In emphasizing the importance of one's attitude toward life, the Epicureans held a position in common with that of the Stoics, although they differed greatly in their attitudes toward the Good, toward knowledge and natural science, toward the gods, and, most of all, toward everyday behavior and participation in the life of society. Two centuries later, in the writings of the emperor Marcus Aurelius, Epicurean thought, especially that emphasizing the transitory nature of all existence, would blend to some extent with that of the

Stoics, but at the time of Lucretius and in the century immediately after, the two streams remained separate. In particular, the doctrine that "the gods exist but they don't care" marked the Epicureans off from other philosophical and theological traditions. The contrast appears clearly in Cicero's *De Natura Deorum*, an artificial debate *On the Nature of the Gods* written in the middle of the first century BC, in which the Epicurean confronts one speaker who argues that the gods not only exist but are concerned with the affairs of men, and another who argues that the gods do not exist at all.

This third position had been known to Greek thought for a long time, but had never won broad acceptance. Those espousing it ran some risk of attack and even prosecution, at least in Athens, and it had never been endorsed by a school or specific tradition of philosophy. But the Epicurean position that the gods need not be propitiated or served, that they gained no advantage from temples, cults, and sacrifices, that all the prayers and gifts of humans were not just disdained but were of absolutely no interest to them, all this ran against the common Greek conception, and if broadly accepted, would have undermined city cults, state worship, and public religion. However, the enthusiastic practice of official and private religion and the widespread acceptance of so-called mystery cults at this very time show that Epicurus' doctrine made no impact at all in the area of religion. Romans, who had expelled the first Epicureans a century before, now apparently had no fear of their ideas, and regarded Lucretius' poem with equanimity. Cicero, himself certainly no Epicurean, praised the style of the poem highly, even if he did not endorse its ideas.

Epicureanism, however, even if without an influence on philosophy or religion in doctrine or practice, brought Hellenism a concept which had hitherto been quite alien to Greek or Roman thought. That concept may have had the greater effect in that although it was implied by the Epicurean system, it was not explicitly asserted, and its influence could be felt in philosophy or theology without necessarily meaning acceptance of the rest of Epicurus' doctrines. This underlying basis of Epicurean thought assumes that people and their problems are in no way a focus of, or even of any importance to, the cosmos. It was, in a way, a corollary of Protagoras' assertion that "man is the measure of all things" as both might be related to Epicurean notions of justice. Protagoras' dictum implied that the only standard humans can apply is a human one, and Epicureanism was willing enough to accept that, with the proviso that human justice was merely conventional, and in any case of relatively little importance in a universe so vast as to dwarf the world in which humans live; and human justice would apply only temporarily until the world's inevitable dissolution. In other words, in the face of Epicurean assertions about the universe, the old Hellenic dichotomy between divine or cosmic justice on the one hand and human law on the other becomes a misstatement of reality. Human law is merely a useful mechanism to enable people to live together, and there is no cosmic law; human good fortune or wretchedness are simply the accidents of atomic behavior. There is no justice, no providence. The quest for either arises out of the mistaken notion that humanity is of any significance to the forces which govern the universe, whether gods, fate, providence or, as the Epicureans have it, chance.

Once such a concept affects the sense of self, a whole series of consequences follow. Religion opens to change. Worship of the gods, which had been human-centered as early as we know it, structured to provide a direct means of exchange between people and gods on a "*do ut des*," "I give so that you give," basis, can shift to become veneration of superior beings or a superior being purely as a recognition of a power beyond human control or even understanding. The religions of the east, whether of Egypt, Palestine, or Syria, all of which were based more on that kind of approach to divinity, could thus find a little common ground with Hellenism. This is not to say that the rapid expansion of eastern cults in the Hellenistic period represented any abandonment of Hellenism in religion. It did not, for these cults were rapidly Hellenized as they spread through the Greek world, in iconography, cult procedure, and doxology. Rather it meant that Greeks, touched by the idea of the insignificance of humanity, could understand to some extent the manner in which Jews, for example, approached their god, or could make sense of the great institutions for divine service which characterized Egyptian society. Of course, not all Greeks after Epicurus shared in this sophistication, any more than those who read Plato's opposition to "bribing" the gods at the end of Book 10 of *Laws* abandoned familiar attitudes. Such conceptualizations or even their potential could have reached only a small percentage of the population, and even that only gradually.

Nevertheless, those whom these concepts reached were the educated, often the purveyors of ideas to kings and statesmen. In the 200 or 300 years after the death of Alexander the Great, when generals and kings were becoming established in their eastern domains, the many philosophical and religious advisers filling the courts were potential sources of such influences. Demetrius of Phalerum, for example, advised Ptolemy I on the cult of Serapis. Antigonus Gonatas was devoted to the Stoic Zeno. Hellenized Jews served under Ptolemy I. All the eastern monarchs with their coteries of philosophers were exposed to the influence of Epicurus' thought, even if many philosophers only reacted to Epicureanism to reject it, and thus might find some common ground with the cosmology of their non-Hellenic subjects. It was not a situation in which a Greek might consider the oriental idea to be "like Epicurus," but rather one in which the minuteness of human interests was in the air, so that religions which operated on that perception could be comprehensible.

Yet, even if one can make something of a case for some Epicurean impact on religious sensibilities, there is no doubt that the Hellenized oriental religions which spread rapidly through the Mediterranean world were most decidedly un-Epicurean. They attributed the creation of the world to their deities: for example, Isis is hymned with the praise that because of her "the celestial sphere and the earth stand."[6] Isis and the other gods were credited with bringing arts to humankind, and with a concern for people which included attention to the healing of even lesser complaints; and in many instances, the proper service of the cult brought immortality to the initiate. All of these ideas were diametrically opposed to Epicurean thought, and Epicurean theology had little or no impact on Greek religious life or practice. As Epicurus' atomic physics had no effect on scientific thought or the development of Hellenistic astronomy or cosmology, so his denial to the gods of any interest in human affairs remained purely a concept for discussion. Philosophers or dilettantes might turn the idea over in their minds or refer to it in their writings, but only a devoted Epicurean like Lucretius would set it up as truth.

If Epicurean physics was ignored and theology and cosmology were rejected, what was left? Only the idea with which we have come to identify Epicureanism – that the end of life is pleasure. Often rejected in a form into which it was distorted, the Epicurean principle, calling for a life program in many ways like that of the Stoics, was a target of attack for centuries because of this endorsement of pleasure. Since it was the antithesis of all other systems of religion or philosophy, each calling for service to some divinity or to some principle of behavior, the adherents of these other systems often felt required to answer the Epicureans, and later thought was to some extent moulded by this necessity. It was a peculiarly difficult problem for those whose beliefs were consonant with the view that humanity was a very unimportant part of the universe. For, with humans unimportant, we gain a kind of freedom. If our actions have no effect on the workings of the cosmos or are insignificant to the gods of the universe, we bear no responsibility to the universe or even to our fellows for our actions, for events flow not from the will and acts of the individual, but from the will and acts of far greater powers. The logic, if pursued to its conclusion, is almost irrefutable, and those who made chance control the universe cut the ground from under programs which called for adherence to systems of ethics or morals, based on a set of principles understandable to and described by people. The alternative, whether one accepts the rest of Epicureanism and its physics and cosmology, might as well be Epicurean ethics and the pursuit of pleasure.

That alternative, however, was generally not chosen except in Epicurean circles or by dedicated Epicureans like Lucretius. Some philosophical thought after Epicurus is marked by an attempt to set prescriptions for conduct on a basis which, on scrutiny, can be seen to be most unstable. Others, perhaps more successful in logic at least, have resort to the hypothesis of some supervening communication which transmits an understanding of the workings of the universe, a communication and an understanding which transcend ordinary human logic and perception. There had been a good deal of this in Plato, and even something of it in Aristotle's concept of fundamental understandings. The concept flourished later among the devotees of the cults of Isis and other deities, as we see in references of the liturgical literature to the hidden knowledge granted to the initiates by the deity. By the time many of the cults reached Rome and the west, the principle of mystical knowledge had become firmly engrained in many of them, and was a concept widely familiar to all classes of the population.

It was a comprehensible answer to Epicureanism, and it was effective. By the time of the Roman domination of the east, philosophy had ceased to trouble itself so obsessively about the problems of knowledge – that is, whether and to what extent sense perception is valid in reaching understanding of the external world, and how one came to know the truth and the good. Issues which Plato had found particularly troublesome had been resolved largely in the manner in which Plato had resolved them. In all this, the exceptional views of Epicurus were almost completely overwhelmed, and after Lucretius, only a small number of determined Epicureans espoused them. Although Epicureanism belonged to a very old tradition in Hellenic thought, that tradition was not to become dominant or more popular. Neither Epicureanism's thoroughgoing materialism in physics nor its abstract mechanics in cosmology proved attractive. Least of all did later thinkers incline to the view of Epicurus that humanity was cast adrift in an impersonal universe, buffeted by forces that acted without purpose or intelligence, unable to influence or even to communicate with the powers that control the cosmos. Hellenism required an attitude that placed humankind at the center, or at least granted it importance, and could not accept the freedom in insignificance implied by Epicureanism.

# 22

# The religious philosophy of Stoicism

## *Stoic ethics, theology, and physics*

Zeno of Citium died in 263 BC, highly esteemed in the Athens where he had made his life and reputation. The eastern Mediterranean, at his birth a congeries of Greek city-states, Macedonian dominions, and Persian imperial territories on to which Alexander was falling like a thunderbolt, was transformed during his lifetime into a more or less ordered arrangement of Graeco-Macedonian monarchies with reasonably firm bases of power and political interrelationships. Athens itself, Zeno's professional home for most of his life, had gone through years of trouble because of its ambition to remain a political factor. During this period political leaders sometimes attacked philosophers as the cause of the city's troubles and this underlined the importance the pursuit of philosophy had played in Athenian public life. The Athenian philosophical schools had brought Epicurus and kept Zeno there, and by founding their own schools in Athens these two greatly increased the scope and intensity of philosophical activity in the city as the third century came to its end.

Of the two new philosophies, Zeno's Stoic school had the more immediate, wide-ranging impact, possibly on account of his own prestige as the philosophical master of King Antigonus of Macedon. After Zeno's death Stoicism found a devoted proponent in his immediate successor, Cleanthes, and then in the next head of the school, Chrysippus, an intellect on a par with that of the master and an energy which outstripped anything in its day. With him, Stoicism reached the last decade of the third century under the guidance of a man who worked over Zeno's doctrines and writings so exhaustively that thereafter it was Chrysippus' books rather than Zeno's which provided the basic material for the study and practice of Stoicism. Writing on each of the three divisions of philosophy, logic, physics, and ethics, Chrysippus produced a staggering output of over 700 books which his enemies like to allege would evaporate if the quotations were removed.

Despite their great number, and their apparent fundamental interest to ancient philosophers, none of his books survives. They were known to Cicero in the first century BC; they provided the fundamentals of Stoicism to Epictetus

25 Chrysippus was conventionally represented as an elderly man, as in this head now in the British Museum, London.

in the latter half of the first and beginning of the second centuries of our era, and they provided most of the materials for Plutarch's attack on Stoicism in the same period. They certainly lasted until the third century, for they could be catalogued by Diogenes Laertius in his life of Chrysippus, and it is a work of

Chrysippus which provides the only attributed fragment of Stoic writing which appears among the papyri of Egypt.[1] Yet ultimately Chrysippus' works, like those of Zeno, were lost to the ravages of time, and we have only fragments, paraphrases, and references to them by others to inform us of their contents.

Certainly Chrysippus differed from Zeno in his stress and prolific writing on logic, which comprehended language and grammar as well as what we would call logic. It was, no doubt, part of his value to educators who came after him that he studied in detail such matters as the formulation of arguments, the nature and uses of elements of speech, in dozens of books which in their number and detail differed from Zeno's emphasis. On the main points of the Stoic theory of knowledge, however, Zeno and Chrysippus seem to have been at one. Only sense perception could provide reliable data, and those data were accepted by a kind of voluntary "assent." Chrysippus, in what Diogenes saw as a contradiction,[2] allowed in one of his works that there were two criteria of knowledge, the sense perception already mentioned, and a second, a so-called prolepsis or "pre-grasping," a certain natural perception of the concepts of universal reality. Self-contradictory it may have been, and a highly suspect piece of epistemology it certainly is, but we are given no reason to believe that it differed violently from Zeno's teaching. Chrysippus also adhered to Zeno's basic tenets in physics. He, like other Stoics, accepted the point that two principles operated in the universe: one, passive, is matter; the other, active, is the reason inherent in a subject, and is in fact god. Chrysippus also held that the substance of god – Zeus – is the whole world and the heavens, that the cosmos came into being from fire, and will eventually be consumed by fire, thence to pass into new cycles of generation and destruction. These are all concepts which underlie most Stoic physics, and it is no surprise to find agreement on these points amongst the major Stoic writers. The Stoics based their ethics on physics, and used their physical theory in distinguishing good and evil,[3] so one would not expect to find Chrysippus breaking with Zeno on basic doctrine dealing with the nature of the cosmos, the fundamental character of matter, or the relationship of the gods to the rest of the universe.

Stoic theology was, in fact, more coherent than many earlier Hellenic conceptualizations of the gods. Chrysippus, we are told, pronounced the view that the cosmos is organized according to reason and providence, is "a living being, rational, alive and intelligent,"[4] and a unity, and that things happen because of destiny. He endorses the practice of divination because of the existence of providence. Here there seems to be some disagreement among Stoics, and Chrysippus himself differs with Stoic colleagues on some other points of detail, as, for example, the identification of the ruling part of the cosmos. All in all, however, Chrysippus probably differed little on basic doctrine from the sentiments in Cleanthes' *Hymn to Zeus*, which hailed that god as the exalted and unique ruler of the cosmos, himself the force of reason which informs all the universe, creation, and matter, including all the lesser deities. Such, in any case, was the accepted Stoic theology. In ethics too, Chrysippus agrees with what we know of Stoic doctrine in general. On the issue of living harmoniously with nature, the foundation of the Stoic creed, Chrysippus defines the concept with precision, writing that "to live according to virtue is the same thing as living according to the experience of what happens in nature,"[5] the ethical principle rises quite reasonably from another tenet, that a creature's first motivation is self-preservation: "what concerns every animal in the first place is its own physical integrity and its awareness of this."[6] Chrysippus defines that nature which our lives should follow as the nature both common to all in the cosmos and that which pertains only to humanity in particular, a refinement of the concept which is different in detail from that, say, of Cleanthes, who was concerned with living in harmony only with the nature of the cosmos.

Stoics came under vigorous attack for some of the extensions of their basic philosophy. Plutarch, who wrote in the late first to early second century of our era, is particularly hostile to the Stoic conclusion that there is no quantification to virtue or vice,[7] a concept which emerges from the Stoic expression that "all sins are equal." Plutarch also enjoyed showing the contradictions in Chrysippus' wrestling with the existence of evil in the world by explicating the doctrine that Zeus created evil in the cosmos so that it has a role, and that "there is nothing in the cosmos that should be cavilled against or condemned."[8] These pronouncements, which seem on the surface to be a kind of moral nonsense, are in fact aspects in detail of statements made in support of the fundamental principle that there is no intermediate between truth and falsehood, that any variance from truth (=virtue) is immediately non-truth, falsehood, vice. Out of this also arises the Stoic position that any action is either in accordance with nature or not, that the philospher will choose only actions and pursuits in accordance with nature, and that virtuous actions, that is, those which accord with nature, are to be chosen, those not in accord, the wicked, are to be avoided, and that all other actions and pursuits are matters of indifference.

While Chrysippus and other Stoics debated the response to such morally indifferent matters as wealth, fame, health, beauty, and the like, or whether virtue alone is sufficient to assure well-being, the disagreements did not affect the fundamental community of Stoic thought on virtue. It is, finally, that sense of the coherence of the cosmos, the ultimate rationality of the ruling deity, that marks the Stoic sense of the universe, humankind's place in it, and the means by which humans can best pursue their destinies. Ultimately, these views require absolutes in virtue and good, absolutes which are violently opposed to Epicurean relativism. These absolutes do, in fact, appear. Chrysippus asserts that "justice exists by nature and not by institution, and so too do law and correct reasoning."[9] Calling for an intuitive perception of the nature of reality and the applicability of this prescription to human life, Chrysippus and other Stoics were forced to abandon sense perception as the exclusive means of achieving knowledge of the good and of developing an ethic. Plutarch and others saw the inconsistency in this, but that inconsistency did not impede Stoicism from gaining popularity in the centuries after Chrysippus, even if this popularity was for a Stoicism of a somewhat simplified form, one concentrating primarily on the ethical aspect of the creed.

Chrysippus' writings, even if available to us only in the form of allusions and quoted fragments, show the state to which Stoicism had evolved by the end of the third century BC. The nature of the creed had been firmly established in the form it would take in subsequent centuries. Although we are not well provided with details of Stoicism in the century and a half between Chrysippus' death and the composition of Cicero's philosophical essays, it is not only Stoic texts we miss but Greek literature in general in the second century. To give us some sense of the current ideas we have only Polybius. His theory of the development of human society "according to nature" has been portrayed as Stoic in origin, but, as I have already noted, the ideas and phraseology of Polybius' discussion can be found in Greek philosophy outside Stoicism. So too his notions of the emergence of justice have some similarities to Stoic terminology, while the idea that the concept of justice emerges out of human social relationships is much closer to the Epicurean position. So too his whole presentation of the natural development of human society has parallels in Lucretius' Epicurean anthropology, but can be related to Aristotle's writings as well. On the other hand, occasional emphasis on the important effect of nature on development may be Stoic, and Polybius' praise of truth "as the greatest god for men"[10] created by nature is very close to some of Chrysippus' views. Polybius' philosophical orientation shows the influence of the ideas of many schools. His views reflect the stance of an intelligent, educated man living when Stoicism was an important philosophical influence and when Epicureanism, along with the later Academics and Peripatetics, could also command some attention. Despite his familiarity with Plato, all his reasoning depends upon an acceptance of the value of the senses – an attitude common to both Stoicism and Epicureanism. He may even have been influenced by the Stoic stress on the importance of providence in cosmic and human affairs. Thus in Polybius we have a man who was a member of no school but was aware of the main ideas of all, who developed his own concepts under the influence of the dominant ideas of the day. Although he made something all his own, what he wrote was particularly compatible with Stoic thought without excluding other traditions from a pragmatic philosophy suitable for a statesman and historian.

There were, no doubt, many such educated men in the Greek cities of the eastern Mediterranean, but we have no more than fragments of their writings, so the extent and nature of the Stoic impact on Greek culture in the second century are very imperfectly known. In another respect, however, we can see that Stoic concepts were in close accord with contemporary developments, and that is in the religious sphere. In this period, Greek religion was moving toward an extensive acceptance of cults which focused on a single deity – or a single deity with associates – who assumed something of a universal nature. The worship of Isis, with the association of Osiris, Harpocrates, and in some instances Serapis, appears all over the Mediterranean in Hellenized form. The goddess is, however accorded a greater role in the cosmic organization than had been customarily supposed for a single Greek deity, and she seems much more a creator, lawgiver, organizer, caretaker than any one Greek deity had heretofore been. She is, in fact, more like the Zeus of the Stoics than any of the traditional city gods of the Greeks, or even Apollo and Zeus of the great national centers of Delphi and Olympia. Her cult was universal not only in the sense that it made its deity a controlling factor in the cosmos, but also in that it crossed city and even language boundaries and was associated with no particular place as a special concern to Isis. All humanity, indeed all the universe, was the goddess' concern, and the cult concentrated on the means by which individuals might serve her and communicate with her. Throughout the Mediterranean in the third and second centuries BC, Iseia – sanctuaries and temples of Isis – sprang up in cities and towns. For many, Isis was the only deity they needed to attend, for she could do all, she cared for all, and she was the dominant force in the world.

Isis, for her worshippers, and Zeus, for the Stoics, were not the only Greek deities to have been regarded as supreme powers. Similar ideas concentrated around Serapis as well as Anatolian and Syrian divinities, Bendis, Atargatis, and the Great Mother. While some of these cults entered the Hellenic Mediterranean and moved west later than did the Isis religion, they shared in that aspect of religion which emphasized the universal power and saving quality of a particular deity. The phenomenon continued well into the Christian era with the spread of Mithraism from Iran into the Roman armies and then on west, and of course throughout this period, the worship of Zeus himself, not as the fundamental principle of reason as he is in Stoicism but as a transformed Hellenic deity. With cult names like Zeus Hypsistos, "Zeus the Highest," Zeus was approached as the highest and most powerful of the gods, and gained the kind of universalism accorded their divinity by the followers of Isis and other deities of more easterly origin.

It is entirely possible that the Stoic Zeus informing the cosmos and the universal deities served by the spreading new cults were interdependent and influential one on another. At the very least, Stoicism provided a kind of philosophical rationale at one level of thought for religious developments which extended more broadly through society. The abstract divine principle proposed by Aristotle was, a century after the philosopher's death, just one of the many ways of hypostasizing the notion of divinity. The fact that Stoicism accepted the existence of other gods as well as the eternal Zeus, the active principle of reason in all matter, made it all the more in tune with the religious developments of the day. What had been in Aristotle's thought a reasoning through to a cause and mover for the cosmos in a purely philosophical effort and had developed in Stoicism as a form of philosophical theology, was in the minds and practices of the multitude much less logical and abstract, much more what we call religion than philosophy, a belief in and relation to divinity which was direct, practical, and mutual. In Stoicism, the abstract divinity Zeus, represented as the principle of reason, served to complete Stoic cosmology. Zeus was the cause of all good and evil, and the difficulty presented by ascribing evil to Zeus was preferable to seeking explanations which would have undermined the supremacy of the active principle of reason. Furthermore the whole *raison d'être* for their complicated physics was the provision of the means of distinguishing virtue from evil, and the solution therefore was the paradoxical assertion that evil has a place in the cosmos, in some way serving the purposes of Zeus, so that nothing in existence, even evil – genuine evil – could be condemned.

The Stoics argued that virtue, an absolute, accrued from an accurate perception of the nature of reality and an understanding of its workings, and that this knowledge could be achieved throught the study and apprehension of the cosmology proposed by Stoic writers. In a sense, it is a restatement of Socrates' dictum that "virtue is knowledge," except that the knowledge of which Socrates spoke was the understanding of the actual nature of virtue or the good, while the Stoics meant understanding of the cosmos, attainable not only through intuition but through sense perception. That knowledge makes it possible to live a life of virtue in accord with nature, and provides the Stoic with the desired attitude of mind toward the experiences of life. For the most part, in the centuries after Chrysippus, the impact of the Stoic position was largely ethical and religious. Even though details of physics might have been dealt with by Panaetius, or, in the next century, Cicero might have learned a great deal of technical philosophy from the exceptionally able and prolific Posidonius, the main impact of Stoic ideas seems to have been the dissemination of the Stoic insistence on the importance of attitude of mind. People could embark on all sorts of activities, could pursue with vigor their careers in politics, war, or anything else of importance, with the assurance that, so long as they had the correct Stoic attitude of mind, they would achieve happiness in success or failure, in triumph or in ruin.

That attitude, based essentially on the principle of "living in accordance with nature," meant the acceptance of any outcome of activity as the natural outcome, in accord with the reasoning principle of Zeus. Whether in fact the everyday discourses ever went so far as to attribute cause to the Stoic reasoning principle, the Stoic ethic as it was conveyed to the non-professional philosopher was sufficiently persuasive that the idea, combining vigorous activity with "tranquil acceptance," became a very popular theme among Roman writers and statesmen alike. It was the aspect of Stoicism stressed by Cicero, and it recurred frequently in the centuries which followed him. In its working out of the paradigms of proper behavior – the justice of the "wise man" – Stoicism offered rules of conduct which it maintained were correct because they were in accord with the reason of Zeus. The Stoic teacher could guarantee that observance of these rules, combined with the proper attitude of mind, would reward the Stoic with satisfaction in life. Living the Stoic virtues meant that one could be comfortable in the manner of one's life, and the cultivation of the proper attitude of mind meant that one would remain undisturbed whatever might be the practical outcome of one's actions.

Insofar as the Stoics divided and classified the virtues beyond the basic rule of living according to nature, they were concerned with modes of behavior according to which the virtuous person dealt with others. The creed propounded some patterns of what we would call moral behavior, operating essentially on the basis of the view that the things people usually sought by wicked acts were either matters of indifference or were downright harmful. The Stoics thus gave an impetus to the spread in Hellenism of a moral code which had some rational, philosophical, and even quasi-religious justification. It went beyond Socrates' acceptance of the generally approved ideas of his time in order to leave his contemplative effort free for the improvement of his soul. The Stoics could justify their prescriptions for behavior in a number of ways: as decreed by the reason of Zeus; as according with the principles of nature; as the modes of behavior which did not pursue the harmful aspects of life, but only the beneficial. What the Stoics had done, in effect, was build a rational basis for the common morality of Hellenism.

For some upper-class Romans, like Seneca, the adviser to the first-century AD Emperor Nero, the Stoic creed may have served well. It was obviously the guide for the Greek slave – later freedman – Epictetus. Throughout the second and first centuries BC, Stoic teachers flourished in the cities of the Greek east and Roman west alike, and their teaching provided the upper classes with a suitable intellectual stance of morality in activity. How much the intellectualism of the philosophic religion penetrated below the upper classes is very difficult to say; Epictetus was probably an exception. Still, the idea that there was some relation between the will of an all-embracing deity and a morality prescriptive of human behavior managed to spread. It certainly found expression in the conception of deities like Isis, who was seen to express virtue along with her power, and who was said in hymns to hold the kinds of generous attitudes toward humanity which exemplified some aspects of virtue encouraged by the Stoics.

However scholastic the major Stoic teachers of the third, second, and first centuries BC might have been, their teaching had the effect of developing a more popular Stoicism which was largely ethical and psychological. The major Stoic doctrines gave Hellenism a philosophical and religious tradition which offered principles of absolute validity on which to base human action. In proposing a cosmos regulated by the reason of a single divinity, with virtue absolute, universal, and knowable, Stoicism drew on both religious and philosophical traditions in Hellenism to create a philosophical religion which could have a practical and programmatic nature. It provided Hellenism with an endorsement of a connection between human morality and divine will. Earlier philosophical traditions had found such an endorsement difficult to propose, and critics of the Stoics, like Plutarch, could easily find the inconsistencies in Stoic doctrine which were inherent in some of their positions. Plutarch and the inconsistencies notwithstanding, however, the Stoic interrelation of human morality and the divinely reasonable cosmos retained a vitality and an attraction for several centuries. The connection between ethics, philosophy, and religion which is characteristic of later Stoic thought permeated other aspects of Hellenism by the first century. It underlay the attitudes of a philosopher like Philo, influenced the views and the universalism of a historian like Diodorus Siculus, and ultimately set the tone and parameters for discussions of ethics, morality, and human conduct in both philosophical and religious contexts. Thus, in its impact on ideas in the sphere of ethics, it had a significant effect on the development of later religion and philosophy far beyond the circle of those who considered themselves Stoics.

# 23

# The struggle to
# govern Rome

*Civil war from the Gracchi to Caesar,
and the final triumph of Octavian*

In 44 BC Gaius Octavius, adopted son of Julius Caesar, set out to claim the inheritance left him by the recently assassinated dictator. He had to face a resurgent Senate, personified by Caesar's assassins, Marcus Brutus, Decimus Brutus, and C. Cassius Longinus, and had also to contend with Marcus Antonius, who had gathered to himself the mantle of leader of the supporters of Caesar and was in possession of the former dictator's funds and papers. Antony had patched up an agreement with the Senate and was, for the moment, in control of affairs. Octavius was aware both of the difficulty of his attempt to assert himself as Caesar's heir, and of the complex politics of the Rome of his day. He could look back upon a century of bloody struggle between the Senate and its opponents and could name a half-dozen or more brilliant military strategists or politicians who had met disaster attempting either to control or to reform the state. He had to find both power and new solutions if he was to establish himself in place of the deified Julius. He was 18 years old.

By the time Octavius was pondering the situation created by Caesar's assassination, the traditional processes of government at Rome had long since collapsed. The Rome of the mid-first century BC was simply not the same city or society which had survived the Carthaginian onslaught and then had overwhelmed all her enemies east and west. The repeated victories in Macedonia, Asia Minor, and Greece had wrought great changes. Apart from the political benefit to be gained at Rome by victorious commanders who returned from the east to take advantage of newly gained fame, the eastern wars produced great economic changes. The state itself not only gained from the levies imposed on the defeated enemies, sometimes vast sums like those exacted from Antiochus III in 188 BC after his defeat, but the generals, officers, and troops carried back coin and treasure as their unofficial reward for service. The plunder from the sack of Corinth, for example, at the end of the Achaean War in 146, scattered Greek art objects all over the city of Rome, to join the river of gold and silver flowing back to Italy. Besides the plunder, large sums were made each year by entrepreneurs, non-senators who undertook the tasks of commissary to the armies and administrator of tax collection and the sequested lands and properties which the state now possessed. In the absence of a system whereby all this cash could be used as capital for investment in productive enterprise, the money had an enormous impact on the Roman economy. It was used primarily for the acquisition of land, always the preferred investment in antiquity, and that, together with the inflow of large numbers of slaves, disrupted the agricultural patterns of Italy.

Before all this happened, much of the good farming land of Italy was in the hands of small landowners who worked their own farms. Roman armies were largely made up of citizens of this class, men who farmed in times of peace and were called up for service in crisis and war. The heavy toll of the Punic Wars reduced their numbers, and gradually, spreading out from the area around Rome, the small farms were replaced by large estates owned by individual rich men. The members of the senatorial class, who had the money to buy land and the slaves needed to work it, rapidly moved into this source of moneymaking which was, by tradition, open to them. The merchants, that is, those non-senators with funds, for whom commerce was open, also increased their wealth and applied it to landholding. The peasants who had inhabited these territories – those who survived – either emigrated from Italy, many settling in southern Spain, or travelled to Rome, where they often became dependants of powerful families. The land itself, which hitherto had been used for the production of cereal crops and the necessaries of life, was converted by the large landowners into production of more profitable commodities like olive oil and wine. The result of this reallocation of land was that Italy in general and Rome in particular became less and less self-sufficient in the production of foodstuffs, depending increasingly on imports of grain from Egypt and Sicily, while at the same time the economic interests of the landowning Senators and merchants called for a foreign policy which preserved existing markets or opened new opportunities for the export of Roman agricultural products.

By the latter part of the second century BC, the effects of all these developments were being felt strongly. The Senate and senatorial class, which had provided coherence in policy and state leadership during the crises of the fourth and third centuries, increasingly came to represent a focal point for resentment and unrest, as the Senators, who still controlled the state and established policy, increasingly served their own economic interests rather than responding to external threats or national needs as perceived by the larger body of citizens. Some of the Senators, probably seeing that their own welfare was tied up with that of the state as a whole, or in other cases using the problems as excuses for steps in their own self-advancement, launched proposals and programs for reform. Because the overall problem was tied up with the existence of the large estates owned by Senators and the control of Rome by the Senate, reforms consistently focused on breaking up the large farms and altering the balance of political power at the expense of the Senate. The Senators, of course, resisted any curtailment of their power and wealth, and the result of the difference in interests was a series of conflicts, prolonged and often violent and bloody, between the Senate and its politically ambitious senatorial opponents.

The first of these were Tiberius Sempronius Gracchus and his younger brother Gaius. The elder of the two, using his office as tribune of the people, in 133 BC attempted a broad land reform, limiting the amount of public land an individual could hold and providing that the tracts thus returned be parcelled out to other citizens. His program came to an end the next year when, contrary to practice, he stood for immediate re-election and was killed in an armed scuffle on voting day. About ten years later his younger brother Gaius held the office of tribune, and began to formulate and implement economic reforms, this time supplementing them with political changes aimed at curtailing the power of the Senate. On top of further allocations of public lands and the establishment of new Roman colonies in south Italy and abroad, he passed the enormously popular grain law which required the government to sell grain to the citizens at Rome for lower than market prices. Even after he was killed in voting day riots a couple of years later and the Senate was back in the driver's seat, it dared not touch that piece of legislation.

The story of the Gracchi exemplifies many aspects of the approach to political and social ethics in the Roman state. The reaction against Tiberius' attempt to gain election as tribune a second successive year, which was contrary to practice even though not specifically illegal, illustrates the importance to Romans of tradition, *mos maiorum*, "ancestral custom," as the Latin put it. Right and proper conduct was often determined by precedent, and the Romans, more than most peoples, put a very high value on the actions of their ancestors and credited them with a strength and moral rectitude well in excess of those of the contemporary generation. It was an attitude not likely to impel Roman statesmen or thinkers to much creativity in setting policy or legislating behavior, and there was, accordingly, not much impulse in Rome to examine political behavior or constitutional and social problems from the standpoint of the need to improve existing circumstances. The Romans were, in other words, even less likely than the Greeks to value novelty, or to break with the past in solving their problems.

The programs proposed by the Gracchi emphasize the extent to which economic crisis was determining political and social developments. Roman leaders, from the second century BC, were forced to adopt policies which dealt first and foremost with economic matters, or at least with a mixture of economic issues and problems concerning the allocation of political power in the state. Thus the legislation of Gaius which gave a greater role in the state and more opportunities for gain to the commercial classes used economic measures to achieve political ends. And behind an attempt to expand the franchise and improve the position of the Italians lay not only the discontent of the allies but the need to broaden the scope of the land allotment legislation to include the lands of the allied cities as well. The overall perception of the political problems of Rome by the Gracchi, in fact, including among others the need to improve the fighting ability of the army, attributed them to economic causes, thus soluble only by economic measures.

The fundamental difficulties remained unsolved after the death of Gaius, and the ascendant Senate did nothing to improve the situation in the last decades of the second century. Expansion into southern France and conversion of part of the area into a province primarily advanced senatorial interests, and a military adventure in North Africa in the century's last decade underscored the corruptibility and incompetence of the generals which the Senate sent out. The army was in poor condition, made up as it was of landowning citizens, for the dwindling number of small landowners left a progressively smaller pool available for service. In the circumstances, the onslaught of a group of Celtic and German tribes, known as the Cimbri and the Teutones, on the new Roman province of Narbonese Gaul in southern France, presented a serious danger. After initial successes in 111 BC, the Germans stayed in Gaul and the Cimbri moved off to Spain, giving the Romans an opportunity to reorganize. The threat provided an opportunity for a general named Gaius Marius, who had come to the fore in 107 as consul, and had taken command of the North African war and ended it in two years. He was a member of the anti-senatorial group at Rome, but now, with the Teutones and the Cimbri pressing on the border, the Senators were prepared to give the tested general what he needed to repel the threat. Marius thus gained unprecedented sequential consulships from 104 to 102 BC, and carried out a fundamental reform of the army. Substituting pay for reliance on the landowning citizens, and offering land grants at the expiry of enlistments, Marius created a professional army which was able to carry the field against both Teutones and Cimbri when they invaded Italy in 102 BC, and in two battles he completely destroyed the danger.

The new army had proved itself in the field, but its structure was to aggravate Roman political and economic problems considerably. Pay for service meant that generals required greater funds than before, and depended either on governments in control at Rome or, failing that, other sources such as wealthy political allies at Rome, plunder from campaigns, even grants from foreign sovereigns. The wishes of these sources and the need for funds inevitably influenced the generals' policies and activities. Secondly, the land-grant system introduced an element into politics whereby important generals could be attacked by refusing the expected grants to their veterans, and Rome would even see armed conflict arise out of the attempts of one faction to clip the wings of an opposition leader by depriving him of this means of rewarding his veterans. As a result of all this the army, while much more reliable as a weapon in the field, was much less trustworthy as a national instrument of policy, and even became a threat to the maintenance of orderly government.

For the moment, however, his army's success assured the ascendancy of Marius and the anti-senatorial forces. The Senate was still a power to be reckoned with, however, and its resistance to reform measures which included compensating the Italian allies for land by admitting them to the franchise led to a hard-fought "War of the Allies" from 91 to 88 BC, which came at the same time as the attack on the Roman east by King Mithridates of Pontus. Out of this crisis emerged a general who had earlier served under Marius, L. Cornelius Sulla, a supporter of the senatorial faction, and control of Rome see-sawed between his forces and those of Marius until 82. There was actual civil war, with the supporters of first one side, then the other, dying in the city in their hundreds and thousands as victims of political murders – proscriptions, as they were called, from the practice of posting the names of intended victims to declare them fair game. In the field, thousands of troops, citizens and allies alike, were killed on each side as the Marians clashed with Sulla's armies. The aged Marius died in 86 BC, and in the end Sulla prevailed, and instituted wide-scale political reform measures calculated to restore the Senate's controlling position in the state, such as legislation limiting the powers and freedom of the senior magistrates, particularly the consuls, and a law returning to the Senate exclusive jurisdiction in the high courts. Finally, on the principle of "do as I say, not as I do," he took measures to prevent any repetition of his own earlier seizure of Rome by force of arms: there was to be no standing army in Italy, and proconsuls – former consuls who had received governorships of provinces – had no military authority and were only ordinary citizens when in Rome; soldiers, when they came back from the provinces, were to disarm and become ordinary citizens.

Sulla's behavior and the nature of the laws he implemented shows a great deal about the Roman political mentality. The idea that the serious troubles which arose from deep-seated disequilibrium in the economic and political life of the state could be controlled purely by legislation illustrates the Romans' exaggerated expectations of the law. This formalist approach also placed faith in the notion that power-seekers could be impeded if deprived of due authority – the almost mystical *auctoritas* – by legislative provisions. Then too, the idea that the Senators would put aside their personal and family interests to govern for the benefit of the state as a whole illustrates the veneration in which the Senate was held then and later, a veneration justified far more by the Senate's antiquity than by its performance.

Within a decade, the futility of Sulla's legislation was obvious. Crisis after crisis at home and abroad rocked the Senate, with domestic armed rebellion, a serious slave revolt, another rising by Mithridates of Pontus, and a seven-year civil war against the Roman general Sertorius in Spain. The Senators could contend with their own enemies at home and those of the state abroad only by granting extraordinary powers to men whom it hoped would not use them against the Senate itself. By 71 BC those chickens had come home to roost, and two commanders were at the gates of Rome demanding exemption from the laws of Sulla. The two generals, Gnaeus Pompeius (Pompey) and Marcus Licinius Crassus, wanted to stand for consul in 70 BC without coming into the city, which would mean giving up their military authority. When the Senate opposed them, the two joined forces and attracted to their colors the very anti-senatorial group they had recently been slaughtering, and forced the Senate to comply. The two took control of the state, and the next decade was filled with the struggle between Pompey and Crassus, a rivalry which provided many crises and opportunities for others to come to the fore. One of these, Marcus Tullius Cicero, was to make his name putting down a famous revolutionary plot known by the name of its leader, Catiline, but was unable to capitalize on his reputation to achieve his own aims. Another, Gaius Julius Caesar, worked his way into such a strong position that by 60 BC he could negotiate on a par with Pompey and Crassus, and make up with them the so-called first triumvirate, an informal political alliance which operated with all the force brought to it by the political and financial strengths of its members. Amongst them, they divided the offices and tasks of government to control the state in opposition to the Senate over the following years.

Caesar was consul in 59 BC, and in that office, he pushed through the legislation which had been agreed by the three in the year before: Pompey's veterans got their land, and his administrative restructuring of the eastern provinces and dependent kingdoms was ratified. Crassus was given the opportunity to reward one of his supporters by allowing him to initiate a prosecution of Cicero which resulted in the ex-consul's exile. In the next year Caesar started on his five-year command of Gaul, a campaign which gave him a great deal of prestige but kept him out of Rome as political order there deteriorated. In 54 BC Crassus took a great army out to Syria against the Parthians, but lost it and his own life in a disastrous battle. Now there were only two contenders for supremacy, making a somewhat trickier situation for Caesar and Pompey, each of whom feared the other's maneuvers in pursuit of sole power.

In those years it was very difficult for Caesar, away in Gaul on campaign, to maintain his political influence in Rome at the necessary level. In nine years of fighting, his armies had ranged over much of modern France, into Belgium, across to Britain, along the Rhine frontier of Germany, and into Switzerland, successfully pursuing the establishment of firm Roman control over the area. Eventually Caesar was ready to return, and requested the privilege of standing for the consulship without surrendering his provincial command, just as Pompey and Crassus had demanded a decade before. The combined opposition of Pompey and the Senate led to open civil war, starting when Caesar violated the law by crossing the Rubicon River in northern Italy in 49 BC. This civil war lasted four years, and after a series of battles which ranged from Greece to Egypt to North Africa to Spain, Caesar was supreme in 45 BC, all of his rivals defeated and dead.

The year before the final battle in Spain in 45 BC, Caesar was moving to formalize the power he held in fact following the defeat of the senatorial army in Africa. He intended to operate as sole ruler, and had so indicated by the title of dictator, which he had used for short times before. Now, in 46 BC, he was proclaimed dictator for ten years by the Senate and the people, and in 44 that term was extended to his lifetime. He consolidated his position by having himself elected consul every year from 48 BC on, and he gathered to himself a range of titles, offices, and powers – such as the rights and inviolability of the tribunes – which gave him technical legal authority for any act. His administrative and political reforms were just beginning when his career was cut short in 44 BC, although he had had time to begin the reconstruction of two great cities, Corinth and Carthage, which had earlier been prominent enemies of Rome. His attitude toward the Senate was apparent from his treatment of the institution: he appointed a flock of his friends and supporters to outweigh the members who had originated more properly from the senatorial class, and these appointees of Caesar's significantly diluted the influence of those who considered themselves "the best men." His control of the Senate was all the more important as he was using that council as the organ to execute his intentions, and he was, in fact, sitting in the Senate house when his enemies struck him down on the Ides of March of 44 BC.

It is impossible to know whether a longer rule would have permitted him to deal with some of the structural problems affecting Roman society and economic life, or even to ascertain if such matters were on his agenda. The nature of some of these problems is clear. Besides the ruination which the civil wars had brought to so many private citizens, the state's finances were in terrible disarray. In a century, Roman civil government had burgeoned into a great establishment, resting on the inadequate administrative base suitable for governing a single city, with many people serving in many different ways over hundreds of thousands of square miles from the English Channel to the Arabian desert. There was no coherent procedure for funding this establishment, and to a large extent it lived off the revenues which it could draw from the stream that was intended for government coffers. At the same time, the generals and provincial governors contending for power used provincial revenues for their own ends. The result of all this was that the revenue-producing provinces became increasingly impoverished, without any concomitant increase in the state's wealth or prosperity. Thus the central authority was perpetually short of funds, and the business of government was subject to the use of great fortunes which had built up in private hands, giving their owners resources more appropriate to states than to private houses. In Rome of the first century BC, where the interests of the men of great wealth were similar in all the myriad areas in which private activity and profit are related to public activity, no policy seriously detrimental to them had much chance of implementation – unless it affected the army.

The army was the great counterbalance to the power of money. Romans needed it to protect the frontiers, to maintain control over the provinces and provincial cities, to keep client kings and petty tyrants in line, to keep overland trade routes open and the seas free of pirates. All this activity, carried on over the lands and cities reaching inland from every coast of the Mediterranean, depended on the army. The Roman state could not live without the army, but it could barely live with it. Once converted to a professional force by Marius, the soldiers did not regard the state and their small farms as the only cause for which they were fighting. As the first century BC wore on, the soldiers increasingly gauged their efforts and success purely in terms of the amount of pay they received, the plunder they were able to win, and the land they were given when their enlistments were over. They equated their interests with those of a commander who could provide them with those rewards. Soldiers were as willing to fight other Roman armies as foreign forces, the more so if they perceived the opposition as attempting to prevent their commander from rewarding them properly. The man who controlled the army controlled Rome, and Caesar knew perfectly well that he owed his position and his power to the troops who followed him.

Another important development of the century was the aura which increasingly came to surround the successful leader and commander. Pompey took on the appellation Magnus, "the Great," which earlier might have been thought unseemly in a Roman. Caesar did not refuse any of a whole series of honors and tributes which verged on treating him as divine. No politician could hope to be successful as a leader of troops if he did not project a successful image, so appearance and propaganda were as important as reality, perhaps even more so. In the long run, the man who projected an image of invulnerability, who seemed favored by the gods and whose character and deeds looked a little greater than human, and who was in no way like most other men, was a man who could win and hold control of Rome. It was a role that a collegial body could not hope to fill, and which had eluded the greatest Romans of the century.

All this Gaius Octavius knew as he surveyed the situation after Caesar's assassination. The outcome of events was uncertain, and the game was very complex. Octavius, now calling himself Gaius Julius Caesar Octavianus to signify his adoption, faced Mark Antony's assumption of leadership over Caesar's partisans. Octavian, trying to get a foothold on power, accepted the overtures of Cicero to support the Senate against Antony, and his rapid success in bringing Caesar's veterans over to his side, combined with some successes in battle, established him as a force to be reckoned with. The outcome of all the jockeying and fighting was that Octavian, instead of coming to blows with Antony, joined him and Marcus Aemilius Lepidus, Caesar's Master of the Horse, in an agreement to share power. They could, and did, dictate to the Senate, and in 43 BC they were formally declared *triumviri reipublici constituendae*, "three men appointed to reconstruct the state," to hold power for five years. The next year saw a new and more ferocious series of proscriptions, destroying a large number of distinguished Romans, including Cicero. In the year after, Antony and Octavian defeated the army which Caesar's assassins had assembled, at Philippi in Macedonia. The losing generals killed themselves, and with them died the last effort to maintain senatorial government.

The situation for the next few years was complicated by the triumvirs' need for money for their troops, the difficulty of obtaining it from the already impoverished provinces, the turmoil created in Italy by Octavian's seizure of lands for veterans, and the reappearance in force of the Pompeians, under Sextus Pompey, Pompey's son, who grabbed control of Sicily. Antony, in the east, solved some of his problems by an agreement with Queen Cleopatra VII of Egypt, while Octavian maintained himself in Italy. Finally, in 40 BC, the two met at Brundisium to re-establish amity, and a treaty was struck the following year to include Sextus Pompey as well. Antony was to control the east, Octavian the west, with Africa going to Lepidus, and Spain, Sicily, and Greece to Sextus Pompey. But the rivals struggled on, and even after the triumvirate was renewed in 37 BC, Octavian ended the career of Sextus Pompey, seized Lepidus and kept him under house arrest, and so gained complete control of the west. In the next year, Antony failed miserably in a Parthian campaign and barely managed to get back to the Mediterranean. He was now even more dependent on the funds of Cleopatra, who had helped him in his preparations for the disastrous war. In the propaganda war which was now heating up between Antony and Octavian, Antony was portrayed as a creature of Cleopatra, with Octavian pointing out, among other things, that Antony had given her and Caesarion – Cleopatra's child who, she claimed, had been fathered by Julius Caesar – some Roman territories in the east, and that Antony himself had divorced the Roman Octavia to marry the eastern queen. Armed conflict was inevitable, and both sides prepared for it. In 32 BC, Antony and Cleopatra collected a great army and fleet and moved them to the west coast of Greece, in preparation for a crossing to Italy. Anticipating them, in 31 BC Octavian landed at Actium and began a blockade of his opponents' forces. Antony and Cleopatra took their fleet against him, and fought an engagement which has become something of a mystery because of Cleopatra's early withdrawal from battle, which led to the total defeat of their forces when Antony sailed his ship off to follow her. Octavian was master of all, and, when he arrived in Egypt in the next year, 30 BC, it took only the suicides of Antony and Cleopatra to ratify his total dominion of the Mediterranean. There was no rival alive to challenge him, and none would arise.

The century of civil war was over, but the years of conflict had changed Roman society. The army was a different institution from what it had been when it conquered Carthage and the east. The Senate barely existed, and governed in name only. Many of the great fortunes had been dissipated, their owners killed, and their treasures spent for soldiers' wages and rewards. Provincial government was almost at a standstill, and the provinces had often served in recent years as campaign grounds. Yet Italy was still wealthy, for the bulk of the plunder from the provinces had managed to find its way there, and the rich potential of her agriculture still existed. There were also many families who had not been destroyed by battle or proscription. By luck or wit they and their fortunes had survived intact, and they were ready to cooperate with a government which promised some stability for the future. There were, in other words, many problems left for Octavian to solve, but there was much in the economy and in Roman society with which he could work.

# 24

# The consular philosopher
## *The life and work of Cicero*

Of all the figures of the century of civil war at Rome, none has had so great an influence on the thought of those who came after him, at the same time provoking such wide extremes of praise and condemnation, as Marcus Tullius Cicero. Born at Arpinum in 106 BC, of an old and prosperous Italian family which had not made any impact at Rome, he was elected consul in 64, and became a factor to be reckoned with in the struggles between the great political leaders. His support was often sought; he was exiled once when he picked the wrong side; in the end, his attempts to preserve the primacy of the Senate brought his death in the proscriptions of 43 BC. At the end of his life, excluded from the politics he loved so well, he turned his attention to the composition of philosophical books based on his lifelong perusal of Greek philosophers. The works which resulted have, like his life itself, met a widely varying response. Montaigne thought his writing "tiresome." On the other hand, Erasmus writes that although he could not stand reading him when he was young, "Cicero never pleased me so much, when I was fond of those juvenile studies, as he does now, when I am grown old."[1] I understand Erasmus' reaction, for I too sympathize more with Cicero's banalities, contradictions, and perplexities, after some experience of life.

Cicero's importance lies not so much in his political accomplishments as in the work of his last years, his expounding of his conception of philosophy, thinking it would add to "the dignity and renown of the state for such weighty and eminent matters to be encompassed in Latin letters."[2] The particular assemblage of Greek ideas, with his own emphases, occasional modifications, or original comments, proved to be enormously influential in later times. For it was to Cicero that men often turned in succeeding centuries in search of guidance from ancient philosophy, and it was his Latin version of Hellenic thought which often passed that tradition on to thinkers who came after, at least in the Latin west. Modern philosophers who deplore his lack of originality, his repetitions, and occasional distortions of earlier views, even sometimes extending to downright misunderstandings of the philosophies he had read or the doctrines he was expounding, attack his work all the more virulently on account of the influence his writings had. His philosophical accomplishment, however, is fully understandable only in terms of his whole life: thought and action combined to form his ideas, which in later times were the more influential as the product of both contemplating and doing.

His background made him, in a way, more Roman than the Romans, more the defender of aristocratic values than many patricians of the oldest families.

26 Marcus Tullius Cicero, a portrait bust in the Capitoline Museum, Rome.

The residents of Arpinum, something over 100 km east of Rome, had held Roman citizenship for about a century before Cicero was born; mere citizenship, however, gave him no particular standing in Rome itself. Even the fact that the family was of old Italian dignity and of no little wealth did not give it much position in the great city, when Cicero's father took the family to live there when the boy was about 10 years old. The young Cicero grew up in a fine house in one of the better quarters of town, and was well educated in all the necessaries which would later fit him for his public career. He even had some military experience, for he served, briefly, at the age of 16 or 17, during the war which Rome fought with her restive Italian allies in the years 91 to 88 BC. He was young enough to stay out of the way during the struggle between Marius and Sulla, although the behavior of the forces of Marius and Cinna in the assassinations of 88 and 87 BC soured him against that faction in Roman politics. When Sulla finally returned from his eastern victories in 83 BC, seizing control of the state and instituting his reforms to re-establish senatorial dominance, Roman public life became, at least for a little while, tranquil enough for Cicero to embark upon a career. From the start, the causes which he chose as advocate show something of his political instincts, and that he had a sense of propriety and rectitude which could overwhelm his political preferences for senatorial pre-eminence. His first case was the defense of one Roscius against a powerful freedman of Sulla, even while the dictator was exercising power at Rome. He later gained a great deal of notice, if not widespread approval, by attacking senatorial misconduct in his successful prosecution of Verres, a Senator who had shamelessly and illegally lined his pockets to an outrageous extent when governor of Sicily.

By the time he began this career, he had already been exposed to the major philosophical ideologies of the time. Turmoil created by Mithridates of Pontus and the war of 88 to 87 BC had driven many to seek safety in the west, among them the heads of the Stoic, Epicurean, and Academic schools of Athens, and Cicero heard them all lecture at Rome when he was still young. At this point in their history all three schools were in a somewhat parlous state. The Academics were in the best position under Philo, who was attempting to make out the case that the views of the school had not changed since the time of Plato. Until this time, the Academy had, in fact, been marked by its increasing adherence to the sceptical view that knowledge – genuine knowledge – of anything was impossible. The position, first proffered in the school by Arcesilaus in the middle of the third century BC, was of course the antipode of Plato's idealism. Philo's backtracking from scepticism was not the final word, however, for his successor Antiochus, who led the Academy during Cicero's later life, reclaimed the name "Old Academy," re-established dogmatism, and made the Academy more of a focus for philosophical discussion than it had been for some time.

During Cicero's youth, the great philosopher of the first century BC, the Stoic Posidonius, was still just over the horizon, and Antiochus had yet to set the Academy back on the path of dogmatism. No school had yet gained Cicero's adherence, but philosophy intrigued him, and when in 79 BC at the age of 27 he found himself having trouble with his voice and decided to withdraw from public life for a time, he took the opportunity to travel and to study. He spent six months in Athens, and there heard discourses of the new leader of the Academy, Antiochus, and also of Zeno the Epicurean. It was a stimulating time for him, and he recalled it vividly in the introduction to the fifth book of *de Finibus*, written some thirty-five years later.

From Athens Cicero went to Rhodes for rhetorical studies, and there met Posidonius, who was not only the leading Stoic of the time, but had made a name for himself as a master of many fields of knowledge. Posidonius was one of the great minds produced by later Hellenism. The Stoic interest in the workings of nature prompted him to extensive writings on physics, and, although his skill as a teacher of rhetoric initially attracted Cicero, the vast scope of his achievements and knowledge led the Roman into other matters as well. Posidonius collected information and wrote on geographical and geological phenomena, such as the peoples and regions of northern Europe, tides, earthquakes, and the like. He was a historian who carried the history of Polybius into later times. He knew, taught, and wrote on mathematics and astronomy. At the same time, his Stoic philosophy produced in him a conviction of the validity of divination, and he wrote explications of that as well. All this made a great impression on Cicero, and from that time on, whatever philosophical school he might adhere to, Cicero remained heavily influenced by Stoic ethics and generally declared his belief in the principles of behavior which can be found in the works of Posidonius and his predecessors.

When he returned to Rome in 76 BC, he launched himself on the political career which in twelve years brought him to the consulship. He moved up the political ladder of office steadily, and by 64 BC, when Caesar's supporters were maneuvering to offset Pompey's leadership and the dominion of the Senate, Cicero found himself in an opportune position to achieve his own ambitions while serving what he saw as the cause of republican government. As the candidate of the senatorial forces in 64, he defeated Caesar's ally Catiline and entered office for the year 63 as the latter prepared for armed rebellion. Cicero considered his successful blocking of the conspiracy, which included the emergency execution of Roman citizens, one of the high points of his career, and he viewed himself from that time on as the savior of the republic. Although his consulship produced no other notable achievement, the suppression of the Catilinarian conspiracy was, in fact, one of the outstanding events of the period, and Cicero left office convinced of his own place in history and in the affections of the Roman people.

He was, in fact, one of the great men of the state, as Caesar and Pompey recognized when they invited him in 62 BC to join them and Crassus in the political alliance to control the state. Cicero's refusal to make the first triumvirate a foursome is certainly reckoned by many a political mistake, and

Cicero could also look on it as such, for his separation from the power of the three meant his immediate eclipse as a star of Roman politics. But the overthrow of senatorial dominance which the league of Caesar, Pompey, and Crassus brought was against Cicero's political convictions, and he had been imbued with enough ethical teaching and knew himself well enough to remain true to his principles. He could always hope for a reversal of fortune.

This reversal never came for Cicero, although one by one, Crassus, Pompey, and Caesar were picked off by foreign enemies, mutual conflict, and assassination by conspiracy. Cicero never made a political comeback, but he did outlast the other three even though the immediate effect of his rejection of their offer resulted in an exile which lasted from 58 until September 57 BC. He went to Greece, first to Thessalonika where he kept in touch with events at Rome by letter and tried to make up his mind about a more permanent location. When he finally was allowed to return, in 57, he found himself doing so almost in triumph, with more influence and public prestige than he had enjoyed before his exile. The triumvirs allowed Cicero to participate fully in affairs, for he was given the opportunity to propose the legislation assigning supervision of the grain supply to Pompey, who nominated him as a member of the commission, and, according to Cicero, told him that he was to be his right-hand man.

He took his new alliance as a realistic move, hoping to detach Pompey from Caesar, and judging that his erstwhile allies among the senatorial party not only had no power, but would not even have been friendly toward him if they had. Privately, as his correspondence shows, he deplored the situation and resented his position, remarking to Atticus that "we must be followers who didn't choose to be commanders."[3] He kept close to Pompey, maintained good relations with Caesar, but, although at the center of affairs, he had no important official duties until his governorship of Cilicia in 51 to 50 BC. There he acquitted himself quite well, but he was out of Rome during the critical period of maneuvering by Pompey and Caesar. By the time he returned to Italy in late 50 BC, the state was on the brink of civil war between the two forces.

As Caesar and Pompey plunged toward war in 50 and 49 BC, Cicero's allegiance was with Pompey, not only because Pompey had promoted his return from exile, but also because he thought that Pompey would maintain the cause of legitimacy in government. Initially, he urged peace, but then seemed to approve first Pompey's steadfast refusal to yield to Caesar, then his concessions in search of peace. When peace did not come, Cicero remained outside Rome as Caesar's march from the Rubicon turned into a rout of his opposition. Then, when Pompey left Italy to pull his forces together in Greece, Cicero dithered for months about the course to follow. His letters to Atticus during the spring of 49 BC give us almost daily reports on events and on his own state of mind. He was in a terrible quandary, for he knew where his duty and the path of courage lay, and he was equally fully aware of the dangers, uncertainties, and disadvantages of openly joining the forces opposed to Caesar. His letters in this period often betray a desire to fault Pompey and sometimes even to praise Caesar; he often expressed his horror of an actual war between the forces; the state as he knew it was dead, but he would forbear to join those who were about to mutilate its corpse. In the end, however, he did throw in his lot with Pompey, and joined the army in Greece which was defeated at Pharsalus in August 48. Then after returning to Italy for a nervous year of waiting at Brundisium for Caesar's dispositions, he was excused on Caesar's return in September 47, the conqueror generously showing the forgiveness he could now well afford. Cicero was finally able to return to Rome.

He was, of course, not part of Caesar's administrative group. There were plenty of reliables for that, so Cicero's life from 47 BC on had little involvement in politics. As the Caesarian forces were snuffing out the last flames of opposition abroad, Cicero took up the literary and philosophical work he had begun a decade before. He had written his *Republic* in 54 BC, and had begun work on his *Laws* before taking up his provincial command in 51, and seems to have returned to that work and taken up others in 46 BC. By 45 BC he had finished the first version of the *Academica*, his study of the means of achieving knowledge, and also *de Finibus*, an account of the views of different philosophical schools in the field of ethics. In 45 he finished the *Tusculan Disputations*, a compendium of philosophical approaches to the major issues of life, such as death, pain, distress, virtue, and happiness. He then moved on to *On the Nature of the Gods*, and then finally in 44 BC, the last complete year of his life, to *On Moral Duties*. It is, in a way, fitting that such should be Cicero's last philosophical work, for it was his view of his "moral duty" which brought about his death.

When Caesar was assassinated in March 44 BC and Rome was again plunged into civil turmoil, Cicero came back into the Senate in an attempt to lead again what he saw as the forces of legitimacy. In September of that year, he delivered a series of speeches in the Senate, violently attacking Antony, Caesar's aide who was supported by large numbers of Caesar's troops and had made off with much of his funds. Cicero and his senatorial comrades were relying on their own forces plus those of Octavian, Caesar's designated heir, who initially, at least, bid fair to be the great rival of Antony. But to the consternation of the senatorial group, the two came to agreement instead of blows, and, with their political and military power now combined and joined with that of Lepidus, they forced the Senate to appoint them as triumvirs – "three men for the settling of the state." Cicero now had not long to live. He was among those on the top of the list of designates for liquidation. He tried to escape, but on 7 December, at his villa near Formiae, he was captured and killed.

Cicero had seen his duty as the obligation to serve and defend a state governed by its traditional laws and institutions. He was also sufficiently interested in his own well-being to want to protect his own interests, both practical and political, and to hesitate to dash himself on the rocks in the performance of a hopeless duty. The doubts, the changes of direction, the political mistakes, all easy for historians to see in retrospect, were natural enough in the circumstances, when not only was a personal future hard to chart, but even more difficult was the assessment of what policies and what leaders were most likely to benefit the state and its citizens. It was even more difficult for Cicero to decide what to do. A convinced believer of philosophy's value and relevance to action, his extensive studies with the contemporary schools made him very aware of the different interpretations and definitions of virtue and duty and the varied assessments of the considerations which he should take into account in determining the course of his life. Although professedly a follower of the Academy, and endorsing its view that the best one can find in pursuit of knowledge is probability strong enough on which to base action, he was also deeply influenced by and sometimes inclined toward the stronger and more absolute moral code of the Stoics. All this left him with pulls in different directions, and reinforced the doubts imposed by practical affairs.

In his philosophical writing, Cicero did not aim at introducing new systems or making major changes in any part of the tradition, but rather sought only to make the tradition accessible to the readers of Latin, and a part of Latin letters. Although from time to time he gives an account of the views of earlier philosophers, he was not interested in writing a "history of philosophy" which would present a coherent account of the development of the ideas or systems of the Greek philosophers. Rather, he chose to present the ideas themselves, and primarily those current in his own day, as they related to the major issues of life, and as they varied from school to school. He did not hesitate to evaluate and comment upon what he found in the works of the Greeks, and although he rarely presented a concept markedly different from what he found in his texts, he often criticized material as inconsistent, as mere quarreling over words, or as just plain wrong. In each work he wrote he focused on a theme – virtue, duty, the state, divination, and the like – and addressed to that theme the views of the Stoics, the Epicureans, the Academics, and sometimes explicitly his own ideas.

We do not have all of Cicero's philosophical works. Some have been lost completely; others, like the *Republic*, of which the greater part now extant was rediscovered in the Vatican Library as late as 1820, are represented only by some books surviving out of the number written, and we fill in as much as we can of the missing portions from quotations or comments by later writers who read them before the losses occurred. Other works have come down to us complete or almost so. Among those damaged worst by time is the *Academica*, a work written in 45 BC and then completely revised, in which Cicero presents his views in defense of scepticism as to the possibility of absolute knowledge. As in most of the philosophical works, the *Academica* takes the form of a discussion among Cicero and some of his friends, with one speaker presenting the views of one of the philosophical schools on a particular subject, and another either criticizing it or offering an alternative view from another school. Cicero himself is prominent among the speakers, more so than in some of the other works, and it is clear from the role he assigns to himself and the statements he makes that he is in complete sympathy with Academic scepticism. In an examination of the dogmatism of the Old Academy, he presents himself defending the scepticism of the New Academy in his own person. The whole epistemological discussion is carried by the stock arguments of the schools of philosophy, and it is generally believed that Cicero's text is based on the works of other philosophers, books which were, so to speak, open on the desk as he worked. Even so, he made the arguments his own, and defended from conviction the arguments against dogmatism and in favor of making judgments about perceptions, reality, and actions on the basis of the probability which perception and reason can generate.

This basic attitude emerges through the dialogues of *de Natura Deorum – On the Nature of the Gods* – written in the same year as the *Academica*, a lively, witty, and clear exposition of the theological views of the three philosophical schools. Here Cicero puts a sceptical argument in the mouth of Cotta, a Roman pontiff whose duties involved the supervision and regulation of Roman religion. Cotta acknowledges this, but points out in his rejoinder that as a Cotta and as a pontiff he is supposed to maintain traditional belief, and so "I always will and always have maintained them."[4] But his belief is based on faith, and he is not convinced by the arguments for the nature of the gods presented by either the Stoics or the Epicureans. The work as a whole thus combines a lucid explication of the different views on the gods in a manner calculated to allow belief, and still discourage the acceptance of dogmatic positions or arguments.

Cicero summarizes the arguments for the existence of the gods at the beginning of Book I of the *Tusculan Disputations*, written a little earlier in the same year. The five books of the dialogue offer the explications of the respondent, an otherwise unidentified "M," about the major concerns of life as proposed by an interlocutor. Book I presents the argument that death is no evil; Book II that pain is not such either; Book III treats the question of distress in general, Book IV the emotional disorders of the soul, and Book V concludes with the argument that virtue is happiness. Much of what is said comes from the more or less standard commentaries of the philosophical schools, and there is enough banality to satisfy the most demanding of preachers. For example, an important argument, that for the immortality of the soul, is made by the usual reasoning one finds in ancient writers: Cicero gives citations of authority using sensation, knowledge, learning and memory as evidence; he uses analogy; he presents statements as obvious; he introduces examples of human behavior to demonstrate belief; he proffers the evidence of etymologies. All this one finds over and over again in ancient philosophical writings, and it carries as much or as little conviction in Cicero as anywhere else. The arguments that pain is no "evil" in Book II are just as weak or as strong, turning as they do primarily on definition, and arguing with some force that the Stoic position is weak if one agrees that pain is "against nature," although Cicero does not acknowledge the Stoic use of the words "not evil" in the moral sense that they are meant. The discussion is less attractive for these theoretical considerations than for his practical comments that fortitude in the face of pain is virtuous because we consider brave and praiseworthy those who exercise such steadfastness; ordinary readers may also find some sense in the comment that complaint about pain does not alleviate it, and that practicing endurance often makes pain more bearable.

None of this is particularly penetrating, although its practical tone assured it a long life among moralists who came later. It all has strong Stoic flavor, as does the discussion of distress in Book III and of the so-called disorders of the soul in Book IV. Approving the Stoic view of distress, Cicero accepts their conclusion that disorders of the soul are created by what we would call "bad attitudes," so that the pursuit of pleasure, money, lust, envy, and all the other sins of feeling bespeaks disorders of the soul which arise from the mistaken belief that the objects of envy, lust, greed, and the like are good. These views make it easy to conclude in Book V, after a brief résumé of early Greek philosophy, that virtue is sufficient for happiness, as the virtue of expelling the disorders of the soul leaves it happy: the "wise man" is always undisturbed and is therefore always happy.

This *vademecum* for behavior benefited from the just completed *de Finibus Bonorum et Malorum, On the Ends of Good and Evil*, which represented Cicero's survey of the ethical theory of the Stoics and Epicureans and the criticism thereof, as well as the ethics of the Academy. Aiming at refuting the Epicureans, Cicero argues definitions and classifications of pleasures, but overlooks the basic idea behind Epicureanism that the limitation of desire achieves maximum equanimity. Seeing the contest as one between virtue and pleasure, Stoicism against Epicureanism, he asserts that the virtues are not merely aids to pleasure, nor morality a mere convention. Perhaps most important, not only in the discussion of Stoicism but in all the moralizations in the work, is his treatment of Stoic sociology and the doctrine of common humanity. From this flow such approved acts as patriotism, the benefiting of others by passing on knowledge, and the service of the strong in protecting the weak. The Stoic idea that "there are bonds of justice between men",[5] expressed here by Cicero, was important for the future, as were his explications of the principles which lie behind and affect human conduct and relations between individual and society – ideas of law, of political association, of pure love between man and wife, of friendship.

Cicero's last philosophical work, the *de Officiis*, usually translated *On Moral Duties*, is written in the form of a letter addressed to his son Marcus, and as any compendium of proper behavior must inevitably be, it is full of commonplace advice and instructions on what seem trivial matters. It is valuable more for its revelation of Cicero's attitudes and upper-class Roman ethics than for its occasional good thought or its adaptations of the statements of other philosophers. Its combination of theoretical observations and concrete prescriptions for behavior (rather than pure abstractions) made it a favorite with later moralists. For example, in proposing the classification of the virtues into four, Cicero's definitions maintained a close bond with everyday life. The first virtue, wisdom, he defined as an accurate perception and elaboration of what is true; the second, justice, so often a philosophical abstraction, Cicero related to society, defining justice as the execution of obligations and the rendering to each person what is due in a proper ordering of organized society. His third virtue, fortitude, relates often to Stoic values, and exhibits many of the best Roman traits of physical courage, humility in prosperity, and endurance in adversity, and calls for participation in public life. The last virtue, temperance, Cicero describes as a kind of self-control in behavior, moderation, and good order.

In this approach to proprieties, Cicero diverges from the usual Hellenic treatment of abstract virtue and stresses the importance of society to the evaluation and determination of virtuous behavior. He shows the influence of the Stoics in stressing the role of nature, for he argues that the moral duties which arise from community life have greater affinity to nature than those which arise from knowledge, with the result that the duties of justice, which relate to treatment of other people, have priority over those arising from knowledge. "Thus it is that human society and community prevail over the pursuit of knowledge,"[6] Cicero alleges (without proof), out of the fact that human society did not arise merely as a means by which people could provide for their daily needs. This whole section of Cicero's philosophical writing is not only an effective revelation of Roman social philosophy, but is also an influential contribution to later political and sociological theory, offering a means of resolving a common problem of practical ethics:

in discriminating between obligations, this class of obligations takes priority, that which relates to human society . . . so that it is not difficult in examining one's obligations, to see which one is to be preferred to which other. And, moreover, even in relating to the community there are levels of obligation, in which it is possible to understand which stands over any other. Thus first there is obligation to the immortal gods, second to one's fatherland, third to parents, then gradually descending to the rest.

From these matters briefly set out it is possible for men to be in doubt about something, whether it be good or bad, but also when two legitimate courses are open which is the better. This is something, as I said before, which Panaetius missed.[7]

Panaetius was not the only Greek to pass by this kind of issue, and it is Cicero, more than any other ancient philosopher, who dealt with this very common and real human dilemma.

Book II deals with much more individual and particular issues of behavior, and the manner in which they relate to one's advantage, while Book III deals with issues in which there is doubt about the moral course of action. We use the short-hand expression, "the conflict between the Right and the Expedient", to define the problem, but the question is somewhat more wide ranging that this would imply. Cicero says that he is dealing with those moral duties called secondary by the Stoics, not the exclusive properties of the wise but those held in common by all humanity. Against true morality, which is understood by the wise only, expediency has no weight. Against ordinary moral obligations, the second-level kind of which we are aware and which apply to us, the tempting counter is the profitable, which is to be rejected in favor of the moral. Acknowledging that there is need of a rule or set of rules for deciding when an unprofitable course of action must be chosen for moral reasons, Cicero proceeds to offer some: "for a man to take something from another, and to improve his situation by the loss of another is more against nature than death, poverty, pain or anything else."[8] There are social interests which all men have in common, and the law of nature which applies to all means that one is prohibited from wronging any man, foreigner or citizen, for any such discrimination disrupts the common human society; and ultimately, in determining courses of action, the objective of the good man should be the well-being of human society.[9]

The rules which Cicero offers are fairly detailed and take into consideration many aspects of human interaction. One is not required to sacrifice all self-interest, for example, but may act in pursuit of self-interest so long as one's acts bring no injury to others. Nevertheless, what is morally wrong can never be expedient – that is, even fulfilling one's self-interest can never lead in the direction of wrong action. In attempting to establish the lines between legitimate self-interest and immoral action Cicero sets up test cases; for example a grain importer, who knows that other ships are on the way to a city where grain is short, is torn between telling that more grain is on the way or concealing that fact to maintain high prices. Cicero decides that following the moral course requires the grain seller to reveal that other ships are on the way, just as the vendor of a defective house ought to reveal the defect even if not asked.

Cicero's *de Officiis* is important for its value to subsequent generations by working out detailed rules of morality and giving examples to clarify issues. It is much more significant, however, for its careful working out of the morality of community interest within the state and even beyond, to all humankind. Cicero had undoubtedly spent a good deal of time in thinking out his views on this matter and he had, in fact, elaborated his political philosophy in his *Republic* and *Laws* a decade before undertaking the ethical essays. Both these political works have come down with serious losses, of the *Republic* almost all of Books IV and V, and a good part of Book VI, while out of at least five books of *Laws*, we lack the end of Book III and virtually all of Books IV and V. Nevertheless, enough of each remains to show the major thrust of Cicero's argument, and some of the basic political philosophy be was expressing.

He builds his political views on what is a sort of social contract notion, emerging from the premise, expressed elsewhere, that the nature of human institutions is dictated by the human desire to live in community. It is not so far from the Aristotelian idea, and much of Book I of the *Republic* is basically a rehash of common political philosophy – the descriptions of different types of Constitutions, the usual explanation of the manner in which they degenerate. Outstanding, however, in all of this, is an argument for equality among citizens of a state in the course of the presentation of the case for democracy of which Cicero makes Scipio the spokesman:

> It if does not please us to equalize wealth, if the talents of all cannot be equal, then the rights in law certainly ought to be equal among those who are citizens of the same state. For what indeed is a state unless a community of law?[10]

Later in the work, in a fragmentary part of Book III, Scipio serves as a proponent of justice, arguing that government with justice is good, and that without justice is inevitably bad; a society without justice, he maintains, does not even deserve to be called a state. In the sequel to this work, the *Laws*, Cicero offers an explication in detail of the regulations which will obtain in a state which is constructed according to the theory of the *Republic*. Specific laws, he says at the beginning of Book II, are created for the safety of the citizens, for the security of states and the peaceful enjoyment of life by humanity. Overall, Cicero's specific legislation repeats, with few exceptions, the regulations of the Roman state in his own time, reflecting the view of the *Republic* that the Roman Constitution was the best in existence.

Cicero's assemblage of Hellenic ethical thought was important because it meant that to many, Academic, Epicurean, and Stoic philosophy was what Cicero said it was. Also influential, however, was Cicero's own contribution to all of this, the formulation of the claim for priority to social goods and social obligations. Many Greek writers had assumed this priority, implicit in Aristotle's statement that man is a social creature. Cicero's explicit claim, however, and his frequent reference to the universal application of ethics requiring that all men, citizen and non-citizen, great and small alike, be accorded the same basic right to fair treatment and moral respect, "that there should be respect for the best men and the rest as well,"[11] placed the idea in a context of writing which had wide dissemination for a long time. Although the universality of ethics and the idea of the existence of a common bond of humanity had been elucidated by Greek thinkers, the idea did not appear so prominently before Cicero presented it. The emphasis on the social nature of humankind and the existence of the universal community thus gained further dissemination in his Latinization of Hellenic philosophy.

Cicero's philosophical writing, even including his own original thought, was basically Hellenic. It owed its genesis to his studies of Greek writers and thinkers, and the essential Hellenization of Roman culture which had taken place by Cicero's time. Latin literature followed Hellenic models in lyric poetry, epic, and historical prose, and the only philosophical writer besides Cicero, Lucretius, however brilliant his Latin, added little to the Epicurean thought which he presented in poetry on the model of Greek writers like Aratus. Cicero's unifying of Greek thought, even if basically a synthesis of Hellenic ideas, created a new philosophical vocabulary in Latin, and established for the first time a tradition of using Latin prose for purposes other than historical, forensic, legal, or documentary.

There was, apart from Lucretius, no philosophy in Latin but Cicero's as the first century BC came to a close. It was Cicero, virtually alone, who provided a window on Greek thought, for Latin writers in genres like the drama did not share any of the earlier Greek tradition of exploring the human condition through their writings. And Cicero's writing belongs to a particular stream of Hellenic thought, selecting almost exclusively that part of the tradition which was rational, verbal, and subject to discussion and argument, over the mystical, non-intellectual perceptions which are directly attained. His approach to religion was almost entirely that of a rationalist, even to the point of acknowledging through Cotta in *de Natura Deorum* that the rational demonstrations of the nature of the gods must be assessed as "not proved," with religion taken on faith rather than from demonstration. Of all Cicero's writing, only the so-called "Scipio's Dream," a part of the *Republic* preserved separately from the other manuscripts, contains much of a mystical element, and that was heavily influenced by Plato. Of the spectrum of Greek thought which ranged from the most rational of Aristotle to the other extreme of religious frenzy in the mysteries, the pragmatic Roman had selected almost nothing but that which was subject to assessment and demonstration. He had dealt with justice, with virtue, with human ethics and behavior, presenting views which depended for their acceptance on the idea that human society was the repository of the highest good, a view which made it possible to judge his arguments against a perception of human society and compare them to what was known and experienced rather than against an abstraction hypostasized to another plane. He had developed a presentation of ethics in which the conclusions could be tested against human experience. For the most part, he had passed by cosmology and the analysis of virtue in an ethics which went beyond humanity. For those who sought their answers in such absolutes, other philosophies would have to be consulted.

# 25

# Bystanders

## *Philosophers and historians of the first century BC*

When the wealthy young Titus Pomponius, Cicero's school friend, retired to Athens in about 85 BC, he was seeking more than mere escape from the political troubles of Rome. In his mid-twenties, Atticus, as Pomponius became known from his attachment to Athens, was making a conscious choice for a life of study, culture, and writing, which he could pursue in the comparatively safe and certainly inspirational Athens of the early first century BC. The philosophical schools, although hardly the centers of great innovative thought, were beginning to recover after the war with Mithridates which had occupied the early years of the eighties, and new leaders were taking the place of those who had fled to Rome. Antiochus, in particular, with his leadership of the Academy and his polemic against the other schools and the Academy at earlier stages, was making Athens a lively place, at least for philosophy students. The city itself, with its architectural treasures on the Acropolis and throughout the lower town, was a delight to Greek and Roman alike. Few cities could rival the magnificence of her buildings, and none could boast so many of such antiquity. Cicero could later reflect that he had frequented the haunts of Plato, Atticus lived among the relics of the past for twenty years, and Athenians spent their lifetimes amidst the memorials of history. Athens had become a place in which the present could resort to the past for inspiration.

More was going on elsewhere. On Rhodes, as I have already noted, was the great Stoic philosopher Posidonius. The influence of the brilliant mathematician, astronomer, geographer, historian, and rhetorician reached far beyond that which he exercised on Cicero, with a scope even wider than that encompassed by the many disciplines of which he was master and to which he contributed. For, although his treatment of Stoic ideas often returned to the principles of the earlier Zeno and Chrysippus, he introduced a number of ideas which seriously changed some basic Stoic concepts. He endorsed Plato's view that the soul had three parts, with reason dominant over the other two, and even more important, he held, like Plato, that the soul is immortal, a striking deviation from earlier Stoicism, for which the ultimate perishability of the soul was fundamental doctrine.

Posidonius' mysticism may have made him move away from the more directly ethical and pragmatic Stoicism, toward the religious orientation of many Stoic themes. The absence of any sizeable portions of Posidonius' writings makes any assessment of the direction of his thought tentative, but it certainly seems to emphasize the "cosmic" side of Stoic writing at the expense of the "ethical,"[1] perhaps with the effect of devaluing the worth of the individual. In any case, he certainly expended a great deal of his writing efforts on expositions of various aspects of the structure of the universe, and he was one of those who actually constructed a working model of the solar system, a mechanism of a sort described by Cicero.[2] Like Plato, he saw philosophy as the route to discovery, and in his conception of human progress, he took the view that advances and discoveries were made by philosophers, the Stoic "wise men."[3] For Posidonius, like any Stoic, the understanding of the nature of god was an integral part of philosophy, and although his view of the divine relied less on the evocation of its role as the rational element in the cosmos, god is still "intelligent *pneuma*"[4] – a term used by later writers on divinity. Posidonius had such impact that he developed a tradition of "followers" who turn up, for instance, in Plutarch's *On the Generation of the Soul in the Timaeus*, associated with Posidonian notions about the separation or non-separation of the soul from matter. Plutarch's exposition of the *Timaeus* shows the Posidonians following Plato into a morass of hypothesis and bald, nonsensical assertions.[5]

Posidonius was not the only Greek of the period to have had a clutch of followers, nor were Rhodes and Athens the only important centers of philosophy. The Academic Antiochus had gone to Alexandria in the eighties, spent some time there, and left disciples to carry on in a school later led by the friend and teacher of Augustus, Arius Didymus. The transplanted Academy, with its now dogmatic Platonism, was opposed by a school of Scepticism founded by Aenesidemus, who wrote extensively, expounding the concepts of Pyrrho, dealing with methodology of inference and methods of investigation. Although there clearly was a vigorous tradition of Sceptic philosophy in Alexandria, the formal school did not develop great influence elsewhere, and even in Alexandria, Platonism, for the most part, was the more influential tradition. Aenesidemus' account of Pyrrho's views is lost, but from the *Outlines of Pyrrhonism* by the later Sextus Empiricus, we have a fairly good idea of what it would have said.

By this time, philosophical speculation had developed a concept of a universe with humanity and the cosmos interrelated in some way through "soul," the Greek *psyche*. The identification and description of the invisible but effective agent of life and thought had fascinated the Greeks from the time of the numerological hypotheses of the Pythagoreans on. What made it up, what it actually did or could do, whether it died with the body or was in some sense immortal had been treated in some considerable detail by Plato, Aristotle, and later writers. Plato's linking of the individual souls with the world soul as elements of that world soul in the *Timaeus* made that dialogue so important to later writers that they produced commentary after commentary on it. Some of these were primarily explications of what Plato meant, occasionally getting one or another Platonic position distorted, while others of these commentaries went beyond mere exegesis to criticize Plato or to propose an author's particular views of the nature of soul. Some writers, like the Peripatetics, were more interested in the soul's effects and capabilities in terms of sense perception and motivation, working from Aristotle's view of the soul as the final cause of the body. Others were more caught up in analysis of the makeup of the soul itself, examining and evaluating Plato's earlier theory of the division of the soul into the three parts, rational, "spirited," and appetitive. All were forced to deal with the Pythagorean numerical proportions relating to the soul, since Plato himself introduced such concepts into the *Timaeus*, and all were also impelled to deal with the question of the divine nature of the soul, an idea which had early penetrated Greek thought. There were fundamental questions which persisted: Is the soul in any way at all material? Is it self-moving and therefore the ultimate genesis of human activity and thought, or is it impelled from outside? Is it immortal, or is it dissolved with the body? Is it the cause of sensation and sense perception, and if not, what is? Does it have parts, or is it a unitary "substance" or agency? If it has parts, what are they, and how are they effective and interrelated? What connection exists, if any, amongst individual souls and with the cosmos? There were repeated efforts to answer these and other questions. Sometimes the answers proposed were offered as conclusive because nothing else seemed to make sense to the writer. At other times they were doggedly argued through lengthy sorites from premises which no one would necessarily grant.

The later Platonists had an elaborate theory of the interrelation of things, an interconnection derived from the existence of the world soul of which all in the cosmos took part, and which provided for a mutual interaction. Many of the aspects of this theory which were current at the time of Posidonius were actually credited to him, and in any case fitted the Stoic notion of god as reason pervading all of the cosmos. With the Stoic conception of reason/god operating upon the other aspects of existence, that is, inert matter, it was not difficult to conceive of the universe as a living thing, intelligent and "ensouled".[6] The attribution of life force to the earth by Cicero[7] is seen by moderns as evidence of a particular Posidonian emphasis on this universal life and soul of the cosmos and its interaction with the subordinate parts of the universe, but whether or not this doctrine of the interrelation of the life and soul of all things was stressed by Posidonius, it was embedded in Platonism before the end of the first century BC. Ultimately it could be incorporated into religious conceptualizations of the relationship between deity and man, and provide a philosophical impetus to the pursuit of union or reunion of human soul with divine. Such conceptualizations of soul suited dogmatists, or perhaps one should say such assertions could only arise in a tradition which had veered away from the insistence on the limits of probability achieved through sense perception, the

Ciceronian attitude which had marked the Academy in an earlier time. With the Academy back on this path, and Stoicism virulently infected, only the beleaguered Sceptics offered Hellenism an alternative philosophy in any formal way. In an Alexandria which had become a major center and jumping-off point for the Hellenized mysteries offering eternal salvation through rapid transmigration, stern Pyrrho attracted few, and none read Cicero.

The Greeks were bystanders to events in this period, anyhow. They hardly needed Epicurus to urge them to cultivate happiness in their private gardens, for the Romans were giving them no opportunity to share in public life. As Sulla, Pompey, Caesar, and Antony ranged through the east in the struggles for power, the Greeks were asked only to pay the costs of civil war, not to influence its course. Hellenism had finally become an exclusively cultural force in the Mediterranean world, and its political expression, even for the client Ptolemaic kingdom, was limited to the maintenance of Hellenic institutions within individual cities. Under the circumstances, the philosophical schools did not face much demand for political philosophy, nor did it seem important to explore the meaning and exercise of justice with young men who would have no opportunity to test out theories against the real experience of civic government. With administration limited for the most part to the maintenance of buildings, festivals, and streets, the dilemmas of the prosperous governing class related more to the allocation of their resources than to any sense of justice. Philosophy could better analyze the social human situation, investigate the universal qualities of human institutions, or enquire into the qualities of human nature that had no relation to government. Thus even Stoics, who earlier had stressed the importance of participation in politics and social institutions, focused more on the elucidation of the nature of the soul than on the behavior of its possessor.

The concerns of the philosphical schools appear also in the religious literature which emerges at this time. That these concerns reached the population outside the great cities is shown in the four Isis hymns of Isidorus found in the small village of Medinet Madi in the Fayum of Egypt. In addition to attributing to Isis the characteristics of an all-powerful deity looking after the needs of humanity in the world which Isidorus knew, the poems praise her and thank her for all the gifts of skill and knowledge which she had given humanity in the distant past. If Posidonius could argue that all material progress had been made through the inventive genius of a succession of "wise men," Isidorus could see that progress as entirely due to the generous ministrations of the deity. In a sense, Isis is the world soul, and certainly the reasonable element in creation which fashioned natural phenomena into objects of value to mankind. There is a historical perspective to the worship and praise of Isis which has some resemblances to the somewhat mystical expression of the divine role in the creation of the universe which can be found in Stoicism and in the Academy.

Some other ideas of the philosophers appear in other kinds of secular composition. The thrust toward the acceptance of universalism in human life, seeing human history as a unity over all the inhabited world for the period of known time, influenced the writing of history. While "universal" history in a sense goes back to the beginning of the art with Herodotus, over the passage of centuries historians had become more conscious of that aspect of their task. Polybius attempted to present his account of the Roman climb to power in the context of the history of the Mediterranean as a whole, but did not try to make his history complete either in time or in place. The first such history which we have in substantial part is that of Diodorus, a Sicilian Greek who wrote in the latter part of the first century BC. His so-called "Library of History" is a compendium of what was known, written, and believed about the human past, from the very beginning of things through all human development, in all places about which Greeks knew anything. It was an ambitious undertaking, and with all its flaws it was well enough regarded in antiquity to assure the preservation of many portions of the work, including the early books which tell us the principles on which he worked and the kind of interpretations he made of ancient traditions about the early history of the world.

Diodorus makes clear his belief that the only kind of history worth writing or reading is the universal, "as the whole is so much more useful than the part, and the complete than the broken,"[8] and it is this unified history which brings together all the important events of man's past. He thought that all history, regardless of the influence of some events on others, was informative, and could provide guidance for action, but that events could be understood properly only in the context of the totality of history. He also wrote his account of earliest times under the influence of the same ideas which we confront in the poems of Isidorus, that is, the view of human and divine history which credits to the Egyptian gods – through whom the Greeks learned about the gods – the role of guidance of the development of human civilization. His account of early history interweaves human and divine actions, and following a long-established Hellenic tradition he gives priority to Egyptian history. He presents as fact, for example, the standard account of Isis, with the death, dismemberment, and reconstitution of Osiris, following, one supposes, the same current text as was later available to Plutarch to form the basis of his *On Isis and Osiris*. He was fully aware of the historical view which credited to Isis or Osiris the discoveries which created human civilization, and he recounted as well the traditional stories of the Egyptian gods generally.

In one respect, he was very different from his Greek predecessors in the writing of history. His work was, in modern terms, academic. It was based more on reading than on experience, and he wrote more as a collator of data than as an observer, even though he had probably seen as much of the world as any modern professor with an accumulation of grants and sabbaticals. But he did not demand of himself or of the writing of history the kind of experience of politics required by Polybius. For Diodorus, the historian need not participate in events or know the frustrations and satisfactions inherent in the attempt to direct a state or city. It was enough to know what statesmen did and other historians said, and Diodorus could sit in his study, weaving together his sources into a single tale, telling us, as he came to points of termination, which predecessor wrote about what. Diodorus considered that his overall knowledge made his work superior to what he used as a basis for writing. Neither Herodotean investigation nor Thucydidean experience was needed for the transmission of a tradition which Diodorus could, in a way, encompass in its entirety. A historian who needed merely to assemble and write, he appeared on the other side of the coin which showed Stoics no longer insisting that philosophers take responsibility for the direction of affairs.

It was a world which suited even the older Titus Pomponius Atticus, now returned to Rome to live, to stand back and advise his friend, the activist philosopher-statesman Cicero. The adviser of caution, discretion, inaction, as we perceive him from Cicero's responses to his letters, was able to remain on good terms with the murderers of his friend, living out the last decade of his own life in perhaps Epicurean detachment from the final civil struggle between Antony and Octavian. He proved that Romans as well as Greeks, even Romans of great wealth, could insulate themselves from politics and pursue lives of study and writing. What a century of Roman rule had done to the Greek east, the next century of monarchical dominion would do to Rome and Italy. As Octavian, soon to be Augustus, gathered into his own hands all the threads which were to be woven into history, most men, even the most talented and wealthy, were becoming bystanders. Hellenism, which had always been able to invest life with meaning by proposing the relevance of human action to history, needed to redefine the arena of that action. Fortunately, it could find that definition within its own tradition.

# 26

# Ordinary people
## *The proprieties of everyday life*

So far we have been floating down the high road of history, attending to the ideas of artists and philosophers. But there is another path closer to the activities of everyday existence that has always been travelled by ordinary people who must work out the rules of behavior in terms of their ordinary daily activities of buying, selling, leasing, marrying, making wills, and carrying on the myriad occupations of commercial and family life. The nature of approved action in private life offers other insights into attitudes toward human conduct, and evidence of its quality and exercise is as important an indicator of ideology as the most thoughtful literary or philosophical texts.

Private life, however, is not an aspect of antiquity into which we have many opportunities to peer. Almost all our evidence about life and thought in the ancient Mediterranean derives from literary sources, with supplementation from inscriptions and from conclusions which can be made from art objects or archaeological discoveries. But ancient literature tells us very little about private life or the ideas, motivations, or principles of ordinary people, and only comedy presented the common folk to any great extent. Even there, it is difficult to fashion much of a view of the realities of private life by piercing the screen of Aristophanic satire or the melodrama of Menander and his imitators. How much was exaggerated, how much real? Nor can more ·precision be attained through the interpretation of archaeological remains. Beyond confirming what we might already guess about the crudeness of living conditions of the poor or the comparative luxury enjoyed by the few who were prosperous or rich, excavation tells us little of the intellectual content of private life. The artifacts with which people lived may tell us something of economic or social trends; we have little idea of the interrelation among the people who used those objects.

Nevertheless, the material remains of ancient towns and cities provide insights into the lives of ordinary people which would never emerge from literature. By this I do not mean just the massive amphitheatres, markets, temples, and public buildings of the great cities of Rome and Athens, but the

291

*27* Portrait of a man buried in the Fayoum, Egypt, third century AD, painted in wax on a wooden board fastened over the head of the mummy. Roman in date, the man depicted was probably not from the poorest class of the population.

more modest homes and shops, particularly in their better-preserved condition in towns like Pompeii, Herculaneum, and Ostia. For after the crowds of people left the great spectacular games, sacrifices, and processions, they wended their way home through narrow streets lined with rows of two-storey houses in some places, four-storey apartment buildings elsewhere, past open shops and taverns, stopping at the corner for a draught of warm wine ladled out of great vases embedded in low brick walls along the sidewalks. Pompeii shows us some middle-class, perhaps even rich, homes, with courts, fountains, gardens, a multitude of rooms with frescoed walls, and floors done in elegant mosaics, a community of some thousands of prosperous families, and Herculaneum, the other side of Vesuvius, is much the same. All across the Mediterranean, in fact, from Greece to North Africa, private commerce was paying off by providing a measure of comfortable living. Towns of stone and brick bespeak the same permanence or long endurance which writers gave human civilization, and warehouses, mills, wharfs, oil factories, fulleries, and the like suggest the source of some of the incomes which built the fine houses of Pompeii, Athens, Tarragona, Volubilis, and Antioch. And the archaeologists' labors have stocked museums with the flotsam of city life: forges, anvils, pots for cooking, storing, and shipping, pins, clips, brooches, armor, nails, pens and inkpots, coins, and so many more utensils of manufacture and commerce. We hardly need the satires of Juvenal to revive images of clanking carts and carriages and shouting vendors pushing their way through the dense crowds of Rome's narrow streets.

We are less well served for information about the countryside and rural life. The airy fancies of Theocritus tell us nothing about real farm life, and the ancient handbooks on agriculture were meant for the wealthy city-dwelling owners, not for the poor slaves who actually did the work. Yet, with all the bustle of the urban centers, most activity in antiquity went on in the hamlets, villages, and towns whose existence depended on farming and whose life related mostly to the land. The sheer weight of population meant that it was mostly the concerns of farmers which made up the greater part of the business of antiquity, so that the rules of behavior for everyday activity were for the most part beaten out in the experience of the inhabitants of the millions of mud-brick houses which made up the country villages of the ancient Mediterranean world. Whatever Cicero and his philosopher friends might think about kindness, generosity, friendship, and honesty, most often the definition of those qualities was made by the interchange between the people who created the basic essentials of life and worked hard to do it.

Life on the farm could be very hard. Although peasant farming was, in many places, unhurried and hardly incessant work, it involved labor in the fields, plowing and tilling behind animals or people, pulling rocks or clearing ditches for irrigation. When this toil ended, the laborers bedded down on skins or cotton cloths in almost windowless houses, perhaps illuminated for short periods after sundown by oil lamps emitting the nauseating odor of burning castor oil. Goods were scarce, tools primitive, and food basic. In most parts of the Mediterranean world, the sparkling streams of which Theocritus wrote were rare treasures, and where water was plentiful it was often turgid, insect-filled, and muddy. The diet was bread, beans, barley mash, cheese, sometimes wine or beer. Although iron tools were in use almost everywhere, they were precious and expensive, and wood was often made to substitute. Clothing was usually made at home and there is no indication that very much effort or art was expended on it. People who lived in stonier lands would pile up flattish stones to make the outside and inside walls of their houses, stretching sticks, rushes and poles across, to be roofed in with mud. Much more common a building material was sun-dried brick, made from blocks cut from a mash of earth and straw while the mixture was still wet. There were many places to which rain rarely came, although when it did, it washed down walls in great rivulets of mud, undercutting foundations, and leaving great gaps here and there. Stone or mud-brick, the houses sheltered animals as well as humans, and courtyards could sometimes be seas of mud through which members of the household would pick their way carefully as they went about their daily tasks.

Although to a large extent, the private life of rural people remains even more remote from us than that of city dwellers, one part of the ancient world has left us a comparative wealth of detailed documentation of the everyday life and business of farmers and village entrepreneurs. Residents of Egypt, throwing away their business and personal papers in dumps which the Nile never reached, ensured that some of what they wrote to one another would survive to be read by us. As a result we have wills, contracts of sale, marriage contracts, letters, leases, and all kinds of agreements made by private parties to add to a goodly number of official documents which have also come down to us. Some of these cast a good deal of light on the bases for commercial and family relationships amongst the Greeks in Egypt. We can discern people's expectations of one another, and assumptions about what makes up normal, fair behavior. We can see the kinds of things they contracted for, what they complained about, what they thought good and bad. And instead of philosophical idealizations, the documents present us real problems and their proposed solutions.

It is probably true that the majority of documents derive from those of the rural population at the upper end of the scale of prosperity – whatever that scale may be in an up-river town in Egypt. They still do not attest a lot of wealth in the villages. For example, in a group of papyri known as the Adler collection, dating to the last decade or so of the second century BC, there are a number of texts which give sale prices for land and houses. A normal price for an aroura – about two-thirds of an acre – seems to have been 6000 drachmas of the copper currency and these prices seem to be consistent from the latter part of the third century BC down to the beginning of the first century BC, despite currency inflations which hit the country from time to time over these years. The prices are also comparable to those of houses, which seem to be, for the most part, between 4000 and 36,000 drachmas, with more at the lower end of that scale. Judged by the prices of other things, none of this is very much money. In a papyrus of 156 BC,[1] the rewards for the return of an escaped slave range from two copper talents if he is found in a temple, to three talents if he is in the house of a man subject to civil action, and in the same text, another escaped slave is reported to have gone off with three items of clothing worth 41,000 drachmas, a figure to be compared with 24,000, 36,000, or even 90,000 drachmas for the value of houses. Elsewhere we read of a woman's robe valued at 3800 drachmas, a man's only robe stolen and pawned for 2700 drachmas, and a child's chiton, or shirtwaist, at 500. A papyrus from the small town of Tebtunis values a woman's chiton at 4000 drachmas, another puts a price of 3000 on a man's robe lost in a fight, while a third claims that a woman's robe which was stolen had a value of 10,000.[2] All of this is very instructive, for it shows that it is possible to pay for a house or a usable plot of land with a sum no greater than that paid for an item of clothing. However one takes such figures, it is clear from these and many other texts that throughout the period of the Ptolemaic rule in Egypt, the 2000 or more drachmas which represent the value of a house does not make that item of property so much more valuable than other, more movable possessions. Houses of sun-dried brick, which, except for the wooden lintels or doors often mentioned in texts, could be made from the mud, water, and straw freely at hand for only the effort or cost of labor, need not have been such costly possessions. Even land, which could be valued in the neighborhood of 6000 to 12,000 drachmas per hectare for a mid-range, seems less precious than some other common items of value.

The relative value of some of these items, clothing against housing, for example, is in itself an indication of the nature of the economy and the low level of wealth among the rural farmers of Ptolemaic Egypt. For these and other prices to make any sense at all, we must assume that they reflect a typical peasant economy in which people are not accustomed to dealing in a market operation, using coinage regularly for exchange. People bartered, for the most part, and had very little money and few things apart from their consumables. This is also demonstrated from wills, showing that inheritances rarely comprised much more than what we, in a different economy, call "real" property, and some clothing. Even the obviously prosperous soldier Dryton, who drew up his will in 126 BC,[3] apportioning his estate amongst his wife, son, and five daughters, detailed land, for the most part – and waste land at that – and some buildings. The other items mentioned to fill out the formulaic "property in land and movables and whatever else I possess" illustrate Dryton's sense of his estate: a horse for campaigning, and armor; six slaves – three adult females and three children; some wells made with baked bricks, and their fittings; a cart and harness; a cow; some undetailed grain and money contracts and movable property. All this is deemed adequate to generate sums designated to maintain the wife and two daughters for four years, and two younger daughters for eleven years after the initial four, with a dowry for the wife as well. The whole is not so impressive, and it is the estate of a man of real substance, one who calls himself a "hipparch of men," that is, an officer, with a son for whom he claims citizenship in one of the Greek cities of Egypt. And wills of other people suggest even smaller possession of manufactured things, while the dowries presented by marriage contracts confirm this impression.

For most of the population of Egypt, and by extension, the rest of the ancient world, philosophical disquisitions about moderation, about the pursuit of luxury, about excessive expense or accumulation of wealth, the issues explored by Epicurus, Zeno, Cicero, and the other philosophers, were irrelevant. There was no luxury to lead people astray. There were very few things, in fact, even liable to attract misbehavior, and crime, when it occurred, usually fixed on the necessaries of life. A typical robbery, for example, committed in 210 BC, involved only the theft of a few grapes to make a little wine and a pruning hook.[4] Even so, it was enough to prompt an official complaint and turn up in our documents. Misbehavior, for the most part, involves physical violence rather than serious theft: a lady is scalded in a bath; a tax collector is assaulted and prevented from doing his job; sacred sheep belonging to village cultivators are stolen.[5] Official and police business is largely taken up with this sort of difficulty, or with petitions arising out of failures to fulfil obligations. Here a woman complains about potential malversation of her dowried house. There a man alleges that someone has improperly billeted himself in his house, while another person complains that his full salary has not been paid him.[6] People don't pay their debts, or the interest thereon, or complain that taxes are being unfairly assessed, while others fail to fulfil contracts or otherwise don't meet obligations to which they had agreed. The pettiness with which the system could get clogged is illustrated by a petition of the middle of the third century BC:

> To Philiscus, greeting, from Harentotes, lentil-cook of Philadelphia. I give in each month 35 artabs [something over 35 bushels] and I work manfully to meet my tax obligation every month so that you cannot blame me for anything. Now the people in the city are cooking pumpkins. For this reason no one buys a dish of lentils from me right now. Now I ask and plead with you, if it seems just to you, that it be allowed me, as they did in Crocodilopolis, to be slow in completing the tax payment to the king. For the first thing in the morning they settle down next to the lentils selling the pumpkins and don't let me sell the lentils.[7]

Propriety, therefore, amongst ordinary people, did not deal with the larger concerns of justice in a society but, as one would expect, with the rights and wrongs of conduct between associates or within families. The papyri are replete with phrases that indicate that all members of the society assumed their obligation to pay what the king demanded; they accepted, as they had no choice, the royal power as legitimate, and saw no reason to expect in return the kind of fairness from that sovereignty that philosophers thought kings ought to offer their subjects. There was not the slightest notion that the government owed any concern to its subjects beyond the care which any prudent proprietor would take for the productive condition of his goods, and this is the view not only of the governor but of the governed. No petitions seek any significant changes of policy; the most that is sought of the government is an extension of time for tax-paying, as in the case of the lentil-cook, or protection, perhaps, from abusive officials, or, much more often, the services of the king or his representatives in righting private wrongs. And the justification for the king's help, either in petitions or official instructions, is the concern to avoid killing the golden goose which is the peasantry.

In this peasant society, with people toiling away to provide livelihoods for themselves and taxes for the king, there were still occasions for dispute and mutual complaint, meagre possessions still providing cause for trouble. These were not the naïvely imagined happy farmers, content with little and sharing what they had in a cooperative tribal or communal society. If we are to credit our documents at all, people lied, cheated, and stole as much as any do, were as

mean and selfish as those of any society we know, and were hardly brought to
virtue by frugality. Even the family solidarity expected in a peasant society
does not apply everywhere, and we have a number of instances in which this
has clearly broken down, perhaps the most obvious being that shown by a
petition in which a father complains of a daughter's neglect,

> for having brought her up from childhood, being my own daughter, and
> having educated her, and bringing her to maturity, when I lost the capabili-
> ties of my own body and was unable to use my eyes, she was not the sort to
> provide me any of the necessities. And when I wanted to get the right thing
> from her in Alexandria, she apologized to me and in the 18th year she agreed
> with a written royal oath at the temple of Arsinoe Actia to give me each
> month 20 drachmas by working with her own body; and if she did not, or
> violated anything of the stipulations of the written document, she was to pay
> me in compensation 500 drachmas or be burdened by the oath.[8]

She did not do as agreed, and the wretched father petitions that his daughter be
brought to account and compelled to fulfill her agreement. It is not natural
justice that the father seeks, for there is no mention of that, and he is lucky that
he has a contract on which to proceed.

Wives and husbands trouble one another as well. Deeds of divorce can be
found as well as marriage contracts, and while they do not specify the reasons
for separation, they show clearly enough that arranged and contractual
marriage is not necessarily the route to assure the permanence of marital bliss.
Wives complain about their husbands in petitions, and rail at them directly in
letters which allege ill-treatment, theft of dowries, and failure of maintenance.
There are complaints by parents of misbehavior and ill-treatment on the part of
the children, as well as the perhaps inevitable squabbles amongst siblings about
property. Outside the family the situation is much as we might expect. There
are robberies and assaults, false oaths and breaches of contract, and all the other
violations of fair practice we might expect to find in commercial relations. The
letters and petitions deal with many such matters, and we even have official
legislation setting out penalties of different sorts, something characteristic of
most ancient law, whereby public offenses punishable by imprisonment or by
fine payable to the state are only those in which the injured party is the state
itself. In this concept of law the commission of wrong is not so much the act
itself but the damage incurred, and retribution is the requisite compensation.
Without pressing the point too heavily, it would still be safe to say that our own
legal system maintains a greater sense of moral wrong than did that of the
Greeks. The realities of life for ordinary people thus differ a lot from the
hypotheses of morality offered by the sages. The frugality or poverty endorsed
by the Stoic Zeno or even Epicurus is a very different kind of restraint from that
which necessity imposes upon the peasant. It is small wonder that the virtues
which Stoic and others spent so much time classifying do not show prominently in the daily lives of people in the countryside of Egypt, where there is

barely room for a sense of community of family and village, let alone the universality of human interest suggested by Cicero.

It has often been noted, usually as a favorable comment, that Ptolemaic Egyptian society was not racist, in the sense that the Ptolemies did not obviously discriminate against the natives, and put the Greeks in preferred positions only because they spoke the language of government. But the virtue here is probably more of convenience than anything else, and we do have some evidence which suggests that Greeks might have treated the Egyptians with contumely, as when a third-century BC petitioner complains of ill-treatment because he is a "barbarian" and doesn't "hellenize."[9] How much his perception was justified, or to what extent the mistreatment arose on ethnic grounds, is anybody's guess. It is true that in a very few decades intermarriage between Greeks and Egyptians had proceeded at such a pace that it is very difficult for us to discriminate between the two groups on the basis of their names in documents or by their ability to use the Greek language. But our petitioner of the third century BC obviously thought that the allegation was a believable one, and his complaint is not strictly language-based, but is a matter of customs and habits.

Our concern with such matters reflects our own ethical values, which are very different from those of these Egyptian peasants whose ethical attitudes might be described as non-existent. Complainants do not describe their persecutors or oppressors as "bad" or use any term of ethical value for them. Even the acts themselves are not so described. The closest the language of the papyri comes to moral judgment is the use of the Greek word *adikoumai*, "I am being wronged, unjustly treated," and its cognate *adikos*, "wrong, injustice." But these words have a very broad spectrum of meaning in Greek, and they subsume what ranges in English from the ethical-philosphical "injustice" through the moral "wrong" to the juridical "illegal" and practical "harmful." More noticeably, value-loaded words like *agathos* – "good, virtuous," – or *kalos* – "beautiful, noble" – or *kakos* – "bad, base" – do not appear in the context of these petitions or even in letters. Petitioners object that what has been happening to them is against the law or against properly made agreements, and they use the Greek word *dike* - "justice, punishment, judicial process, correct treatment" – when they are seeking legal rectification. The point is reinforced by informal documents like letters, such as one written in the middle of the second century BC by a wife to her husband who, under the god's command, had sequestered himself in the Serapeum of Memphis. She tells of the difficulties she and their child have confronted, and revealing that she knows he has been released, calls him home:

I am completely disgusted. However, since your mother is also taking it hard, you would do well to be here in the city on her account as well as ours, unless a greater necessity restrains you. You will be gracious also by taking care of yourself so that you stay healthy. Farewell.[10]

She is one angry wife. But furious as whe is, she does not charge her husband with wicked behavior or use any words of ethical or moral judgment. The wife is angry because she has been inconvenienced or harmed, and her mother-in-law is taking the situation hard for the same reason. The question of "right and wrong" or ethical behavior is simply not present. Like most letters which deal with issues like these, there is no assertion of motives of abstract value. These people are in an ethical condition quite different from that of Cicero, who, not wanting to commit himself to the risk of joining Pompey in Greece, neverthe-less ultimately abandoned his safety in Italy because he believed that was what he ought to do. Such elevated matters were naturally not the concern of the peasants of Ptolemaic Egypt. But their documents show that in those concerns which they did have, the selling, buying, and leasing of property, the arrange-ments for marriage, divorce, and inheritance, borrowing and repaying of money, in banking, laboring, hiring, and the many other business matters which engage the attention of rural people, law, necessity, and physical force were enough to maintain most rights over self and property, or to punish the occasional violations when they occurred. The society was, in a sense, con-strained by the kind of law which Epicurus described as an agreement to prevent mutual harm, and not, as Cicero was, by values which served no practical good but aimed at some higher, though debatable, good. Life was harsh, and left little room for generosity, kindness, selflessness, liberality, or scrupulous honor.

All this finds some confirmation in a genre quite removed from the legal documents and the letters, but one still fairly reflective of the ideas and attitudes of an agricultural population. This is the fable, a literary or narrative tradition of great antiquity in Greek, and one which reveals everyday attitudes toward different kinds of behavior in precisely the kinds of situations which occur in the documents. Greek fables, most of which are attributed to a sixth-century BC resident of Samos named Aesop, had been told as early as the days of Hesiod, but, maintained for the most part in an oral tradition of narrative prose, were not elevated as "literature" until quite late. Even such collections of the fables as were made served primarily to put the material at the disposal of orators and others who might find a use for it, and such early collections as that made by Demetrius of Phalerum in the fourth century BC have been totally lost to us. It is not until the first century, when a freedman of Augustus named Phaedrus produced a Latin verse collection, and then later in the century a Hellenized Italian named Babrius did the same in Greek verse, that the fables appeared in a format conducive to the preservation of a specific text.

The genre of fable is a popular form of story-telling which may share the characteristics of folk-tale, fairy-tale, myth, animal story, and many other types of narrative, but is distinct from any of them in providing a little lesson in behavior. I avoid using the term "moral" to describe the lessons of the fable, because, for the most part, the lessons have nothing to do with morals or ethics. They are the sentiments of the under-class, as Phaedrus says in the prologue to

299

*28* By the fifth century BC, when this Athenian cup was painted, Aesop and his fox were established in Hellenic tradition, the portrayal of Aesop himself suggesting the painter thought his background non-aristocratic. (Vatican Museum)

his Book III, remarking that the fables originated with slaves who used them to present views they would not state openly. In these tales, the powerful are often defeated or outwitted in an manner which illustrates shrewdness, and the fables also serve as exemplars to warn against precipitate action, thoughtless greed, gullibility, or the like. The narrative is often an animal story, in which a hare, or a fox, or a wolf comes to grief by following some natural human propensity attributed to the animal nature. A dog with meat in its mouth drops and loses it when it snaps at its reflection in water, thus losing what it had by trying to get more.[11] A snake is saved from death and then bites its benefactor: when asked its reason, it replies "so that one may learn not to benefit the wicked."[12] One after another, the fables create a simulacrum of a human situation and teach a lesson in good sense. Generally speaking, trouble comes not as a punishment for a moral slip, but because a mistake is made in assessing a situation: a braggart is caught because the means of unmasking are easily at hand, a cheat is outwitted because the intended victim is cleverer than expected, or a bully is overcome by some minor difficulty which by his own nature he cannot solve. In those few instances which introduce ethical or religious concepts, the fable so affected is late, or that appendage to it does not appear in early texts, so that this aspect can be attributed to Christian influence on the tradition. Indeed, the story of the ungrateful snake is almost the antithesis of a tradition of kindness and humane values.

The topics range over the whole scope of human concern, from close associations of family and friends to the larger realm of government and kings, but they are always treated in a metaphorical, though very simple, way. The lessons are also given in a manner comprehensible to those without education and are predicated on the assumptions and attitudes of ordinary people. The necessity for unquestioning submission to rulers, for example, is an essential element of the tale of the frogs who asked the god Jove for a king. When the frogs complained that the block of wood which the god had thrown to them was inert and useless, Jove sent them a water snake which terrorized them. When Jove heard of their further complaints, he told them "since you did not want to bear with your good one, you now must endure a bad one."[13] The fabulist assumes that one must put up with a ruler, good or bad, until he is removed by a higher power, an attitude we would also find among the tax-paying peasants of Ptolemaic Egypt, although the fables suggest that they might like to see the tables turned.

Throughout the collection, it is peasant wisdom at its best which is exemplified, as in the fable of the lark which was content to remain in its nest in the ripe grain so long as the farmer was waiting for his friends to help him reap. Only when the farmer became concerned that the ears would over-ripen and hired some reapers did the lark tell its offspring, "now it is really the time, children, to flee this place, when he himself is reaping and not depending on his friends."[14] It is a tale which provides a lesson for the farmer, not the lark, and it is a practical, not an ethical lesson. The whole fable tradition illustrates the nature of didactic interests of ordinary people, and confirms in a sometimes lighter vein what peasant wisdom appears to be in the documents – essentially self-interested and concerned with issues of survival rather than virtue. Rare indeed was the marginal farmer who could reflect on his duty while struggling to wrench from the soil his own livelihood and his assessment to the king, a fact very early recognized by Peisistratus, the sixth-century BC Athenian tyrant when he did not reprove the farmer who grunted that he would like "to pay Peisistratus a tithe of these labors." For ordinary people, abstract justice, divine or human, and the creation and validation of codes of ethical conduct were so far removed from the usual concerns of life that they were not so much irrelevant as unknown.

These characteristics of this material may be related more to the nature of the texts, particularly the legal documents, and the part of society which produced them, than to the particular culture. That is, the pragmatic attitudes in papyrus and fable may belong to peasant societies in general rather than to the ancient world in particular. Certainly legal documents from many societies eschew moralistic remarks. On the other hand, popular tales of many later societies have a high level of didactic, ethical content, and private letters can present some aspect of the moral thought of the writers and readers, as they do for Cicero. In any case, the letters, petitions, and other documents taken together with the fable material give us no basis on which to suggest that ethical ideas emerged from the rural population. We find what we should expect, that ideology was molded by the upper-class writers as expressions of philosophy, rather than the mass population which received little benefit from the ethics promulgated by the rich and powerful. The documents merely portray that world to which the gentility of upper-class ethics was not applied.

# 27

# To rule the nations

## *The Augustan accomplishment and the ideology of the age*

When Octavian returned to Rome from Egypt in 30 BC, the survivor of the bitter contest for control of Rome, and the ruler of the vast Roman domain with all its armies, wealth, and population, he was still only in his early thirties. The fourteen years since Caesar's assassination had given him plenty of time to reflect on the needs of the state and the manner in which he might organize his own administration to avoid an abrupt termination like Caesar's. It was clear to him that Caesar's packing of the Senate with a motley crew of his own supporters to the prejudice of the dominion of the old senatorial families had elicited the very bitterest resentment. He had also learned from his successful contest with Antony that the citizens of Rome and Italy could be rallied to the principle of their supremacy over the provincial residents of the realm. But the mistakes of others provided only a partial chart for his course through the tricky waters of Roman politics, and with the possibility of a long life ahead of him, he was vitally concerned to avoid serious mistakes of his own which over a long period would give rise to opposition and conspiracies. His success in devising arrangements to maintain his own control over affairs without arousing hostility is a measure of his creative political genius.

Octavian's dispositions for governing Rome started from his position as its military leader, supreme commander of all the armies, with loyalty sworn to him by all citizens, not just the soldiers in his armies. He also stood for and was elected to the consulship annually, which provided him with the *auctoritas* for the conduct of public business as a magistrate. Then, proceeding to measures calculated to meet the political, social, and economic needs of the times, in 28 BC he arranged for the resignation from the Senate of those of Caesar's appointees who came from unfitting backgrounds and did not meet the standards for membership in the senatorial class. That "purification of the Senate" followed a number of measures aimed at encouraging the growth of the citizen class as a body made up primarily of Romans and Italians; every citizen was expected to marry and produce children; citizens were not allowed to marry freedmen, a prohibition strictly enforced on Senators.

29 The so-called "Prima Porta" statue of Augustus, originally at the imperial villa north of Rome. The iconography on the cuirass is part of Augustus' message that a new day has dawned for Rome, and the emperor himself is portrayed as an Apollo-like young man, even on a statue carved after the great man's death. (Vatican Museum)

By 27 BC he was ready for a symbolic act: he renounced all the special powers which the Senate had conferred on him and "transferred the state from my power to the control of the Senate and the Roman People,"[1] the manner in which his statement of his accomplishments carved over his mausoleum in the

Campus Martius claimed the re-establishment of the ancient Roman Constitution. The Senate, which he was to use as his major instrument of administration, recognized his accomplishment by granting him the extraordinary title "Augustus." Thereafter, as he rebuilt the financial and military administration of Rome, Italy, and the provinces, he was careful to use the normal constitutional offices and procedures in implementing his will, introducing and passing legislation, and making administrative arrangements. He improved the army, kept standing troops out of Italy, established a guard for himself in Rome, and created a whole supplementary army of non-citizens, who were rewarded by citizenship after twenty-five years of service. He reorganized Rome's finances, administering a public treasury called the fiscus and occasionally using some of his own enormous "personal" wealth for state purposes.

All this made government in the time of Augustus, and Augustus himself, something new in the experience of Rome, and in its scale qualitatively different from the kind of absolute monarchy known in the east. Augustus very quickly had to develop the machinery for administering his vast financial empire, arranging not only for the reliable and honest collection of his income but for the maintenance of controls over its expenditure and the orderly transfer of funds from one place to another. Bureaucracies existed in places like Egypt, but some of his frontier provinces had little administrative infrastructure, and Augustus faced the need to integrate existing channels of government with new offices and procedures which suited the new situation. Where he could, he left people and their jobs undisturbed, but at the top, he appointed a group of financial and administrative officials, freedmen and slaves, whose status depended completely on their position on his staff. These men administered his personal property and the fiscus, served as private and confidential secretaries for maintaining communications with public officials and his own agents abroad, and carried on all business for which he did not wish to use the regular magistrates of the state. In addition to these personal officials at Rome, he had large numbers of agents for personal and public business at work in the provinces which he administered, answerable directly to him. It was a complex and far-flung network which stretched from the Atlantic Ocean to the Euphrates.

Not every province of the realm fell directly to the administration of Augustus and his agents. In the formal devolution of authority, those provinces which did not need his direct attention were left to the administration of the regular officials of the state. Senators served as proconsuls in the supreme government of provinces, and their subordinates, also members of the senatorial class, were dispatched with the authority of the Senate. Younger members of the senatorial order could follow the time-honored route to high office and distinction, so long as Augustus was favorable to their advancement. For Augustus retained the reality of power, and the Senate's discussion of business, the people's election of magistrates, the policy and legislation adopted by both Senate and people were all carried on in the context of Augustus' known views, and rarely, if ever, was anything done in the face of his disapproval. Thus, even in those provinces subject to senatorial administration, residents knew that ultimate decisions were taken by Augustus and it was to him that they could resort as the highest court of appeal against wrongdoing. As a result, even the allotment of the heavily populated interior provinces of the empire to the Senate did not slow the tendency for all people in the Mediterranean to look to one man in Rome as the source of all power and help.

That help was expressed in many forms, but it was particularly welcome in that material form which help so rarely takes – money. He disbursed pay to the legionaries, the provincial auxiliaries, and pensions to the retired soldiers. The funds for all this came out of a special treasury which Augustus administered, made up of a combination of some of his own wealth and some of the regular public tax revenues, and the procedure assured his financial, and thus real, control over the armies. Another important service in the provinces was Augustus' frequent assignment of detachments of the army to road- and bridge-building tasks. Finally, the establishment of a small but efficient standing fleet – again paid for by Augustus – with detachments at Ravenna and at Misenum to range east and west, meant that it was Augustus whom the provincials and everyone else could thank for keeping the sea clear of the perennial scourge of pirates.

All Augustus' dispensations created a new and very different form of administration for the provinces, particularly in the east. In Egypt, which had recently been a monarchy, the king was no longer relatively accessible down the Nile, with communications relatively tight. The focus of government moved to distant Italy, for the chief of the country, the Prefect of Egypt appointed by Augustus, was only an official and not a sovereign, so that recourse to the highest power called for a long sea voyage. Furthermore, for the Egyptians and those Greeks for whom the royal cult had any significance, that divinity was now remote and never seen. He also spoke Latin, as did his prefect and most of the headquarters staff in Alexandria, so that what was said or sent to them might have to pass through the medium of interpreters or translaters if they chose not to deal with it in Greek. On top of all this, the establishment of Roman rule brought an influx of Roman and Italian businessmen and commercial agents, many of whom eventually acquired property in Egypt and settled in Alexandria or even occasionally in the country. To them, Roman law applied, introducing a third legal system on top of the familiar Greek and Egyptian law for any who had to deal with these Roman citizens.

In other parts of the eastern Mediterranean, the development of the system of Augustus brought different changes. Asia Minor and the Levant had long been familiar with Roman tax collectors and Italian businessmen, although after Mithridates' solution to their annoying presence, there may have been fewer of them after 88 BC. What was new was not the Roman presence or the domination of their officials, but a new chain of command which controlled the worst elements and put the provincials on a new footing with government.

Again, direction emanated from far-off Rome, and operated with consistency on policy lines which were not created from expediency to serve the emergency need of temporary governors or generals. The provincials also found themselves, city to city and province to province, more on a par with one another, the striking differences in administration generated by the very varied officials of earlier times smoothed out by the establishment of some universal rules and procedures. In practical ways, people everywhere were moving closer to one another through their common dependence on and subservience to the distant ruler in Rome.

Augustus, of course, certainly did not represent himself as master, and his memorial is explicit that he "accepted no office given contrary to ancestral customs."[2] His role was that of servant, first of the Senate, then of the Roman people, and then of all the people in the cities, towns, and villages of the realm. Master or servant, his regime certainly benefited them all. He piled one *euergesia* – "beneficial action" – on another: ending the civil wars, reforming the administration, paying the soldiers, protecting the seas, building roads. He also brought a measure of border security which the Mediterranean basin had never known before. It is a measure of the success of Augustus' military strategy that except for the Rhine-Danube region, all this territory remained little troubled by war during his lifetime. In Germany, when newly won territory could not be held, Augustus ordered withdrawal to the Rhine, and the forces held there and along the Danube, so that military operations in the wild and unsettled regions of central and northern Europe slowed to a minimum. Elsewhere, Augustus did as little campaigning as possible, securing Syria by an agreement with the Parthians, and in Asia Minor maintaining the system of buffer and tributary kingdoms which gave no trouble. Before his reign was over, Augustus was able to claim his achievement of tranquillity everywhere. The priests could order the doors of the Temple of Janus closed, the ancient symbol that the state was at peace, and an act which "in the whole age since the city was founded is conceded to have been closed only twice, in my period of leadership the Senate voted to be closed three times."[3]

The Augustan peace was his greatest accomplishment, not only in the annals of history but in the minds of men of his own time. Compared to the improved administrative machinery, the new buildings, the standing army and fleet with their set salaries and reliable pensions, the end of the civil wars and the imposition of peace along the borders were towering achievements. They seemed almost superhuman in scope, and even in Rome, where Augustus discouraged extravagant honors, the man responsible was surrounded by symbols which bridged the gap between his humanity and the world of the gods who looked after the state. Even his official name blurred the line between man and god. He was *Imperator Caesar Divi Filius Augustus*: the first part made the traditional salute to a victorious general, the next named him "Caesar, son of a god," and the honorific Augustus certainly dragged some of the divine aura with it when it was borrowed from the gods. But god, god-like, or

30 Ingres went back many times to rework his illustration of Virgil reading the *Aeneid* to Augustus, as the poet stands in front of the ruler, who holds his upraised hand above the reclining figure of his sister Octavia. (La Salle University Art Museum, Philadelphia)

ordinary man, Romans were inclined to concede him an adulation which exceeded anything any earlier Roman had achieved.

To all this Augustus added another whole aspect of reconstruction and renewal – the rebuilding of Rome's existing monuments and the construction of new. The importance Augustus gave to this activity is suggested by its emphasis in his "statement of his accomplishments," the inscription at his mausoleum built in the Campus Martius which was copied in both Greek and

308

Latin on monuments in a number of places in the realm. The work was more than a matter of rectifying the neglect which had allowed sacred buildings to deteriorate during the century of civil conflict, and certainly a much greater concept than that of demonstrating munificence and generosity. In a Rome where piety toward the traditional gods of the state was still strongly felt by many, the repair of so many religious edifices served both to assert the endorsement by the gods of the current regime and to propitiate their continued help and protection for Augustus and Rome. And iconography, as in the reliefs on the Altar of Peace, related in explicit visual images the benefits Augustus had arranged for the state, as well as his performance of the state's duties to the gods. In addition, the remaking of the physical city carried a message to far more than the Roman inhabitants. Now Rome was the foremost city of the world, not only in the power of her arms but in her nature as a physical entity. Rome would not only be the locus of power; it would be the center of the world from which would radiate the new age's art and culture throughout the entire empire.

Monuments could be planned, paid for, and built. Ideology was a more difficult matter. The ideology was also not entirely clear. The *Res Gestae* – Augustus' account of his acts – is replete with practical benefits he brought to his countrymen, which show his piety, fairness, and generosity. But the virtue of Augustus was not the ideology of the state, and ideology was something which Augustus could neither describe nor prescribe nor inscribe in stone. Notwithstanding Shelley's claim that "poets are the unacknowledged legislators of the world,"[4] the ideas of poets are taken up most positively when, like the decisions of successful politicians, they lead where the people are going. Augustus could not have decreed an ideology, even if he could have devised one, and ordered or encouraged the literati to disseminate it. It was something which could only emerge from the hearts and minds of Romans of the day, expressing their perception of the new era, and the best Augustus could do in its formulation was to offer an example and advantage to Romans so that the new ideology would center on him. He could not force it, but induce it he might.

\*

When Aeneas, the fated founder of the Roman race, tarried in Carthage, seduced by love of the Carthaginian queen Dido, to help her build the city, he was violating more than the divine scheme which ordered him to take his refugees from Troy to settle in Italy. To Romans he was acting, however unknowingly, as a king of accessory before the fact to create what would become the greatest single threat to the survival of Rome and the Roman people. Virgil, in telling the tale, describes in vigorous poetry the bustling construction, as the walls and towers rose around the city, and the houses and temples within took shape to the sawing and hammering with which the refugees from Tyre and from Troy filled the brilliant North African air. Virgil could imagine the area well enough to convey the dramatic wooded hillsides of the Tunisian coast, plunging in places right down to the sea. When he takes us through the forests hunting with Dido and Aeneas, fleeing before a sudden storm to the cave where Dido's passion for the Trojan leader drove their personal and public lives into an emotional tangle, he creates an imaginative narrative which poses all the personal, moral, and philosophical questions which had plagued Cicero and still remained unsolved in the age of Augustus. The romantic tale is attractive enought in itself to have become a fixture of western art, music, and literature, but for Roman readers it had more than romance, was more than mere drama of fiction.

To a modern reader, Aeneas seems callow in his surreptitious departure from Carthage, even though he had been told by the gods that it was his destiny and responsibility to leave, and seek Italy. Remaining would have suited Aeneas perfectly. He would have had prestige as king, power as leader of the combined Punic and Trojan forces, love, if that counted, with Dido, and all this in tranquillity for the foreseeable future. Against this, duty meant undergoing the perils of the seas again, an unknown journey, the likelihood of conflict, personal loneliness, and although there was the certainty of success, there was no assurance of the kind of personal satisfaction which he had already achieved in Carthage. But the dramatic conflict is almost specious, for every Roman knew how Aeneas should have acted and how in fact he did act. In Ciceronian terms, in fact, the antithesis between Aeneas' duty and what appeared to be his self-interest was a false opposition, for there could never be conflict between virtue and true expediency, which always lay in the direction of fulfilling the strictures imposed by the principles of right conduct. In these terms, however arduous the path of obedience to the gods might be, for Aeneas that was the route which would bring him to genuine self-benefit. Virgil so constructed his narrative as to show what features of character might be necessary to a man who would choose the part of duty and *pietas* in preference to that of narrow self-gratification and personal pleasure. No Epicurean could praise or even justify Aeneas' behavior; no Stoic could do anything else. A Roman might want to emulate Aeneas' achievements, but he might not want to assume his personality, and that is precisely the point of the lesson which Virgil would have his generation take. Virgil's Aeneas shows us a man whose sense of ends allows the employment of even disreputable means to ensure that the gods' work is done. Virgil did not permit him the character traits of grace, thoughtfulness, scrupulous openness, or any of the other saving qualities of gentility, but sacrificed them all in the cause of demonstrating how singleminded he could be once back on the path of duty. Writing in the full awareness of the nature of the Augustan era and the terrible century which had preceded it, Virgil created his *Aeneid* (unfinished at his death in some unknown respects but fortunately saved for us in defiance of the author's explicit instructions to destroy it) as a distillation of all that the author saw as Romanism, written at a time when the national character needed redefinition.

The questions posed, Roman as they were in emphasis, had by Virgil's time felt the influence of Hellenism, so that the issues he treated and the solutions he described were an amalgam of Greek and Roman concepts and moral attitudes. The resolution of the story of Aeneas in the final victory of duty – *pietas* toward the gods and fidelity to comrades – shows a fundamentally Roman devotion to state and state religion. On the other hand, Virgil's justification of the pursuit of that duty as the ultimate human role is only morally conceivable in the context of a century of philosophical assertion that concord with nature is the highest good. The *Aeneid* insinuates the history of Rome into the natural order, with the Roman state taking on a providentially planned role in the fulfilment of the divine plan for the world. Thus all that is done in the service of the growth of the Roman state accords with nature's plan, and what may seem imposed as a duty on Aeneas or anyone to fulfil his particular assignment is in reality the divine revelation of this role in the cosmos, the work set out for his hands in the universe.

The endorsement of action in accord with nature is Hellenic; that such accord may be found entirely in service to an existing state is peculiarly Roman. If there were any doubt about the ideological intention of the work, it would be stilled by Aeneas' discovery of Rome's future in Book VI. Having descended to the underworld, the hero meets his recently deceased father, who parades before him the heroes of the Rome to come, beginning with the earliest legendary builders of the state and continuing down to the Augustan age. The description of these men, together with the imagery on the magnificent shield which was presented to Aeneas, focuses all the metaphors of Virgil's long epic on its fundamental meaning, that human virtue and achievement are measured by the extent of a contribution to the success and growth of the human political state. As Augustus was great because he renewed the Roman state and brought it back from its dark years of fratricidal conflict, Aeneas was great because he would win through manifold difficulties to establish his people in a new land. His importance in history and in morality was not what he was as a man – kindness, generosity, courage, honesty became irrelevant – but his importance lay solely in what he did. We need not, in other words, like our heroes.

There remain obscurities in the *Aeneid*. Like any great work of literature it shows levels of meaning and ambiguities left by the poet, some deliberate and some inherent in the creation of symbolic statement. Some modern readers see Virgil's statement as a deeply pessimistic pronouncement on his own time, while others find in the epic a burst of optimism for the future. There are obscurities which are probably unfathomable, like the identification of the unnamed child to whom Aeneas' father refers at the end of the catalogue of Roman heroes, a reference imprecise enough to be seized upon by Christian writers as a prediction of the coming of Christ. But these are obscurities and

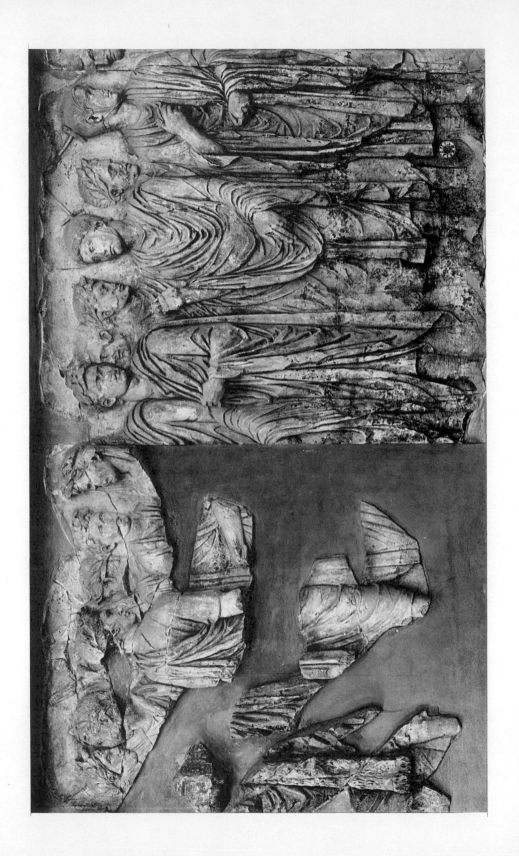

31  The *pietas* of Aeneas (and Augustus) is a prominent aspect on the Altar of Peace which Augustus built and dedicated in 9 BC. In this large monument, over 11 by 10 meters in plan, and more than 6 meters in height, and now reconstructed under a shelter in Rome, one panel shows Aeneas sacrificing to the gods, another, Augustus in sacrifice to Peace.

ambiguities of detail only, and their interpretation can in no way affect the fundamental message of the *Aeneid* – that Rome has a special mission in the world, and that the servants of Rome thus join in the great cosmic work of creating the future, as father Anchises says to Aeneas:

> others will better fashion bronze into breathing images – that I believe – and others will draw living faces from marble. Others will plead cases better in the law courts, and will describe the passageways of the heavens and tell the rising stars. You, Roman, will rule the peoples by your authority. These are your arts, and to impose your order in peace, to spare the conquered and humble the proud.[5]

Woven by Virgil into his epic as a pronouncement at the beginning of history, the lines serve equally well as an assessment at the end of hundreds of years. They describe almost precisely the Augustan accomplishment. If there is a tinge or more of regret on the part of the artist that his role and accomplishments are subsidiary, there is enough of the detachment of the philosopher – at least the Roman philosopher – to attach greater weight to the creativity of statesmen and soldiers. Yielding the palm to the men of action was a poetic acknowledgement of the validity of Cicero's precepts that gave first place to obligations to society and to the goods which benefited social life. It was an ideology which suited Romans, and one which could be taken up by Augustus, his contemporaries, and the successors to all of them.

*

The ideal of service to the state was the dominant ethic of the Augustan age. It was an ideal of behavior which Augustus prompted by his own example, and which Virgil shared also with other writers and poets of his day. The most obvious and uncompromising of these was the historian Titus Livius – Livy – whose almost interminable narrative of Roman history was a demonstration of the efficacy of that virtue in the past and the penalties of its abandonment in the present. Large segments of Livy's history are lost, but there are enough books at the beginning and in the sections treating important periods of Roman history, like that of the Punic Wars, to give us a clear idea of the manner in which he weaves together information which ultimately derives from oral tradition into a narrative which make sequential sense, and goes beyond political history to draw a moral lesson as well. That moral was twofold: Roman virtue had deteriorated badly from its early high level, and Roman virtue was exemplified in self-sacrificing service to the state. Livy's history is filled with repetitions of these judgments, and with examples which are introduced to prove their truth. The early books in particular lend themselves to this demonstration, as the virtuous wisdom of the early king Numa is trotted out in Livy's account of the establishment of Roman religion, while the devotion to the state of successive kings leaves little room for the self-aggrandizement and luxurious living so often associated with the lives of monarchs. It was only the last of the kings, Tarquin the Proud, who allowed himself to slip badly, and his career was cut short by Roman virtue which intervened to end the line of kings and establish the republic. From that time on, the steady growth of the state was the story of more self-sacrifice, now of individual men and families, who one after another exhibited that simple and hardy Roman virtue which Livy thought had been lost in the prosperity and comfortable living of his own times. There was no other state, Livy thought, "to which greed and high living came so late, nor in which so much scarcity and frugality lasted so long."[6]

Livy's was an old Roman idea. It had been voiced not only by stern moralists like Cato, whose ultra-conservative politics and philosophy might have prompted many to dismiss the notion, but even by radicals like Julius Caesar. If Caesar could write that of all the Gauls the Belgians were the most courageous "because they were most distant from the settled life and humanizing influences of the province . . . and those things which tended to effeminize spirits least penetrated to them,"[7] then the notion of the degeneration of Roman society must have been a fairly generally held idea. What is unusual about Livy's use of the theme of deterioration is its introduction as a main principle in the interpretation of history. In Livy's history of Rome, Roman spirit and its terrible decline are the explanation both for the growth of Rome to world domination and the recent troubles which had afflicted it.

Livy's second moral theme, that of self-sacrificing service to the state, was more particularly Roman and more appropriate to the needs of Augustus' new regime. The proposition that the virtues of the old Romans could be revived and applied in Augustan times also appears explicitly in Livy's preface, and his approach to history as art coincided exactly with Augustus' conception of the kind of political activism suitable for the future Roman state. With the Senate now the formal, if not real, forum for Roman decision-making, and Augustus an actual locus of power and his bureaucracy the means of administration and communication of decisions, there was a real need to limn some genuine and important role for the surviving Senators and members of the old governing class. That role could be one of service – demonstrable participation in government by faithful execution of the tasks of administration. The Roman upper class could, as it were, take the examples of service and virtue from the pages of Livy's history and emulate them in the fulfillment of Augustus' requirements for the city and the empire. They could do so in their contributions to the decoration of the city, to the life of religion, to the needs of the citizens. They could imitate the great men of old in brave leadership of the armies and in the modest assumption of necessary offices. They no longer need seek immortal fame in the attainment of the highest power, for they could find it in outstanding service.

There were other writers of the day who saw in this program an acceptable

315

ideal for human conduct. The poet Horace took a break from his preferred topics of the joys of the countryside and of love to pen six poems on national themes, the so-called "Roman" odes which begin Book III of his odes, praising the new order and extolling the benefits which Augustus had brought to the state. Like Virgil in his *Fourth Eclogue*, Horace wrote of an unnamed savior who was to come to rescue Rome, an idea which was prevalent in many places and amongst many peoples. Most, if not all, readers would associate the idea with Augustus, and the explicit praise which Horace offered the ruler, elsewhere calling him the "best guardian of the race of Romulus,"[8] makes the poet's opinion clear. The themes of his Roman odes, service, dutiful work, submission to legitimate authority and the fulfillment of self through the state, are all part and parcel of an ideology based on an almost universal Roman hope which Horace also expressed, that the new era had really arrived, that Rome would not slide back into internal disputes and the savagery of civil war. Of the present, Horace had only praise. It was a time when "faith and peace and honor and traditional modesty and neglected virtue would dare to return."[9] The question which must have unsettled all minds was that of the future. What would happen when Augustus was gathered to the gods?

Augustus himself was doing his utmost to ensure that his peace would live after him. He had worked very hard and with great success to ensure that the great majority of the members of the distinguished and potentially powerful senatorial families were satisfied with the prerogatives and distinctions that they held in lieu of real authority. There were campaigns – but usually not too dangerous – in which to win military glory. There were the regular magistracies of the state by which to perpetuate senatorial status for their families, and by which an occasional wealthy or deserving member of a non-senatorial family might rise to that status. There were provincial governorships at the disposal of Augustus and the Senate, and countless lesser offices for the younger and aspiring members of the upper class. For the knights, traditionally the second class of Romans and made up of wealthy families without senatorial rank, Augustus formally confirmed that position and established it as a genuine part of Roman aristocracy. Officer ranks in the army, certain provincial governorships, appointments to Augustus' staff were among the privileges either ratified for them or newly allotted. There was every reason to be confident that they too would be supporters of the regime and would want it continued after Augustus' lifetime. The same was true of the population of Rome and Italy as a whole, which was enjoying peace for the first time in over a century, and would neither seek change nor follow anyone who offered it in the unlikely case that one such should emerge. After some years of peaceful administration, Augustus began to make arrangements for an eventual successor, and after a number of his preferred choices died prematurely, he adopted as his own son Tiberius, the son of Livia by her first husband. By this time Augustus was well advanced in years, and had grown old in secure tenure of his position as the chief man of the state, its *princeps*, "first man," as he was formally called.

Decades of patient work had created a new form of government, principate we call it, whereby government was carried on by one man in the name and through the agency of many. An ideology of service and adherence to ancient morals had evolved, assisted by Augustus' own example, in which he even exiled his daughter Julia for sexual misbehavior. As he led the Senate to the formulation of legislation which would guide the Roman people back to virtue, so he would enforce it on his own family. It was another opportunity to demonstrate to the Romans that in him they had not a master but a servant.

He was not such a stickler for form in his approach to the provincials. There, accustomed as people were to sovereigns with divine qualities, Augustus appeared as another, perhaps more successful and powerful, in a long series of rulers who were gods, had been worshipped as such, and for whom formal cults had been established. Augustus allowed, if not encouraged, them to continue the practice in connection with his own reign and person. He was inscribed as pharaoh, with his own cartouche, in Egypt, as had been native rulers for millennia, and the Greek royal cult of the Ptolemies now became the imperial cult focused on Augustus. Elsewhere in the free Greek cities, honors were voted to Augustus in the same manner that the Greek cities had honored a Ptolemy, a Seleucus, or an Antiochus. Throughout Greece, Asia Minor, and Syria, idealized representations of Augustus were set up with those of the other gods, and even in Italy and the more Roman regions of the realm, the genius of the ruler received veneration in the same manner as the genius of the master of a household was worshipped in traditional Roman religion. But Augustus did not force this. The Jews, who would have been appalled at even the suggestion of incorporating a statue of Augustus into the Temple worship in Jerusalem, were perfectly free not to do so, and they showed their respect in ways that did not offend their religious sensibilities. Elsewhere, if citizens chose to place Augustus among the gods, they were also free to do so, although at Rome itself so direct a statement was discouraged.

By the end of the reign the impact of Augustus on religion, at least in the east, had been a heavy one. For the residents of eastern cities, who had been used to see kings and consuls lead armies back and forth across their lands, the remoteness of this ruler who had brought peace across the whole Mediterranean fostered the sense of his affinity to the gods. It had never been hard for Greeks to accept that certain men of outstanding accomplishment were rewarded for their achievements with a grant of immortality or divine status, or were gods in the first place. The same Greeks would have no trouble accepting Augustus as such. As the reign progressed and peace held while prosperity grew, people had more and more for which to thank the ruler, the son of a god, a god himself. At the same time Rome became increasingly the center for all, a kind of Mount Olympus on earth whence all dispensations for humankind emanated. Augustus' reign had done more than save Rome or even transform the realm. It had made Virgil's lines in which Anchises prophecied to Aeneas that Rome would rule the nations come true in a manner which made Rome and its ruler seem part of the great line of authority and dominion reaching from the gods down to earth, with Rome and Augustus' authority justified as originating in the divine order.

# 28

# The first
# Christian century

## *Imperial Rome*
## *and provincial Judaea*

As Augustus' life was drawing to an end, a young Jewish boy was growing to maturity in far-off Judaea – what the Romans called Palestine. Although it would be a few decades before Jesus and his followers would come directly to the attention of the government of Rome, there would be several confrontations before the century was over, just as there would be between the imperial government and the Jews as a whole. The nature of these conflicts, and ultimately the environment which Christianity would face in its migration from Judaea westward across the empire, were influenced directly by the developments in the structure of government and the concept of the ruler which took place in Rome during the reigns of Augustus' immediate successors.

The first of these was Tiberius, who came to power immediately upon Augustus' death in AD 14. Not initially a member of Augustus' family, which he joined later first as Augustus' stepson, then as his son through adoption, he knew perfectly well that he had not been Augustus' first choice for the succession when in his fifties he began to rule. Initially, he insisted that the Senators and others avoid paying him exaggerated honors, following both the form of the Augustan period and attempting to continue its reality by assigning genuine power to the Senate. But he did not find life in the city congenial: the Senators did not accord him the same unquestioning respect as they had extended to Augustus, and he was suspicious of many around him. As a result, he abandoned Rome completely and carried on the administration at long range from the island of Capri through an executive officer, Sejanus, the commander of the Praetorian Guard. Eventually, however, believable reports that Sejanus was plotting against him reached Tiberius, and after having the prefect executed, he turned back to the uncongenial task of direct administration. For the most part, he did well during his reign, with the empire and the provinces ably administered.

Tiberius died in 37, and was succeeded, for a short reign, by Gaius who, according to report, filled the palace with sexual licentiousness extending to incest with his sisters. Much more serious was his break with Augustus' tradition of restraint in accepting or seeking honors and symbols of authority or public expressions of worship. Gaius insisted that the trappings of eastern kingship be extended to Rome, and announced his own divinity with the statement that he was *dominus et deus*, "lord and god," with his sister-wife as goddess. It was a claim offensive to Roman probity, and disturbing, when honored, to some of the provincials as well. He was still a young man, likely to rule a long time, when he was killed in 41 by a palace cabal worried about the direction events were taking. With no heir, the potential for confusion called for quick action, and the Praetorian Guard saluted as ruler the late emperor's uncle, Claudius, who had neither expected nor wanted the position. The sources imply that Claudius had weaknesses of mind or body or both, but his reign, from 41 to 54, was in fact reasonably successful in returning the imperial court to some measure of respectability, and he carried on the duties of government with efficiency. The diffidence with which he accepted honors and the care with which he dealt with provincial matters emerge in a famous letter addressed to the Alexandrians, a document which also illustrates the kinds of issues which might require attention from Rome. Responding to an embassy sent him on his accession by the citizens of Alexandria, Claudius accepts some of the honors which they beg to be allowed to offer him, but deprecates the establishment of a priesthood to him or the building of temples for his worship; he then goes on to deal with matters affecting the civic administration of Alexandria. The text concludes with an even-handed but monitory treatment of issues raised by recent internal disorders in the city, conflict between the Alexandrian citizens and the Jews which had created very serious civic turmoil, "war, rather, if one must speak the truth."[1] Claudius writes of the series of riots, persecutions, killings, and ravaging of property inflicted on the Jews during the reign of Claudius' predecessor, a pogrom carried out, according to the Jewish philosopher Philo of Alexandria, with the connivance of the emperor's governor in the city. Referring to these events in his letter, the emperor requires that the Alexandrians treat the Jews gently and not interfere with their religious practices, while he commands the Jews to end their attempts to aggrandize their position in the city. The document not only casts a great deal of light on the social problems of Alexandria and the emperor's response to unrest, but demonstrates that the deification of the emperor and the augmentation of the ruler cult sought by Claudius' predecessor Gaius had not only failed to take hold, but were positively repudiated as the next reign began. Rome was not, at least in Claudius' time, to expect the ruler to be accorded divine honors which might be offensive to some, and Rome would act as protector of the religious sensibilities of peoples under its domain.

By the time Claudius died in 54, the realm was in as good a condition or better than it had been on the death of Augustus four decades earlier. His successor Nero, however, plunged the palace into turmoil again. As time went on, seeking security and independence of action, he murdered his half-brother and his mother, and ordered the suicide of his adviser the philosopher Seneca. His personal peculiarities aroused the hostility of Senators and soldiers alike, for Roman stolidity could make little sense of Nero's predilections for Greek drama, music, and poetic performances, and found the emperor ridiculous in his pursuit of praise from terrorized audiences, and in his pressure on judges who gave him awards out of fear for their lives. Senators whom he suspected of plots fell to his assassins, and his reign of terror consolidated the opposition of the upper classes under the leadership of the army. An army revolt in Gaul prompted an attack on the emperor by his Praetorian Guard in 68, and Nero fell on his own sword on a by-road outside Rome while fleeing from pursuing soldiers. He was the last of the emperors related to Augustus, and his death brought a year of conflict over the succession.

To read Roman historians, one would think that almost all of the important action in the first half of the century took place in the imperial palace at Rome, and much of that in its bedrooms. Although we know from ancient documents on papyrus and stone of the steady work of the armies and the imperial and senatorial officials throughout the provinces, almost nothing of their activity turns up in the conventional historical sources. This kind of writing, not only in Roman times but for a millennium and more after, focuses on rulers, as though the flow of history gains its direction and impetus mostly from them. The view that "history" is to a large extent the actions of rulers emerges from a fascination with their power and authority, and as they increasingly tended to claim divine authority for their positions and divine endorsements for their acts, the emperors, kings, princes, and what you will came increasingly to exclude all other centers of power. Augustus' arrangement whereby the legal authority, the Senate, chose to follow the recommendations of an accepted leader, gave way to a formulation in which the accepted leader evolved into the legal authority itself. Eventually, the leader and legal authority, working under divine dispensation, came to personify the state itself, so that history was the history of the king. The French monarch's "I am the state" was not a boast; it was a statement of fact. By the end of the first century, as their historians betray, the Romans were well on their way to this conception of monarchical power.

There is much more to the story, in Roman as in any other times. Right through the reign of Nero, despite the startling or absurd behavior of the emperors and their families and freedmen in Rome, life in the city, in Italy, and the provinces proceeded almost undisturbed. Many people were prosperous, the imperial fleet maintained order at sea and protected trade from piracy, while the army guarded the borders from incursions by foreigners, and the soldiers, quartered for the most part in the peripheral provinces, were not a great burden on the population in the interior of the empire. The imperial administrators carried out their tasks of tax collection and army management without seriously disturbing the daily life of the urban centers or the little villages. Citizens sent their sons to the gymnasiums in the Hellenic centers of the east, served in the municipal offices as they had for generations, and the rich shouldered their burdens of providing civic necessities and took their accustomed share of offices and honor for doing so. Religious centers prospered greatly, not only from the encouragement offered by occasional imperial generosity, but from the increased travel which the peaceful state of the world now made possible.

Thus the fight over the succession which took place in 68 and 69 was primarily a matter for the army and the senatorial leadership at Rome. The candidate of the army in Spain, Galba, was accepted by the Senate, and before the year 69 was out, three other candidates had contested power. From this "year of the four emperors" only one emerged, Titus Flavius Vespasianus, the experienced general and candidate of the eastern armies. By the end of the year he was in Rome, had been declared emperor by the Senate, and was setting to work to repair the damage left by Nero and the struggle over the succession.

By the time Vespasian began to take hold of the machinery of government, there seemed to be no alternative to the imperial scheme if the whole Mediterranean was to continue to look to Rome for government. Despite Tacitus' later lament for the dead republic, of which "nothing of ancient and virtuous custom" remained,[2] no Senators, either in his time or earlier in Vespasian's, seriously considered the notion that the reins of government could pass back to the Senate. It was enough that Vespasian continued to use the institution of the Senate for the formalization of law and policy, beginning, for example, with the *Lex de imperio Vespasiani* – "The law regarding the governing authority of Vespasian" – which the new emperor arranged to define precisely his authority over the vast bureaucracy of imperial government which had by now grown up. There was also to be administered the emperor's private property, which Vespasian had taken as rightfully his, as a kind of inheritance from the Julio-Claudian line which had ended with Nero. He thus also assumed management of the enormous wealth and vast estates which his predecessors had owned, taking on, through his freedmen and slaves, the management of the far-flung personal empire which Augustus had first assembled, and which by Vespasian's time had grown much greater. By the time he died and the realm was handed over to his elder son Titus in 79, a massive job of reorganization of an enormous state had been accomplished.

Titus came to power having had the advantage of a great deal of experience from tasks assigned to him by his father. Although not all the leaders of the Senate and army were convinced that rule should pass by inheritance alone, Titus' demonstration of military competence in leading the forces in a serious war in Judaea, combined with his accession to the accumulated private wealth of his father, meant that there was little opportunity to make any serious contest of his assumption of government. He ruled, however, only two years, until 81, just long enough to complete the conquest of Judaea and to show the beneficence of the emperor when he came to the aid of Pompeii and other towns devastated by the eruption of Vesuvius in 79. On his death in 81 his younger brother Domitian took power, for a reign that lasted until 96 and thoroughly soured the historian Tacitus and others on imperial government. Titus had continued his father's manner of frugality and modesty, but Domitian was a very different kind of personality, and his divergence from the tradition of Augustus and Vespasian brought the end of the Flavian dynasty.

Domitian found his parallels and patterns in the absolutism and divinity of the eastern kings who had preceded Roman dominion, but who had passed on a pattern of kingship which persisted in many of the eastern provinces. The emperor was a god in Egypt, in many of the cities of Asia Minor, Syria, and North Africa, and Titus' devastation of Judaea and debilitation of the Jews in his suppression of the great revolt removed the last significant group of provincials in the east who resisted the concept of the divinity of the emperor. Domitian demanded in Rome what he found was given freely in the east, but the Senators and upper classes in the capital were not as ready to follow the patterns of worshipping the ruler as the provincials had long done. The emperor found himself regarded with hostility by the elements who had received his father with open arms, and had he not been able to count on the loyalty of the army, he would have been in serious trouble. Even the army was kept loyal primarily by higher pay for both ordinary soldiers and their officers, which Domitian had implemented early in his reign, as trouble along the German borders of the Rhine and Danube increased the need for troops there, while at the same time the outbreak of serious combat made service in the legions less attractive. The rise in pay was largely successful in its object of attracting new recruits, and Domitian was largely able to contain the German tribes and keep the army loyal to him. He was thus able to reign for fifteen years in the teeth of opposition, almost to the end of the century, before succumbing to a palace plot in 96. With the end of Vespasian's dynasty the Senate asserted its demand for the selection of the aged but very highly respected Nerva, who came from a distinguished and old Roman family. His adoption of the respected general, Marcus Ulpius Trajanus, meant that on his death in 98 the empire could be passed peaceably on to new and competent hands. Under the guidance of Trajan and his successors, the imperial idea would gain revived respect, as the realm passed into the second century and a new era.

At the end of the first century the emperor was still the figure to whom the army, the Romans, and the provincials looked for authority. The experiences of imperial government and the knowledge of the kinds of men who had occupied power had given a great impetus to the development of a moral and ethical theory of monarchical government, and philosophers had done much to develop ideas of what a ruler should be and what a citizen ought properly to do in a state governed by a single man. Most of this examination of government was carried on in the tradition of Stoicism, and only by those members of the upper classes who practiced philosophy or were interested in the teachings of philosophers. In Rome, the most influential philosopher by far was Seneca, the

Spanish noble who was engaged by Agrippina, the mother of Nero, as tutor to the young prince, and who, together with the army leader Burrus, effectively administered Rome during Nero's first five years of rule. As Nero exhibited worse and worse traits, moving from the murder of his mother to that of even his closest advisers like Burrus, Seneca could hardly see in him an exemplification of the benefits of Stoic teaching, and eventually, the philosopher became a burden to the prince, who ordered his suicide. The calm manner in which the old Stoic proceeded to his arrangements excited the admiration of the Romans, who liked such things, and his courageous death is recorded in the pages of Tacitus' *Annals* as an example of brave resistance to tyranny, the old philosopher saying at the last, "I leave you the best thing which remains to me, the example of my life."[3] Seneca's standard for imperial behavior, like that of the later Greek philosopher Dio of Bithynia, known as the "Golden-mouthed" was abstract, based on ideals like service, wisdom, magnanimity, justice, and all the other stock virtues which the Stoic "wise man" will exemplify as he carries on his life in accord with nature. That the ruler should be that "wise man" of virtue was only an ideal, but one that was so disturbing to the real rulers that Seneca was ordered by Nero to commit suicide and Dio with many other philosophers was banned from Rome by Domitian. The ideal was dangerous, for it implied thast the ruler who did not meet it should not govern, and that power should be earned and not inherited.

Against this intellectual and political background were played out the events of the first century in Judaea. At the start of imperial administration, Augustus ruled Judaea through his client king, Herod the Great, an arrangement which was of material benefit to the country and earned Herod Augustus' close friendship, as well as praise throughout the Greek world. The king built lavishly throughout the land, vigorously embarked on the dissemination of Greek culture, celebrated quadrennial games of the Greek type both in his own new city of Caesarea and in Jerusalem, and stretched out to help in the re-establishment of the Olympic Games in Greece. He kept his kingdom at peace, despite conflict with the religious leaders of the Jews, and was rewarded for his success by the addition to his kingdom of border territories which Augustus found troublesome. In the heart of the old Jewish state, Jerusalem, Herod built a temple which would provide the focus of worship until its destruction during the Jewish war of 70. His reign, however, ended under the cloud of his own mixed-up relations with his wives and the bitterness between him and his sons, so severe as to lead Augustus to remark that he would "rather be one of Herod's pigs than one of his sons."[4] He died in 4 BC, dividing the realm amongst three remaining sons, and the Jewish territories passed again under divided rule.

Of the three sons, Antipas, who was allotted the title of tetrarch and the territories of Peraea, across the Jordan, and Galilee, where Jesus spent most of his life, had the longest and most successful reign. Like his father, he built extensively, avoided conflict with the Jews in his dominions, refrained from putting images on his coins, and kept his domain peaceful. When his brother, Philip, also a tetrarch, died in 34, his lands to the north-east of the Sea of Galilee were first joined to the province of Syria, and three years later to the remainder of Judaea under the kingship of the emperor Gaius' friend Agrippa, who had taken charge of what had been the most troublesome part of King Herod's bequest. That was the heart of the old kingdom, comprising Samaria, Judaea, and Idumaea, which the eldest of the three brothers, Archelaus, had originally taken, but which fell to direct Roman administration after Augustus deposed him for maladministration.

Thus the land was administered by Roman procurators for thiry-five years, in the period which saw Jesus's life and crucifixion during the tenure of office of the fifth procurator, Pontius Pilate. That world-shaking event, which happened in 30, was to the Roman administration one of the aspects of the religious disruptions which had been manifesting themselves during Pilate's administration. The governor had been forced to use troops on several occasions. Just about as soon as his appointment began in 26, a general strike broke out over the appearance in Jerusalem of the standards with Emperor Tiberius' image on them, and the governor was forced to back down in the face of the choice between removing the offending banners or killing the offending Jews. The first was the more politic course, if he was not to face the possibility of a much greater and more embarrassing rebellion in his new province. A similar incident occurred later when the placement of dedicatory shields with merely the name, not the image, of the emperor caused an uproar. There were other incidents focusing on religious issues, and one ultimately caused Pilate's recall to Rome in 36. Next, the procurator appointed by Gaius, who came to power in 37, had to deal with troubles as well, and the emperor himself almost provoked a serious incident. We hear a good deal about the religious troubles of the reign of Gaius, not only from the Jewish historian Josephus but also from the philosopher Philo of Alexandria, who was a member of an embassy of 39-40 to the emperor from the Jewish Alexandrians. That community had been very badly mauled in the course of 38, when a series of riots, allowed by Gaius' prefect Flaccus Avillius, resulted in the desecration of synagogues and the maltreatment of the Jews. Philo's diatribe *Against Flaccus* contains graphic descriptions of pillage, starvation, force-feeding of pork, assaults, murders, torture – progressing in fury to the burning alive of men, women and children, the rending of the half-burnt bodies, and the ultimate penalty of crucifixion. Although the riots were over by the time of the embassy to Gaius, the Jews were petitioning for protection of their status in Alexandria for the future, a plea that would not be answered until the reply of the next emperor, Claudius, in 41. Gaius, as the ambassadors were to find out to their dismay, was no friend to the Jews. Responding to the destruction of an altar in Judaea, the emperor had given orders to set up a colossal statue of himself in the Temple of

Jerusalem, and furious at the governor's caution in wanting to delay, was urging speed when his personal friend, Agrippa, intervened and begged him to desist.

Agrippa, a grandson of Herod the Great, had been a close companion of Gaius before his accession, and soon after the death of Tiberius, the new emperor transferred the old tetrarchy of Philip, Herod's son, away from the province of Syria and gave it to Agrippa to rule as king. By 38, Agrippa had also been given the territories of Galilee and Peraea when their tetrarch, Antipas, was banished. All sources agree on the great favor in which he was held by Gaius, and it was due to this affection that Agrippa's intervention in the affairs of Jerusalem in 40 was effective. Gaius was killed in 41, but Herod Agrippa ruled for three more years until 44. With his death came the end of the independent Jewish kingdom, for Agrippa's domains were reassigned to administration by a procurator. Now, however, the Roman province was much larger, for Judaea had been reunited under Agrippa, and the new emperor decided to leave it that way. Thus the Roman governor who assumed control of the area in 44 governed all of Judaea, all the way from Trachonitis and Galilee in the north to Idumaea in the south, the modern Negev. It was, considering the inhabitants, rather a large brief, and it turned out to be troublesome: the governors were repeatedly called upon to put down rebellions, religious riots, and clashes between Jews and other groups in the province.

Josephus, who commanded Jewish forces in the great war of 66–73 and wrote a history of these events, is at pains to associate the trouble with extremist religious elements and rapacious Roman governors, whose interaction generated periodic outbreaks of violence throughout the reigns of Claudius and Nero. Sometimes trouble came as a consequence of a supposed insult of a religious nature, at other times it was caused by religious assassins called *sicarii*, and on still other occasions by turmoil generated by figures who claimed to be prophets and attracted groups of adherents. Ultimately, a minor incident in Caesarea where some young thugs managed a crude insult to a synagogue led to open conflict there between the Jews and Roman troops. The balance tipped back and forth between insurrection and restraint until the rebels seized the fortress at Masada in the summer of 66 and refused to sacrifice in Jerusalem on behalf of Rome and Augustus, thus eliminating any possibility of reconciliation.

The war thus kindled lasted in full ferocity until the capture of Jerusalem in August 70, and dragged on until May 73 with the fall of the fortress at Masada and the suicide of its some 900 defenders. During this period the countryside was subjected to continual ravages, the cities to the most terrible sieges. Gradually, the Roman army under its general Vespasian reduced the resisting forces. By late 68, most of the Jewish forces were bottled up in Jerusalem, but the turmoil over the succession at Rome in 68 gave the defenders of the city some respite. Finally, Titus advanced against the city with the Roman army.

32 Part of Herod's Temple still stands in Jerusalem. The veneration of the building persists among some Jews, and this wall, called the "wailing wall," is an object of pilgrimage for many who stand before it to pray.

Josephus, recounting anecdotes of military heroism as well as civilian suffering like that of the mother who cooked and ate her baby, exonerates the Romans from responsibility for the seige, blaming the defenders for bringing it on themselves. He portrays Titus, for example, as claiming that not he but the rebels were responsible for their sufferings, as he gazed upon the ravines oozing putrefying flesh from the corpses of the dead thrown from the walls. Even the burning of the Temple, which ended the siege, occurred despite Titus' attempts to avoid its destruction and save it, and, as Josephus tells the tale, "the flames had their start and their cause from the people to whom it belonged."[5] When it was all over, the city burnt and the defenders killed or captured, more than a million were dead, if Josephus' sometimes exaggerated figures are to be believed here. The trial was so long, the battle so hard, the losses so severe that the accounts of the operations in the next years and the final fall of Masada are anticlimactic.

It is difficult to imagine today the terrible impact of the destruction of the Temple in August 70. Frightful though the losses were in life and freedom, the destruction of Herod's great second Temple brought the end of a way of life for the whole Jewish people. No longer could the prescribed sacrifices be carried out; no longer would the priests, garbed in the manner so lovingly spelled out by Philo or Josephus, carry out the people's duties to their God. Not only the inhabitants of Judaea but Jews all over the world had lost the focus of their religious life. Since that religious life was indissolubly tied to the sense of the interaction of God with his people, whom he rewarded or punished as deserved, the events of 70 could only be interpreted as the will of God. For the great community of Jews in Alexandria as well as those in Judaea, the destruction of the Temple was a statement about their situation in the world. The war which dragged to its end in 73 was a political event which might effectively terminate the view of God and God's country which the Jews had held for a thousand years. Only if there could be a reconstitution of the Temple and the Temple cult could there be traditional Judaism. And only so long as Jews could hope, plan, and work for a restoration of the Temple and the institution of Israel as God's ruling nation could there be a political Judaism. There had been destruction and rebirth before, in the exile of 586 BC and the return a half-century later in 538 BC, and in the independent Jewish state from 142 to 63 BC. It could happen again, and political Judaism flickered on in that hope.

All this history interacted with the development of Christianity in its formative years, as Jesus and the apostles lived their lives against this background of political revolution and religious ferment. As the political situation deteriorated in Judaea, Paul carried out his mission overseas. It was in 62, shortly before the outbreak of war, that James, the brother of Jesus, was stoned to death at the behest of the High Priest, and Paul himself was probably still alive, and possibly Peter also, when the war broke out in 66. Our earliest Greek narrative accounts of Jesus and the early church, the Gospels of Mark, Matthew, and Luke and the Acts of the Apostles, were composed or translated either while these stunning events were in train or, at least, were still fresh enough in memory to influence ideas and phraseology. And the development of Christianity can hardly have failed to have been affected by the destruction of the Temple and the center of the Jewish cult in 70. By the end of the first century the Mediterranean was on a new course, even if that fact was sensed by only a few. With the accession of the emperor Trajan, even Roman government would develop on new lines, while in the east, nascent Christianity was offering a fundamentally different interpretation of the meaning of history. Roman political institutions had demonstrated their durability, and men could still look with confidence to a material life protected by the imperial legions. For the rich, the powerful, the well-born, and well-connected, the promise of the golden age of Augustus was still bearing fruit. The century which had begun with the advent of a new regime was ending, its concept still intact. Even with "bad" emperors, Virgil's prophecy that Rome would "rule the nations with justice" had turned out mostly true. It was only the poor, the weak, the slaves who had nothing, and the Jews who thought that they had lost all, who found the earthly paradise wanting.

# 29

# Philosophy and religion among the Jews

## *Philo, Apocalypse, Jesus, and his followers*

When the commission of Alexandrian Jews went to Rome in 39 to protest against the treatment of their community, Philo, who was one of the group, was an old man. Of great repute amongst the Jews of Alexandria, he knew the leading men of the city, had contact with such international figures as Agrippa, and even numbered in his own family the young Tiberius Alexander, who later served as prefect of Egypt and then as general of Vespasian and Titus for the conquest of Judaea and Jerusalem in 70. Philo himself was completely Hellenized, with a familiarity with Greek literature and culture which may have dominated his philosophical interpretation of Judaism. Some modern readers think so, while others argue that his thought is still strongly Jewish, with Hellenic conceptualization only as its mode of expression. Whatever the case may actually be, the issue is more important for an understanding of Philo the man than of his writings, a vast store of discussion of biblical and religious matters, which stand alone for interpretation. The writings, of course, were all in Greek, and although for the most part they deal with Hebrew Scripture, it is Scripture of the Septuagint, and the interpretations often introduce Greek ideas, Greek literary figures, and Greek philosophical concepts and terminology, taken from the Greek literature and philosophy which Philo knew well.

Despite this extensive Hellenic orientation and culture, Philo's writing is very different from that of any Greek up to his own time. Apart from the prolixity and repetitiveness which often tire a reader, his scope is so limited that he rarely offers the thrill of discovery which so often rewards the reader of an equally copious writer like Aristotle, while his allegorical treatment of Scripture as metaphor for moral action carries abstraction to an almost intolerable level. He is, in short, responsible for a lot of writing which is no pleasure to read. A modern admirer who has written of his work frankly admits the possibility of boredom. He is, therefore, probably the least-read today of all ancient philosophers of whose work a significant amount remains; but his omission leaves aside a most important linchpin in the evolution of ideology among Greek thinkers. His importance shows in the daunting corpus of his work; even after losses a large mass of writing was preserved, copied, recopied, and cited by Christian writers who took enough interest in it to count Philo as one of the Christian fathers. The breadth of his readership shows even in the survival of his works, for some are now preserved only in the Armenian translation of the fifth century, while others which survive only in part are mined from the texts of Eusebius, Procopius, and other ecclesiastical writers or Byzantine chroniclers. He was, in short, influential.

Virtually every philosophical or theological notion Philo had is expressed through allegory, and allegory carried far beyond anything hitherto attempted. He used it to explain individual persons named in the Bible, their actions and their relations with each other, as, for example, in the fall from paradise, Adam represents Mind, Eve is Sense perception which can beguile Mind, and the seduction of Eve into eating the fruit of the tree of knowledge by the serpent is the seduction of sense perception by pleasure. One great Hebrew historical personage after another is reduced to allegory:

> Abraham used instruction as the leader on the road bringing him to the good . . . Isaac used a nature which listened to itself and learned on its own, while the third, Jacob, used training exercises, corresponding to the laborious efforts used for contests.[1]

Every item in the attire of the high priest had its particular allegorical significance, and each feature of the ark of the tabernacle had meaning apart from its decorative value. All this allegory invested Scripture with a constantly repeated moral guidance, as allegory after allegory provided specific instruction after instruction to be followed by the disciple who seeks to find God and to achieve the state of virtue.

The achievement of virtue depends on an understanding of the nature of human beings, which in turn comes through allegories like those of Adam and Eve, defining human mind and sense perception and the manner in which mind falls under the influence of sense perception to the extent of being dominated by the passions of the flesh. Thus the Genesis 2: 24 text, "Because of this a man shall leave his father and mother and cleave to his wife, and the two will be one flesh"[2] becomes an allegory of sense perception dominating mind, and goes on to include the serpent in Eden, portrayed as a creature crawling on the ground to represent pleasure. This antipathy to the pleasures of the body pervades all of Philo's work, and is made explicit allegorically in a number of ways, of which one of the most common is the use of Egypt to represent flesh, and the migration from slavery there as the escape from the bonds of sensual passion. The same horror of sensual, and in particular, sexual pleasure appears in the allegorical treatment of the story of Joseph and Potiphar's wife, with the dramatic representation of the almost irrepressible demands of pleasure and fleshly lust. That mind must always be watchful against the baneful influences of sense perception, and that bodily pleasure is the undoing of virtue in the soul are two themes to which he repeatedly returns. Philo can find these ideas recurring over and over again in Scripture because he resolutely reads it as a creation of Moses in which the great lawgiver presents history as allegory for human behavior. Thus is it Moses, with all the wisdom and divine aid which Philo attributes to him, through whom God has transmitted the wide-ranging prescription for living.

Because of the inherent allegory, Scripture's prescription for living goes beyond the explicit legislation recorded by Moses, and includes the modes of life called for by the allegory as well. Indeed, although Philo does acknowledge that adherence to the literal, as well as the allegorical, law is required, there is no doubt about his stress on the allegories. In *On the Migration of Abraham*, his allegory of the patriarch explicating the characteristics of behavior which permitted Abraham to disentangle himself from sense-perception and the lower world of the passions, the literal meaning relates to the body, while the allegorical relates to the soul. The allegory is extended to include Sarah, "who is *phronesis*,"[3] with whom Abraham had not been able to mate productively until he had reached a state of improved soul. *On the Migration of Abraham* is thus a complete allegory for the migration of the soul toward that state wherein it has broken away from the grasp of the body, the fleshly passions, and the maleficent influences of sense perception to join finally to virtue.

Much the same concept emerges in the elaborate allegory of the "two wives, one of them loved, one hated,"[4] which Philo makes into an allegory for a contest between the "wives" pleasure and virtue, to which every soul is mated. Pleasure, says Philo, comes sidling up to the soul, offering all sorts of seductive rewards; virtue, bringing along a whole company of good qualities such as holiness, justice, prudence, and the like, warns of the qualities which pleasure brings in her train. There are nearly 150 qualities named in a list of words which includes such bad traits as "unjust, low-class, untaught," and on and on and on. All this will pleasure bring, says virtue, while she will only bring one good, valuable if strenuous, and that is labor. This *ponos*, the Greek word used here for the kind of labor to which Philo refers, is the necessary ingredient to the life which aspires to all the goods and virtues. The good to which the mind aspires is the state of virtue, a state which once reached by the soul permits it to escape from sense and to penetrate with the intelligence into the world beyond sense perception.

It is a Platonic idea, and in Philo it takes a particular character. Establishing the Ark of the Covenant as an allegory of the makeup of God in *Questions and Answers on Exodus*, p. 68, Philo presents a complete, coherent, and clear account of his concept of the deity. Elder than the one, the beginning, is "that which exists," or "the existent," in Greek, *To On*, unreachable by any aspect of human understanding. From it emanates an aspect which Philo calls the Logos, a Greek term which means "word" or "reason." The Logos, which Philo calls the "truly seminal substance of existing things," is accessible to the appropriately educated mind, and emits two powers, "creative power," and "royal power"; from the creative power comes a "beneficent power" while from the royal power comes the "legislative," or "putative power"; all these terminate in the "world of ideas" which is represented by Philo as "below" the aspects of deity. The concepts may be represented schematically

*To On* – "The Existent"
Logos
Creative Power    Royal Power
Beneficent Power    Legislative Power
World of Ideas

In this scheme, all but the ultimate Existent is knowable and approachable by mind, but God in self is not knowable by mind or anything else, in any way at all, and all the terms for God and God's nature refer not to the reality of God but to God's manifestations in action.

Philo's concepts taken all together make a coherent philosophical whole, details of which show specific Stoic or Platonic influence as well as Philo's general familiarity with Greek philosophical ideas. Again and again his philosophical conceptualization is couched in Greek terms and ultimately determined by Hellenism and his Greek education. Thus it is entirely natural that a number of important Greek ethical and philosophical problems turn up in his writing, even though they are not significantly relevant to the main thrust of his thought. The argument that every good man is free is essentially Stoic, for example, marshalling typically Stoic arguments and Greek citations of Alexander, the philosopher Calenus, Greek history, and heroes to show that only the "wise man" is free, exhorting in Stoic terms that souls raised properly "will come to an end, not so much in Zenonic terms as oracular, to live according to nature."[5] He brings in repeatedly the idea that "inequality is the source of injustice," which may "disappear in equality, which is the spring of justice," as he says in the account of his embassy to Rome,[6] and repeats in the more philosophical works. Philo believes that nature "has created all to be free,"[7] so much so that in punishment for homicide, servants are also protected against being killed, for, although unequal in fortune, they are equal in nature, and "in the law of God, the canon of justice is not fitted to fortune, but to nature."[8] Even more interesting is what might be seen as a transformation of a Protagorean "Man is the measure of all things" view into something both Hellenic and his own. Humans, asserts Philo, have the greatest resemblance to God, with the soul "the most clearly related to heaven, the purest part of existence, and to the father of the universe."[9] This leads to the justification of the law against homicide and the valuing of humanity for its resemblance to God rather than for itself. His Jewish theological orientation has its influence, but it is an influence which must work on a philosophical outlook trained in Hellenism, and which must express all of its insights in Greek terms. And there is little doubt that he was thinking of Hellenism when he wrote that God exists and is and has been eternal; that God is one; that the cosmos has been created; that the cosmos also is one, and that there are not a plurality of worlds; that God cares for the cosmos.[10]

These ideas and most of the rest of Philo's writings were understandable to Hellenized Jews and to Greeks in general, and some of his notions might even have seemed valid. Certainly his argument against pleasure and his proposition of training the mind to use sense perception without becoming influenced by it were old ideas to the Greeks. Even his particular rendering of the structure of God, with "The Existent" an unknowable being with intelligible manifestation, however much it could be regarded as Philo's own conceptualization, belonged quite solidly in the tradition of Greek metaphysical speculation about the nature of the supreme power. He had, after all, done what every Greek philosopher before him had done or tried to do in some respect: relate a metaphysical construction of the cosmos to an ethical conception of human nature and the requirements for human behavior. Herein lies a very important aspect of Philo's influence. To those whose beliefs included an acceptance of a single, eternal creator of the universe, Philo's "Existent" was an acceptable concept. Most Jews and many Greeks could be believers here. That the creator made one world, not many, and cared for it would be completely palatable to Jews, and although many Greeks might reject one or other or all those conditions, many others would agree with all three: creation, singleness, and divine providence. But that The Existent did not communicate directly with humans and humanity's world, that even the most perfected soul could not approach and know God but could at best penetrate only to manifestations which were intelligible to mind – from such a concept many Jews would retreat, leaving the field of acceptance largely to Greeks. Even many of Philo's ethical views which involved a devaluing of sense perception and its objects would find Greeks more sympathetic than Jews, for Greeks had long read such things in Plato and his followers. The very notion that there was a world of intelligible ideas separate from the world of sense, a notion which Philo used in his interpretation of the two Genesis accounts of the creation of humanity to assert that God first made the idea of Adam, and then only after and in imitation of it the fleshly man – all this was Greek, not Jewish.

Whether Philo's ideas, or ideas like them, were shared by many Jews of his own time is impossible to ascertain. It does seem clear, however, that they did not exert much influence on the Jewish texts of his own times which have come down to us, so he did not affect the Jewish tradition which survived the cataclysm of the first century. But there were many whose minds were still receptive to such ideas even if they were primarily Hellenic. These Greeks and Hellenized easterners who were also receptive to other religious and philosophical ideas current in the first century could provide a ready audience for Philonic ideas, even if at second hand and not as readers of his cumbersome allegories. Within a few decades of his death his metaphysics and ethics would both have a very sympathetic reception.

Among Philo's works is a pleasant little essay entitled *On The Contemplative Life*, which deals with a little community of ascetics called Therapeutai, near Alexandria. Philo is full of praise for the abnegation of the flesh practiced by these Jewish mystics, who gave away all their possessions to come together for a life of prayer and divine service in a little cluster of simple houses in the country. Abstinence marked much of their lives, and they fasted every day until nightfall, while they had only the simplest and most inexpensive houses, household articles, and clothing. Their prayers, contemplation, and gatherings focused on Scripture, and they sought knowledge through contemplation, with the guidance of the Mosaic code. Philo had already written about the Essenes, another ascetic group whose members were spread about Palestine, but his work on that group is lost. What we know about them comes from the summary remarks of Josephus, who described them briefly.[11] Like Philo's Therapeutai, the Essenes were an ascetic group, disdaining money, allowing their clothing to fall to pieces before renewing it, and adopting children rather than procreating in the normal way in marriage. They treated the property of any member of the community as common to all, and travelling members had on their arrival in any town all the facilities at the disposal of their brethren there. Their activities were focused on worship, they believed in the immortality of the soul, with reward and punishment after death, and were absolutely indomitable in the face of efforts to make them renounce their faith.

There were about 4000 Essenes, Josephus tells us,[12] only a tiny proportion of the Jewish residents of Judaea, and the rest, insofar as they were members of any sect recognized by Josephus, were Pharisees, Sadducees, or proponents of the so-called "Fourth Philosophy." Josephus, who after some investigation began "following the system of the Pharisees, which was nearest to that called the Stoic by the Greeks,"[13] wants us to believe that the Pharisees were the dominant religious and ideological leaders of the Palestine Jews in the first century. He describes the Essenes, if cursorily, at least favorably as living simply, respecting God's will as determinate albeit with some room for human free choice of vice or virtue. All the comments which Josephus makes about these various Jewish sects, particularly the Pharisees, have been pressed to yield what scholars want to hear about the opponents of Jesus, so his statements, almost surely tendentious, that the Jews followed the precepts of the Pharisees, are accepted without question in the interpretation of the New Testament. As a result, the Judaea of Jesus' time is often portrayed in the categories of Josephus' descriptions: the Pharisees accepted and expanded an oral tradition of scriptual interpretation, and were not limited by the literal text, in contrast to the Sadducees, who accepted only those parts of the Law which were explicit in Scripture.

Our author also mentions another faction, the "Fourth Philosophy," but in his now safe position among the Romans, is not overly anxious to expatiate at any length on this group, which led the Jews into their disastrous revolt and made him one of its most prominent military leaders for the first part of the war. Josephus ties this "Fourth Philosophy" to the leadership of one Judas of Galilee, a rebel who was defeated and killed while leading a revolt at the end of the first century BC. He may thus wish to date it by implication, and tar the whole concept by association with the condemnation which he expressed for the rebellion at the beginning of his Book XVIII of *Jewish Antiquities*. The leadership of that revolt, like most of the resistance to Rome, centered in Galilee, the district in which Josephus himself was appointed to command in the later war, and this was also the region of most of Jesus' ministry three and a half decades before the outbreak of the great war in 66.

A troublesome bunch, these Galileans, as also were many of the Jews of the rest of Judaea. The "Fourth Philosophy" remained a virulent ideological infection long after the death of Judas the Galilean, and the eruption of a final revolt even as late as the second century of our era shows that it was still alive and well at the time that Josephus was writing at the end of the first century. Josephus tries to lay the blame for it on increasingly oppressive Roman administrators, and bad government may have had some share of the responsibility for exasperating the populace. Overall, however, the success of this "Fourth Philosophy" and its tenacity in the minds of some Jews of Judaea shows the extent to which political behavior was influenced by a scriptural authority which led them to expect success in taking on an enemy of overwhelming material superiority. This long-standing authority stood behind an attitude and an expectation which were almost equally old. Through Jewish literature and behavior runs the theme that the Covenant with Abraham assured the Jews of ultimate victory over their enemies, and that reverses, destructions, deportations, and captivities were caused not so much by the power balance between them and their enemies but by the state of the relationship betwen them and their God. Literature now centuries old made their troubles a retribution by God for failure to obey the Law, for injustice to people and impiety to God, for impurity of eating and living. The educated could read Scripture and tell of its promise to the unlettered in the synagogues, in their gatherings and in their homes, and the partisans of the "Fourth Philosophy" could capitalize on this hope for national renewal.

However, even the activists of the "Fourth Philosophy" probably reached few of the great mass of believing Jews. These are the people who lived not only in Jerusalem but in the countless little towns and hamlets across the country-side. Outside the Temple and the temple cult they focused their religious lives on the synagogues large and small which were maintaining Judaism away from the sacrifices and rules of the priests. These country people still centered their lives on their flocks and crops as had their ancestors for generations before, living by the rules of Deuteronomy and Leviticus, which were still as suitable for them as they had been for the agricultural economy of the early Hebrews. Life in the villages, with their squat, almost windowless houses lining dusty streets, had changed little if at all in centuries. Transportation was provided by foot or donkey, and only the more prosperous had or needed carts. Biblical scenes of girls drawing water from the public wells were repeated countless times daily. People found it difficult to make the pilgrimage to Jerusalem, if they could go at all, and had to make do with whatever worship they could carry on at home. Demons, like those cast out by the old-time prophets, still came from time to time to blight lives, and Satan and his gang lurked as always to bring disaster. The Jews of the hills of Galilee in Jesus' time were much like the Israelites of the days of Abraham, Isaac, and Jacob, of David, Solomon, Josiah, and Ezra.

It was not so in the cities, and by cities I mean much more than Jerusalem. Those founded by Herod and his sons, like Caesarea in Samaria and Tiberias in Galilee, were thriving centers in the first century, big, prosperous, and to a significant extent Hellenic. They had their gymnasia, temples, and other public buildings which promoted Greek life in the area, as well as the synagogues which were needed by the local Jews. Life in urban areas like these could be conducted in Greek, and probably was for the most part. Certainly Greek was the language of the court of Herod and in the capital cities of his sons, as it was in the port of Caesarea, which along with Jerusalem even had games of the Greek type. The high level of Greek culture is apparent in the work of Josephus. Educated in Judaea, he nevertheless wrote perfectly respectable Greek prose, and his many allusions to earlier works in Greek show a broad familiarity with Greek literature and culture. He also tells us, incidentally, of a number of contemporaries who could boast similar accomplishments,[14] and his audience, doubtless, was that element of Hellenized Jews of Palestine on whom Josephus' pro-Roman account of the war might be hoped to have some effect, particularly coming from one who had fought the Romans so vigorously in the early years of the revolt.

There were also the Greek – that is, non-Jewish Greek-speaking residents of Caesarea, Tiberias, and the other cities and towns of Judaea. There were enough of them to kill tens of thousands of Jews at the beginning of the conflict, as Josephus tells us.[15] Whatever these people's relationship had been to the Jews before the war, there were a lot of them, obviously, and it was undoubtedly through association with all these Greeks that the Jews of the cities became Hellenized. It is also clear, furthermore, that there were significant numbers of Hellenized Jews in the cities, and that they had suffered at the hands of the Romans. The Roman procurator Florus, for example, as part of what Josephus portrayed as deliberate provocations of the Jews, had generated a disturbance in Jerusalem which resulted in his executing about 3600 Jews there, " daring . . . to take men of equestrian rank and flog them . . . and nail them to the cross, men who even if Jewish were nonetheless Roman in dignity."[16]

Jews, then, could be divided in a number of ways, and made up a number of different groups and different kinds of groups. There were those who remained outside the influence of Hellenism and those who were very Greek. Most of the Hellenized were in the cities, although not all those in the cities were so. Outside the urban areas were those whose lives remained essentially rural and had been little changed either in cultural or material ways. There were also other small groups like those of the community which withdrew to Qumran near the Dead Sea, some of whose writings were only discovered in the middle of this century. In addition there were, as we read in the pages of Josephus, repeated appearances of prophets, whose call to the people elicited an enthusiastic response on their part and nervousness on that of the government. One of them, who came out of Egypt, roused great crowds who followed him into the desert, prompting quick repression by the Roman government. Another was John the Baptist, of whose mission and murder by Herod (Antipas) Josephus gives a brief account. There were crowds who followed John, as Josephus tells us, and "Herod killed him, although a good man who was urging on the Jews the cultivation of virtue and behavior toward each other in justice and toward God in holiness to join in baptism."[17] It was an act which, according to our author, brought God's ruin on Antipas' army in punishment. The story makes political sense and fits with the treatment of other prophets of the period who collected people around them.

Josephus does not tell us much about Jesus or the Jews who followed him. Unlike the story of John the Baptist, it was not a closed issue when Josephus was writing, and the crucifixion was of enough note in Josephus' time to attract the attention of the contemporary, Tacitus, who reported it briefly in *Annals*.[18] But those around Jesus did not fade away as had those around John. Members of the early Christian community had sufficiently attracted the attention of Nero as to be blamed for the great fire at Rome, and to be executed. There were again persecutions during the reign of Domitian, when Josephus was in Rome, and that too was a period of increasing hostility toward the followers of Jesus on the part of Jews who had survived the terrible war with Rome and were trying to carry on their religion without the focus of the Temple in Jerusalem. All of this is more than enough to suggest to Josephus that he pass over Jesus' life in silence or, at most, briefly.[19]

That leaves us little besides the Gospel accounts to guide us to an understanding of the Jews, Jesus, and those Jews who followed him in his lifetime or in the years immediately after he appeared to some of them in resurrection. The Gospels, however, were unfortunately not written to inform us about Jesus and his followers in the early decades of the church, but to explain and propagate the faith. For some, they were records of things done and said; others might use them as guides along the road which Jesus had pointed out. In Jesus' lifetime and in the early years after the crucifixion the things done and said were primarily, if not exclusively, seen as extensions of what had been done and said by prophets from the time of Jeremiah. The Gospels could serve to explain and clarify this, to correlate and make coherent Jesus' warnings of the coming last days, Jeremiah's warning again, repeated immediately before the event because the time was near. This belief in the arrival of the kingdom of God had an old and honorable history in Judaism, and there was nothing heretical about it or even about the belief that the time was at hand. Those who followed Jesus were Jews who had become convinced that God's promise for

337

*33* Early in the development of Christianity, Paul was as prominent in iconography as the disciples. Here, on the sarcophagus of Junius Bassus, who died in 359, St Paul joins St Peter in flanking a beardless Christ. (Crypt of St Peter, Rome)

Israel was about to come true, and even in writings in Greek intended for those who might never have known Judaism, Jesus' proclamation of the last days comes through as a fundamental part of his message.

Jesus' period of preaching was very short, probably lasting only for the years 28 and 29 in Galilee, terminating in 30 in Jerusalem. The people to whom he gave his message and who responded to it were mostly the country folk of the north, Galileans whose Judaism was perforce remote from the Temple in

Jerusalem. None of his immediate followers seem to have come from the Hellenized Jews of more urban areas, and the Gospels, in fact, are at some pains to identify them as ordinary working people. The particular following of Jesus represented a force in Judaism which was different again from that of the groups Josephus names. They seem to have been unaligned in terms of the divisions of the times, yet sufficiently open to religious fervor to be pulled out of their ordinary occupations to follow a charismatic religious leader. During Jesus' lifetime and for a while after, this movement was, as has always been recognized, a Jewish movement, and when the disciples settled in Jerusalem after the crucifixion, they did so as Jews. If there was any conflict between them and other Jews – Sadducees, Pharisees or priests – it was because they gave priority to Jesus and his declaration of the coming kingdom of God and the life and preparations necessary to enter therein, and because they were actively carrying that message amongst other Jews.

Within a decade they were reaching out beyond Jerusalem and then even Palestine to the communities of Jews who had emigrated from their homeland and had settled among the Greeks and Romans. There were many such communities, some of them large, even beyond the great Jewish center of Alexandria. They had early reached as far as Rome, and there is a story that even two centuries before the crucifixion Jewish visitors to Rome had attracted enough attention to provoke their expulsion from the city. By Jesus' time there was a sizeable community in the capital, one prosperous enough to build the large synagogue of which the ruins stand today near Rome's airport. To the east, Tarsus, a large and culturally active Hellenic settlement accommodated a Jewish community which produced Saul, a devout Pharisee who was to experience conversion and under the name Paul become a leader of the early church. This Saul knew Greek and was born with Roman citizenship, as a result of his father's acquisition of that status in some way not reported to us. This dignity, in no way commonplace in the east at this stage in the development of the Roman Empire, came to a family which, as Jewish, was not allowed full citizenship in its own city of Tarsus. That the family had Roman citizenship illustrates the fact that Jews of the diaspora could attain a status not available to all their non-Jewish compeers. Paul shows the same thing for the Jews of Tarsus as the Roman Jewish knights demonstrated for Jerusalem.

In the first century there were communities of Jews with their synagogues all over the Greek and Roman world, in cities like Tarsus, Athens, and Corinth, to mention but a few, and in some places, like Egypt, scattered about the countryside. In their close ties to Judaea, the Jews all over the Mediterranean reproduced the divisions of the homeland. Saul/Paul, as I have noted, was a Pharisee. Essene-like communities turned up elsewhere. In Egypt there were Philo's Therapeutai and, as we learn from an old Hebrew manuscript found in Cairo at the end of the last century, a group had left Judaea to settle in Damascus, its members covenanting with one another to observe the Law as it was no longer followed in Judaea itself. All these groups, inside Judaea and out, and all this organization of Judaism, changed with the catastrophic historic reverse of 70. Then there was no longer a Temple to which taxes should be sent, or sacrifices made in accordance with the rules of Scripture. The central rite of Judaism was gone, and some fundamental issues of interpretation no longer relevant. The matter of the relation of the Essenes to the Temple, their admission, and their sacrificing, and many of the points at issue between Sadducees and Pharisees disappeared into the flames of August 70.

The destruction began a critical period, one in which the Christians finally pulled away from Judaism completely. The Jews faced the problem of maintaining the faith and service to God although the Temple had been destroyed, while the Christians began to abandon the Temple cult when they turned from the unsuccessful proselytizing of the Jews to the great Gentile world outside. Yet these early Christians remained highly sensitive to the Judaism of their own times, and there was a tension in their ranks between the so-called "Judaizers," the Christians who called for adherence to Jewish ideas as part of Christ's message, and "Hellenizers," those primarily of Gentile origin who felt no particular loyalty to Jewish tradition. Thus Jewish decisions in the crisis produced by the destruction of the Temple affected Christian development. Jewish Christians had been demanding that the followers of Jesus also follow the Law. With the Temple gone, what was the law? and if modifications were called for, who had the authority to prescribe them?

Overwhelmed by the sense of loss and desolation, some could only express despair until God's kingdom should arrive, an expectation like the hope and proclamation of good news by Christians. Two works of apocalyptic vision, 2 Baruch and 4 Ezra, purporting to be the work of prophets of centuries before but today generally agreed to have been composed after the destruction of the second Temple, vividly evoke the anguish of the times. As Baruch cries out:

> Blessed is he who was not born,
> or he who was born and died
> But we, the living, woe to us,
> because we have seen those afflictions of Zion,
> and that which has befallen Jerusalem.

> Awake, and gird up your loins to mourn,
> and raise lamentations with me,
> and mourn with me.
> You, farmers, sow not again,
> and you, O earth, why do you give the fruit of your harvest?
> Keep within you the sweetness of your sustenance.
> And you, vine, why do you still give your wine?
> For an offering will not be given again from you in Zion,
> and the first fruits will not again be offered.

Henceforth, do not speak anymore of beauty,
and do not talk about gracefulness.
You, priests, take the keys of the sanctuary,
and cast them to the highest heaven,
and give them to the Lord and say,
"Guard your house yourself,
because, behold, we have been found to be false stewards."[20]

How this differs from those words, penned just a little earlier, and attributed to another Jew, Mark:

And so the Lord Jesus, after speaking to them, was called up into the heavens and sat down on the right side of God. But, they, going out, carried the message everywhere, the Lord working with them, strengthening the word through accompanying signs.[21]

But there were other Jews who resolutely resisted these conclusions. For them the traditions of the interpreters of the Law had meaning. Through all the changes which had overtaken the nation of Israel after Alexander defeated the Persians, the exigencies of the times called for both resolution and flexibility. For the survival of the Law and its observance, men wise in Scripture explained what Moses meant to be done in the face of the cirumstances they knew. Those who had defended the validity of this expansion of the Law and called for its observance had by the late first century collected a great body of detailed rules for living. Observance of these rules, they claimed, was required of the Jew who sought right living. Like much of the Mosaic code, the accumulated legislation dealt with everyday life and ethics. Besides the rules of Temple life, sacrifice, and priestly activity, Moses and his interpreters prescribed for festivals, purity, family life, commerce, and agriculture. All of this legislation remained relevant to everyday life, for there still remained the villages, farms, and families to be regulated, and there were even still Jews in the cities who had survived the war and were prepared to try to continue to live holy lives. While the authors of works like 4 Ezra might throw up their hands and abandon hope for the future, life nevertheless would go on. Learned men could help the survivors make something valuable of it.

Ultimately, apart from the proclamation of the kingdom of God by Jesus and his followers, all of the approaches to religious life fashioned by first-century Jews were rejected by Christians. The literalism of the Sadducees they never considered, while the Pharisees were made into Jesus' enemies as the Gospel account evolved. Christians early abandoned any connection between a revival of the political kingdom of David and the kingdom of God which they believed was approaching; as a result, they had nothing in common with the independence movement of the "Fourth Philosophy" and took no noticeable role in the revolt of 66–70. Even the ascetic movement, like that in which the Essenes and Therapeutai took part, which did attract some Christians, never came close to dominating the ideology of most of them. And the elaborate structure of rules, like that illustrated by the Mishnah, which could serve as a means of relating to God by self-regulation, was rejected in favor of approach to the Father through the Son. Finally, after Bar Kochba and the definitive failure of the revolt in the second century, the Jews came to terms with their situation. But even before the revolt of 66 things were changing, and the destruction of the Temple was a kind of seal separating the groups, Jews from Christians, Jews from Greeks. Thenceforth, the roads went in different directions.

# 30

# Early Christian thought

## *The concepts of*
## *the New Testament writings*

By the middle of the second century, the followers of Christ – the Christians – were well aware that they had parted company with the Jews. In their past lay the great debate between those who saw themselves as Jews and their movement as one to which all Jewish law and custom applied, and those who saw the coming of Christ as a rupture with the past, symbolized by the story of the tearing of the veil in the sanctuary at the moment of Christ's death. Those of the latter persuasion had won out, and the generation which lived this conflict and the generation which followed passed on to their heirs a body of writings which we have come to call the New Testament. These writings too had passed through some trial and debate; the middle and latter part of the second century was the period which saw the development of a consensus about which should be regarded as legitimate additions to the body of sacred Scripture which the Christians had inherited from the Jews. This consensus, which eventually evolved into a canon, or official list, has preserved for us a collection of accounts of Christ which are interpretations of his life in both historical and religious terms, a report of the earliest apostolic activities, letters dealing with theology and church organization, and an example of mystical vision recorded in writing. This collection, not all parts of which are by any means always mutually consistent either factually or ideologically, was for the most part the work of the second half of the first century. It is a record of the concepts of some Christians in the two generations after Christ's death, telling us what they believed Christ had done and said and what those acts and words meant.

This collection is the earliest written evidence we have of the experiences of Christ and the content of his message. As a result, all the works have generated enormous controversy over interpretation, genuineness, attribution, and date. These disagreements existed as early as the time of the first church fathers, but they have been greatly amplified in the last century with the advent of what practitioners call scientific New Testament criticism. In some areas there is a modern consensus, such as that which sees some interdependences among the three synoptic – viewable together – Gospels of Matthew, Mark, and Luke, with the fourth Gospel, John, representing a very different tradition. A number of the letters said to have been Paul's are accepted by all modern critics as genuinely the work of the apostle, while disagreement remains about others. Not all modern students agree that all the letters said to have been written by John are the work of the writer of the fourth Gospel, and there are disagreements over which parts of certain letters might be seen as later interpretations. Beyond all this, there is a lot of controversy over the nature of the sources used by the Gospel writers, the compiler of Acts of the Apostles, and the relation between these sources and, let us say, the letters of St Paul, which most people agree predate the composition of any of the Gospels.

The resolution of these issues influences fundamentally the determination of what was said and done by Jesus and the early apostles, questions which are significant for historical or theological reasons, or both. Descriptions of early Christianity, the "primitive" church, and the like, depend on distinguishing that which is early and that which relates to the second or later centuries in the Gospels, in Acts, and in the various apostolic letters. A lot of what is said is certainly true, at least in general terms, about the division of the early Christians between the so-called Judaizers who wanted to hold to Mosaic law and those who would allow most of its details to be abandoned. And a great deal of what has been written about specific aspects of the material, explicating Paul's theology, for example, from his letters, or attempting to understand certain ideas or attitudes in early Christian writing as they emerge from the texts, is valid and has great value in helping us understand the development of Christian thought. But I do not think that we can create a reliable account, at least in any detail, of what Jesus said and did and thought during the two or three years of his ministry, nor have I any confidence in the reconstructions of the details of the evolution of the church and the attitudes and actions of the apostles in the two decades after his crucifixion, the period of so-called "primitive Christianity." Too much had happened, too many historical, theological, and doctrinal issues had been debated and perhaps not even resolved between the day of the crucifixion and the time when the earliest Greek Gospel was committed to writing. Thirty to fifty years or even more had intervened, years in which the movement was defining itself with the intense activity and vitality so characteristic of any new ideology. For every "historical" fact which can be argued from the text, the assertion can be made of its later inclusion in the record to justify later doctrine or liturgy. The earliest evidence of what anyone thought is that of St Paul, and it is clear from his letters that certain "historical" events mentioned in Acts as predating his activity must in fact have come after him.

So, it seems to me that we really do not know very much about Jesus, the apostles, and the Christian movement – apart from St Paul – until about the last quarter of the first century. Then the Gospels emerge, at the earliest in the decade before the destruction of the Temple in 70, more probably in the period after that event. Whatever we make of these writings for historical reconstruction, they very quickly became the basis of the whole Christian movement. What they said happened was, for all intents and purposes, more important than what might actually have happened, since people believed them. If there is causation in history at all, it arises as much or more from what people believe about an event as from its objective fact. The importance of the New Testament is certainly much more in its effect on the minds and acts of subsequent generations than in its information about the experiences of an earlier generation, and to understand some of this influence, we need not enter into the debates about sources, about attribution, or about early and later material. We can deal with texts which, apart from the usual manuscript problems and variations, can be taken as wholes, certainly complete and having an impact by the middle of the second century. In them, a number of specific theological, philosophical, and ethical themes vital at the end of the first century came to dominate western thought for the next 2000 years.

One of the strongest and most consistent ideas, running through all the works and affecting attitudes toward other matters as well, is the concept of the impending arrival of the kingdom of God. The Gospels repeatedly tell of Jesus' words of warning, exhortation, and explanation of the life to be lived in the face of the impending end of life as it had been lived so far. The idea remained current even a generation later, in apostolic times, for the First Letter of Peter refers to the time of writing as "the end of the ages."[1] Variously attributed and dated over a wide period – from the middle of the first century to the beginning of the second – whatever solution to the dating problem one chooses, the letter shows that people were still expecting the kingdom to arrive imminently for some decades after Jesus' death, and the Revelation of John demonstrates that the idea persisted at least until the latter part of the century. This apocalyptic vision, the notion that the world as it had existed so far was coming to an end, and was to be replaced by the perfection of the kingdom of God, had been a part of Jewish thought for at least two centuries by the time the Apocalypse, or Revelation, of John was penned, and writings like 2 Baruch and 4 Ezra are roughly contemporary with the creation of the earliest Christian books, including the Revelation. The doctrine was preached by John the Baptist, and it was Jesus' message. For Christians, however, unlike Jews, the announcement of the arrival of the kingdom was one of the fundamental keystones of belief, for it was connected with Christ's role in its proclamation, organization, and salvation of living and dead. For Christians, there was also hope for the present. True believers could make lives which would make them eligible for inclusion in the kingdom. To the writers of 2 Baruch and 4 Ezra the travails of Israel were part of the events which precede the last days, and all Israel must perish under the heel of evil power as part of the end of the world as it is, but should not be. The writer of Revelation on the other hand, saw the "beast" – Rome, Nero, or whatever – as the agent of the evil one, slaughtering some of the virtuous and seducing others, but for those who stood fast there was a promise of reward in the new age. The tumultuous destruction of the cosmos which would accompany God's final victory over all the demonic angels and forces of evil would usher in a new heaven and a new earth, and there would stand the new Jerusalem.

Much in Revelation draws on Jewish apocalyptic literature, and specific parallels can be found with its Jewish antecedents. Its writer refashioned those antecedents, however, to make a prophecy quite different from that which had been given to the Jews for two centuries. While "seeing" events much like those described in Daniel, Baruch, and Ezra, the writer of Revelation gives the faithful an ally in Christ, an assurance of ultimate personal victory along with the cosmic victory of God, and he portrays the "beast" and its master Satan not as agents of God, but as the enemies of God and God's faithful in Christ. It is a distinction very clear to Marcion, writing in the second century. It is also a distinction implicit in all the exhortations of Jesus as reported in the Gospels, and it is a fundamental concept of God's plan to which the Sermon on the Mount is a corollary. Revelation and all the other apocalyptic passages are at one with the words of Jesus as he urges his followers to abandon the things of this world and emulate the lilies of the field:

> Not everyone saying to me "Lord, Lord," will enter into the kingdom of the heavens, but the one doing the wish of my father in the heavens. Many will say to me on that day, "Lord, Lord, did we not make prophecies in your name, and in your name did we not cast out demons, and in your name did we not do many miracles?" And then I shall say plainly to them, "I never knew you; go off from me, workers of wickedness."
>
> Everyone then, who hears these words of mine and does what they say will be like the thoughtful man who built his house on rock. And the rain fell and the rivers rose and the winds blew and fell upon that house, and it did not fall, for it was established on rock. And everyone hearing these words of mine and does not do what they say will be like the foolish man who built his house on sand. And the rain fell and the rivers rose and the winds blew and struck that house, and it fell, and its fall was great.[2]

The words to which his hearers are to listen are the moral pronouncements of the Sermon on the Mount, clearly to be taken not as a call to make this world better but to reform the self to make it ready to enter the new Jerusalem.

The end did not come as quickly as Jesus said it would. He had claimed that it would come before all those to whom he spoke had "fallen asleep," but all his hearers died and the kingdom of heaven still did not arrive. The promise of the First Letter of Peter and Revelation was not fulfilled. Christians began to wonder; an answer to their doubt emerged in a second letter attributed to Peter, which justified the promise by asserting "that one day for the Lord is just as a thousand years, and a thousand years are just as one day,"[3] and explaining the delay as offering time for repentance. But this apologetic response, drawing upon the "thousand years" of Psalm 90: 4 which serves rather to celebrate the power of God, is much later than the other writings of the New Testament. Probably belonging to the end of the second century, it was unknown to those who drew upon the Gospels, Acts, Revelation, and the other letters; coming long after the apostolic age, it still insists now that, at least, the last days and the kingdom of heaven are at hand. Although rejected by many early Christian scholars and theologians, its ultimate inclusion in the canon of "true" Scripture shows that the apocalyptic vision of the impending kingdom of God and the protection afforded by genuine Christian living were still important parts of mainline Christianity, and its presence along with the other sacred books helped to assure that this would remain the case.

Other themes of the early Christian books relate to the particular role and position of Christ in Christian thought. By that I do not mean specific statements of dogma like that of virgin birth or other individual miracles, which are much easier to accept by an act of will or faith than are the dictates of Christ's sermons as prescriptions for behavior actually to be followed. What is peculiarly Christian, and appears in Christian writings as early as Paul's letters, is a Christ exhibiting an ambiguity which permits a whole range of conceptualizations of him as God, as man, as intermediary between God and man, as spirit, God's logos and resurrected flesh, and as savior. All of these emerge from the earliest writings, ratified and preserved for the future. Whether or not all were part of the Jesus known to the early apostles, all had their impact on later thought and belief. Whether, for example, Jesus thought of himself and represented himself as the expected Messiah of the House of David is a historical, rather than theological or ideological, question, for the apostles certainly thought that was the case. And the writers of the Gospels either found traditions which depicted Jesus as relating himself to earlier prophecy like that of Isaiah, or they created them to make the point clear. Thereafter, Christians accepted the idea that God had revealed Jesus' advent through prophecy, and one of the great quests for Christian writers was the discovery of yet more of these predictions than those recorded by the Gospels. In a similar manner, the Gospels, Revelation, and the early apostolic letters offered a number of comments not only on the mission of Jesus but on his nature, providing the possibility of interpreting the incarnate Christ both as human and divine, or in some way as a combination of both. The potential of interpretation not only passed an open issue on to succeeding generations and provided an opportunity for savage doctrinal quarrels in succeeding centuries, but the desire and necessity to understand the nature of Christ led to increasing Christological speculation and pushed to the fore the Christ-figure. The ultimate resolution in the Trinity, with consubstantiation of God and Christ and the Holy Spirit, came from the problems of understanding Jesus as Gospels and apostles wrote of him.

To Paul, twenty-five years after the crucifixion, Christ's nature and role in the cosmos were clear. Writing to various communities of his converts on many matters, he expended a great deal of effort to ensure that they would understand what their acceptance of Christ actually meant, how the Spirit worked in them once they were part of the body of Christ, and that the coming of Christ represented not only salvation but a change for the world. As his views were a dominant influence on the thought of Christians who came after him, some moderns, Christians and non-Christians basically sympathetic with the ethical pronouncements of Jesus but not with the power and theology of the church which later emerged, find in Paul a convenient scapegoat on whom to blame everything thought to have gone wrong. The idea is unfair and wrong, and only has to recommend it that it eliminates the need to confront and understand Paul's difficult and often ambiguous Greek. While Paul does write as an organizer, attempting to establish authority in the church and regularity of belief and conduct, and offers many opinions about details of administration which later came to control decisions, he was concerned for the church only because it and its Christians were part of the body of Christ; it was not the welfare of the church for which he was concerned, but the purity and reliability of faith. While his theology was authoritarian, it was expressed in terms of the authority conferred on it by Christ which ultimately derived from the father. To sweep Paul is to sweep away all the confidence of the early Christians in the revelation given them through Christ as sacrificed and risen Lord. Paul's letters present Christ's sacrifice as part of God's plan whereby the "powers and principalities," the supernatural agents of evil, actually precipitate the events which will bring their destruction in the apocalyptic period which is to follow the crucifixion. The death of sin with the death of Jesus' physical body leads to God's victory over the power of evil.

Paul's letters acknowledge the paradoxical nature of some of this teaching, with a claim that salvation is achieved through the faith that takes its potency through the cross rather than through human wisdom:

> For it is in the wisdom of God that the cosmos does not know God through wisdom, since God decided to save the faithful through the foolishness of the message. When the Jews ask for signs and the Greeks look for wisdom, we proclaim a crucified Christ, to the Jews a stumbling block and the pagans folly, but to those who have been called, Jews and Greeks, a Christ who is the power of God and wisdom of God.[4]

It is a ringing declaration of the manner in which the purpose, act, and meaning of the crucifixion contradict all normal human wisdom and logic, proclaiming the faith which is the fundamental attitude needed by Christians for their successful transit of the last days. The concept of faith, stressed so heavily in the letters, became an indispensable part of the religious attitude of Christians, and this faith was, at least in the view of Paul, independent of observance of the Law.

The wider, Greek-speaking world to which Paul's letters penetrated had much in common with the apostle, and his deliberate choice of language appropriate to Greek religiosity meant that however Jewish his thought may have originally been, couching that thought in Greek rather than Aramaic inevitably bent it to Hellenic meanings – an illustration of what McLuhan meant by his remark "the medium is the message," but at a deeper level. At the same time, there were enough similarities between Christian concepts and some current in the world of Paul's time to make it possible for him to use terminology familiar to non-Christians. For example, the idea of a savior who would come to the world to rectify it was a concept which had long penetrated Judaism and some of the Greek mystery religions. At the same time, the mystical notion of a *pneuma* – the Greek word which we translate "spirit" but which in Greek is close also to the meaning of our word "breath" – was commonly used by the religionists of the mysteries to express the concept of the infusion of divinity which participation in worship brought to the initiates. It was part and parcel of the change which came over the individual when he saw the God, or "converted," an experience which brought Paul himself to Christ on the road to Damascus. Many would take the spirit of which Paul writes as that same *pneuma* akin to soul which was of the breath of humans as of the breath of God, not as the independent entity implied by much of Paul's writing. Many others might assume that the Christ who appeared to Paul and whom the Christians worshipped was the same as that exalted redeemer, known to other religious thought, who would come from God to bring about the end of the world in preparation for the last judgment – but without Paul's perception of the coming and death of the redeemer as a sacrifice necessary to free individuals from sin. Lastly, Paul's idea that the redeemer, Christ, still lived, that he could and did appear to people and by the action of the *pneuma*, which was in some way independent of while yet part of God, Christ, and humanity, he passed to the individual the grace which freed from sin – these were combinations of earlier ideas difficult for Jews and Gentiles alike.

It is hardly surprising, therefore, that Paul's letters advert to these themes again and again. It is precisely because they were so difficult to express or apprehend correctly that he comes back again and again to the same points, sometimes using the same words over and over again, at others trying new modes of expression. Even so, he did not neglect those other aspects of behavior which we have been accustomed to call "Christian virtues": Christians are to put off all the wickedness of earthly life, and clothe themselves "in feelings of pity, kindness, humility, gentleness, patience and over all these, love, which is the unifying bond of completeness,"[5] to "love one another and the whole human race."[6] The entire Law is summarized by the behest, "Love your neighbor as yourself,"[7] and the virtue associated with the Christians, "the fruit of the spirit (*pneuma*) is love, happiness, peace, patience, kindness, goodness, faith, gentleness, self-control,"[8] while in Romans[9] he adverts again to the theme of brotherly love, and goes on to urge the extreme Christian position of loving one's enemies.

Paul does not turn away from the moral prescriptions defining the Christian life in the period before the end of the ages in favor of metaphysical refinements of Christian doctrine on faith and the meaning of Christ. He too calls for the Christian love – *agape* which appears so prominently in the Gospel and letter attributed to the apostle John, and demands adherence to the Christian virtues. However, the focus of his extant letters is determined by the need to clarify his perception in the face of ideas which too easily distracted new converts from the difficult, but fundamentally different and more valuable, doctrine of Christian redemption on an individual basis through faith and Jesus. This, to him, was what his preaching was all about.

Many of the subsidiary points in the letters should be understood in the same way. The injunction to obey civil authority in Romans 13: 1–7, with its assertion that authority and the state are put in place by God, and the concomitant justification for Christians to pay their taxes, illustrates the kinds of concerns which preoccupied early Christians while they waited for the arrival of the kingdom. Paul's repeated exhortations against sexual immorality may have obsessed both later Christians and their opponents, but the obvious preference which the letters show for chastity is an almost incidental aspect of the prescription for Christian life, the main focus being Christ, the meaning of the crucifixion, and faith. And if Paul is to be blamed for a recommendation of chastity that later generated a Christian obsession with that issue, he is not responsible for the notorious command that wives be subservient to husbands as the church yields to Christ, in Ephesians 5: 22–4, since that letter is almost certainly not from his pen. Written by Paul or not, however, Ephesians was accepted early into the group of Pauline letters; read along with the other early Christian writings, it was one of the accepted and influential expressions of legitimate thought. It carried a concept which is not stressed elsewhere, that under God's predetermined plan the Christians were part of the scheme whereby Christ was designated from the beginning to unify everything on earth and in heaven. God had made Christ ruler of all, the head of the church which is Christ's body, and Christ himself fills the cosmos. The focus is on unity, making all humankind one, which became a feature of Christian thought and may owe something to Greek philosophy.

The authority which the apostle Paul's authorship brought to these letters later was spread over another text, one which began to be accepted into the collection of Pauline letters at the end of the second century, but was well known long before then. Probably written just at the beginning of that century, or in the latter years of the first, the so-called Letter to the Hebrews is a brilliant composition in excellent Greek, with many connections to Greek philosophical thought, especially Platonic. It may have been an apologetic addressed to the Jews, as many think, or may be, as is more likely, directed to Christians themselves, in the manner of Paul, exhorting allegiance to the new faith and dealing with the problem of carrying on life as the years stretch on and the kingdom does not arrive. How did the followers of Christ stand in relation to salvation as ordinary life presented recurring temptations to sin? How ultimate was the Christian message, how much could Christ's sacrifice cleanse? To these questions the author of Hebrews had a clear answer. The Christian message was final, a new Covenant which brought the potential of perfection. It is through Jesus, the supreme high priest, that the faulty first Covenant is replaced by the second and perfect one, and it is in the new Covenant that Jesus is mediator. As in earlier times, purification could only be achieved through blood, and since the things purified by blood were, like the Law itself, only reflections of heavenly realities, Christ's death served to cancel the sins which had occurred in violation of the earlier testament, the Law. But it is a one-time sacrifice, cancelling sins before the coming of Christ, but with no such effect for the future. The writer warns that, "If we sin willingly after gaining the knowledge of the truth, there is no longer left a sacrifice for sins, but a frightful expectation of judgement, and the zeal of the fire which consumes enemies."[10] The point made here of the scriptural statement of divine vengeance differs violently from a use Paul made of the same text to argue for human forgiveness and kindness to enemies. The doctrine of a one-time redemption from sin looks away from divine mercy toward Dante's *Inferno*.

Well before Hebrews was written, a completely different sort of Christian literature had begun to make its way into the world. At some time in the four decades after Paul's last letter, the first of the three synoptic, or "viewable-together," Gospels appeared, and before the first century was over, in all probability all three of the Gospels of Mark, Matthew, and Luke were being read. That none of the three was the first-hand account of the disciple to whom tradition attributes it is now generally accepted, but dates, interdependence and mutual influences, stages of composition and editing are intensely debated matters. All this happened between the fifties of the first century and the beginning of the next. When all who had known Jesus had died, the Gospels and other written material were all that was left to tell the tale. Christianity is, therefore, to a significant degree a religion of the Gospels, and what the Gospels tell us to believe is what we tend to accept. Whenever these beliefs were formulated and recorded, within a century they were firm Christian doctrine, accorded authority because of the apostolic authorship which tradition accepted for them.

In the three synoptic Gospels there is a great common body of incidents and events, and often identical language, and for the most part, they all organize the material in the same basic way. The three are closely related, although the nature of that relationship is not one agreed upon by all modern critics. All three purport to tell the story of the life, teaching, and death of Christ as simple, first-hand narratives, and, although they differ occasionally in the details included and here and there even contradict one another, all together they provide the basis for the Christ story which is their legacy to western humanity. They do, however, have different objectives, which means that they place different emphases on their material, and they are each written in a very different style of Greek. Mark is vividly dramatic, in a Greek that is often abrupt and unclassical to modern readers, with passages which some have taken to prove that the text is a document of translation. Matthew's Greek, on the other hand, corresponds more to the classical Greek which moderns call "better," and it has a carefully worked-out structure, breaking it into five parts. Almost every incident in Matthew can be found in Mark, but there are rearrangements, notably in pulling together statements of Jesus made at various times in other Gospels, into the one, coherent address which we know as "The Sermon on the Mount." Matthew's major addition to Mark's material is the long genealogy tracing Jesus' ancestry back to David, along with the story of Jesus' birth, the visit of the Magi, and the unparalleled account of the flight into Egypt by which the child was saved from the evil designs of Herod.

All this preliminary additional material reveals a special interest on the part of the Gospel writer to present Jesus as a lawgiver parallel, although of course superior, to Moses, to fix Jesus in the history of prophecy, lawgiving and divine revelation as the specially chosen emissary of God, much as Moses had been earlier for the conferring of the first Law. It is a story of the manner in which the savior who is to bring the replacement for the Law is himself brought to humanity by God, and in an even more extraordinary and miraculous way than that by which God had saved Moses. Matthew's narrative, however, stood quite independent of its significance. The account of the virgin birth was fixed as an integral part of the Christ story, along with genealogy from David, the story of Magi sent by Herod when he heard of the birth of the King of the Jews, and even the flight into Egypt which certainly puzzled many, as the story is omitted, or rejected, from Luke's fuller account of the infancy of Jesus. Matthew's highlighting of miracles, his provision of the end which Mark lacks (apart from the added verses 16: 9–20), in which Jesus actually does appear to Mary Magdalene and Mary mother of James and then later to the eleven disciples in Galilee – all this adds to the growing sense of the miraculous which verifies Jesus' words and acts and helped to focus Christian attention on the person of Jesus at least by the end of the first century. The overall picture would all be quite plausible and impressive to Matthew's Hellenic audience, and because the Gospel deals with the life of Jesus, rather than the views of an apostle, like the letters of Paul, whatever Matthew added to Mark made and makes a strong impression on later Christians.

Some of the additions are minor, but there can be great importance even in minor expansions like that in the description of the institution of the Eucharist. After Mark's words "For this is my blood of the covenant, which is poured out for many," Matthew adds the all-important four words "for release from sins," to give the particular Christian twist to the sacred meal familiar to Hellenes for centuries. On a much grander scale of composition, if not of implication, is the organization of the Christian ethic as a cohesive whole presented by Jesus as the

Sermon on the Mount. Although like all of Jesus' ethical exhortations this long passage is based on the premise that the kingdom of heaven is near, and describes how believers should live while awaiting the day, because of its fullness it has tended to be taken as a prescription for life in normal times. As one might expect, Jesus' words present the basic morality of Judaism as expressed in the ten commandments, but with expansions: "thou shalt not kill" is extended to preclude anger with other humans; "thou shalt not commit adultery" is now taken to forbid divorce except in the case of fornication; the prohibition of false witness now excludes any oaths at all, and anything more than simple affirmative or negative statement is said to come from the devil. But there is also an emphasis on gentleness, mercy, and forgiveness. It is the turning of the other cheek, the going of the second mile, the prohibition of resistance even to the wicked, the order to love the enemy. Here Jesus also presents his rejection of any value placed on money or wealth, forcing the choice between service of God or of money. Here is the injunction to store up treasures not on earth but in heaven, a command explained by the psychological insight: "For where your treasure is, there will your heart be also."[11] Worldly goods themselves are not malevolent, but the consideration of worldly goods as treasure leads the heart to emphasise the things of this world rather than the requirements which bring a life ready for the kingdom of heaven. All this moral prescribing is wrapped and interleaved with instruction for prayer, in a discourse that begins with the beatitudes, the celebration of the followers as the light of the world is then highlighted by the Lord's Prayer and the golden rule of treating others as one would be treated, and concludes with a reminder of the coming kingdom of heaven and the promise that those who follow Jesus are building their house on rock.

Matthew's creation of a single, all-encompassing expression of Jesus' moral and religious teaching is one of the great outpourings of the human spirit. It endures still to tantalize Christians with ideals which they feel they cannot meet, even allowing for the fact that the call to abandon the things of this world is made in the expectation of the imminent arrival of the next. From the time of its composition, it has stood as a résumé of Christian teaching, whether taken as the ideal of the church or the revealed words of God through Jesus. It has justified the formulation of formal liturgical service and the life of the hermit, it has led to asceticism and monasticism. But above all, it has been interpreted as the core of Christ's teaching and life, a towering reminder to Christians of the teachings of the early church, words which often called the most spiritual away from the man-made institutions built on Christ, back to the message which they felt he brought from God.

The third of the synoptic Gospels, Luke, while broadly corresponding in content to the other two, is nevertheless quite different in its approach to the Jesus story. Not only is it in excellent Greek with a proper classical introduction, it is the severed early chapters of a much longer work on the history of the church, the later part of which appears in our texts after the fourth Gospel as a separate work entitled The Acts of the Apostles, and must be considered together with it as a single example of early Christian writing. The overall effect, import, theology, and conception of the two are the same, and they weave a cohesive and acceptable account of the manner in which the apostles, and therefore their disciples, received the teaching and spirit of Christ in a manner which gave authority to apostolic and church preaching. In Luke, the account of Jesus' appearing to the apostles after the crucifixion is very different from and much longer than that in Matthew. Two disciples see Jesus on the road to Emmaeus, and immediately go off to Jerusalem, where they find the eleven assembled to hear their tale and tell them of another appearance, to Simon. Suddenly Jesus is there again, frightening them all greatly. The events are made dramatic and literal. "A ghost has not flesh and bones," Jesus says, offering his hands and feet for them to touch. "Do you have anything here to eat?" he asks,[12] and to prove his corporeality he eats a grilled fish before their eyes. He goes on to explain to them that all the events of the immediate past were what he had been telling them earlier – "opened their minds to understand the writings"[13] – and called them as witnesses.

The Gospel leaves no doubt that the resurrection was in the flesh, nor of its precise significance. By focusing on the appearance to the apostles, Luke clothes them with the particular authority conferred by Jesus' risen person. Added to the knowledge they had of him in life came that insight brought when he "opened their minds" in resurrection, all of which authority would be enhanced when they received the "power from on high."[14] They then go off to Bethany for the ascension, a story picked up by Acts; Jesus promises the apostles again that they will receive the power from the Holy Spirit, and departs to heaven. Next comes Pentecost, and Jesus' recent promise is fulfilled, in a suitably dramatic and portentous manner. As the apostles were gathered for the holy day in one room,

> there was suddenly from the heaven a sound like the force of a driving wind, and it filled the whole house where they were sitting, and separating tongues as if of fire appeared to them, and settled down on each one of them. And they all were filled with the Holy Spirit [pneuma] and they began to speak in other tongues, just as the spirit [pneuma] gave them the ability to speak.[15]

The noise brought in others, devout from all nations who were living in Jerusalem, and each could hear the apostles preaching in his own native language. It was amazing. Peter used the occasion to give a sermon on Christ which resulted in about 3000 immediate conversions. The ministry of the apostles had begun.

All this validates the apostles' preaching and transmission of God's message, the Holy Spirit having given them not only the truth but the ability to perform miracles. It endorses the idea that the apostles had unique access to truth, a view which not only establishes the reputation of the Gospels and other "apostolic" writings as inspired, but created the authority of the church as well. As the story in Acts proceeds, the apostles draw more and more people into the church, and after the martyrdom of Stephen, the scattering of the disciples leads to successful evangelism in Samaria. Then, in Paul's absence, Peter received the word which permitted him to baptize the first pagans when the Holy Spirit descended on them. Acts thus details and justifies the first expansion of the preaching into the Gentile world, and with its account of the Council of Jerusalem shows how the pagans were first exempted from the requirements of traditional Jewish law. The apostles are now, in concert with the Holy Spirit, legislating for the church, and the process of interpretation of Christ's words through progressive revelation begins. Success follows success, miracle follows miracle, and Paul goes out into the world and founds churches throughout Asia Minor and Greece. After his return to Jerusalem he meets a prosecution there by the Jewish leaders, is detained by a Roman administration which fails to find any fault in him, and would have been freed had he not himself as a Roman citizen requested trial before the emperor. The story is carried only as far as Paul's arrival in Rome, but it is enough.

Luke and Acts have skilfully woven theology into their accounts so that the narrative itself justifies doctrine. The story itself, rather than mere assertion, is proof. Christ shows himself in gentleness, love, and forgiveness of sinners, kindly toward the poor and weak, the merciful surrogate of the loving God. Even the sinners have their chance; all they need is repentance. The apostles in Acts call men to the same repentance, themselves guided by the Christ who taught them in life and came to them in resurrection; they are themselves informed by the Holy Spirit which from time to time moves men to accept the apostles' message. Although the Jews in stubbornness resist, and Paul in sadness rather than anger is always forced to turn from the synagogue to the pagans, that very resistance is the means God uses to turn the apostle to evangelize the Gentiles, to bring them into the body of the faithful and receive the mercy of the Father in repentance through Christ.

The last of the four Gospels in our collection, the Gospel of John, is so different from the three synoptics that it is classed separately and always considered aside from them. It is not that the three synoptic Gospels give a more "historical" account of Jesus, although most readers assume they do because they seem more heavily narrative, but that John gives an essentially different picture. The locale is different – Judaea for almost all the story instead of Galilee – and the time implied by the number of Passovers is much longer, perhaps as much as four years. Jesus' personality is very different from the gentle shepherd of Luke and Matthew or the moral preacher in all three other Gospels. In John he is more remote, a much more exalted and god-like figure. If he is the Word made flesh, it is not very human flesh. Even at the end, his last words on the cross are not the anguished "My God, my God, why have you deserted me?" of Mark and Matthew, mentioned as a cry coming immediately before the final words of Luke, "Father, into your hands I place my spirit [*pneuma*]." Even these bespeak too much humanity for John. Jesus says, "I am thirsty," but only to fulfill Scriptural prophecy, and his last words are the unafflicted and remote, "It is finished."

John is also much more Hellenic than any of the other Gospels, even the well-written Luke, and shows acquaintance with Greek philosophical notions prevailing in the first century. It is difficult not to see the language of Philo behind the aligning of logos and God in the opening verses, and the whole story which John is about to tell is there in the prologue. The human Christ of the synoptic Gospels of whom we tell small children, the "holy infant so tender and mild" on whom we build our Christmas story, is replaced by an abstract logos not portrayed in human birth, of a virgin or anything else, but rather simple "made flesh." And from the prologue on, the Gospel of John and the Jesus it portrays proceed deliberately, explicitly, and unflinchingly toward the denouement on the cross, from start to finish in full knowledge of what was to happen and its meaning.

The point is made again and again, in phrases that have become so familiar through their selection for church liturgy, homily, and sermon. John the Baptist knows the story fully, in advance, recognizing "the lamb of God that takes away the sin of the world."[16] Jesus of course knows it, and broadcasts it the very first time that words of his are quoted, in the conversation with Nicodemus whom he tells, "Thus God loved the cosmos so that he gave his only begotten son, so that every person believing in him might not perish but have eternal life."[17] He repeats the message again and again, in parable and in metaphor: "I am the bread of life"; "I am the resurrection"; "I am the way, the Truth and the Life."[18] We know all these phrases because we have heard them over and over again, and we have heard them so often because they express, perhaps better than the other Gospels, a perception of Christ which goes far beyond the historical to reflect an intuition of the essence, an intuition transmitted so forcefully as to channel the intuitions of spiritual people for almost twenty centuries. And the words which John gives to Christ also have a fully developed doctrine of the effectiveness of the Eucharist, as Jesus more than once speaks of himself as spiritual food. There is meat and drink also for the transubstantiation debate, for communion and excommunication, for literal or metaphorical interpretation of the sacrament, and John's words lay the groundwork for much of the mystery and dogma of the later church. Here as in so many other places the language goes far beyond anything said in any of the other Gospels to establish the metaphysics of Christ and his relation to the cosmos, beyond reason and beyond sense to evoke a Jesus passing human understanding, a kind of Jesus who can say, "Truly indeed, I say to you, before Abraham existed, I am."[19]

It is a metaphysics and assertion of reality beyond human experience, more acceptable to Gentiles with a background in Greek philosophy and particularly in Platonism, than to Jews firmly rooted in their own scriptural tradition.

John's own thought processes are so deeply imbued with the notion of two levels of existence, the heavenly and the earthly, that he inevitably uses language that makes God's and Christ's world the genuine world of truth, a concept which helped to make Christian thought easily acceptable to educated Greeks of the time. The Jesus of John is not the ultimate messenger of the Father proclaiming the long-prophesied and now imminent end of the world and arrival of the kingdom of God, but the eternal existent logos-Son of God, temporarily turned to flesh and this world from the higher plane to provide people with the means of casting off earthly sin so as to reach the other world and eternal life. It is also a concept of Jesus less related to the end of life as we know it. The Jesus of John is not only eternal with God in the past, he is also eternal in the future, his nature unchanging, his message the same, his promise of purification and eternal life available to humanity for all time to come.

This, essentially, is John's contribution to Christology, perhaps a confusing contribution, because it is so different from those of the other Gospels. It is not just the narrative and words but the insight which is different, and the Gospel has been viewed by Christian believers as an account on a level of meaning different from and perhaps deeper than those of the synoptic Gospels. Treating John as metaphor or symbol has meant that it could be accepted along with the other Gospels as revealed truth, despite its apparent historical or factual discrepancies. Thus made part of the corpus, John contributed its mystical, symbolic, and metaphorical interpretation of Christ as an alternative to the literal interpretation, an intuition which although sometimes regarded as heretical when enunciated, was always available to private faith. And as part of the revered literature, the Gospel of John brought that Johannine emphasis on love so prominent in Christ's discourse at the last supper and in the First Letter of John, which also starts with reference to the logos which existed from the beginning, and exhorts the Christian community to guard against sin, but, like the Gospel, focuses on love.

It is this Johannine concentration on love, love of God for Jesus, Jesus for his people, the people for God, Jesus, and one another, that has established the tradition of Christianity as a religion of love. This perception has survived the concentration of the other Gospels and letters on salvation and the apocalypse, and even the behavior of churches and the preachings of clerics. Among some Christians over the ages and many of the present time, the nexus of mysticism and human and divine love has provided the central meaning of Christianity, for the platform erected by the Johannine writings is strong enough and broad enough to support an entire religious life, even leaving aside the ideas of all the other early writings. John's statement "In the beginning was the Word" could be taken to complete the historical account of the Old Testament; and the Gospels and ancillary letters, with the Old Testament behind them, could be taken to make Christianity the "complete answer" to anything. To others still, John's more remote and ideal Christ could be taken to justify and validate any private intuition about Jesus and his message, allowing for an insistence on "every man his own priest." in a religion which could be variously ecstatic, ethical, ascetic, or highly intellectual.

This whole body of early Christian literature, once it came to be accepted as the standard literature of the early church, gradually took on more authority, until it reached the status of revealed truth. Meanwhile, other early works, like the Shepherd of Hermas, the Gospel and revelation of Peter, and some letters like those of Clement, fell by the wayside. Of interest for what they tell about the early church, the exclusion of these works from what came to be the New Testament meant that they had little or no influence on later Christian thought, and today they are read only by a few historians of religion and theologians. What was to be said to subsequent generations had been established. Interpretation might well be necessary, but its scope was limited by the basic texts which stood as the accepted truth. And the message was available in the language which could reach all the literate from Syria to Spain. Any old Aramaic writings, if such had indeed ever existed, had been discarded. The message had been decided, and the medium was Greek.

That the language of the New Testament was Greek meant that it was understandable to almost all in the east and the educated in the west, but its significance was even greater than this. That the gospel writers should frame their accounts and their quotations of Jesus in Greek meant that inevitably Christianity was quickly forced to think in concepts expressible in Greek, and her thinkers and advocates to present their ideas in the philosophical and religious language of Hellenism. That the first generation succeeded in doing this meant that the pattern was firmly established. John could use the Greek word "logos" for Christ in an atmosphere which knew Philo's logos as the closest aspect of the unapproachable Existent One - God - to which the human mind could attain. The implications would be clear to any familiar with the Platonic two-tiered universe. As time went on and the promised arrival of the last days faded in immediacy, that essentially non-Hellenic aspect of Christianity also received its Greek cast as salvation came more and more to be seen as promotion to God's higher existence. The influence of Hellenic modes of thought on most of the works in the New Testament is so pronounced that many of the most characteristic Greek philosophical ideas make their appearance in these earliest Christian writings. We can find the Greek concept of human nature as defined as a compound of matter, soul, and *pneuma*, or spirit; we see the Platonic preference for soul and spirit over matter; we see the striving after knowledge of the ultimate reality with the Christian solution of knowing God through salvation; we can trace the resemblances of liturgy and act to the forms of Hellenic mysteries; most of all, we can see the influence of Plato given new life and vitality in Christian philosophy as Christian thinkers discount the importance of this world in confronting preparations for the next. Slaves remain slaves, masters their rulers, and the authority of temporal powers stays in place. Until the apocalypse, the demons wander the world to delude the unwary and afflict the sick, the wrongs of humankind will not be righted, and the poor will always be with us. If the Platonist denied that this world even exists in reality, the Christian waits for it to end, either in apocalypse for all the cosmos or in personal salvation in heaven.

Within this core of early Christian thought lie the seeds of many beliefs and attitudes; the New Testament is the center from which many different roads began. Christian gnosticism could find its roots here, as could the concern for loving treatment of others and the feeding of the poor for which Christians became known in later antiquity. Salvation in Christ and through Christ, Jesus himself present in the faithful, which could be so understandable in terms of mysteries which promised merging with and becoming the god, gradually developed into an elaborate doctrine of life after death which would have been unrecognizable even in Christ's time to Jews and Greeks alike. One idea, however, which had begun to emerge in late Greek ethics, and which might have taken a great deal of support from Christian notions of the soul, failed to develop in Christian thought. The principle of the basic equality of all humans to which Cicero alluded and which he supported to some extent, and which was endorsed by some of the later Stoics, was passed over by most of the early Christian writers. Even though all souls might be thought to be equal in God's love, that concept was not carried forward from theology to social philosophy. Apart from the warning in James' letter that Christian congregants should not despise lower and poorer members of their synagogues, social equality was not at the heart of Christian concerns. This may be due in the first instance to the fact that it would not seem to be a very important matter in view of the impending end of the world. As time passed and Christian regulation of life in this world seemed more and more necessary, the definition of ethical behavior answered more to the words of Jesus and the apostles than to a theoretical and not very prominent construct of Greek philosophy.

Christian ethics thus focused on the golden rule first, and then on the pronouncements of the ten commandements, as they applied to the lives of Christians and their communities. In Jerusalem, the Christians at first shared all their possessions, but that pattern quickly yielded to the more normal life of private property and trade. The commandment to treat others as one would wish to be treated, which, as Jesus said, comprehended all the other commandments, meant that the Christians made a special effort to aid the poor, the sick, and the helpless. There was no notion of addressing the problem which produced the unfortunate, but Christians did follow Jesus' exhortation to help them. They were also more scrupulous than some in their commercial practices, or were at least said to be so by some of their non-Christian contemporaries. They were either treating others as they would wish to be treated themselves, or were including commercial honor in the commandment against stealing, as Jesus had carried that against killing to prohibit anger also.

The Christians had support for their ethical system in a validation which the Greeks had never been able to achieve. From the time of Plato, the search for the definition of justice and the other virtues had foundered on the need to establish definitions or moral codes in some absolute way, not subject to the familiar relativism of human values. Plato's hypothesis of a transcendent world of ideal forms served to provide the potential for this validation, but the removal of that world beyond sense perception or even the reason of more than a very few meant that any such absolute verification was not very accessible or communicable. The Christian solution, like that of the Jews, was to see their morals and values as revealed word, truth with the absolute validity of an unambiguous divine message. Insofar as Christ or the ten commandments were explicit, the ethical requirement was clear and accepted without question. In any matters on which there was doubt or lack of clarity, the doctrine of the Holy Spirit infusing the apostles provided the means of resolution. In later centuries, the continuing activity of the Holy Spirit, not only in Christian leaders but in all the faithful, helped to solve new problems as they arose. Behind it all stood the two commands of Christ: "love your brother as yourself," and "do unto others what you would have them do unto you," explicit, unambiguous, and with the authority of God behind them. Difficult of fulfillment as they might be in the long years which stretched on when the end of ordinary life did not come, they could still provide the ideal and the basis of an absolute ethic.

Of course, not everything was so easy. Absolute clarity and authority do not always command absolute acceptance or understanding. Even the commandment "Thou shalt not kill," which might have been seen to be reinforced and deprived of the possibility of exceptions by Christ's own demand that wickedness be not resisted, was quickly "reinterpreted in the light of changing conditions." The initial fear that Christians might not serve in the army quickly dissipated, as large numbers of Jesus' followers showed themselves as willing as any to shoulder military burdens and slaughter barbarians in defence of civilization. The pursuit of heretics also seemed to take precedence over following those particular words of Christ. The cynic of the second century and later could find any number of instances in which Christian practice and precept differed violently from the words of Jesus in the Gospels. It has not been difficult to build the myth of a simple, beautiful, and moral Gospel perverted by arrogant men and venal human institutions.

Myth it is, for if there was any perversion of the message of Christ found in the early Christian writings, that perversion arose under the influence of other parts of that message as reported in these same authoritative works. So much of what romantics have excluded from their views of Jesus' true words, rejecting the emphasis upon faith instead of good works, the doctrine of sin and its redemption through Christ, the apocalyptic preachments, the assumption of an eternal reality on a different plane from that of existence, the denigration of flesh and the senses, the assertion of authority, all these are as much in the discourses of Jesus in the Gospels as are his expressions of love, kindness, gentleness, and sometimes humility. As early as we know it, Christianity was

*34* Salvation, the Last Judgment, paradise and the miseries of the damned became central in Christian thought. This polyptych by Rogier van der Weyden (1400–1464) illustrates the vigor which the conception exercised in later paintings as well as in the writings of the early church fathers. (Hospice at Beaune)

infected with the long-standing hostility to the everyday world, the world accessible to the senses and significant to the body. The non-rational, mystical aspect of Hellenism which was so much part of philosophy in the writings of Plato and which survived the onslaught of the science of Aristotle and the materialism of Epicurus to lodge, somehow, even in Stoicism, was given an even more vital role to play in human history through Christianity. Whether these early Christian writings received this orientation through Hellenized Judaism or directly from Hellenism in the creation of the first Christian texts in Greek, it is impossible to say. In any case, even if the immediate origins of this conceptualization of reality are uncertain, its effects on the texts and on human thought are clear. For almost a thousand years, the central concerns of human thought would not be the things of this world and what could be understood and done about them, but the nature of the next and the manner in which it could be reached.

# 31

# The core of Hellenism

*Plutarch, Christianity,
and the ideas which persisted*

In the first century, Greeks living in the territories under Roman control could look forward to the future with some confidence. No longer were generals sent out from Italy against Mithridates, only to end up fighting one another and requisitioning vast sums from the cities to do it, and their troops no longer swept over the land like locusts. The economic recovery allowed by peace was enhanced by Augustus' administrative reforms and the construction projects which the emperors and their friends undertook in the cities, and all the provincials benefited from the ready cash which the now solvent Rome put in the hands of the soldiers. With the end of the Roman civil wars, city and countryside alike became safer for residents, and Augustus' standing fleet made the Mediterranean safer for those who had to travel. While no Greek leader could hold the hopes with which Mithridates had burst out of Pontus, all could settle for the secure future which Hellenism now seemed to have.

The past century had been terrible for the Greeks. The presence of so many intellectuals in Italy and in Roman-dominated Alexandria shows how uncomfortable the mobile had felt in Greece, Anatolia, or the Levant. Those who could, voted with their feet. By the time Plutarch was writing in the latter half of the first century, he presented the depopulation of Greece as an accepted fact. In one of his philosophic-religious essays, Plutarch's favored explanation for the diminishing numbers of oracular places or agents is "the common scarcity of men which the earlier quarrels and wars have brought about,"[1] of which Greece had the greatest share.

But now that the troubles were over, times were good. Although no Greek city had any importance on the international scene or more power than was necessary to keep its streets clean and its festivals going, Plutarch thought well of the political situation which tightly restricted the ambitions of civic leaders, an attitude no doubt due in part to the prosperity of his family and his own dignity at the shrine of Apollo in Delphi. He also thought well enough of the ruling authority of Rome, and condemned city leaders who "rouse the multitude, nonsensically exhorting imitation of the actions, thoughts and activities of their forefathers, which are not compatible with current times and circumstance."[2] Almost a century of history gave him good reason to abandon any expectation of political life for Greeks apart from civic, honorary, or administrative service under the Romans. By the time he was born, Augustus was long dead, his settlement firmly in place. Plutarch knew Nero's regime; the emperor's devotion to things Greek was more impressive to him than to the Romans who observed Nero's vicious criminality. Plutarch saw how, even after that emperor's assassination, the strength of Roman institutions meant the continuance of imperial power under Vespasian, who put administration on an even firmer footing. Plutarch lived through Domitian's attack on the philosophers, which he must have viewed with mixed feelings; those attacked were Stoics, who followed a creed that Plutarch didn't like at all, but still they were philosophers and ought to have been respected.

He travelled to Italy and visited Rome, and his old age took him into the reign of Hadrian, another Hellenophile who had much greater success than Nero, with an enduring reputation as one of the "five good emperors" of the second century. The signs of recovery and better times to come were hard to miss. The optimism natural to the prosperous could be reinforced by the age, and Plutarch's writing shows his inclination to have faith both in the ability of men to improve their characters and the likelihood that some will actually do so.

It is not Plutarch's optimism alone which is a creature of the recovery. His massive outpouring of writing derived from the confidence that Hellenism remained an important force in the world. His collection of parallel lives of famous Greeks and Romans uses the examples of great men of the past to teach moral lessons, but they are moral lessons based on what Plutarch took to be the continuing validity of Platonic thought. His other works, a dauntingly large collection of essays known as the *Moralia* – some good, some bad, some interesting, others dull, and some even falsely attributed to him – serve as a kind of library of Hellenism. With philosophy there are essays in history, biography, and literary criticism. His interests led him to write of Roman religious antiquities, the myth and cult of Isis and Osiris, numerology, obscure facts about the shrine of Delphi, and many other details of history and religion. His philosophical works range from serviceable little efforts like *On Not Borrowing* and *Advice on Political Activity*, to more technical studies of Plato's *Timaeus*, or physical and biological speculation in *On the Face which Appears in the Orb of the Moon* and *Whether Land or Sea Animals Are More intelligent*. In all this he shows detailed familiarity with the doctrines of Plato, Aristotle, the Epicureans, Stoics, and later Academics, and a wide range of theories and propositions in physics, mechanics, optics, biology, astronomy, geometry, and mathematics. He emphasizes or decorates his points with passages from all the great classics of Greek literature, either remembering the texts themselves or having seen apt phrases in compendia. His own reading probed into all the significant books composed before his time, and his writing had almost the scope of an Aristotle.

But not the originality. Even with all the losses in our Greek texts, we can usually come up with earlier examples of any concept he puts forth. His loyal reiteration of ideas he has found in his books may be a typical example of Greek conservatism, but it may also be due to the omnipresent problem of the scholar, with so many ideas from other people that he has no room for any of his own. Plutarch packs in so much that a large number of the entries in collections of "fragments" of earlier writers on physics, astronomy, biology, and the life are dug out of the rolling hills of his prose, and without his great output, we would be much the worse off in understanding the evolution of all the manifold branches of philosophy and science.

Some of what he tells us about his forerunners in philosophy is simply informative, while his own intellectual standpoint emerges from other remarks, like this comment about Socrates' accomplishment:

> Receiving philosophy full of phantasmas and myths and superstitions from Pythagoras and his group, and in complete Bacchic frenzy from Empedocles, he made it accustomed to use wisdom in connection with everyday activities and to seek it with controlled argument.[3]

Plutarch detested superstition, the conventional fears that meteorological phenomena, odd zoological freaks, and the like might bode ill or well for people. He devoted a whole essay, *On Superstition*, to an attack on what were, in fact, very common views among the Greeks which reflect the non-rational side of Greek religion, taken up with cult attention to the gods to avoid their displeasure, to propitiate demons, to attempt to turn aside the threats of portents. Plutarch completely rejects the idea that divinity can be the cause of evil or be tyrannical, he derides as superstition the anthropomorphic iconography of the gods, and he characterizes the fear of evils pursuing a man after death as

> making fear longer-lasting than life and tacking on to death the notion of eternal evils. . . . Some deep gates of Hades open, and rivers of fire and rivulets of Styx are mixed together, and darkness is filled with multifantastiform images bringing horrible visions and agonizing sounds, and along with these, judges and chastisers and chasms and inmost depths loaded with an infinity of miseries.[4]

Plutarch's cool, intellectual religion would have none of this. To him, divinity was the Platonic conception of god as a "pattern of all goods." It is a divine force which works in ways which may not always be clear at a given time, but which are basically understandable to humanity, and follow the same principles of right and wrong in the pursuit of moral virtue.

Throughout his work Plutarch writes on the assumption that the human virtues – the everyday virtues of honesty, temperance, courage, frugality, and the like – suit this world and the cosmos. For the most part, there is no metaphysical justification of virtue; it is convenient and advantageous in itself. In a curious little work, *How to Gain Benefit from Enemies*, he shows how the inclination to avoid being a target for one's opponents helps to induce one to follow a life of virtue, and thus enemies are useful in providing lessons in one's faults. The work is particularly noteworthy in urging kindness and generosity to enemies, who are thus beneficial in providing the opportunity for the exercise of that virtue. It contains a praise of "Christian" generosity which goes beyond most Greek ideas of human kindness, and even passes the biblical notion of helping one's enemy in order to "heap coals of fire" on his head. But again, there is no abstract or transcendent justification for this kindness. Plutarch recommends it because it is useful, beneficial in bringing good repute.

In most ways Plutarch was a typical Greek intellectual, and his work shows most of the characteristics of Hellenism as it had evolved over the centuries. Untouched by Christianity, but imbued with all the ideas of Greek writers in all fields, his writing focused mostly on the rationalistic tradition of Greek thought without completely rejecting some of its more mystical aspects. Basic to his ideology, as to that of Hellenism generally, is a respect and affection for humanity, an inclination to accept humankind with all its imperfections as the best and most important thing in the cosmos. He even touches on the most extreme, if rare, expressions of Greek egalitarianism, in *The Symposium of the Seven Wise Men*, an imaginative account of the witty and wide-ranging conversation of the seven sages of Greece who go to dinner at the house of Periander, tyrant of Corinth. At one point, as each offers one piece of advice for a ruler, Solon, who, in character, had advised the monarch to convert his rule into a democracy, defends the Athenian position:

> "and indeed," he said, "the Athenians still listen to one herald and one ruler, the law, having a democracy. Now you are terrific at perceiving the meanings of crows and jackdaws, but you don't hear sharply the voice of equality."[5]

Democracy as equality is not very strongly stated, but then, in most Greek thought equality was not the fundamental characteristic of democratic Constitutions. Plutarch even presents the suggestion of economic egalitarianism, for, as the wise men each offer one suggestion for best preserving democracy. Thales said that the best democracy was the one "having its citizens neither too rich nor too poor."[6]

These were ideas which had erupted in the administration of Athens in the late fifth century BC, but they had not played much of a part in political Hellenism at any time afterwards. They were not a significant part of Plutarch's thought either, for he, like most Greeks of his time, was concerned with the philosophy and principles of individual happiness and virtue rather than of statecraft. The history of Greece had made earlier Greek political ideas obsolete, perhaps even dangerous in some cases. Arguments over the superiorities of monarchy, aristocracy, and democracy in the writings of Herodotus, Aristotle, Polybius, and others were irrelevant to the real political scene; Plato's political thought had never been taken up; and Isocratean ideas of a union of all Greek states in a great crusade would have brought Roman repression.

Certainly the evanescing political power of the Greek cities had its effect on ideology and philosophy, but there is no doubt that the developing tradition from Socrates on had given each generation more to think and write about. After Aeschylus, Herodotus, Sophocles, and Thucydides, there was a much more formal approach to the discussion and study of ideas once Socrates had established the pursuit of philosophy as a discipline. With Plato's Academy, Isocrates' school, and later, Aristotle's Lyceum, Zeno's Stoa, and Epicurus' garden, Athens throve on disputation and polemic, and each succeeding generation produced more of both, verbally and in writing. The discipline and the schools spilled out of Attica, out of Greece to cross the Mediterranean, south and east to Egypt and the Levant, westwards to Italy, Spain, and the Maghreb. A full 500 years after Socrates, they handed over to Plutarch a Hellenism rich in a great variety of approaches to the study of the universe, the earth and its creatures, human society, psychology, and ethics.

This was a much wider world, and gave scope to the scientific and naturalistic interests of those who wanted to investigate its wonders. One of these was the Roman Pliny, who carried on that aspect of Hellenism much more than his younger contemporary, Plutarch. As his nephew tells us, the elder Pliny perished in the course of his too-curious approach to the erupting Mount Vesuvius in 79, his interest in natural phenomena too great to let him miss viewing this extraordinary and terrible phenomenon closer at hand. He left his nephew and the safety of his ship, went ashore to risk the sparks, pumice, and soot belching from the crater, and never returned.

He left behind his great work on natural history. Following the Aristotelian writings in scope, but not the master's analytical grouping according to function, he recorded a vast amount of data on both animals and plants. Like Plutarch, he made great use of compendia which presented information which had accumulated over the centuries, but unlike the Greek, Pliny's exclusive focus on natural history meant that he put down just about everything he knew or could find in his sources. The work is a demonstration of the amount known or thought to be known about the world in all its reaches and details. Although written in Latin, the *Natural History* is very much in the tradition of Greek scientific writing as it had evolved over the centuries to delve into all the physical, geographical, astronomical, and biological phenomena accessible to human examination and analysis. It brought to the readers of Latin in the west the culling of the work of generations of Greek writers in one whole area of science, just as Cicero had done for much of philosophy. And like Cicero's writing, Pliny's served as a basis of knowledge for a long time for those who read only Latin.

Latin writers like Pliny and the Stoic Seneca illustrate the influence Hellenism had on Romans, and the use that was made of it. Neither contributed much, if anything, that was new, but for both Romans, as for Plutarch, the riches of the tradition were adequate to answer the problems they posed, to provide, reworked in their own styles and with their own emphases, guides for life in the new and expanded world of the Roman Empire. That Hellenism, even if we judge it only by what has survived to our own time, was not only varied in scope and approach, but also often expressed uncommonly deep and perceptive insights into human nature and man's condition. Even literature intended for popular consumption like the epic and Athenian tragedy often wrapped exciting narrative and drama around a core of ideas which communicated certain attitudes about human behavior and the problems which produced it. None, of course, was propagandistic in the sense of attempting to inculcate an idea or a program, but they were strongly ideological in the sense that they expressed concepts, often fundamental concepts, which were part of Hellenism and molded it for the future. Even contradictory ideas and principles were expressible, and tragedy in particular often built dramatic action around the conflict between two principles, both of which were part of the tradition and each of which would have been endorsed by some of the viewers.

Athenian tragedy was only one of the vehicles which carried Hellenism. There were fundamental opinions about human knowledge, how it is possible and even whether it can exist, rooted in the questionings of Sophists of the fifth century BC. Again, Greeks lived with contradictory views. At one extreme was Protagoras' assertion that knowledge is possible only in human terms, with its implication that knowledge itself is a human phenomenon; at the other extreme was Platonism, which asserted that knowledge was a transcendent perception of eternal verities. For many, that approach was not useful, and Aristotle's endorsement of sense perception, which was followed by Stoics and others who asserted that sense perception was all we have, persisted through Hellenism alongside the continuing Platonic categorization of the senses as subject to deception and productive of only a collection of opinions which have no solid grounding in truth.

Tensions of that sort were characteristic of Hellenism for much of its history. Athenians who were familiar with epic and Sophoclean notions that people were buffeted by ill-understood forces, and could measure their performance better by their response to the uncontrolled cosmos than by success in it, could also support the teachings of a Protagoras, who did not seem to worry about the problem in that way. It was the same society which pragmatically told the Melians that they were wasting their future in trusting in the gods, and at other times prosecuted Anaxagoras for impiety and hounded Alcibiades from command on suspicion of desecration of sacred images. While the rationalist position may have been that of a small minority, and the god-fearing – superstitious, Plutarch would say – piety that of the masses, the two positions always coexisted in Hellenism. The subliminal tensions account for some of the vibrancy of tragedy and other poetry. Philosophy at times attempted to mediate between the ideas and actions of popular religion and the most abstract formulations of some thinkers, but even popularized, the ideologies of the philosophers never overcame the attractions of the old and new cults. At the most, philosophy might, over a long period, affect the conceptualization of divinity, but it never had much effect on the flourishing centers of sacrifice and healing. Despite the most vigorous attacks by cynics and the insistence of Epicureans that the gods had no care for man, the old-time religion blended with the new in all the conventional activities by which Greeks tried to influence the actions of the gods. There was still plenty of "superstition" for Plutarch to complain about.

Early Christians saw Plutarch as an ally in their struggle against pagan ideas. It was specifically pagan cult that they opposed, and Plutarch's categorization of some of it as superstition seemed to give confirmation of Christian belief on the part of one who had no involvement with either Jewish or Christian groups. His exposition of the idea that the daemons, or demigods, could die even seemed to coincide with the belief held by some Christians that Jesus had actually destroyed some of these devils who had inhabited the world up to his own time. In addition to his condemnation of pagan belief, Plutarch had the extra attraction to Christians of his high moral tone, the frequent bald reiteration of so many of the virtues which the Christians were incorporating into their own ethics. He provided a kind of round-up of all the ethical values and arguments for their usefulness and validity which had developed over centuries of Hellenism, and his belief that divinity can be the cause only of good coincided with Christian confidence in the nature of God, even though it left unsolved the problem of the existence of evil in the world which Greek metaphysics and ethical speculation had worked so hard to resolve. Christians could also sense in Plutarch a brother under the skin in his Platonism, a tradition which had so influenced Philo and which was infusing Christian philosophy as it developed under the guidance of Hellenized Christians and later generations of Greek-speaking Christians and new converts among the Hellenized.

Pliny, Plutarch, the Christians, and many others east and west in the Mediterranean, peoples of many different places and of widely varying stations in life shared a Hellenism which had become common to all by the first century. There were different choices among the varying traditions of Hellenism – rationalism, mysticism, and philosophical dogmatisms like Platonism, Epicureanism, and Stoicism, but the selection was made as among contemporary alternatives. To Plutarch and others of his day Hellenism was by no means a tradition of the past, and they were quite different from writers of the next generation, who often wrote in a self-conscious attempt to reproduce the "classical" Greek of early Athens. The competing philosophical schools were very much alive in Plutarch's day, and, as some of his own writing shows quite clearly, the differences were deep and strongly felt. But for all the differences, all schools shared the same basic assumptions about the human condition which was characteristic of Hellenism. All agreed that human life was ameliorable, even if only by controlling personal responses to circumstances. All agreed that human life ought, in fact, to be made better, and all the philosophical schools, at least, brought their proffered improvement down to the level of the individual. There was also great confidence in the promise of words and argument: writing, discussion, and debate could lead teachers and followers of philosophy to a better understanding of humankind and the cosmos and the relationship between the two. All this presupposed a healthy optimism about the potential of human reason, for even the Platonists with their distrust of the senses believed that reason was the instrument to be used in the apprehension of the ideal forms.

Out of these attitudes grew a number of important ideas. By Plutarch's time, Greek intellectuals were agreed on the legitimacy of individual happiness as a human goal. Many imposed on government, even the emperor at Rome, a responsibility to act as the servant of the people rather than their master. The maintenance of the Augustan achievement of peace and prosperity was, in this construction of affairs, the task for which the great imperial power was properly wielded. The emperor was not to use his position and wealth in the pursuit of luxury, gluttony, personal aggrandizement, or other vices but was to be a model of hard work, restraint, charity, temperance, and beneficence to all the peoples of the realm. It was not a mission to which an emperor like Domitian felt especially called, but the intellectuals persisted.

The analysis of government and society had been a very long-standing concern of Hellenism, and Greeks had sought stability in political and social institutions and worked out reasons for changes and deterioration in constitutional structures. Even those, like Polybius, who saw a certain inevitability to change looked for structures which would resist collapse longest, and, from Aristotle's time on, most had seen the greatest strength in a sharing of power among the different elements in society. These discussions emerged for a city-state mentality which never quite lost the sense of the nature of society as a structure in which all elements had a rightful share, so that suppression and oppression created pressures for change which would always produce revolution. The city-state mentality did not serve the situation of the world-state of Rome, but the person of the emperor could still be incorporated into the general political framework of Hellenism when he was seen as a kind of father-figure looking after the whole society.

The philosophical schools had been playing around for some time with the universality of humankind, and Cicero himself had brought the idea into Latin.

It admirably suited the world as it took shape after the time of Augustus, and it fitted the Christian conception of humanity united under God the Father. It also began to appear more and more appropriate for the people in the empire as the citizenship spread to all corners and all provinces. Plutarch and his family, St Paul, and countless other individuals and families of all sorts of ethnic groups could count themselves citizens, either as a regular grant after military service or as an honor or reward for some particular action or service. After the Julio-Claudian emperors who came from Roman families, even the imperial power was no longer held only by this group, for Vespasian's accession to power brought Italians into the picture, and the Spanish Trajan showed that residents of the provinces need not consider themselves excluded. The advent of the Roman world-state gave political unity to that enormous portion of humankind living within its borders. After the next century, however, and the service ethic of Marcus Aurelius, the political ideas of earlier Greek philosophers ceased to have any real relevance to government, and concepts of balanced power, mixed Constitutions, and autonomy and sovereignty of citizens fell into disuse.

Another idea from Hellenism, however, was gaining ever greater force. From Socrates' first proposal of the supreme value of the improvement of the soul, that aspect of the human being was a major focus of philosophers' attentions. Plato's permanent mark on philosophy in his treatment of the soul was not just the recording of Socrates' views on the matter, or even the insistence on the soul's immortality which may or may not have gone back to the master. It is rather the new dimensions in his treatment of the soul with his elaborate myths in *Timaeus* and elsewhere, portraying the individual souls flitting up from the world and, after suitable refinement and purgation, down again to occupy another body in a new life. While Aristotle's approach to understanding the soul dealt with function, that is, the manner in which the soul – whatever it is – perceives and learns, the Platonic hypothesis of an entity which retained individual identification through more than one life retained an attraction and was repeated. While we do not have the works of later writers in the Academy, and the issue was not significant for Philo's exegesis of Scripture, Plutarch again is our evidence for the continuation of the tradition. More than once, and not just in passages discussing Plato's work, Plutarch gives a myth of the soul's migration to another plane, or to the moon, there to be punished or purified before its return to life on earth. Of the Christian use of this concept of the soul little more need be said than that Christian thought moved to adopt the Platonic kind of immortality and made the saving of the soul the primary object of Christian act and belief.

As much as was lost of Greek rationalism and practicality with the domination of Platonism in philosophy and its preservation in Christianity, the sense of individual personality for each human being was carried on in the notion of the personal soul. The notion of the individual soul passing from this life, into immortality, with its own personality and its owns sins and good works still attached, with its aim of happiness in the survival of the discrete individual soul, became characteristic of western religious thought. In the many centuries of western history, if nothing else had remained from the Greeks, this idea of the eternal existence of each of us carried enough of Hellenism's value of humanity to mark western society fundamentally.

# 32

# The future of the past
## *Hellenism and humanity*

From the therapy of the soul to the graduated income tax is a long stretch. The society which has created the latter, however, ultimately derives from the one which produced the former, and has grown through centuries according to ideas and values which have their roots in the ancient world of Greece, Rome, Judaea, and the Christian Mediterranean. It is possible to look back over the 2000 years which have passed since the beginning of Christian times to show how these values molded the ideas of churches, nations, and philosophers, how the ebb and flow of regard for the human species interacted with the development of institutions and activities to create our world. I am not suggesting some kind of sociobiology of the intellect which argues that there is a "genetic" relationship between the seminal ideas of society and the growth of social structures, but rather, that human institutions are built on assumptions about human nature and are based on values, whether stated or tacit, so that these fundamental presuppositions about humanity determine the future once they are laid down.

When early Christians debated the relative value of faith and good works, they were reproducing in a new area of thought the long-standing Hellenic antithesis between the pursuit of absolute truth by reason, and reconciliation with appearances according to the senses. If Christianity could derive human value out of humankind's relation to the creator, along a Philonic tradition which exalted the human by its similarity to God, it also had to respond to the aspect of Hellenism which dealt with the whole populace of a particular unit as the aggregate which made up sovereignty, not as a servant mass. As early as we have information, political Hellenism recognized divisions among the populace, and the theory of social organization developed in response to the realities which that recognition encouraged. The realities were the civic conflicts of an often savage nature; encouragement was the acknowledgement that different social and economic groups had entitlements against others merely by the fact of their membership in the state. So long as political Hellenism remained important to the administration of affairs, that is, down

372

into the period of Roman control of the east, political thinkers debated the levels of power to be allocated to the several divisions of society. Even Roman constitutional practice was forced into this mode of analysis when subjected to the scrutiny of a Greek like Polybius.

This was not the individualism often imagined in romantic portrayals of Greek society. There is very little to support a notion that *particular* individuals were seen as endowed with specific or even general rights against the society; but individuals as members of society were entitled to participate in the society's activities. *Ad hoc* decisions for the general welfare might perfectly well override any individual's desire for life; at the same time, whole segments of society might agitate quite violently to give their members a greater share in the overall general wealth. Athens carried this idea furthest, but many other cities faced the same issue. Political theory that dealt with matters as they seemed to be then attempted to delineate some principles on which power and wealth could be allocated to offer stability to civic institutions. Even with the rapid spread of monarchical institutions after Alexander, political theorists held to a doctrine that called upon the kings to be the "best" men, to rule with the welfare of the populace as their goal. That notion was even at the heart of so Utopian a scheme as Plato's, which aimed at leadership by the philosopher who could perceive the transcendent forms through reason.

Although a short look into the future in AD 100 would reveal a society in which the monarchical principle was at one of its heights in human history, and which would show a tendency in philosophy and religion to encourage self-realization independent of social structures, the long-range view which we can take today makes it clear that the social aspect of Hellenism has resurfaced time and time again. In fact, in recent centuries it has been pressure from those convinced by this aspect of our traditions that has made for the most startling changes in western society, from the time of the social contract libertarians of the seventeenth and eighteenth centuries to the modern advocates of mutuality in community. Certainly it is hard to imagine how the Enlightenment, eighteenth-century political liberalism, or even the Industrial Revolution could have emerged from Plato's reasoned search for the good, or in the absence of a tradition which included ideas about the everyday world ranging from political accommodation of the poor to Cicero's willingness to act on the basis of probability.

A thousand years of Hellenism evolved a number of approaches to the problems of human life, on both social and personal issues. But because Greek perceptions were almost always couched intellectually and verbally, rather than, say, by meditation, they were readily communicable, not only to other Greeks but to future generations as well. It would be fair to say that the Homeric idea of the human condition always remained a part of Hellenism, just as did the Socratic search for right understanding, once they were enunciated. So too, as long as Homer is a part of our education, or tragedies or Plato or the Bible are read, the attitudes about ourselves which inhere in them will continue to mold our society. The influence is even more pervasive than that, for almost all writers and thinkers from St Paul to Sartre were raised on an intellectual diet of Hellenism, so that even if future generations forget the ancient past, they are still rooted in its ideas, reworked and reproduced by more modern writers. This is no less true of those convinced by the highly abstract and symbolic modes of expression of modern anthropological attempts to demonstrate an archetypal human social universality by the evidence collected in a tradition of Aristotelian observation. However useful these strategies of research may be for understanding cultures other than our own,[1] they and we still perceive human acts and their explanations within the parameters of a conceptualization of humanness imposed by the tradition established by Hellenism. We see what we are, in a sense, or we see the way we think.

"The way we think" has been in large part the focus of this investigation, as I have presented some fundamental aspects of western ideology as they have emerged through Greek and Roman history. Our way of thinking about ourselves and our institutions has been decisively molded by the basic intuitions about the human being which are expressed by texts like the *Iliad*, the *Oresteia*, Plato's *Republic*, and other ancient works, and we understand these works in terms of the conceptions which in part they themselves laid down. If westerners live out their lives in a world separate from the gods or God, if, ultimately, we have made of Christianity a religion of this world and not of apocalyptic renewal, if we retain our anthropocentric orientation in spite of the evidence of the almost invisible minuteness of our world and galaxy in the universe, we do so because our heritage thus far precludes us from thinking in any other way. Inherent in this conception of humanity and society is a tacit acceptance of a fundamental tension between what is good for humanity and the disregard of humankind apparent in the workings of nature, a perception which had been with us since the *Iliad* and which has provided the starting-point for much of our social and personal ethical thought. It is also Hellenism which has provided us with the concern to resolve the apparent contradiction between what seems good for the group and what seems good for the powerful few, the old *nomos–physis* controversy, which Nietzsche thought to resolve by choosing *physis*. It is inherent in our ideological nature not to choose either irretrievably, however, so that we prefer, rather, to deny the view that "humbugs and dilettantes have always tried to mix the two conceptions."[2] Sophocles' *Antigone* still prevents us from choosing sides with conviction.

So we often waver, in our moral judgments and in our social institutions, between differing conceptions of what is best for us. But whether we select a Nietzschean optimism by which "what is good for General Motors is good for the country," or endorse Roosevelt's ideal of governing so as to increase the material well-being of those who have little rather than those who have much, we operate within the parameters which constrain our goals to human welfare. And in the debate, the best in us, like the best in Hellenism, tends to come down on the side of Roosevelt: not only the Socratic and Athenian answer, but that of the theoreticians of politics and kingship, who argue that the whole populace is the sovereign institution, and that the governors must govern in the interests of the whole, not the powerful. Greeks, it seems, had no idea of the "trickle-down" theory of economics, which only seems really to work in periods of rapid economic expansion.

We will also be pulled between the extremes of absolutism and relativism, between a Platonic conception of the good which represents perfection, perceptible by humans through their reason, and an Epicurean insistence that the good, and justice, are merely human agreement to abstain from mutual harm. Today, as in much of antiquity, the Platonic conception probably dominates, at least for philosophers, theologians, and some social planners, but again, the inheritance of the past leaves us with the Platonic confidence that to some – experts, today, not philosopher kings – answers are accessible, and our ideology includes the notion of approaching the truth.

For the foreseeable future, then, we are stuck with our heritage. Some of us will continue to strive for the absolute good by reason and argument, words and not inspiration, while others will insist on making the best of the world as it looks to us. But even these disparate aspects of Hellenism share not only the Greek reliance on words, thought, and debate, they also stem from the Hellenic attitudes toward the cosmos which place humanity at the center, and which assume a human nature which is not inherently evil. Milton's reworking of pagan epic to Christian ends still retains enough Hellenic self-confidence that "I may assert Eternal Providence, and justify the ways of God to men."[3] Teilhard de Chardin begins his study of humanity with the remark that without the assumptions of "The pre-eminent significance of man in nature, and the organic nature of mankind . . . I do not see how it is possible to give a full and coherent account of the phenomenon of man."[4] Humanity at the center, a part of nature, and the human being no more nor less than a natural creature come to us from Hellenism. To the notion of the fall from grace we oppose the Hellenism of the perfectibility of humanity. The two ideas and the tension between them have molded our society. Without them both, we would not be what we are. We may choose the first on faith, but we cannot deny the validity of the other ideal.

# Maps

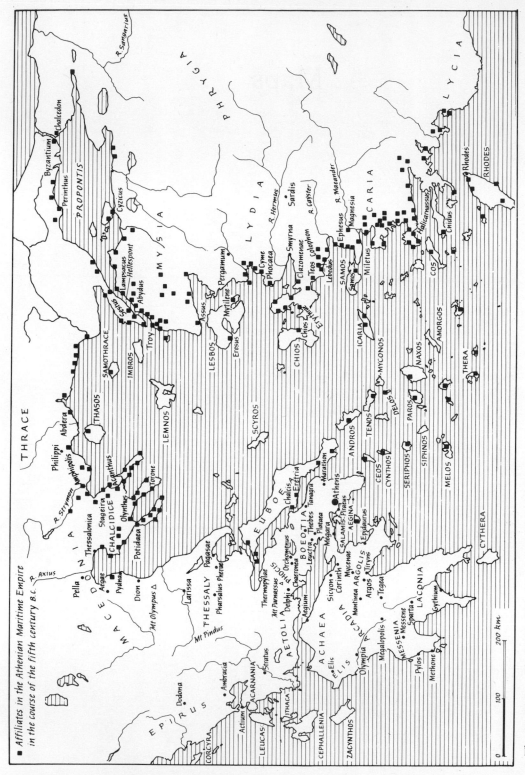

1 The Aegean world, showing the cities controlled by Athens

■ Affiliates in the Athenian Maritime Empire
in the course of the fifth century B.C.

378

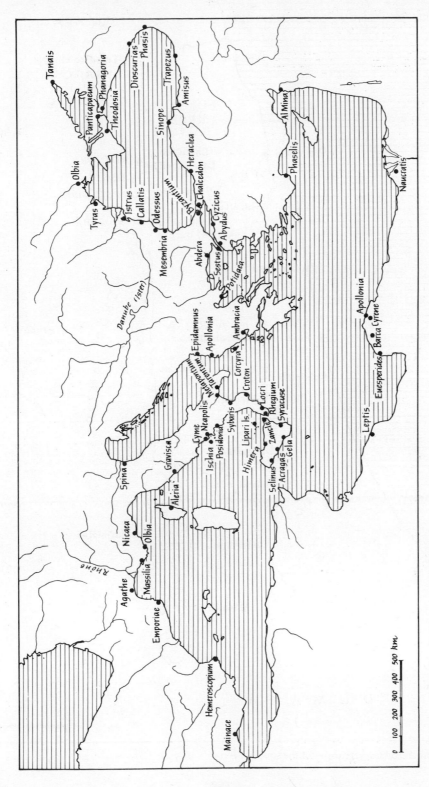

2 The scope of Greek colonization 750–550 BC

0  100  200  300  400  500 km

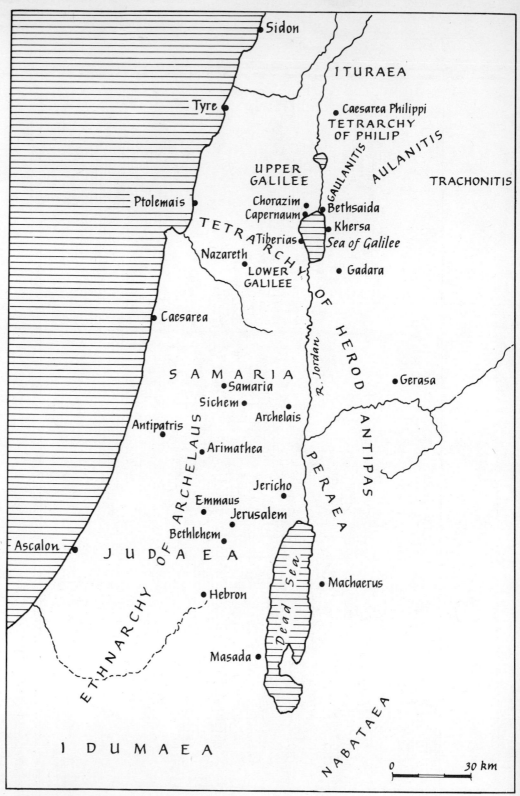

*3* Roman Judaea: territories of the sons of Herod

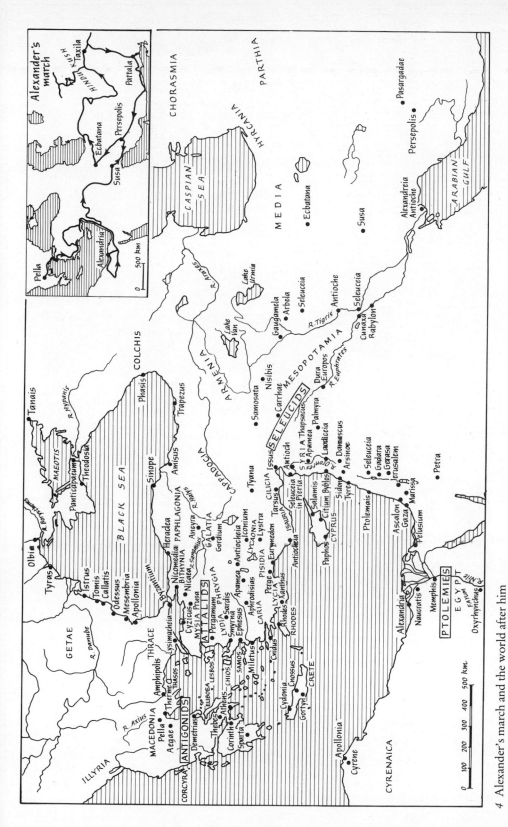

4 Alexander's march and the world after him

Note: The extent of city founding by Alexander's successors is suggested by including a number of cities which they named after themselves and their consorts.

# Chronology of people
# and events BC 1000–AD 100

| BC | Italy and the west | Greece, the Aegean, and Anatolia | Palestine, Syria, and Egypt |
|---|---|---|---|
| 1000 | | End of palace-centered Bronze Age kingdoms | David king of Israel to c. 975<br>Reign of Solomon c. 975–935<br><br>c. 935, southern kingdom of Judah left to Rehoboam after separation of Israel under Jeroboam |
| 900 | | | |
| 875 | | | Ahab king of Israel<br>Prophets Elijah and Elisha |
| 800 | 814 – traditional date of founding Carthage | Homeric epics<br>Hesiod<br><br>776 – traditional date for establishment of Olympic Games | |
| | Foundation of Syracuse in Sicily, Sybaris in south Italy; Naples colonized | | |
| 750 | 753 – traditional date for founding of Rome | Colonization of Chalicidice<br>Movement into Hellespont | Activity of Isaiah<br>Fall of Samaria and Israel to Assyria (721) |
| 700 | Period of kings of Rome (753–509) | Development of new, heavy (hoplite) armor<br>Tyrannies in many Greek cities (700–600) | |
| 675 | Zaleucus lawgiver at Locri, south Italy | "Lycurgan" reforms at Sparta | Psammetichus king of Egypt 664–610 |

| Date | | | |
|---|---|---|---|
| 650 | | Beginnings of Greek colonies in the Black Sea area | Foundation of Cyrene in North Africa; Establishment of Greeks at Naucratis c. 625; Activity of Jeremiah |
| 625 | | Traditional date of 621 for first Athenian lawcode of Draco | Discovery of Book of Deuteronomy (621); Defeat of Egypt at Carchemish by Nebuchadnezzar of Babylon (605); Judah a vassal of Babylon |
| 600 | Massilia (Marseille) founded by Phocaeans | 594 – traditional date for the Athenian year designated as the archonship of Solon; 585 – an eclipse of the sun which the philosopher Thales is said to have predicted | Final fall of Jerusalem in 586; Beginning of the Exile |
| 575 | | Poetic, and possibly political, activity of Solon; Reign of Croesus of Lydia (560–546) | Reign of Amasis of Egypt (570–526); Reign of Cyrus of Persia (559–530) |
| 550 | Western Greeks defeated by Carthaginians and Etruscans (540) | Peisistratus establishes tyranny at Athens (546); Homeric epics written down; Activity of Theognis of Megara; Defeat of Croesus by Cyrus (546); Ionian Greeks subject to Persia (545) | Liberation and restoration of Jews by Cyrus of Persia (538) |

| BC | Italy and the west | Greece, the Aegean, and Anatolia | Palestine, Syria, and Egypt |
|---|---|---|---|
| | Activity of Pythagoras in south Italy | Beginning of tragic performances in Athens | Cambyses king of Persia (530–522) Persian conquest of Egypt |
| | | Death of Peisistratus (528) | |
| 525 | Etruscans defeated at Cumae (524) | | Darius king of Persia (521–486) |
| | | | Building of second Temple in Jerusalem (520–515) |
| | | | Activity of prophets Haggai and Zechariah |
| | 509 – traditional date of expulsion of kings from Rome and establishment of republic | Expulsion of tyranny from Athens (510) | |
| | Roman treaty with Carthage (508) | Reforms of Cleisthenes (508) | |
| 500 | | Activity of Hecataeus of Miletus (historian) and Heracleitus of Ephesus (philosopher) | Jewish colony at Elephantine, Egypt (papyri dating from 498–399) |
| | | Beginning of revolt of Ionian Greeks from Persia (499); Ionians back under Persia by 493 | |
| | Secession of Roman plebs and grant of concessions to them | Persian attack on Greece Battle of Marathon (490) | Revolt of Egypt from Persia (487–485) Death of Darius, Xerxes king of Persia (486) |
| | Gelon tyrant of Syracuse | Second Persian invasion of Greece; Athens captured; Battle of Salamis (480); Battle of Plataea (479); Persians retreat to Ionia | |
| | | Establishment of Delian League against Persia under Athens' leadership (478) | |
| | | Pindar's first *Olympian* ode (476) | |

475 Syracuse defeats Etruscans at Cumae (474)

Production of Aeschylus' *Persians* (472)

Athenians exercise compulsion on allies, e.g. Carystos and Naxos

Birth of Socrates (*c.* 469)

First victory of Sophocles (468)

Thasos revolts from Delian League and forced back (465); League now really Athenian Empire

Anaxagoras the philosopher arrives in Athens (date disputed)

Ostracism of Cimon from Athens (461)

War between Athens and Sparta (461–451)

*Oresteia* of Aeschylus (458)

*Prometheus Bound* produced (?)

Death of Aeschylus (456)

First production by Euripides (455)

Treasury of League transferred from Delos to Athens (454)

5-year truce between Athens and Sparta (451); Pericles' law defining Athenian citizenship

Palestine under Xerxes of Persia (486–465) and Artaxerxes I (465–423); Attribution of composition of Job, Proverbs, Song of Songs, Ruth, Malachi, Obadiah, and many Psalms

Revolt against Persia by Egypt Athenian Egyptian campaign (462–454)

Ezra (or, alternatively, as late as 398)

450 Twelve Tables of law at Rome

Beginning of construction of Parthenon (447) Sculpture of Phidias

Revolt of Euboea, generating Pericles' campaigns of 446

Nehemiah; the restoration of the walls

| BC | Italy and the west | Greece, the Aegean, and Anatolia | Palestine, Syria, and Egypt |
|---|---|---|---|
| | | 30 years' peace between Athens and Sparta (445) | |
| | | Activity of Herodotus the historian | |
| | | Protagoras, Hippodamus at Athens | |
| | Athenian foundation of Thurii in south Italy (443) | Pericles dominant in Athens | |
| | | Sophocles treasurer of League (443/2), then general (441/0) | |
| | | Production of Sophocles' *Ajax* and *Antigone* (c. 441) | |
| | | Activity of Sophists in Athens | |
| | | Euripides' *Alcestis* produced (438) | |
| | | Athens excludes Megara from League harbors (432) | |
| | | Outbreak of war between Athens and Sparta (431) | |
| | | Production of Euripides' *Medea* | |
| | | Activity of Socrates (to 399) | |
| | | Production of Sophocles' *Oedipus Tyrannus* and perhaps *Trachinians* | |
| | | Activity of Hippocrates of Cos, physician | |
| | | Death of Pericles (429) | |
| | | *Hippolytus* of Euripides (428) | |
| | | Revolt of Mytilene (428) and recapture of Mytilene and Mytilenean debate in Thucydides (427) | |

| BC | Italy and the west | Greece, the Aegean, and Anatolia | Palestine, Syria, and Egypt |
|---|---|---|---|
| | | Athens surrenders to Sparta (404) Oligarchy (tyranny) of the Thirty established at Athens; political activity of Theramenes and Critias | |
| | | Posthumous production of Sophocles' *Oedipus at Colonus* (401) | |
| | | Xenophon and 10,000 Greek mercenaries join Cyrus the Younger's attack on his brother Artaxerxes, Persian king (401) | Prophet Joel |
| | | | Book of Tobit (5th or 4th century) |
| 400 | | Execution of Socrates (399) Activity of Socrates' students, Antisthenes the Cynic, Aristippus, and Eucleides of Megara, to about mid-century | |
| | Final defeat of Veii (396) and victory of Rome over Etruscans | Activity of Plato (to 347) | |
| | Rome sacked by Gauls (390) | Activity of Isocrates (to 338) | |
| | | Plato's Academy founded (387) | |
| | | Birth of Aristotle (384) | |
| | | Sparta dominant Thebes expels Spartan garrison (379) | |
| | | Second Athenian League founded (378) | |
| 375 | | Thebes defeats Sparta in Battle of Leuctra (371); period of Theban supremacy begins | |
| | Dionysius II tyrant of Syracuse (367) Plato in Syracuse to educate him | Aristotle in Athens to join Academy (367) | |

First plebeian consuls in Rome (366)

Second visit of Plato to Syracuse (361)

Dion, uncle of Dionysius II and pupil of Plato, rules Syracuse (356–354)

350

Timoleon active in Sicily 344–337, ending the tyrannies and defeating the Carthaginians at Crimesus (341)

Rome fights Samnite Wars (343–341, 327–304) and Latin War (340–338) to achieve dominance in central Italy

Thebes wins Battle of Mantinea against Sparta (362)
Death of Epaminondas ends Theban supremacy

Activity of Diogenes the Cynic (to 323)
Philip II king of Macedon (359)
War begins between Athens and Philip (357)

Birth of Alexander the Great (356)
Sacred War, Philip in Central Greece (356–352)

War between Athens and her allies (to 355)

Demosthenes active in Athens

Death of Plato (347); Speusippus head of Academy; Aristotle leaves Athens

Peace of Philorates between Athens and Philip (346)

Aristotle tutor to Alexander the Great (343)

Aristotle leaves Macedonian court (339)

Battle of Chaeronea (338); Philip supreme in Greece

Death of Isocrates (338)

Philip assassinated (336)
Alexander's destruction of Thebes (335)

Beginning of Alexander's march east (334)
Alexander's victory at River Granicus

Approximate date of books of Chronicles, Ezra, Nehemiah

| BC | Italy and the west | Greece, the Aegean, and Anatolia | Palestine, Syria, and Egypt |
|---|---|---|---|
| | | Isis worship attested in Greece | Alexander defeats Darius at Issus (333) |
| | | | Alexander takes Syria and Palestine (332) |
| | | | Alexander founds Alexandria in Egypt (331) |
| | | | Alexander's final victory at Gaugamela (331) and Darius' death (330) |
| | | | Alexander in India (327–325) |
| 325 | | | Callisthenes, Aristotle's nephew, executed (327) |
| | | | Alexander returns to Susa (324) |
| | | | Death of Alexander at Babylon (323) |
| | | Antipater regent in Greece Lysimachus controls Thrace, Antigonus western Anatolia | Ptolemy rules Egypt as satrap |
| | | Death of Aristotle (322) Theophrastus head of Lyceum in Athens | |
| | | | Conference at Triparadeisus (320) ratifies areas of power |
| | | | Antigonus attempts supremacy (320–301) |
| | Agathocles controls Syracuse (317–289) | Murder of Philip III Arrhidaeus (317) | |
| | | Athens under control of Demetrius of Phalerum (317–307) | |
| | | Activity of Crates, Cynic philosopher | |
| | | Activity of Menander | |

| West | Greece / Athens | East |
|---|---|---|
| Agathocles' war with Carthage (311–306) | Polemon becomes head of Academy (314) | Seleucus captures Babylon, beginning Seleucid era (312) |
| | Arrival of Zeno in Athens (ca. 313) | Renewal of agreement on zones of power (311) |
| Agathocles lands in North Africa (310) | Murder of Alexander IV (310) | |
| Romans defeat Etruscans at Lake Vadimo (310) | Demetrius son of Antogonus captures Athens (307) | |
| | Legislation against philosophers at Athens Departure and return of Theophrastus (307–306) | |
| | Epicurus founds school at Athens (306) | Antigonus assumes title of king (306) followed by Demetrius, Ptolemy (305), Seleucus, Lysimachus, Cassander |
| | Zeno's school founded (dated variously) | |
| | Battle of Ipsus (301), death of Antigonus | Activity of Euclid in Alexandria |
| | Death of Cassander (297) | |
| | Demetrius gains control of Macedonia (293) | |
| Plebian assemblies gain decision-making power at Rome | Death of Theophrastus, Straton head of the Lyceum (287) | |
| | Demetrius captured (285) and dies in captivity (283) | Death of Ptolemy I (283) Ptolemy II reigns in Egypt (285–246) |
| | Deaths of Lysimachus and Seleucus (281) | Antiochus I, son of Seleucus, reigns in Syria |
| | Gauls invade Greece (279) | |

300

393

| BC | Italy and the west | Greece, the Aegean, and Anatolia | Palestine, Syria, and Egypt |
|---|---|---|---|
| | Expedition of Pyrrhus of Epirus to south | Antigonus Gonatas, son of Demetrius, repels Gauls and takes rule of Macedon (276) | Activity of Callimachus, Theocritus |
| 275 | Italy to help Greek cities, ended in 275 | | Apollonius of Rhodes in Alexandria |
| | Embassy of Ptolemy to Rome (273) | | Aristarchus and the heliocentric astronomic theory |
| | Surrender of Tarentum in south Italy to Rome (272) Rome dominant from Po to Straits of Messina | Death of Epicurus (271) Death of Polemon, head of the Academy Succession of Crates | |
| | Hiero general, then king at Syracuse (270) | | |
| | | Unsuccessful Athenian war (Chremonidean) against Antigonus Gonatas | Translation activity rendering Hebrew Scriptures in Greek Septuagint |
| | Roman army crosses to Sicily to help Mamertines (264) War with Carthage (264–241) | Death of Zeno (263) Cleanthes head of Stoic school | |
| | | Eumenes (263–241) establishes Pergamum as independent power, and begins architectural and cultural activity there | Composition of Book of Ecclesiastes (300–200) |
| | Activity of Archimedes, mathematician and inventor | | |
| 250 | | Activity of Aratus of Soli, poet; Hieronymus of Cardia, historian | Ptolemy III reigns in Egypt (246–221) Seleucus II reigns in Syria (246–226) Third Syrian War (246–241) |
| | | Expansion of Achaean League under leadership of Aratus | |
| | | Death of Antigonus Gonatas (239) Reign of Demetrius II in Macedon (239–229) | |
| | Romans occupy Corsica and Sardinia (237) Hamilcar lands Carthaginian forces in Spain | Chrysippus succeeds Cleanthes in Stoic school (232) | |

| | Activity of Eratosthenes | | |
|---|---|---|---|
| | | Athens independent of Macedon (228) | |
| | | Rome involved in Illyria | Sicily and Sardinia made Roman provinces (227) |
| 225 | | | |
| | Antiochus III "The Great" reigns in Syria (223–187) | | |
| | Antiochus III in control of Palestine | Philip V king in Macedonia (221) | |
| | Ptolemy III reigns in Egypt (221–204) | Second Illyrian War (219) | |
| | | | Second Carthaginian War begins (218) Hannibal's victories in Italy (218–216) Battle of Cannae (216) |
| | Battle of Raphia (217) returns Palestine to Ptolemaic control | Alliance between Hannibal and Philip V (215 or 214) | |
| | Antiochus' expedition east Seleucid Empire restored Antiochus' return (204) | Rome fights Philip V in First Macedonian War (211–205) | |
| | Ptolemy V king in Egypt (204–181) | | Scipio lands in Africa (204) Hannibal recalled to Carthage (203) Romans defeat Carthage at Zama (202) Carthage surrenders |
| 200 | Aristophanes of Byzantium head of library of Alexandria | Romans defeat Philip V at Cynocephale (197) ending Second Macedonian War (200–197) | |
| | After Battle of Panium (200) Palestine remains under Seleucid control | Flamininus announces "Freedom of the Greeks" at Isthmian Games of 196 | |
| | Composition of Books of Sirach, Ecclesiasticus (c. 200) | Beginning of war between Rome and Antiochus III (192) ended by Roman victory at Magnesia (189) | |

395

| BC | Italy and the west | Greece, the Aegean, and Anatolia | Palestine, Syria, and Egypt |
|---|---|---|---|
| | | Antiochus withdraws from Europe and western Anatolia (188) | Death of Antiochus III (187) Seleucus IV (187–175) and Antiochus IV (175–163) successors |
| | | | Ptolemy VI Philometor king in Egypt (181–145) |
| | | Perseus (179–167) king in Macedon on death of Philip V (179) | |
| 175 | Polybius in Rome as hostage (167) | On conclusion of Third Macedonian War (171–168), Macedon divided into four separate republics (167) | Roman embassy to Egypt, ordering Antiochus IV to end invasion and leave (168) Rebellions in Palestine (169–168) |
| | | | Maccabean revolt brings religious freedom (164) and political independence (142) Period of composition of Book of Daniel |
| | | | Service of Jews in Egypt to Ptolemy VI Philometor; probable period of composition of Letter of Aristeas |
| 150 | Third Carthaginian War (149–146) Carthage razed Africa made a Roman province | Fourth Macedonian War (148) and Achaean War (146) Macedon made into Roman province; sack of Corinth | Ptolemy VIII Euergetes reigns in Egypt (145–116) |
| | Stoic philosopher Panaetius arrives in Rome (144) | | Dispersal of intellectuals from Alexandria |

Serious defeat of Roman army at Numantia, Spain (137)
Tiberius Gracchus tribune at Rome (133) and is killed in following year

John Hyrcanus high priest in Jerusalem (135)

Attalus III wills Pergamum to Rome (133); it is made into province of Asia (129)

125

Gaius Gracchus tribune at Rome (123–122)

Southern Gaul made into province (121)

Ptolemy VIII reconciled with Cleopatra II (118)
Amnesty decreed
Turmoil in Egypt after death of Ptolemy VIII in 116

Polybius dies after 118

Movement of Cimbri and Teutones south (111), Teutones in Gaul, Cimbri in Spain

War with Jugurtha in North Africa (111–105)

107: first of Marius' six consulships
Marius reforms the Roman army

Birth of Cicero (106)

Roman defeats by Cimbri (105)

Marius defeats Cimbri and Teutones (102)

100

Approximate date of Lucretius' birth
War between Rome and Italian allies (91–88)

Approximate date of Isis hymns of Isidorus

Sulla's march on Rome (88)
Civil war in Rome

Outbreak of war against Mithridates VI of Pontus (88), leading to Sulla's campaigns in Greece and Asia Minor

Marius seizes Rome (87)

Death of Marius (86)

Sulla captures Athens (86)

397

| BC | Italy and the west | Greece, the Aegean, and Anatolia | Palestine, Syria, and Egypt |
|---|---|---|---|
| | Civil war at Rome (83–82) on Sulla's return | End of Mithridatic War (85) Philosopher Posidonius active at Rhodes | King Tigranes of Armenia annexing remaining Seleucid territory in Cilicia and Syria |
| | Sulla dictator at Rome (82–80) Sullan reforms and legislation Cicero's earliest extant speech War against Sertorius in Spain (80–72) | Bithynia bequeathed to Rome (80) Activity of Antiochus of Ascalon as head of Academy in Athens and in Alexandria Cicero in Athens (79) hears Antiochus at Academy, in Rhodes meets Posidonius | |
| | Sulla retires (78) Cicero returns to Rome (76) | | |
| 75 | | Mithridates renews war, defeats a Roman army (74) | |
| | | Roman victories over Mithridates (72) Mithridates in Armenia | |
| | Pompey and Crassus consuls (70) Birth of Virgil Cicero's speeches against Verres | | |
| | Birth of Horace (65) | Mithridates back in Pontus (66) | |
| | Cicero consul (63) Caesar pontifex maximus Conspiracy of Catiline Birth of Augustus | Pompey creates provinces of Bithynia, Cilicia, Crete Death of Mithridates (63) | Pompey's reorganization of the east terminating Seleucid monarchy (64), Syria made a province, independent Jewish state ended. Hyrcanus governs as "High Priest" |
| | "First Triumvirate" – Pompey, Crassus, Caesar (60) | | |

| | | Ptolemy XII Auletes recognized as king by Romans (59) |
|---|---|---|
| Caesar Consul (59) | | |
| Caesar begins Gallic campaigns (58) | | |
| Cicero's exile and return (58–57) | | |
| 55 – approximate date of Lucretius' death | | |
| Cicero's *Republic* (54) | | Crassus defeated and killed by Parthians (54) Death of Ptolemy XII (51), accession of Cleopatra VII (51–30) |
| | | Book of Wisdom |
| | Cicero governor in Cilicia (51–50) | |
| **50** | | |
| Activity of Diodorus Siculus, historian | | |
| Caesar crosses Rubicon River in North Italy (49) renewing civil war | | |
| | Caesar defeats Pompey at Battle of Pharsalus (48) | Caesar in Alexandria, winter of 48/47, establishes relationship with Cleopatra Activity of Arius Didymus in Alexandria |
| Caesar dictator (47); extended for ten years (46) | | |
| Many of Cicero's philosophical works written 45–43 | | |
| Caesar assassinated (44) | | |
| Second Triumvirate (43): Antony, Octavian, Lepidus Murder of Cicero | | |
| | Caesar's killers defeated at Philippi (42) | |
| | | Antony in the east (41–32) |
| Pact of Brundisium between Antony and Octavian (40) Virgil's fourth *Eclogue* | | Herod appointed tetrarch (41), governs 37–4 |
| Triumvirate renewed (37) | | |

399

| BC | Italy and the west | Greece, the Aegean, and Anatolia | Palestine, Syria, and Egypt |
|---|---|---|---|
| | | | Antony's failed campaign against Parthia (36), Antony and Cleopatra co-operate, then marry |
| | | Antony and Cleopatra bring fleet to Greece (32), defeated at Actium (31) by Octavian | |
| | Octavian supreme (30) | | Antony and Cleopatra suicides (30) Octavian annexes Egypt |
| | Virgil completes *Georgics* (29) | | |
| | Octavian's "purification" of the Senate (28) | | |
| | "Restoration of the Republic" Octavian given the title Augustus (27) | | |
| 25 | Horace's *Odes* 1–3 (24–23) | | Start of rebuilding of Temple by Herod (20) |
| | Death of Virgil (19) | | |
| | Secular Games (17) Horace's *Carmen Saeculare* | | |
| | End of Livy's *History of Rome* (9) Augustus' Altar of Peace dedicated | | Birth of Jesus in about 7–6(?) |
| | Tiberius retires to Rhodes (6) | | Death of Herod (4) |
| BC Beginning of Christian Era AD | | Paul born at Tarsus between 5 and 10 | Philip the Tetrarch builds Julias |

400

Death of Augustus (14)
Tiberius succeeds (14–37)

Antipas founds Tiberias (c. 17)

25

Pontius Pilate Procurator (26–36)
Preaching of John the Baptist (27)
Jesus preaching in Galilee (28–9)
Crucifixion of Jesus (30)
Death of Philip the Tetrarch (34)
Martyrdom of Stephen
Conversion of Paul

Death of Tiberius (37)
Gaius succeeds (37–41)

Gaius gives Herod Agrippa I territories of
Philip and Lysanias, with title of king (37)
Persecution of Jews in Alexandria (38)

Philo's embassy to Rome (39–40)

Gaius killed (41)
Claudius succeeds (41–54)

Death of Herod Agrippa (44) Judaea
administered by procurators

Letter of Claudius to the Alexandrians

50

First mission of Paul

Paul in Corinth (50–2)

Death of Claudius (54)
Nero succeeds (54–68)

Arrest of Paul (58)

Paul in Rome (61–3)

James, brother of Jesus, killed (62)
Rising of Alexandrian Jews (66)
Rising of Judaea

401

| BC | Italy and the west | Greece, the Aegean, and Anatolia | Palestine, Syria, and Egypt |
|---|---|---|---|
| | Suicide of Seneca (65) | | Procurator Florus crucifies some Jews in Jerusalem (66) |
| | | | Rebels control Jerusalem |
| | | | Josephus joins Romans (67) |
| | Vespasian (69–79) in power after war among four claimants | | Vespasian reconquers Galilee (69) |
| | | | Titus' siege of Jerusalem (70) |
| | | | Burning of the Temple |
| | | | Fall of Masada (73) |
| 75 | Vespasian dies (79) | | |
| | Reign of Titus (79–81) | | |
| | Eruption of Vesuvius (79) | | Period of composition of Gospels (or after 60) |
| | Death of Pliny | | |
| | Burial of Pompeii and Herculaneum | | |
| | Josephus in Rome | Activity of Plutarch (to c. 120) | Composition of 2 *Baruch* and 4 *Ezra* |
| | Domitian (81–96) succeeds Titus | | |
| | Activity of Epictetus | | |
| | Nerva (96–8) | | |
| | Trajan (98–117) | | |
| 100 | | | |

402

# Bibliography and Notes

Resisting the tendency to proliferate annotation and bibliography, I have held both to as tight a limit as I could. For the most part, I have referred in the text only to works quoted, or for which some exceptional case could be made for annotation. I have also indulged in argumentation in the notes or references to modern scholarship only in such cases in which I felt the issue was of some real importance to my own argument, and for which some recent discussion seemed to me to call for acknowledgment. Apart from that, I have cited neither those with whom I agree, not those whose conclusions I do not accept. Members of the first group will, I hope, bask in the warmth of tacit approval, while the others I greet from a respectful distance.

I have been equally chary of bibliographical entries, aware that for Greek literature, L. Doherty's bibliography to her translation of Jacqueline de Romilly's *A Short History of Greek Literature* (1985) reports almost everything important in the way of texts, translations, and critical studies, while the *Cambridge History of Classical Literature* serves the same purpose for work on Greek literature before 1985, on Latin before 1982. The discussions in these works, as well as the articles in Luce's *Ancient Writers*, or the interpretative essays in Daiches and Thorlby's *Literature and Western Civilization* are good starting-points for further reading on Greek and Latin writers. Because these volumes list modern English translations, I only give references to translations which relate to my text but are not listed in one or other of these, and I have been reluctant to list interpretative studies apart from the very recent, unless they relate particularly to the concerns of my text; in those noted "bibliography," the reader will find particularly well-organized, well-selected, or full guides to earlier work.

I have provided a slightly wider scope for fields distant from the study of Greek and Roman literature, but even so, I limit myself to recent books and suggest those offering convenient bibliographical reference. Where possible, I have referred works to those chapters of mine to which they are most relevant, but there is, inevitably, greater breadth in many of those cited. For Jewish, Christian, and biblical studies in particular, works cited range over more than the subject matter of the chapter for which they are listed.

## GENERAL REFERENCE WORKS

Africa, T. W. (1974) *The Immense Majesty, A History of Rome and the Roman Empire*, New York, Thomas Crowell. Bibliography.
*Cambridge Ancient History* (1970) Cambridge, Cambridge University Press, 3rd edn in progress. Bibliography.

Cambridge History of Classical Literature, I, Greek Literature (1985); II, Latin Literature (1982), Cambridge, Cambridge University Press. Bibliography.

Crawford, M. (1978) The Roman Republic, Hassocks Sussex, Harvester Press.

de Romilly, J. (1985) A Short History of Greek Literature, Chicago, University of Chicago Press. (Transl. of Précis de littérature grecque, 1980). Bibliography.

Fine, J. V. A. (1983) The Ancient Greeks: A Critical History, Cambridge, Mass., Harvard University Press.

Hornblower, S. (1983) The Greek World, 479–323 BC, London, Methuen. Bibliography.

Koester, H. (1982) Introduction to the New Testament I, History, Culture and Religion of the Hellenistic Age; II, History and Literature of Early Christianity, Philadelphia, Fortress Press. (Transl. of Einführung in das Neue Testament, 1980.) Bibliography.

Luce, T. J. (ed.) (1982) Ancient Writers: Greece and Rome, 2 vols., New York, Charles Scribner's Sons. Bibliography.

Wilkinson, L. P. (1975) The Roman Experience, London, Paul Elek.

## GENERAL INTERPRETATIVE WORKS

Daiches, D. and Thorlby, A. (eds) (1972) Literature and Western Civilization, I, The Classical World, London, Aldus Books.

de Ste Croix, G. E. M. (1981) The Class Struggle in the Ancient World, from the Archaic Age to the Arab Conquests, Ithaca, Cornell University Press. Bibliography.

Dodds, E. R. (1964) The Greeks and the Irrational, Berkeley, University of California Press.

Guthrie, W. K. C. (1962–81) A History of Greek Philosophy, 6 vols (from the Presocratics to Aristotle), Cambridge, Cambridge University Press.

Havelock, E. A. (1978) The Greek Concept of Justice, from its Shadow in Homer to its Substance in Plato, Cambridge, Mass., Harvard University Press.

Lloyd-Jones, H. (1983) The Justice of Zeus, 2nd edn, Berkeley, University of California Press. (First published 1971.)

Meeks, W. A. (1986) The Moral World of the First Christians, Philadelphia, Westminster Press.

Rist, J. M. (1982) Human Value: A Study in Ancient Philosophical Ethics, Leiden, Brill.

Simon, B. (1978) Mind and Madness in Ancient Greece: The Classical Roots of Modern Psychiatry, Ithaca, Cornell University Press.

Snell, B. (1960) The Discovery of the Mind: The Greek Origins of European Thought, New York, Harper & Row. (Transl. of Die Entdeckung des Geistes, 1946.)

Vidal-Naquet, P. (1981) Le chasseur noir: formes de pensée et formes de société dans le monde grec, Paris, François Maspero.

## PREFACE

1 Jaegar, W. (1934) Paideia: Die Formung des Griechischen Menschen, I, Berlin and Leipzig, Walter de Gruyter & Co. (Volume II appeared in 1936.)

## 1  INTRODUCTION

1 It is the theme of many of his works. See in particular Mohammed and Charlemagne (1939) London, Allen & Unwin. (Transl. of Mahomet et Charlemagne, 1937.)

2 Much less, I believe, than the sociobiologists try to tell us. See Rose, S., Kanin, L. J., and Lewontin, R. C. (1984) *Not in Our Genes: Biology, Ideology and Human Nature*, Harmondsworth, Middlesex, Penguin.
3 Penfield, W. (1975) *The Mystery of the Mind: A Critical Study of Consciousness and the Human Brain*, Princeton, Princeton University Press.

## 2   THE ENVIRONMENT OF HELLENISM

Burkert, W. (1985) *Greek Religion, Archaic and Classical*, Oxford, Basil Blackwell. (Transl. of *Griechische religion der archaischen und klassischen Epoch*, 1977.)
Dumézil, G. (1970) *Archaic Roman Religion*, 2 vols., Chicago, University of Chicago Press. (Transl. of *La Religion romaine archaïque*, 1966.)
Ehrenberg, V. (1960) *The Greek State*, Oxford, Basil Blackwell.
Eliade, M. (1978, 1982) *A History of Religious Ideas* I, *From the Stone Age to the Eleusinian Mysteries*; II, *From Gautama Buddha to the Triumph of Christianity*, Chicago, University of Chicago Press. (Transl. of *Histoire des croyances religieuses*, 1976, 1978.)
Ferguson, J. (1970) *The Religion of the Roman Empire*, Ithaca, Cornell University Press. Bibliography.
Fontenrose, J. (1978) *The Delphic Oracle: Its Responses and Operations, with a Catalogue of Responses*, Berkeley, University of California Press.
Lyttelton, M. and Forman, W. (1984) *The Romans: Their Gods and their Beliefs*, London, Orbis.
Metzger, B. (1984) "A classified bibliography of the Graeco-Roman mystery religions 1924–1973 with a supplement 1974–1977," *Aufstieg und Niedergang der Römischen Welt*, II (17), 3.
Rykwert, J. (1976) *The Idea of a Town: The Anthropology of Urban Form in Rome, Italy and the Ancient World*, Princeton, Princeton University Press.
Vernant, J.-P. (1980) *Myth and Society in Ancient Greece*, Hassocks, Sussex, Harvester Press. (Transl. of *Mythe et société en Grèce ancienne*, 1974.)
—— (1982) *The Origins of Greek Thought*, Ithaca, Cornell University Press. (Transl. of *Les Origines de la pensée grecque*, 1962.)
Wordman, A. (1982) *Religion and Statecraft among the Romans*, Baltimore, Johns Hopkins University Press.

1 In several contexts, and in particular, in (1961) *General Economic History*, New York, Collier books. (Transl. of *Wirtschaftgeschichte*, 1923.)
2 See the description in Burkert, *Greek Religion*, pp. 237–42.
3 For a critical survey see Kirk, G. S. (1970) *Myth: Its Meaning and Functions in Ancient and Other Cultures*, Cambridge, Cambridge University Press. A coherent and convincing critique of the structuralist approach is offered by Burkert, W. (1979) *Structure and History in Greek Mythology and Ritual*, Berkeley, University of California Press, pp. 10–14.
4 Burkert provides the most recent and concise summary, in *Greek Religion*, pp. 1–4.
5 Gould, J. (1985) "On making sense of Greek religion," in Easterling, P. E. and Muir, J. V. (eds) *Greek Religion and Society*, Cambridge, Cambridge University Press, p. 33.
6 ibid., p. 32.
7 Expressed in much of his writing. Cf. e.g. (1966) *The Savage Mind*, London, Weidenfeld and Nicolson (transl. of *La Pensée Sauvage*, 1962) and the summarizing 1977 Massey Lectures *Myth and Meaning*, Toronto, University of Toronto Press (1978).

8  For most Greek intellectuals, the narrative aspect of myth had lost connection with object or cosmic reality as early as the sixth century, and from that time on could be taken as a series of misleading statements about divinity or as evidence of human ignorance.

9  Burkert, W. (1983) *Homo Necans: The Anthropology of Ancient Greek Sacrificial Ritual and Belief*, Berkeley, University of California Press (Transl. of *Homo Necans*, 1972.) p. 296: "Sacrifice as an encounter with death, an act of killing that simultaneously guarantees the perpetuation of life and food, grew up out of the existence of the Palaeolithic hunter and remained the formative core of the sacred ritual." Burkert (p. xiv) joins those convinced by Lorenz, K. (1966) *On Aggression* (London, Methuen) and although he does not want to "hypothesize about genetic fixation of 'human nature'" (p. xv), he slips into expressions like "this indicates that religious ritual is advantageous in the process of selection, if not for the individual, then at least for the continuance of group identity" (p. 26) and asserting a "biological-functional view of ritual" (p. 27).

10  This seems best demonstrated by Mikalson, J. D. (1983) *Athenian Popular Religion*, Chapel Hill, University of North Carolina Press, showing, *inter alia*, that in law court arguments, the evidence of divine attitudes as shown in matters such as success at sacrifice was readily accepted by opposing parties in pleading, but was merely interpreted differently; Mikalson also argues that we cannot really demonstrate the shift in religious attitudes which has been so often asserted for the period after the middle of the fifth century.

11  Plato, *Phaedo* 118. I owe the reminder of this to Sir Moses Finley, who mentions it in his introduction to *Greek Religion and Society* (see note 5).

12  For a short survey of oracular response at Delphi, with brief bibliography, see the recent discussion by S. Price, "Delphi and divination," in *Greek Religion and Society* (see note 5), pp. 126–54.

13  Ideas put forth by G. Dumézil (1970) *Archaic Roman Religion*, Chicago: Chicago University Press. (Transl. of *La religion romaine archaïque*, 1966); (1969) *Idées romaines*, Paris, Gallimard.


3  IN THE BEGINNING

Clay, J. S. (1983) *The Wrath of Athena: Gods and Men in the Odyssey*, Princeton, Princeton University Press.

Luce, J. V. (1975) *Homer and the Heroic Age*, London, Thames & Hudson.

Parry, M. (ed.) (1971) *The Making of Homeric Verse: The Collected Papers of Milman Parry*, Oxford, Clarendon Press.

1  Plato, *Republic* 606 e, refers to the "praisers of Homer, saying that this poet had educated Greece," an idea found as early as Xenophanes (fr. 10). The reason for Homer's importance is argued by Havelock, E. A. (1963) *Preface to Plato*, Cambridge, Mass., Harvard University Press, as being the fundamentally oral nature of Greek society, for which Homer served as a kind of "tribal encyclopaedia," formidable opposition in Plato's time; cf. also the implications of a wider interpretation of "oral," as noted in note 4 below.

2  Enunciated in the papers collected in Parry (ed.), *The Making of Homeric Verse*, and restated in Lord, A. B. (1960) *The Singer of Tales*, Cambridge, Mass., Harvard University Press. The fundamental argument of the thesis, that the repetitious use of epithet demonstrates the "traditional" nature of the poetry, is attacked now by Vivante, P. (1982) *The Epithets in Homer: A Study in Poetic Values*, New Haven,

Yale University Press, arguing the poetic value of the epithets. Aesthetic criticism has increasingly felt the Parry thesis a Procrustean bed for literary approaches to the epic, neglecting, it seems to me, the poetic potential of oral expression. The subject of the oral tradition still evokes a great deal of controversy. That there was a long tradition leading up to the formulation of the *Iliad* of our texts is agreed, but the nature of that tradition and the manner in which it was used to create the epics is much debated. In addition to works cited in other notes here, the issue has been discussed recently by Kullmann, W. (1984) "Oral poetry theory and neoanalysis in Homeric research," *Greek, Roman and Byzantine Studies*, 25, 307–23, and Thornton, A. (1984) *Homer's Iliad: Its Composition and the Motif of Supplication*, Göttingen, Vandenhoeck & Rupprecht.

3 The material, and the earlier discussions, are reviewed by Luce, J. V. (1975) *Homer and the Heroic Age*, London, Thames & Hudson.

4 Just what the nature of this oral tradition was, and its potential for freedom, need not be limited to the categories of the Parry-Lord thesis. The subject should not be considered without reference to Finnegan, R. (1977) *Oral Poetry, Its Nature, Significance and Social Context*, Cambridge, Cambridge University Press, which sets forth the evidence for the diversity of types of oral composition and emphasizes the importance of interaction between poet and audience. On writing, see Chapter 4, note 1.

## 4 THE WRATH OF ACHILLES

Griffin, J. (1980) *Homer on Life and Death*, Oxford, Clarendon Press.

1 Without assuming that the scope of potential in the oral tradition is so restricted as to force the conclusion that the epic was created in writing while the skill was very limited in its application, as Mueller, M. (1984) *The Iliad*, London, George Allen & Unwin, pp. 163–5, hypothesizes a "master poet" whose lengthy activity accounts for repetitions and inconsistencies. The evidence against extensive use of writing in composition of the *Iliad* has been recently reviewed again by Kirk, G. S. (1985) *The Iliad: A Commentary, vol 1: books 1–4*, Cambridge, Cambridge University Press, pp. 11–14, in an introduction which summarizes the generally held theory of lengthy development of the epic tradition and maintains Kirk's view of an eighth-century date for the creation of the *Iliad*.

2 M. Mueller, *The Iliad*, pp. 173–4, summarizes and maintains the argument that "Book 9 represents a late stage in the growth of the Iliad," while accepting it, of course, as the work of his final poet. Most recent work accepts the embassy episode as an integral part of the *Iliad*, with little or no argumentation. Vivante, for example (see note 1, Chapter 3), makes no distinctions in his treatment of the epithets in that scene, just as MacCary (see note 4 below) makes the episode integral to his discussion, while Schein, S. (1984) *The Mortal Hero: An Introduction to Homer's Iliad*, Berkeley, University of California Press, passes over it in note 35, p. 125, distinguishing the approach of analytical scholars from those who "recognize merely a narrative inconsistency arising from Homer's reworking of a traditional story", briefly also, against the idea of the late reworking, Lloyd-Jones, *The Justice of Zeus*, p. 16.

3 *Iliad* xx. 425.

4 The recent proposal of "an 'Achilles complex' as the thematic core of the Iliad, and a formative stage in the development of every male child," (p. 95), in MacCary, W. T. (1985) *Childlike Achilles: Ontogeny and Phylogeny in the Iliad*, New York, Columbia University Press, has at least the merit of explicating carefully the

tradition out of which such interpretations emerge, as well as reviewing the structuralist and "humanistic" approaches to the Achilles story.

## 5 THE PROBLEM OF MORALS

Murray, O. (1980) *Early Greece*, Hassocks, Sussex, Harvester Press.
Podlecki, A. J. (1984) *The Early Greek Poets and Their Times*, Vancouver, University of British Columbia Press.
Snodgrass, A. (1980) *Archaic Greece: The Age of Experiment*, Berkeley, University of California Press.

1 Hesiod, *Works and Days*, 250, etc.
2 Thucydides I, 13. 1.
3 Alcaeus, Muller 59.
4 Theognis, 183–90.
5 Theognis, 39–52.
6 Solon, fr. 24 Diehl=Lattimore, R. (1960) *Greek Lyrics* (translated), 2nd edn, Chicago, University of Chicago Press, fr. 4.
7 Solon, fr. 3 Diehl=Lattimore 2.
8 Solon, fr. 5 Diehl=Lattimore 3; Aristotle, *Constitution of Athens* 12; Plutarch's version of the verse (*Solon* 18) has Solon giving "power" to the populace.
9 Solon, fr. 1 Diehl=Lattimore 1.

## 6 FIFTH-CENTURY ATHENIANS

Davies, J. K. (1978) *Democracy and Classical Greece*, Hassocks, Sussex, Harvester Press.
Kerferd, G. B. (1981) *The Sophistic Movement*, Cambridge, Cambridge University Press.
Roberts, J. W. (1984) *City of Socrates: An Introduction to Classical Athens*, London, Routledge & Kegan Paul.

1 So claimed by Pericles, Thucydides II, 64.
2 The allusion in *Frogs* 1032 shows that Aristophanes had read *Works and Days*; Thucydides (3.96) knows the story of his death. Outside Athens, Herodotus (2.53) knew the *Theogony*, but saw Hesiod as contemporary with Homer. References by historians should be expected, and prove little. Much more significant is vase-painting, everywhere rife with scenes and quotations from Homer, while mythological and mundane scenes offer little that can be tied to either *Theogony* or *Works and Days*.
3 The dating here illustrates the many chronological problems which bedevil interpretation of this period. Although most scholars concur that these economic measures are part of developing policy which makes sense for the 450s and 440s, a strong effort has been made by Mattingly, H. (1966) *Ancient Society and Institutions: Studies Presented to Victor Ehrenberg*, Oxford, Basil Blackwell, pp. 193 ff. to redate the relevant inscription to the 420s and thus relate Atheniansm imperialism to the Peloponnesian War.
4 In Athenian coinage, there are 100 drachmas per mina, so the 3 drachmas per mina, if correctly interpreted from the decree, means 3 per cent.
5 To give a rough equivalent, this would provide salary for about 36 million days of work at the rate paid a skilled craftsman. A half-talent would keep a trireme at sea for about a month; 200 warships for six months would cost 600 talents.

# Bibliography and notes

6 Population figures for Athens vary widely according to the means used to provide estimates and the classes – slaves, resident aliens, women, and children, citizens as a whole – included in the estimate. It is a reasonable conjecture, based on Justin II.9, that 10,000 Athenians served as hoplites at Marathon in 490, suggesting a number for those of the male citizenry able to finance the cost of arms. Discussion may be found in Gomme, A. W. (1933) *The Population of Athens in the Vth and IVth Centuries B.C.*, Oxford, Basil Blackwell. A recent study seeking to determine numbers serving in the higher offices, Badian, E. (1971) "Archons and strategoi," *Antichthon*, 5, 17–19, supports a hypothesis that in 431 BC the number of those in the upper two classes, based on wealth, was 1800, and that of these, not more than half, in all probability, would be able and willing to serve unpaid as archons in the early fifth century. A figure of 2000 for the leisured classes might seem over-generous when confronted with the figure of 5040 proposed for the whole citizen body in Plato's *Laws* 737 e. De Ste Croix, *Class Struggle*, p. 599, n. 23, proposes "at least" 1000 knights (the most prosperous of the non-aristocrats, if not members of the aristocracy) for the late fifth century.

7 There is a good deal of debate on the question of the relationship, and the period of Anaxagoras' stay in Athens. In Diog. Laert. II, 7, the year of his arrival is reported as the archonship of Callias, which is variously interpreted for dating purposes. Comment generally puts Anaxagoras' arrival toward the middle of the century; cf. the recent discussion by Sider, D. (1981) *The Fragments of Anaxagoras*, Meisenham am Glan (esp. pp. 1–11), which contains texts, translation, and commentary on the fragments with the extensive bibliography. There is dispute whether Anaxagoras was so close an associate of Pericles, despite the statement of Plutarch, *Pericles* 4 ff., that he influenced Pericles' intellectual development, and with the relationship between the two attested as early as Plato, *Phaedrus* 270 a.

8 Plutarch, *Pericles* 36.4, reports the two spent a day in an ethical discussion, and *Moralia*, 118 e–f quotes Protagoras' descriptions of Pericles' demeanor on the death of his two sons.

9 This is the view expressed by Kerferd, *Sophistic Movement*, in particular Chapter 2, "The Sophists as a social phenomenon," for a survey of the relationship to Pericles, the reception in general in Athens, and the hostility directed toward the Sophists. Kerferd's excellent treatment of the Sophists as philosophers and teachers, and of their place in the history of Greek thought, shows them as much more significant as thinkers than has generally been stated.

10 The expresssion used by Jaeger, Werner (1945) *Paideia* I, Oxford, Oxford University Press, p. 297, characterizing the Sophists as "constantly wandering from city to city." Whether or not we agree with Jaeger that this mobility represented "such utter independence," it is important to an understanding of their effect.

11 Many of the visits and their dates are discussed by Untersteiner, M. (1954) *The Sophists*, transl. K. Freeman, Oxford.

12 Again there is disagreement, but Guthrie, *History of Greek Philosophy* II, p. 262, has no trouble with the story about Xerxes.

13 Ehrenberg, V. (1943) *The People of Aristophanes*, Oxford, Basil Blackwell, p. 201, takes the view "that the public was, to some extent, acquainted with the prominent sophists and with some of their doctrines."

14 Guthrie provides an excellent survey of the sources for Socrates' life and the conclusions which may be drawn therefrom, in *History of Greek Philosophy* III, pp. 325-77 for sources, pp. 378–416 for Socrates' life and character.

15 Cf. Ehrenberg, V. (1954) *Sophocles and Pericles*, Oxford, for Sophocles' life, dates, and relationship with Pericles.

16 Sophocles would have been over 80, but Ehrenberg, V. (1968) *From Solon to*

*Socrates*, London, Methuen, p. 351, accepts without discussion the evidence of Aristotle, *Rhetoric* 1419 a.


## 7 DIVINE AND HUMAN JUSTICE IN FIFTH-CENTURY HELLENISM

Connor, W. R. (1984) *Thucydides*, Princeton, Princeton University Press.

Hogan, J. C. (1984) *A Commentary on The Complete Greek Tragedies: Aeschylus*, Chicago, University of Chicago Press.

Knox, B. (1983) "Sophocles and the polis," in *Sophocle*, Fondation Hardt, Entretiens 29, Geneva.

—— (1985) "Euripides: The poet as prophet", in *Directions in Euripidean Criticism: A Collection of Essays*, Durham, Duke University Press, pp. 1–12.

Rosenmeyer, T. G. (1982) *The Art of Aeschylus*, Berkeley, University of California Press.

Scodel, R. (1984) *Sophocles*, Boston, Twayne. Bibliography.

Waters, K. H. (1985) *Herodotus the Historian: His Problems, Methods and Originality*, London, Croom Helm. Bibliography.

1 This is the "deliberate deception which draws the victim on to fresh error, intellectual or moral, whereby he hastens his own ruin," which Dodds (1951) *The Greeks and the Irrational*, Berkeley, University of California Press, pp. 38–9, sees as one of the evil spirits truly feared in the archaic age, an aspect of popular belief from which Aeschylus was trying to lead the Athenians, into a higher level of morality, from the "daemonic, as distinct from the divine," as Dodds puts it, pursuing his developmental model of Greek thought. That both meanings, blindness or "subjective" meaning, and ruin or "objective," are found from Homer on, is shown by Doyle, R. J. (1984) *ATE: Its Use and Meaning: A Study in the Greek Poetic Tradition from Homer to Euripides*, New York, Fordham University Press.

2 The arguments against authenticity of Griffith, M. (1977) *The Authenticity of Prometheus Bound*, Cambridge, have convinced many, but Conacher, D. J. (1980) *Aeschylus' Prometheus Bound: A Literary Commentary*, Toronto, University of Toronto Press, reviewing the argument and history of the controversy, finds the ancient inclusion of the play into the Aeschylean corpus not yet successfully challenged.

3 Lloyd-Jones, *Justice of Zeus*, p. 102, sees no change, but in a Zeus, ruler of the universe, consistent with the Zeus of the other plays of Aeschylus; cf. the discussion in Conacher, *Aeschylus' Prometheus Bound*, pp. 98–137, and especially pp. 128–31.

4 The question of whether Aeschylus intended his treatment of the Areopagus as an expression in favor of or opposed to the reforms of the powers of that body in 462/1 is quite irrevelant to an understanding of the poet's treatment of the moral order, but that issue may be explored in Podlecki, A. J. (1966) *The Political Background of Aeschylean Tragedy*, Ann Arbor, University of Michigan Press, pp. 80–100.

5 Havelock, E. A. (1957) *The Liberal Temper in Greek Politics*, New Haven, Yale University Press, pp. 52–64, shows Aeschylus' familiarity with Sophistic "scientific anthropology" (p. 52) in his treatments of the learning of the arts, the alternative view which Conacher, *Aeschylus' Prometheus Bound*, p. 97, chooses, and with which I agree.

6 If West, M. L. (1971) *Early Greek Philosophy and the Orient*, Oxford, is right that the influence of the east was strongest during the period of Persian domination of Greek areas, *c.* 550–480, there would have been opportunity for Persian dualism to

have reached Greece. Pythagoreanism, however, was dualistic, according to Aristotle; cf. Kirk, G. S. and Raven, J. E. (1957) *The Presocratic Philosophers*, Cambridge, Cambridge University Press, pp. 240 and 241 n.l.

7 Quoted in Diogenes Laertius IX, 51. My translation follows the interpretation of Kerferd, G. B. (1981) *The Sophistic Movement*, Cambridge, Cambridge University Press, pp. 86–93. In much of what follows I accept Kerferd's interpretation of Protagoras' thought.

8 I translate "ignorant" and not, as so often, "unfeeling, inhuman" (*LSJ*) or "callous." *LSJ* cite no parallel for the meaning of "unfeeling," and the natural sense of "unknowing" parallels charging Zeus with "knowing" to sneak into Amphitryon's bed, but not "knowing" to save his dear ones, in the preceding lines. (Liddell, H. G., Scott, R. and Jones, H. S. (1940) *A Greek English Lexicon*, Oxford, Oxford University Press.)

9 Cf. similar statements in Sophocles, *Philoctetes* 416 ff.

10 Neither to me nor to W. Arrowsmith who, in his introduction to his translation of *Orestes*, in Grene, D. and Lattimore, R. (eds) (1959) *The Complete Greek Tragedies*, IV, Chicago, University of Chicago Press, p. 190, found "stupidity" in Apollo's dispositions.

11 Knox, B. M. W. (1964) *The Heroic Temper, Studies in Sophoclean Tragedy*, Berkeley, University of California Press, shows not only that the downfall of the Sophoclean hero is unmerited, but also the characteristic of that hero in asserting character and attempting to impose his or her will on a universe uncontrollable and unfathomable, persisting in the face of all persuasion and opposition to pursue a course judged right, while divine justice remains beyond the reach of human understanding.

12 It is worth noting the Athenians' comment in Book I. 76, where they praise themselves in their treatment of their subjects for being more cognizant of justice than they are constrained to be, regarding justice more as a matter of generosity than external morality.

13 E.g. Antiphon I. 31, *Prosecution for Poisoning*, which concludes, "I think that those who are wronged are a concern to the gods below."

14 And, as pointed out by Carne-Ross, D. S. (1985) *Pindar*, New Haven, Yale University Press, pp. 1–2, the victory ode itself had a very short tradition, and by the time of most of the extant Athenian tragedies, was a moribund genre.

15 E.g. *Pythian* III. 29–30.

16 Cf. *Pythian* VIII. 95 ff. Carne-Ross, *Pindar*, pp. 58–9, points out the explicit statement of *Nemean* VI that it is through the victory that the victor somehow resembles the immortals.

17 *Pythian* VI. 139–40; *Nemean* VI. l ff.

18 Fragment 50 (Bowra).

19 Fragment 152 (Bowra).

20 Only the occasional remark or fragment gives us hints that he might have treated politics (*Nemean* XI. 79–80), or mystery religions (Fragment 121 (Bowra)).

21 Jacoby, F. (1913) "Herodotus," *RE* Supplement II, col. 482. On the other hand Hunter, V. (1982) *Past and Process in Herodotus and Thucydides*, Princeton, Princeton University Press, p. 295, applies such terms as "scepticism, logic, rationality," to Herodotus as well as Thucydides.

22 As the view may be influential for its location, I cite T. S. Brown in *Encyclopaedia Britannica*, III, 1974, s.v. Herodotus. Dealing with alternate interpretations of fact and motive, Brown finds an ambivalence which extends more generally to divine action.

23 III. 38.

24 The god is fond of giving prophecies: VI. 27.

25 It is worth pointing out that, in the oracle reported in I. 13, the retribution on Gyges in the fifth generation is not expressed as justice, *dike*, but *tisis*; and there are many dynasties terminated by royal murders for which no vengeance is asserted either by oracle or by Herodotus. The retribution falling on a later generation has been seen as important in Herodotean thought, but this passage is one of the few in which it is explicit; it is at best only implied by the troubles which fell on Periander of Corinth, V. 92, and there is a much broader morality to the story of Glaucus, VI. 86, who wished to break his oath in regard to a deposit, and in consequence for even contemplating such a thing, was left without later descendants in Sparta.

26 I. 207.

27 It will be clear that my views of Herodotus' treatment of oracles concur with the results of Lachenaud, G. (1978) *Mythologies, religion, et philosophie de l'histoire dans Herodote*, Thesis, Lille, 1976, pp. 225–305.

28 VII. 12 ff. The story, in which the advice comes to each in a dream, also shows Herodotus' awareness of the rationalist explanation of dreams.

29 Well expressed by the comment of Fornara, C. (1971) *Herodotus, an Interpretive Essay*, Oxford, Clarendon Press, p. 89.

30 Exceptions, like Apollo's direct intervention to save Croesus, or the revenge taken on Cambyses for his sacrilegious treatment of the Apis bull, III, 29–30, should be read with his warning of VII. 152 in mind: "I am obliged to report what is reported to me, but I am not obliged to believe everything; let this word of mine suffice for the whole account."

## 8 SOCRATES

Vlastos, G. (1971) "The paradox of Socrates," in Vlastos, G. (ed.) *The Philosophy of Socrates: A Collection of Critical Essays*, New York, Anchor Books, pp.1–21.

1 Plato, *Apology of Socrates* 29 d.

2 Good starting places would be Guthrie, *History of Greek Philosophy*, III, pp. 323–75; Lacey, A. E. "Our knowledge of Socrates," in Vlastos (ed.) *The Philosophy of Socrates*, pp. 22–49.

3 This is the position, essentially, of the recent general work on Socrates, Santas, G. X. (1979) *Socrates: Philosophy in Plato's Early Dialogues*, London, Routledge & Kegan Paul, commenting "that it is only Plato's Socrates that is of major interest to the contemporary philosopher," p.x.

4 *Apology* 30 b.

5 *Crito* 50 ff.

6 This passage has struck many as inconsistent with other Socratic statements on obedience to law, and A. D. Woozley makes much of its logical contradiction with *Apology* 29 d, "Socrates on Disobeying the Law," in Vlastos (ed.) *The Philosophy of Socrates*, pp. 299–318. Although I am in sympathy with the attempt to explain the *Crito* and absolve Socrates from this charge by Kraut, R. (1984) *Socrates and the State*, Princeton, Princeton University Press (with a good bibliography), I am not sure his approach, especially pp. 73–6, succeeds in dealing with a matter which I think is much more pragmatic than logical. Santas, *Socrates: Philosophy in Plato's Early Dialogues*, pp. 43–56, argues against inconsistency on the grounds that the principles at stake are not identical.

7 *Memorabilia* IV. 8. 10.

8 Doubt; but not the extreme position of Chroust, A.-H. (1957) *Socrates, Man and Myth, The Two Socratic Apologies of Xenophon*, London, Routledge & Kegan

Paul, which argues that any information about Socrates is legend, deriving from one or more of the fictitious traditions which grew up from the fourth century BC on.

9 Cf. Xenophon, *Memorabilia* IV. 4. 13–25, portraying Socrates as identifying what is just with what is lawful, not only in respect to laws, but unwritten *nomoi*.

10 According to Xenophon, *Memorabilia* I.3.1, repeated in IV.3.16, Socrates' behavior and advice followed that of the Delphian priestess, who set up the "nomos of the city," as the guide to pious behavior.

11 Explicit, *inter alia*, at Xenophon, *Memorabilia* IV. 4.13.

12 This may help to resolve the contradiction between *Crito* and *Apology* 29, which is made much of by A. D. Woozley in Vlastos (ed.) *The Philosophy of Socrates*, pp. 299–318.

## 10 THE PURSUIT OF POWER

Cawkwell, G. (1978) *Philip of Macedon*, London, Faber & Faber.
Ellis, J. R. (1976) *Philip II and Macedonian Imperialism*, London, Thames & Hudson.

## 11 PLATO

Raven, J. E. (1965) *Plato's Thought in the Making: A Study of the Development of His Metaphysics*, Cambridge, Cambridge University Press.
Rowe, C. J. (1984) *Plato*, Hassocks, Sussex, Harvester Press.

1 In what I say here, I should emphasize that I am not concerned with why Plato reasoned as he did, or the conditions under which his development of philosophy operated, either to reinterpret in the manner of Crombie, I. M. (1964) *Plato, The Midwife's Apprentice*, London, Routledge & Kegan Paul, or to explain, as Havelock, E. A. (1963) *Preface to Plato*, Oxford, Basil Blackwell, does, that Plato worked under the constraints of the contemporary change from oral communication to literacy. Rather, I deal with the text as it stands, and how it is most reasonably read by most interested parties, from Aristotle to present-day readers.

2 *Laws* 739 c.

3 *Laws* 743 c.

4 If this is not immediately obvious, cf. *Laws* 631 b: upright laws furnish all good for those who use them; 697 b: for the state dispensing honors, the goods of the soul take priority; passages like 727 a and 770 d elevating the importance of the soul, the latter referring to the good citizen who directs all efforts to achieving excellence of soul.

5 Marx, K. and Engels, F. (1847) *The Communist Manifesto*.

6 Platonists will be familiar with this style of presentation as a myth to convey the potency of the theory of the Forms, rather than as a claim that it was developed literally in this manner.

## 12 THE REAL WORLD OF CITY POLITICS

1 I believe that he meant both to be accepted, and since ancients made no discrimination between the two kinds of analysis, both aspects of the *Timaeus* could have the impact they did. I am not alone here; see Rist, J. M. (1964) *Eros and Psyche, Studies in Plato, Plotinus and Origen, Phoenix*, Supplementary Volume VI, Toronto, University of Toronto Press, pp. 11–12.

2 Cf. *Phaedo* 76 d–e; 79 a; 102 a–b.

## 13  ARISTOTLE AND THE MIDDLE WORLD

Barnes, J., Schofield, M., and Sorabji, R. (1980) *Aristotle: A Bibliography*, Subfaculty of Philosophy, Oxford.

1 *Metaphysics* 1086 a 36–b 5. Cf. also *Metaphysics* 1039 a 24ff., 1078 b 30–3, 1033 b 26–1034 a 8.
2 Cf. *Sophistical Refutations* 183 b 35 ff. for his originality.
3 As the argument from the sphericity of the surface of water, *de Caelo* 287 b 35 ff.; cf. also 306 a 16–18.
4 Even sometimes producing error, as in *de Anima* 418 b 20 ff.
5 *Nicomachean Ethics* 1094 b 13 ff.; 19–27.
6 *Politics* 1320 a 33, 35; cf. the concise indication of the nature of the sovereignty when different segments hold power in *Politics* 1290 b 1–3.
7 *Politics* 1039 a 33–7.
8 *Politics* 1288 a 1–32.
9 Worked out in *Posterior Analytics* 99 b–100 a.
10 *Posterior Analytics* 100 b.
11 *Nicomachean Ethics* 1095 b 14–1096 a 4.
12 E.g. *Nicomachean Ethics* 1098 b 20–29, 1101 b 13–27.
13 *Nicomachean Ethics* 1106 b 36–1107 a 2.
14 Cf. *Politics* 1253 b 15–1255 b 40.
15 *Nicomachean Ethics* 1102 a 5–6.
16 *Nicomachean Ethics* 1178 b 8–24; cf. also 1077 b 27–36.
17 For which see in particular *de Caelo* 286 b 10–289 a 10.
18 Cf. *Metaphysics* 1072 b 3–5.
19 *Metaphysics* 1072 b 25–30.

## 14  POINT OF DEPARTURE

Fox, R. L. (1973) *Alexander the Great*, London, Allen Lane.

1 Even those who do not want to admit that the *Alexander Romance* is good evidence for early and diverse training in Hellenism (see Samuel, Alan, "The early elements in the Alexander Romance," *Historia*, XXXV, 427–37) nevertheless emphasize the breadth of Alexander's exposure to ideas of the visitors to the court: Fox, *Alexander the Great*, pp. 50–51, and 508. Alexander's Hellenism may also be judged by the remarks in Isocrates' *Seventh Letter* (argued as genuine by Merlan, P. (1954) "Isocrates, Aristotle, and Alexander the Great," *Historia*, III, 60 ff.) written to the prince when he was about 14 years old, describing his reputation as "*philanthropos, philathenaios, philosophos*," and agreeing with what he hears of Alexander's abnegation of formal disputation, and choice instead of traditional rhetoric for study.
2 The evidence of the presence of some of the later kings in the circle at Mieza is admittedly constructive, but is taken without question, for example, by Fox, *Alexander the Great*, p. 56, including among the students perhaps Hephaestion as well as the sons of Antipater and the royal pages. The identification of those who were pages in Alexander's youth is not certain or complete; there seems to be agreement that the body would include Ptolemy, Lysimachus, Perdiccas, Peucestas, and Leonnatus, as well as some others. Berve, H. (1926) *Das Alexanderreich auf Prosopographische Grundlage*, Munich, Beck, I, pp. 37–9, discusses the institution, and II, p. 330, considers Ptolemy's inclusion "probable, as for all Macedonian nobles' sons." Ptolemy, as well as Nearchus, Erygius and

Laomedon, was close enough to Alexander in 337/6 to be exiled by Philip at the time Alexander intruded himself into the arrangements for a marriage to the daughter of Pixodarus (Plutarch, *Alexander* 10; Arrian, *Anabasis*, III. 6.5).

3 It was to Demetrius of Phalerum, who had ruled Athens from 317 to 307, and had studied under Aristotle's successor Theophrastus, that Ptolemy turned for help in the foundation.

4 Justin XV, 3.2.6.

5 Arrian, *Anabasis*, VII, 3.4.

6 *Politics* 1318 b–1319 b.

7 An important characteristic, and observed with approval in antiquity; cf. Arrian, *Anabasis*, VII, 28.1, and Samuel, Alan (1983) *From Athens to Alexandria: Hellenism and Social Goals in Ptolemic Egypt*, Louvain, pp. 76–82.

8 Plutarch's description of Olympias as taken up with orgiastic cults, *Alexander* III, 6, does not suggest this as a direct influence on Alexander.

9 Arrian, *Anabasis*, VII, 28.1.


## 15   A WORLD OF KINGS

Bagnall, R. S. and Derow, P. (1981) *Greek Historical Documents: The Hellenistic Period*, Chico, Scholar's Press. Referred to as Bagnall-Derow, it includes translations of inscriptions and papyri, with short commentary.

Fraser, P. M. (1972) *Ptolemaic Alexandria*, Oxford, Clarendon Press.

Grant, M. (1982) *From Alexander to Cleopatra: The Hellenistic World*, New York, Charles Scribners' Sons.

Préaux, C. (1978) *Le monde hellénistique: la Grèce et l'Orient (323–146 av. J.- C.)*, Nouvelle Clio 6, Paris, Presses Universitaires de France. Bibliography.

Walbank, F. W. (1981) *The Hellenistic World*, Hassocks, Sussex, Harvester Press. Bibliography.

1 Diodorus Siculus XX, 53.

2 Welles, C. B. (1934) *Royal Correspondence in the Hellenistic Period*, New Haven, Yale University Press, No. 6 (Bagnall-Derow 11).

3 For the evidence collected, see Swinnen, W. (1973) "Sur la politique religieuse de Ptolémée Ier," *Les Syncrétismes dans les Religions Grecques et Romaines*, Travaux du Centre d'Études Supérieures Spécialisés d'Histoire des Religions de Strasbourg, Paris, pp. 115–33.

4 Theocritus, XVII; The Adoulis Decree *O.G.I.S.* 54 (Bagnall-Derow 26) claims the Heraclid connection on the paternal side for Ptolemy III, Dionysus on the maternal.

5 *O.G.I.S.* 212 as restored, and *O.G.I.S.* 219 (Bagnall-Derow 16); cf. Justin XV, 4.

6 Athenaeus, *Deipnosophistae* VI 253 e.

7 Plutarch, *Demetrius* 10.3.

8 Pausanias I, 8.6. According to Diodorus Siculus XX, 100, with the approval of the oracle of Ammon at Siwah, they built and dedicated a precinct called the Ptolemaion.

9 *Sylloge*³ 398 (Dittenberger, W. (1915–24) *Sylloge Inscriptionum Graecarum*, Leipzig, (Bagnall-Derow 17)).

10 *Politics* 1285 b 30.

11 E.g. Welles, *Royal Correspondence* Nos. 10–13 (Bagnall-Derow 18); *Milet* 3, 125 (*Ergebnisse der Ausgrabungen und Untersuchungen seit den Jahre 1899*, vol. I, part III, *Das Delphinium von Milet*, by Kawerau, G. and Rehm, A., Berlin, Königliche Museen, 1914) under the year 279/8; *Sardis* 7 (I), I (*Sardis: Publications of the*

*American Society for the Excavation of Sardis*, vol. VII, *Greek and Latin Inscriptions* by Buckler, W. H. and Robinson, D. M., Leiden, Brill, 1932).
12 Josephus, *Against Apion* II. 39.
13 Callimachus, "Hymn to Zeus," 78–9.
14 Theocritus, XVII, 16–18.
15 Similar attitudes appear in XVI, addressed to Hiero II of Syracuse.
16 Revolutionary enough, and widely enough known, to prompt the contemporary head of the Stoic school in Athens, Cleanthes, to urge that he be executed for impiety; Plutarch, *Moralia*, 923 a.


## 16 THE CONNECTING OF EAST AND WEST

Salmon, E. T. (1982) *The Making of Roman Italy*, London, Thames & Hudson.


## 17 THE BRIDGE OF ATHENS

1 *Deipnosophistae* 253e.
2 Diogenes Laertius, V, 37.
3 Diogenes Laertius, X, 10.
4 Diogenes Laertius, X, 26.
5 For a discussion of the range of meanings of *hedone*, "between gross sensual 'pleasure' and entirely spiritual 'joy'," cf. Merlan, P. (1960) *Studies in Epicurus and Aristotle*, Wiesbaden, sec. 1, esp. pp. 1–37, which also serves as an introduction to the controversy over the use of the word.
6 Diogenes Laertius X, 128–9.
7 Diogenes Laertius X, 132.
8 Diogenes Laertius X, 6.
9 Principal Doctrines 33 (Diogenes Laertius X, 150).
10 Described by Cicero, *Academica* II, 145, in the famous parable whereby Zeno illustrated perception by holding his hand open, assent by the hand with the fingers a little closed, comprehension with the fingers closed in a fist, and knowledge with the left hand gripping the right fist tightly, a condition only possible for the "wise man."
11 Diogenes Laertius VII, 87.
12 Recently, Sandbach, F. H. (1985) *Aristotle and the Stoics*, Cambridge, Cambridge Philosophical Society Supplementary Volume 10, has attempted to put some distance between Aristotelian and Stoic doctrines. I think that the argument will not convince many to disregard what seem to be clear similarities and reactions to ideas in Aristotle's texts; I do not intend to suggest here a Stoic innocence of Aristotle's work.


## 18 POLYBIUS AND THE ROMAN TRIUMPH

Gruen, E. (1984) *The Hellenistic World and the Coming of Rome*, Berkeley, University of California Press.
Walbank, F. W. (1972) *Polybius*, Berkeley, University of California Press.

1 Polybius XVIII 44.2–3.
2 Polybius XVIII 46.5
3 Polybius XXIX 27.6
4 Polybius VI 4.13.

5 Polybius VI 5.1.
6 Polybius VI 51.4.
7 Polybius VI 47.7

## 19  THE JEWS IN THE MEDITERRANEAN WORLD

*The Cambridge History of Judaism*, I, *Introduction: The Persian Period* (1984), Cambridge, Cambridge University Press. Bibliography.

Kaufmann, Y. (1966) *The Religion of Israel, from its Beginnings to the Babylonian Exile*, Chicago, University of Chicago Press. Abridged transl. from Hebrew of *History of the Religion of Israel*, 1937–56, vols I–III.

—— (1977) *History of the Religion of Israel*, vol. IV, *From the Babylonian Captivity to the End of the Prophecy*, New York, Ktav Publishing House. (Transl. from Hebrew of *History of the Religion of Israel*, 1937–56, vol. IV.)

Nickelsburg, G. W. E. and Stone, M. E. (1983) *Faith and Piety in Early Judaism: Texts and Documents*, Philadelphia, Fortress Press. Translations of texts of II, BC, I AD.

Pearlman, M. (1973) *The Maccabees*, London, Weidenfeld & Nicolson.

Reinhold, M. (1983) *Diaspora: The Jews among the Greeks and Romans*, Sarasota, Samuel Stevens. Translations of literary texts, inscriptions (including coins), and papyri.

Schmidt, W. H. (1984) *Old Testament Introduction*, New York, Crossroad. (Transl. of *Einführung in das Alte Testament*, 1979.)

1 Joshua, Judges, 1 and 2 Samuel, 1 and 2 Kings, based on annals such as the cited "History of Solomon," "Annals of the Kings of Israel," "Annals of the Kings of Judah."
2 Leviticus 5: 21–6; 25: 35 ff.
3 Deuteronomy, 10: 18; 14: 28; 24: 10–21; 26: 12–14 ff., etc.
4 All translations of Old Testament texts are from *Tanakh: A New Translation of The Holy Scriptures According to the Traditional Hebrew Text*, 1985, Philadelphia, The Jewish Publication Society.
5 Leviticus 19: 33–4.
6 Cf. 1 Samuel 22: 21.
7 Isaiah, like other prophetic books, including Jeremiah, on which I draw below, is a complex editorial creation, drawing on a number of sources; see Schmidt, *Old Testament Introduction*. I am not concerned here to discriminate among the various aspects of the tradition, or to attempt any precise chronological determinations.
8 Isaiah 1: 23; 10: 1, 2; 32: 1, 17; 42: 3–4, 7.
9 Isaiah 1: 11, 14–17. Cf. also, 59: 12–14, by one of the followers of Isaiah.
10 E.g. Amos 2: 6–7; 5: 21–4.
11 Deuteronomy 30: 11–14.
12 Deuteronomy 9: 4–5.
13 Jeremiah 31: 29–30.
14 Jeremiah 31: 34.
15 [*Demosthenes*] 52, 20.
16 Psalms 24; God is the creator to whom only the pure and virtuous may resort.
17 E.g. Psalms 7; 119.
18 As in Psalms 7; 58; 94; etc.
19 Psalms 9–10; 41.
20 Psalms 9–10; 113; 146.

21 Such as Proverbs 21: 3, repeating the prophetic theme that "To do what is right and just is more desired by the LORD than sacrifice."

22 Job 12: 2.

23 Job 27: 2–12, concluding: "I will teach you what is in God's power."

24 Job 38: 3–4, 12–13.

25 Job 42: 2–3.

26 Job 29: 11–17; 31: 16–32.

27 Job 31: 15.

28 The Ptolemaic period in Palestine is now well served by Hengel, M. (1974) *Judaism and Hellenism: Studies in their Encounter in Palestine during the Early Hellenistic Period*, London, SCM Press, with full bibliography of the extensive literature. (Transl. of *Judentum und Hellenismus. Studien zu ihrer Begegnung unter besonderer Berüksichtigung Palästinas bis zur Mitte des 2. Jh.s v. Chr.*, 1973.)

29 2 Maccabees 6: 12–17.

30 2 Maccabees 12: 2–23.

31 For example, the writer of 1 Maccabees emphasizes the hostility toward Jews in the Greek cities of the coast, and the eulogizing hymn of 1 Maccabees 14: 4–15 ends with lines which would be in place in Hebrew texts of half a millennium earlier. See also 1 Maccabees 2: 42; 2 Maccabees 9: 5, 11–17 for service to the law and God's hand in striking Antiochus.

32 The centrality of apocalytic thought to Daniel's prophecy of the Time of the End marks a shift in emphasis also, but is not particularly Hellenic, any more than the treatment of resurrection in Daniel 12: 2 and 2 Maccabees 7: 14.

33 Repeating Ecclesiastes 8: 15.

34 Ecclesiastes 2: 24; cf. the same idea in 5: 17.

35 Ecclesiastes 5: 9.

36 Ecclesiastes 9: 2–3.

37 Ecclesiastes 3: 19-23.

## 20  THE EGYPTIAN CONNECTION

Bowman, A. K. (1986) *Egypt after the Pharoahs: 332 BC–AD 642, from Alexander to the Arab Conquest*, Berkeley, University of California Press.

1 Josephus, *Jewish Antiquities* XII.387 and XIII.62 ff., is supported in designating the Onias in Egypt as Onias IV, the son of the high priest, by 2 Maccabees 4: 32–8, against Josephus' error of Onias III in *Jewish War* I.33 and VII.423.

2 Josephus, *Against Apion* II.49 ff., and *Jewish Antiquities* XII.65.

3 The date is highly controversial; survey and English translation in Charlesworth, J. H. (1985) *The Old Testament Pseudepigraphica*, II, New York, Doubleday, pp. 7–34 (select bibliography, p. 11). It will be clear from my discussion that I incline to a different explanation of the text from that of Shutt in Charlesworth.

4 Cf. Josephus, *Contra Apion* II, 53–5.

5 *P. Tebtunis* 5 (Bagnall-Derow 45).

6 Welles, C. B. (1934) *Royal Correspondence in the Hellenistic Period*, New Haven, Yale University Press, nos 73–4 (Bagnall-Derow 49).

7 Diodorus Siculus XVII, 52.6: 6,000 T in his own time, but this probably does not include Alexandria; Strabo C 798 (XVII, 1.13) gives the figure of 12,500 T which he found in a (now lost) speech of Cicero.

## 21  THE IMPACT OF MATERIALISM

Clay, D. (1983) *Lucretius and Epicurus*, Ithaca, Cornell University Press.

Strozier, R. M. (1985) *Epicurus and Hellenistic Philosophy*, Lanham, University Press of America.

1 Cf. Diogenes Laertius X, 133.
2 Lucretius, *de Rerum Natura* IV, 478-99.
3 The sympathetic explication of Asmis, E. (1984) *Epicurus' Scientific Method*, Ithaca, Cornell University Press, is quite clear about the difference between Epicurus and Aristotle; cf. esp. p. 327.
4 *de Rerum Natura* V, 1170–1.
5 *de Rerum Natura* V, 1145.
6 Vanderlip, V. F. (1972) *The Four Isis Hymns of Isidorus and the Cult of Isis*, Toronto, Hakkert, Hymn I.9; cf. for these concepts in this and the other hymns (texts and translations).


## 22   THE RELIGIOUS PHILOSOPHY OF STOICISM

Inwood, B. (1985) *Ethics and Human Action in Early Stoicism*, Oxford, Clarendon Press.
Rist, J. M. (1969) *Stoic Philosophy*, Cambridge, Cambridge University Press.
Rist, J. M. (ed.) (1978) *The Stoics*, Berkeley, University of California Press.
Sandbach, F. H. (1978) *The Stoics*, London, Chatto & Windus.
Solmsen, F. (1979) *Isis among the Greeks and Romans*, Cambridge, Mass., Harvard University Press.

1 *P. Paris* 2, of the second century BC, a fragment of the work *Concerning Negative Judgements*.
2 Diogenes Laertius VII, 54.
3 Plutarch, *Moralia*, 1035 c-d,
4 Diogenes Laertius VII, 142–3; cf. 138.
5 Diogenes Laertius VII, 87.
6 Diogenes Laertius VII, 85.
7 Cf. Plutarch, *Concerning Stoic Self-Contradictions*; esp. *Moralia*, 1038 c ff. and *Concerning Common Conceptions: Against the Stoics*.
8 Plutarch, *Moralia*, 1051 b; cf. 1050 e-f.
9 Diogenes Laertius VII, 128.
10 Polybius XIII 5.4.


## 23   THE STRUGGLE TO GOVERN ROME

Sherwin-White, A. N. (1984) *Roman Foreign Policy in the East, 168 B.C. to A.D. 1*, London, Duckworth.


## 24   THE CONSULAR PHILOSOPHER

Lacey, W. K. (1978) *Cicero and the End of the Roman Republic*, London, Hodder & Stoughton.
Rawson, E. (1975) *Cicero: A Portrait*, London, Allen Lane.

1 Quoted from King, J. E. (1945) Introduction to his translation of *Tusculan Disputations*, Loeb classical Library Cicero vol. XVIII, Cambridge, Mass., Harvard University Press, pp. xxxi, xxxii–xxxiii.
2 Cicero, *de Natura Deorum* I, 7.
3 Cicero, *Letters to Atticus*, IV, 6.2.

4 Cicero, *de Natura Deorum* III, 5.
5 Cicero, *de Finibus* III, 67.
6 Cicero, *de Officiis* I, 157.
7 Cicero, *de Officiis* I, 160–1.
8 Cicero, *de Officiis* III, 21.
9 Cicero, *de Officiis* III, 31.
10 Cicero, *de Republica* I, 49.
11 Cicero, *de Officiis* I, 99.

## 25  BYSTANDERS

Annas, J. and Barnes, J. (1985) *The Modes of Scepticism: Ancient Texts and Modern Interpretations*, Cambridge, Cambridge University Press.

1 These are the antitheses used by Rist, J. H. (1982) *Human Value: A Study in Ancient Philosophical Ethics*, Leiden, Brill, p. 81.
2 Cicero, *de Natura Deorum* III, 97, mentions such a device as demonstrating the rational design of the heavens.
3 Seneca, *Ep.* 90, in disagreeing with the theory, sets out Posidonius' anthropology at some length.
4 Stobaeus, I, p. 34.36, ed. Wachsmuth.
5 Plutarch, *Moralia*, 1023 b-d.
6 Diogenes Laertius VII, 143.
7 Cicero, *de natura Deorum* II, 81–3.
8 Diodorus Siculus I, 3.8.

## 26  ORDINARY PEOPLE

Hunt, A. S. and Edgar, C. C. (1932, 1934) *Select Papyri*, 2 vols, Loeb Classical Library, Cambridge, Mass., Harvard University Press.

1 *UPZ* 121 (Bagnall-Derow 121).
2 The evidence for these and references to additional prices may be found in Samuel, Alan (1984) "The money economy and the Ptolemaic peasantry," *Bulletin of the American Society of Papyrologists*, XXI, 187–206.
3 *P. Grenfell* I, 21 (Select Papyri 83), one of the few wills in which precise items of property are named.
4 *P. Gurob* 8 (Select Papyri 334).
5 Respectively, *P. Enteuxis* 82 (Bagnall-Derow 117). *P. Tebtunis* 39 (Bagnall-Derow 96), *P. Tebtunis* 53.
6 *P. Tebtunis* 776 (Select Papyri 271) *P. Enteuxis* II, *P. Enteuxis* 48 (Select Papyri 270).
7 *P.S.I.* 402 (Select Papyri 266).
8 *P. Enteuxis* 26 (Bagnall-Derow 126), of 220 BC. A similar complaint, resolved by a son's agreement to pay 2 dr. per month, is *P. Enteuxis* 25.
9 *P. Col. Zen.* 66.
10 *U.P.Z.* 59 (Bagnall-Derow 144).
11 Babrius, fable 79; Phaedrus, Book I, fable 4.
12 Phaedrus, Book IV, fable 20 (or 19); cf. Babrius, fable 143.
13 Phaedrus, Book I, fable 2.
14 Babrius, fable 88.

## 27 TO RULE THE NATIONS

Gransden, K. W. (1984) *Virgil's Iliad: An Essay on Epic Narrative*, Cambridge, Cambridge University Press.

Millar, F. (1977) *The Emperor in the Roman World (31 B.C.–A.D. 337)*, Ithaca, Cornell University Press.

1 *Res Gestae Divi Augusti* 34. For a recent translation see Reinhold, M. (1978) *The Golden Age of Augustus*, Sarasota, Samuel Stevens, pp. 92–102; other texts and bibliography as well.
2 *Res Gestae* 6.
3 *Res Gestae* 13.
4 From "Defense of Poetry."
5 Virgil, *Aeneid* VI, 847–53.
6 Livy, *History of Rome*, Preface.
7 Caesar, *Gallic Wars* I, 1.3.
8 Horace, *Odes* IV, 1.
9 Horace, *Carmen Saeculare* 57–9.

## 28 THE FIRST CHRISTIAN CENTURY

Balsdon, J. P. V. D. (1979) *Romans and Aliens*, London, Duckworth.

Leaney, A. R. C. (1984) *The Jewish and Christian World, 200 B.C. to A.D. 200*, Cambridge, Cambridge University Press. Bibliography.

1 *P. Lond.* 1912.73–74 (Select Papyri 212).
2 Tacitus, *Annals* I, 4.
3 Tacitus, *Annals* XVI, 62.
4 Macrobius, *Saturnalia* II, 4.11, a pun on the similarity between the Greek words for "pig" and "son."
5 Josephus, *The Jewish War* VI, 251.

## 29 PHILOSOPHY AND RELIGION AMONG THE JEWS

*Aufstieg und Niedergang der Römischen Welt*, vol. II, 21: *Religion: (Hellenistisches Judentum in Römischer Zeit: Philon und Josephus)* (1984), Berlin, De Gruyter. (Most articles in English).

—— vol. II, 25: 1 (1984): Sanders, E. P. "Jesus, Paul and Judaism"; Wilcox, M. "Jesus in the Light of His Jewish Environment."

Sanders, E. P. (1977) *Paul and Palestinian Judaism: A Comparison of Patterns of Religion*, London, SCM Press. Bibliography.

Sandmel, S. (1979) *Philo of Alexandria: An Introduction*, Oxford, Oxford University Press.

Stone, M. E. (ed.) (1984) *Jewish Writings of the Second Temple Period: Apocrypha, Pseudepigraphica, Qumran Sectarian Writings, Philo, Josephus* (Compendia Rerum Iudaicarum ad Novum Testamentum, Section 2, vol. II), Philadelphia, Fortress Press. Bibliography.

1 *On Dreams* I, 168.
2 The passage and its meaning are discussed in *Allegorical Interpretations* II, 50.
3 That is, "good sense"; *On the Migration of Abraham* 126.
4 *On the Birth of Abel and the sacrifices Offered by him and his Brother Cain* 19–45, based on *Deuteronomy* 21: 15–17.

5 *Every Good Man is Free* 160.
6 *Embassy to Gaius* 85.
7 *On the Contemplative Life* 70.
8 *On the Special Laws* III. 137.
9 *On the Decalogue* 132–4.
10 This is the summation, almost a creed, in *On the Creation* 170–2.
11 *The Jewish War* II. 119–61.
12 *Jewish Antiquities* XVIII. 18–22.
13 *The Life* 12.
14 Such as the rival historian, Justus of Tiberias, who was "not without the experience of the education carried on among the Greeks," *Life*, 40.
15 *The Jewish War* II, 457–80.
16 *The Jewish War* II, 308.
17 *Jewish Antiquities* XVIII, 117.
18 Mentioning, in *Annals* XV, 44, that the Christians, blamed by Nero for the fire at Rome, took their name from the Christ executed by order of Pontius Pilate in the reign of Tiberius.
19 Most students agree that the passage mentioning Christ in *Jewish Antiquities* XVIII, 63, is a Christian interpolation.
20 2 Baruch 10: 6–18, translated by Klijn, A. F. J. (1983) in Charlesworth, J. H. (ed.) *The Old Testament Pseudepigraphica*, I, *Apocalyptic Literature and Testaments*, London, Darton, Longman, & Todd.
21 Mark 16: 19–20.

## 30  EARLY CHRISTIAN THOUGHT

Childs, B. S. (1985) *The New Testament as Canon: An Introduction*, Philadelphia, Fortress Press. Bibliography.
Sanders, E. P. (1985) *Jesus and Judaism*, Philadelphia, Fortress Press. Bibliography.

1 Peter 1: 20.
2 Matthew 7: 21–7.
3 2 Peter 3: 8–9.
4 1 Corinthians 1: 21–5.
5 Colossians 3:12–14.
6 1 Thessalonians 3: 12.
7 Galatians 5: 14.
8 Galatians 5: 22.
9 Romans 12:14–20.
10 Hebrews 10: 26–31.
11 Matthew 7: 21.
12 Luke 24: 39–41.
13 Luke 24: 37.
14 Luke 24: 49.
15 Acts 2: 2–4.
16 John 1: 20.
17 John 3: 16–17.
18 John 6: 35; 11: 25; 14: 6.
19 John 8: 58.

## 31 THE CORE OF HELLENISM

1 "On the ceasing of oracles," *Moralia*, 413 f.
2 "Advice on Political Activity," *Moralia*, 814 a.
3 *Moralia*, 580 c.
4 *Moralia*, 166f–167 a.
5 *Moralia*, 152 d.
6 *Moralia*, 154 e.

## 32 THE FUTURE OF THE PAST

1 The reader may have noticed by now that I have resisted the temptation to point up aspects of Hellenism by contrasting them to perceived differences in other societies, oriental, American (Indian), or the like, along lines like those which Max Weber, for example, laid down in (1963) *The Sociology of Religion*, Boston, Beacon Press (transl. of "Religionssoziologie" in *Wirtschaft und Gesellschaft*, fourth edn, 1956), attributing the differences between western and eastern cultures to fundamental religious attitudes. The activity can be interesting, even illuminating, as, for example, Dumont, L. (1985) "A modified view of our origins: The Christian beginnings of modern individualism," in Carrithers, M., Collins, S. and Lukes, S. (eds) *The Category of the Person*, Cambridge, Cambridge University Press, pp. 93–122, but I hesitate to embark on an enterprise which would probably cast more light on my own thought processes than my subject.
2 Koestler, A. (1941) *Darkness at Noon*, transl. D. Hardy, New York, Macmillan, p. 157.
3 *Paradise Lost* I, ll. 24–5.
4 (1977) *The Phenomenon of Man*, London, Collins, Fount Paperbacks, pp. 32–3. (Transl. of *Le Phénomène humain*, 1955.)

# Index

# Index

# Index

Forms, Plato's theory of, 146, 360; rejection by Aristotle, 151, 157–8; *see also* Plato, theory of Forms
Fortune, 213
*Fourth Eclogue* (Virgil), 316
"Fourth Philosophy", 334–5, 341
free will, 32, 334
freedom, 154–5, 199–201, 240, 251; of the Greek cities, 209–10
*Frogs* (Aristophanes), 73
Furies, 79–80

Gaius, 325
Galba, 322
Galilee, 324, 326, 335
games, 23, 96; in Judaea, 324, 336
Gaugamela, Battle of, 163
Gauls, 175–6, 187, 193, 209, 265
Genesis, 216
genius, 25, 317
gnosticism, 359
God, 214–19, 220–21 (illus.), 222–3, 225–6, 231–3, 331–2, 334–5, 347, 350, 352–5, 358, 360, 370, 372; as enemy, 224
gods, 7, 17, 21, 23, 25–6, 42–3, 50, 54–5, 57, 77, 79–80, 88, 90–91, 170; 174, 187, 202, 241–2, 248, 250, 258, 288–9, 374; "anthropological" interest in, 99; in Aristotle, 156; authority of, 112; capabilities of, 84; in Cicero, 279, 284; as enemies of humanity, 75–6; foreign, among Jews, 215; Hellenization of, 169; in Herodotus, 100; in law pleadings, 95; justice of, 83; Macedonian, 168; in Pindar, 96; in Polybius, 213; as reified absolutes, 145; at Rome, 307, 309–11, 317
golden rule, 353, 359
Good, 149–51, 155, 196, 202, 212, 246–7, 252, 284; as the Prime Mover, 156
Gorgias, 68–70, 89
Gospels, 343, 345–7, 351–8, 360; composition of, 328, 344, 351; influence of, 351; as sources for Jesus' life, 338, 344
Gracchus, Gaius, 264
Gracchus, Tiberius Sempronius, 264
Greek unity, 31, 35, 62–4
guilt, 56

Hamilcar, 190
Hannibal, 207–8, 210
happiness, 7, 150, 155, 196, 248, 259–60, 280, 310, 366, 369–70; as Aristotle's final end, 152, 154; instability of, 99
harmony, 133
Harpocrates, 258
Hasmonean dynasty, 233, 239–40
healing, 19–20, 26, 232, 251, 368
Hebrews, Epistle of Paul to, 350–51
Hector, 40–42
*hedone, see* pleasure
Hellenization, 180, 238, 241, 245, 288, 298, 311
Hera, 77
*Heracleidae* (Euripides), 85
Heracles, 174

*Heracles* (Euripides), 84, 87
Herculaneum, 292
Hermes, 15
Hermes Trismegistus, 170
herms, mutilation of, 94
hero, Sophoclean, 85–6, 411
Herod Agrippa, 325–6
Herod Antipas, 324, 326, 338, 352
Herod, the Great, 324
Herodotus, 31, 49, 62–3, 68, 74, 96–8, (and illus.), 100–101; rationalism, 97
"heroic" code, 31–2, 36, 40
Hesiod, 49–52, 51 (illus.), 55, 57, 63, 181
Hiero, 186, 189–90
Hieronymus of Cardia, 176
Hipparchus, 241
Hippias, 68–9
Hippias, son of Peisistratus, 77
Hippocrates, 119–20
Hippodamus, 67
*Hippolytus* (Euripides), 86
*Historia Animalia* (Pliny), 148
Holy Spirit, 347–8, 354–5, 360
Homer, 33 (illus.)
Homeric epic, 28–30, 32–5, 46, 51, 55, 62–3; influence of, 34, 181, 241; Plato's hostility to, 136
Horace, 316
housing, 292–3, 295
*How to Gain Benefit from Enemies* (Plutarch), 365
*hubris*, 85–6
human community, 226, 280–83, 289, 298, 307, 350, 369–70, 373
human nature, 3–6, 8, 91, 120, 128, 131, 182, 184, 196, 367, 369, 374–5; in Aristotle, 149, 164, 166; and Christianity, 372; in Philo, 330, 332–33; in Plato, 141, 143–4
human value, 7–8, 131
*Hymn to Zeus* (Callimachus), 181, 184, 255
Hyperbolus, 117

ideology, 3–4, 6, 8–11, 62, 233, 238, 241, 309, 311, 314–17, 334, 342, 365, 367–8, 374–5
*Iliad*, 28–9, 31, 34, 36–45, 56, 230
immortality, 19, 22, 251, 279, 359, 361
*imperium*, 188–9, 239
Indo-Europeans, 15, 24
Io, 77
Ionian philosophy, 1, 74, 97, 105, 203
Ionians, 64
Iphigeneia, 79
*Iphigeneia in Tauris* (Euripides), 87
Ipsus, Battle of, 173
Isaiah, 347, 215, 217–19
*On Isis and Osiris* (Plutarch), 289
Isis, 21–3, 168–9, 250–51, 258, 289; hymns to, 241, 288
Isocrates, 69, 124, 129
Israel, kingdom of, 214–15
Issus, Battle of, 162
Isthmian Games, 96, 209

James, brother of Jesus, 328
James, letter of, 359

427

# Index

# Index